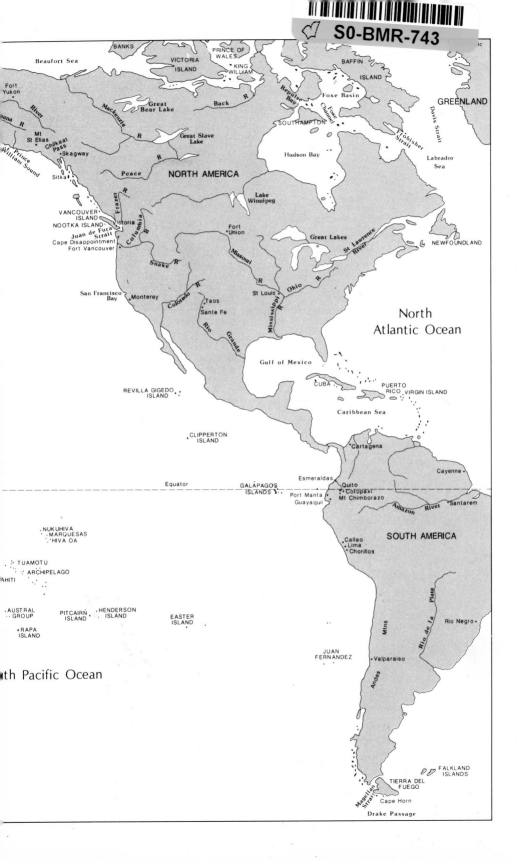

BANKS

Beaufort Sea

PRINCE OF
WALES

VICTORIA
ISLAND

KING
WILLIAM

BAFFIN
ISLAND

Fort
Yukon

River

Mackenzie

Great
Bear Lake

Back

R

Repulse
Bay

Foxe Basin

Foxe
Channel

GREENLAND

aana

R

Mt
St Elias

Chilkaat
Pass

R

Great Slave
Lake

SOUTHAMPTON

Davis Strait

Fröbisher
Strait

Skagway

Peace

R

NORTH AMERICA

Hudson Bay

Labrador
Sea

Prince
William Sound

Sitka

Frazer

R

Lake
Winnipeg

St Lawrence

River

NEWFOUNDLAND

VANCOUVER
ISLAND

Victoria

Columbia

R

NOOTKA ISLAND

Juan de Fuca
Strait

Cape Disappointment

Fort Vancouver

Snake

R

Fort
Union

Missouri

Great Lakes

North
Atlantic Ocean

San Francisco
Bay

Monterey

Colorado

R

Taos

Sante Fe

Rio

Grande

Snake

R

St Louis

Mississippi

R

Ohio

R

Gulf of Mexico

CUBA

PUERTO
RICO

VIRGIN ISLAND

REVILLA GIGEDO
ISLAND

Caribbean Sea

CLIPPERTON
ISLAND

Cartagena

Cayenne

Equator

GALÁPAGOS
ISLANDS

Esmeraldas

Port Manta

Guayaquil

Quito

Cotopaxi

Mt Chimborazo

Amazon

River

Santarem

NUKUHIVA

MARQUESAS

HIVA OA

Callao

Lima

Chorillos

SOUTH AMERICA

TUAMOTU

ARCHIPELAGO

AHITI

AUSTRAL
GROUP

PITCAIRN
ISLAND

HENDERSON
ISLAND

EASTER
ISLAND

Mins

Rio de la Plata

Rio Negro

RAPA
ISLAND

JUAN
FERNANDEZ

Valparaiso

Andes

th Pacific Ocean

FALKLAND
ISLANDS

TIERRA DEL
FUEGO

Magellan
Strait

Cape Horn

Drake Passage

DATE DUE

NEW LANDS, NEW MEN

THE FRED H. AND ELLA MAE MOORE
TEXAS HISTORY REPRINT SERIES

The Texas Revolution
By William C. Binkley

Spanish Explorers in the Southern United States, 1528–1543
Edited by Frederick W. Hodge and Theodore H. Lewis

Through Unexplored Texas
By W. B. Parker
With a new introduction by George B. Ward

Texas
By Mary Austin Holley
With a new introduction by Marilyn McAdams Sibley

A Ranchman's Recollections
By Frank S. Hasting
With a new introduction by David J. Murrah

The History of Texas
By David B. Edward
With a new introduction by Margaret S. Henson

Army Exploration in the American West, 1803–1863
By William H. Goetzmann
With a new introduction by the author

A Texas Scrap-Book
By D. W. C. Baker
With a new introduction by Robert A. Calvert

Progressives and Prohibitionists
By Lewis L. Gould
With a new introduction by the author

Exploration and Empire
By William H. Goetzmann

Women in Early Texas
Edited by Evelyn M. Carrington
With a new introduction by Debbie Mauldin Cottrell

The Texas State Capitol

Lone Star Blue and Gray
Edited by Ralph A. Wooster

NEW LANDS, NEW MEN

AMERICA AND THE SECOND GREAT AGE OF DISCOVERY

William H. Goetzmann

William H. Goetzmann 2001

TEXAS STATE HISTORICAL ASSOCIATION
AUSTIN

Library of Congress Cataloging-in-Publication Data:

Goetzmann, William H.
    New Lands, new men : America and the second great age of discovery / William H. Goetzmann.
    p.   cm.—(Fred H. and Ella Mae Moore Texas history reprint series)
    Includes bibliographical references and index.
    ISBN 0-87611-148-7 (cloth : alk. paper)
    1. Explorers—United States—History. 2. United States—Territorial expansion. 3. Discoveries in geography. I. Title. II. Series.
E179.5.G63   1995
910'.973—dc20   95-34673
                                   CIP

Number sixteen in the Fred H. and Ella Mae Moore Texas History Reprint Series.

*To all those modern explorers, from the peerless
navigator Captain James Cook to the
Challenger Seven who
perished in the service of civilization*

PREFACE

THIS BOOK is the third and final work that I intend to write about Americans and exploration. I think of these books, written now over a period of nearly thirty years, as an unusual kind of trilogy, filling out a historical horizon that I have had in mind since the very beginning. Rather than a continuing chronological series, each book has grown out of the previous one, exemplifying larger and broader horizons of experience—of the aims, techniques, and significance of exploration as a cultural process that provides a special insight into the minds and spirits of men and nations, particularly Americans.

Army Exploration in the American West dealt with the United States government's role in the exploration and development of the American West before the Civil War. It focused upon the work of a small but important group of men, the United States Army's Corps of Topographical Engineers. The subject of my next book, *Exploration and Empire*, was all of the explorers, from mountain men to highly trained members of the United States Geological Survey, who opened up, described, portrayed, and analyzed the West. My intent was to show how exploration as a process meant exploration and reexploration of a vast region in response to changing cultural demands. In this story the Corps of Topographical Engineers was seen in a larger context, and its work thus took on a subtly different meaning.

The West continued to be the focus of my attention, because its exploration, settlement, and exploitation marked the real definition of the aspirations of most Americans, who saw their republican and democratic nation stretching from sea to sea in North America. The West seemed to be America's land of the future, that place which allowed us to be, for a long time, a forward-looking, because underdeveloped, nation. The West, as I saw it, was a vast colony that seemed to be a stage upon which hopes for the future could be endlessly projected. I had not as yet seriously confronted the problem that stimulated and aroused Frederick Jackson Turner—the end of the frontier. Indeed, I was not as yet even concerned with the meaning of that event, and I had not sufficiently considered the extent to which the concept "frontier" really had other dimensions.

As I set to work on the present volume, in an intellectual climate informed by the United States having assumed the role of guardian of the free world on a global scale, America's western adventure began to assume a new meaning—that of a centrally important model or experiential example of a process that was really global in scope, and so powerful as to seem, at the present time, irreversible. That process constituted a new frontier experience: the emergence of a culture of science which was carried over the globe, just as it had spread into and governed our knowledge and goals in the American West. I was able to see this revolutionary process at work more clearly, because my historical lens had opened wider, and because this book was written when it was—during a period of American global responsibility, and during a time when we first began to realize the awe-inspiring consequences of a second Great Scientific Revolution.

Thus, in a very real sense, this volume is a product of its time, though it casts back to that earlier period when the consequences of the first Great Scientific Revolution were being felt. One of these consequences was the spawning of a new nation, the United States, based upon the natural law principles of the Scientific Revolution. Another was a worldwide Second Great Age of Discovery in the midst of which America as a nation was born, and into which Americans eagerly entered on a global scale. The story of the exploration of the North American continent and the American West was still part of the general horizon of historical experience, but it had shrunk to a proper place and a different meaning in the larger historical context, as indeed the whole American experience should be viewed—though by a world historian more qualified than I to tell the story. However, in viewing the American experience through a larger lens, spanning at least two centuries, which saw the important scientific roles played by all sorts of explorers, I have been able, I hope, to see more clearly the inevitable emergence of a transnational culture of science, and something of the consequences that have attended its ascendance. On an intellectual level in the United States, it has governed the national philosophy, from Scottish common-sense realism at the onset of the Republic to the pragmatism that currently governs all our lives, despite high-sounding protests to the contrary. And since a nation's philosophy permeates its significant activities, so America's growing place in the world culture of science can be seen through the activities of its explorers, who were very much a part of the scientific process. In fact, the spread of science can be seen more clearly and dramatically through the activities of explorers reaching out to all parts of the globe, than through looking at any other human endeavor. Hence, the reason for this book.

The sequence of my exploration trilogy calls to mind a similar sequence created by my great predecessor here at the University of Texas, Walter P. Webb. He, too, started with a small but important group of men, the Texas Rangers, operating on a large and wild frontier. He then turned his attention to the whole of the Great Plains, and then finally enlarged his scope to a description of "the four-hundred-year boom" described in *The Great Frontier*. It seems that quite by accident—though in an academic context that has not changed so very much—I have followed the same path. I only hope that I have left the same sense of "history as high adventure" in the wake of my labors.

Since artists were an integral part of the growing culture of science and its handmaiden, exploration, I have grouped the illustrations in this book into "portfolios" that are intended to be as much a part of the story as the prose text. They serve a purpose much more important than that of illustration, because they are intended to demonstrate just how art shaped science's way of seeing, and vice versa.

William H. Goetzmann
Austin, Texas

CONTENTS

BOOK THREE
THE BOOK OF TIME

INTRODUCTION

Re-Thinking
New Lands, New Men

I AM DELIGHTED to see the third volume in my exploration trilogy, *New Lands, New Men*, reprinted. Because of its strong narrative thrust, I do not think that it received proper attention when it was first published in 1986. It is, however, a distillation of nearly three decades of thinking about the history of exploration in the context of intellectual and cultural history as well as the histories of science and art. It is also the story of America's emergence on the world scene in an age that spanned both Enlightenment and Romantic enthusiasms. Indeed, a major thesis of my narrative is that the investigation of all the exotic phenomena of the globe and their description in countless exciting narratives, scientific illustrations, paintings, prints, and even photographs became perhaps the primary influence on the formation of western civilization's Romantic yet scientific world view.

This was also the time when Americans became fascinated with other peoples, or in current parlance "the other." The literary scholar Edward Said has made much of this Hegelian term that is a useful, though slippery, concept. In Said's interesting writings it has been almost exclusively used to confront

European and sometimes American imperialism. Being anti-western, Said says little about Arab imperialism, which has stretched from Spain to the Indies and the Asian subcontinent, and which functioned historically as the engine of the African slave trade. Moreover, this important phenomenon has been largely overlooked by black Americans who paradoxically adopt the names of their Muslim captors rather than their ancestral African tribal names.

Clearly imperialism and even racism have not been exclusively western phenomena. Just as clearly, a fascination with other lands, other peoples, other geographies, and other ecologies has not necessarily been solely motivated by imperialistic aims, nor has it resulted invariably in political and social conquest. Donald Lach's magisterial works on the impact of the Orient on western civilization demonstrate that Oriental influences not only flowed into Europe (and America) but that they have greatly enriched Euro-American cultures without colonizing them.

Outright imperialism or the intent to dominate, control, and exploit other people is clearly wrong. In most cases it has resulted in calamities and injustice on a massive scale. It has also resulted in racial degradation today called "racism." Much of the activity of the explorers whom I discuss in *New Lands, New Men* (Emerson's term) were bound up with worldwide imperial competition, particularly with Britain in the nineteenth century. Except for the quest for a North American continental nation, however, Americans were almost uniquely uninterested in colonial possessions. A careful reading of *New Lands, New Men* makes this clear. Even Commodore Perry did not aspire to colonize Japan, only to open it up to western or world trade. Nor did the vast majority of Americans covet all Mexico; many deplored Trist's treaty of 1848 that created an American West. Nonetheless, when one is dealing with exploration one is always in some sense dealing with imperialism.

Therefore this book can be considered a study in imperialism. Indeed the careful and critical study of imperialism is in my view one of the top priorities for historians and social scientists, though its focus need not always be upon western cultures.

Along with exploration came a fascination with other races at first projected as monsters in the Renaissance, then most often as inferior peoples. Like the American Indians, the Euro-Americans thought of themselves as "the human beings" and all others as something else, despite the Pope's having proclaimed all peoples as humans with immortal souls as early as 1537. American explorers, like their European counterparts, were not solely interested in destroying indigenous populations despite the sometimes careless use of the World War II terms "holocaust" and "genocide" by people less interested in fact than in moral one-upsmanship. In my story, I have indicated American explorers' fascination with races and to them exotic peoples that led to the emerging sciences of anthropology, cultural geography and sociology—social sciences that, while exciting, have in the long run proven to be inadequate for the understanding of other people. This kind of study of other peoples, of course goes back to Aristotle and Herodotus in the western world, but it was systematized in the first Great Age of Discovery by the Spaniards who were very conscious of color, and probably created the categories of mestizo, mulatto, etc. Illustrated Spanish charts exist that show graduations of color correlated with status. In 1776, the German, Johann Blumenbach, tried to turn such categorizations into what became the "science" of anthropology as he and his students investigated what he had decided were the five basic races of mankind. In the United States, Dr. Samuel George Morton collected human skulls from around the world and tried to measure racial cranial capacity as a measure of intelligence by filling the inverted skulls with pellets of one sort or another. He based his experiments on the idea that the larger the brain the more intelligent the person. This reasoning has not entirely died out, unfortunately. Major John Wesley Powell, near the turn of the nineteenth century, bet his friend W J McGee that Powell's brain was the larger of the two because he was more intelligent. He won, though he never lived to gloat about it. In more recent times, scientists have carefully measured both Einstein's and Dillinger's brains. Dr. Morton's 165 skulls can be seen even today, racked up like billiard balls in the Museum of the College of Physicians and Surgeons in Philadelphia.

Clearly, for explorers and even for closet scientists, race was important. So was racial discourse, as explorers and missionaries invariably made vocabularies of the languages of peoples with whom they came in contact. The U.S. government created a whole institution, the Bureau of American Ethnology, in 1879 to study North American indigenous peoples. Many of its publications, including the early works of the cultural relativist Franz Boas, who believed linguistics to be the key to understanding, were vocabularies. Indeed, out of the studies of native peoples in the Second Great Age of Discovery, Boas and others developed the concept of cultural relativism upon which the best hopes for the mutual toleration of "others" on the globe currently rest. Thus the study of race was not always "racist." Even explorers and soldiers were not always "racist." Richard Burton and Lawrence of Arabia come to mind, but so does Captain John G. Bourke of the U.S. Cavalry, who knew more about the Apaches than even the Apaches themselves. Explorers and anthropologists knew that they had to relate to native peoples if they were to learn about them. They also had to *depend* upon them—a point that I have, alas, not made sufficiently clear in my narrative. Were I to rewrite the whole book, I would in the strongest terms emphasize how much the explorers depended upon the natives they encountered. To some extent I hope I have done some of this in the work as it stands, as I also, in the picture sections, at least hinted at some of the rudenesses and even brutalities that the explorers inflicted on native peoples.

In *New Lands, New Men*, I was intent upon establishing the idea, hinted at by historians such as J. H. Parry, of a *Second Great Age of Discovery*, distinguished from the Columbian Era by its emphasis on science and its viewpoints and emerging institutions. Beyond this, I had in mind Thomas Kuhn's idea of the paradigm of science, in which he lauded "normal science" as opposed to "great man science." In a lecture to the American Association for the Advancement of Science, "Paradigm Lost," I expanded normal science to include exploration and its attendant institutions. This expansion, of course, added tremendously to the number of people who participated in what I have called "the culture of science." This has, I hope, created a more sophisticated social and institutional context for Kuhn's celebrated concept.

However, despite some improvements in the literature, most historians of science focus on the great "discoverers." This is not to discount the Newtons or Darwins, however, but rather to note the tremendous ripple effect of the raising of questions such as those that preoccupied them. It is also to suggest that often great scientific questions, even great shifts in values, are the result of travel and mobility. Looking back at the earth from vehicles in outer space or out into the galaxies via the Hubble Space Telescope has created a new perspective in our time, even if the B-29s over Hiroshima did not.

Discovery in a geographical sense has changed its meaning for most people today. In my exploration trilogy, especially in *Exploration and Empire*, I went to some pains to distinguish between "exploration," which is a mental and physical process of searching, and "discovery," which is a happenstance along the way. I probably should have gone further and said "a *perceived* happenstance," since indigenous peoples all over the globe knew about their own territory, though few made an effort to inquire much about other lands and ecologies. It really took Captain Cook's charts to "create" Polynesia, though we now know that "the argonauts of the western Pacific," as they have been called, knew relatively little about the other cultures that dotted the Pacific. In fact, if one discounts the land-bridge theory, indigenous peoples appeared to know little beyond regional knowledge. Sacajawea, for example, knew nothing of Upper Missouri geography until she entered her homeland, the Snake country west of the Jefferson Fork of the Missouri. We do know, however, for example, that Athabascan peoples must have migrated at some point from Canada to Arizona, where they became Apaches. We also have convincing legendary evidence, via the Spanish savant, Oviedo, that North American tribes migrated into the Valley of Mexico and helped change the Mexics into Aztecs. Still, curiosity, science, technology, and mobility greatly heightened inquiry into global places and peoples. They stimulated what, since Alfred Crosby's *The Columbian Exchange*, we have called "encounters" rather than discoveries in order to encompass the knowledge of indigenous peoples.

Stephen Greenblatt in *Marvelous Possessions: The Wonders of the New World* adds a "new historicism" dimension of linguistic criticism to the history of exploration. Through the analysis of discourse, he illustrates the "wonder" that dazzled early explorers.

More recently I have been fascinated by Lisa Bloom's *Gender on Ice: American Ideologies of Polar Expeditions*. Her work in "New Historicism" is dedicated to the propositions that Arctic explorer Robert Peary was not only a symbol of masculine imperialism (she seems to take his statement at the Pole, "mine at last," to mean that like Byrd at Antarctica he meant to establish a "Little America" colony at the North Pole), but that he was guilty of "racism" and fraud. Some recent scholars assert, for example, that the black explorer, Matt Henson, unaided by

Peary, was the first to set foot on the North Pole and that he was never given enough credit. Henson himself believed this to be the case. And in his time, despite the number of pictures Peary took of him at the Pole, he was largely obscured by the relevant American institutions. It has been said, too, that Peary victimized the Inuit or Eskimos with whom he lived and by one of whom, like Henson, he had a child whom he adopted. The Inuit, however, didn't believe he had victimized them and had nothing but friendly thoughts about their "encounter" with him.

As for "masculinity," Ms. Bloom, who is unique in her investigation of this aspect of Peary, does not question the close relationship between Henson and Peary for obvious reasons of ethnic sensitivity. She does, however, suggest that Peary does not give his wife credit for her expedition with him around Inglesfield Gulf and across Greenland in 1892. Had Peary made a great deal of Josephine Diebitsch-Peary's journey it would, of course, have made Arctic exploration feminine-imperialist as well as masculine-imperialist.

Naturally, to Bloom and others, Peary's and Henson's North Pole discovery is after all, a fraud perpetrated by the two men and the National Geographic Society. Frederick Cook, of course, discovered the Pole and was unfairly challenged by Peary, says Bloom. Wally Herbert, sponsored by the National Geographic Society in his polar explorations, contended in *In the Noose of Laurels* (1989) that Peary missed the Pole by sixty to eighty miles. This became gospel in some quarters despite its definitive refutation by Thomas D. Davies and the Foundation for the Promotion of the Art of Navigation, who by using modern photogrametry in 1990 conclusively proved that Peary had indeed reached the Pole or within five miles of it. The Davies committee added, "And, on a personal note, we cannot but hope that this marks the end of a long process of vilification of a courageous American explorer." Apparently it did not, especially if one is set upon finding fault and nothing else with American civilization.

The National Geographic Society has also been castigated for picturing indigenous peoples in their traditional garb, i.e., bare-breasted native women, as if the preponderance of the *Geographic*'s articles were devoted to this "masculine" and "racist" mission. This kind of ridiculous vilification equating the *National Geographic Magazine* with *Playboy* negates several very good points that could be made and which suggested themselves to me as I was concluding *New Lands, New Men* though I was only able to devote pages 419–421 to them. The National Geographic Society did and still does let itself appear as a U.S. government agency—perhaps because it was original-ly formed by men like John Wesley Powell, Henry Gannett, General A. W. Greely, and Grove Karl Gilbert, all part of the U.S. government's scientific establishment, though a lawyer, Gardiner Green Hubbard, was its first president. The National Geographic Society still enjoys good relations with the U.S. government and its various agencies. This, however, does not mean that its activities—financing expeditions, sending pho-tographers all over the globe, and popularizing geography—are imperialistic. Quite the contrary: the *National Geographic Magazine* acquaints over sixteen million people world-wide with "others." If, however, making imaginary explorers, even discoverers, of its readers is wicked, it is guilty. It also continues the romanticism of the Second Great Age of Discovery by making such places as Iowa and the Arctic equally exotic.

As I have suggested, however, the *Geographic*, in supporting latter-day exploration, often touts mere stunts. Peary's reaching the Pole is one of them, as I imply in "The Hero" chapter of *New Lands, New Men* (pages 444–453). Since Peary, it has become even more of a stunt. Two American and uncounted numbers of Russian submarines have coursed across the Pole under the ice since 1958. In April 1968, four amateur explorers reached the Pole by snowmobile, while Wally Herbert with four men (no women) in an overland expedition claimed to have reached the Pole in 1969 after a sled journey of fourteen months aided by air drops of supplies. But earlier in 1968, Ann Bancroft of Minnesota had reached the Pole with a party led by Will Steger, and the same year Jean-Louis Etienne reached the holy pole alone, on skis and pulling his own sled. Of course, Admiral Richard Byrd had flown over it in 1926 and countless satellite photos have made it a familiar place. It still, however, like the moon, does not belong to the "imperialist" United States.

Ernest Hemingway once wrote, "If I could have made this enough of a book it would have had everything in it." I would have written a great deal more about that fascinating Anglo-American, Henry Morton Stanley. I would have written not only of his exploration of the Congo and his cruelty to the natives (as pictured on page 387) but about his ridiculous 1887 march from the mouth of the Congo through the dense Itruri Forest (Jungle) and finally to Lake Albert, just south of the Sudan, to rescue Amin Pascha (a German) from the clutches of the already dead murderer of General "Chinese" Gordon, the Mahdi. Amin Pascha refused to be "rescued," but Stanley's grueling stunt still sold newspapers.

And, having gone through all his papers at Yale, I would have told the story of Hiram Bingham and his "discovery" of the "lost city of the Inca," Machu Picchu. I would have written of what really happened on Bingham's Yale Peruvian Expedition in 1912; that he was really intent on beating Annie Peck, an intrepid female explorer, to the top of Mt. Coropuna, then thought to be the highest point in South America, because he didn't believe women should be explorers. And I would have written about how, while trekking down the Urubamba River trail in search of new Inca ruins, his muleteer told him about the "cloud city" that his family had farmed for generations, which actually led to the momentous rediscovery of Machu Picchu. I would have written about how Bingham was unimpressed by the find, and rushed away to beat Annie Peck to the top of South America, and how only after failing to do so did he turn his attention to the Incas and his "Lost City." I would have written all about this with some relish, but was beaten to it by Bingham's own son, Alfred Bingham, an honest man, who told the whole story, just as it was, in a masterful biography of his father that has been largely overlooked: *Portrait of an Explorer: Hiram Bingham, Discoverer of Machu Picchu.*

This and many other stories of exploration not so heroic spring to mind, as do the stories of intrepid female explorers discussed by Elizabeth Fagg Olds, head of the Women's National Geographic Society, in her intriguing *Women of the Four Winds.* I would write more about Annie Smith Peck; Delia J. Akeley, who crisscrossed Africa, virtually duplicating Stanley's feats, as she collected specimens for the American Museum of Natural History; Margaret Harrison, who crossed Siberia and explored Outer Mongolia; and Louise Arner Boyd, who explored northeast Greenland further and more thoroughly then even Peary had done. Beyond this, I would somehow have worked in Englishwoman Isabella Bird Bishop, who wrote *A Lady's Life in the Rocky Mountains,* but who is best known for her daring expeditions to Tibet and the "Golden Chersonese." Or I would have devoted a whole chapter to Fanny Bullock Workman of Worcester, Massachusetts, who with her husband, Dr. W. Hunter Workman, not only bicycled over the Atlas Mountains to the Algerian Sahara, but for years, while Peary struggled with the Pole, also explored the entire Himalayan frontier of northeast India—Karakoram Ladakh, Nulva, Sura, the Punjab, and Balistan. I recommend her wonderful travel books, published between 1895 and 1917. Which is to say that exploration is a physical and mental adventure that does not and never has excluded women. Indeed, who could forget the Norse woman-warrior, Freydis, who landed on the north shore of Newfoundland around the year 1000. There, beating her bared breasts with a Viking sword, she chased away a Beothuk horde that had cowed her male Viking explorer-companions.

As this book goes into what is perhaps its final reprint I can't help echoing Hemingway: "No. It is not enough of a book, but still there were a few things to be said"—in this case perhaps a whole volume of things. One of these things, however, that still strikes a chord with me—largely an armchair explorer like Thoreau—is something Marlow wrote in Joseph Conrad's *Heart of Darkness*: "Now when I was a little chap I had a passion for maps. I would look for hours at South America, or Africa, or Australia and lose myself in all the glories of exploration."

William H. Goetzmann
Austin, Texas, 1995

PROLOGUE

The great maritime conquests, those of the end of the fifteenth century and sixteenth century, had ended with the conquest of the planet's *useful* ocean routes. Two centuries later, the situation changes completely: The voyages around the world had no other goal than to obtain new information about geography, the natural world, and the mores of different peoples.

—FERNAND BRAUDEL

i

SOME time ago, in another book, I wrote, "The nineteenth century, for Americans as well as for Europeans, was an age of exploration. During this period all of the islands of the sea were charted, the Antarctic discovered, and the interiors of the continental land masses opened up to the mobile citizens of the western world, who came to them with Christianity, ideas of progress, new techniques in science, and dreams of romantic imperialism." In the years since I wrote those words, I have come to realize that all of this activity formed part of a lost horizon of the western world's cultural history. The lost horizon, I would assert, is a "Second Great Age of Discovery," founded on the world-spanning work of at least two centuries of scientific exploration that followed closely upon the Scientific Revolution of the seventeenth century that culminated in the cosmological works of Isaac Newton and the epistemology of John Locke. It was the ever-growing belief in science and the idea of linear progress that made the new Age of Discovery stand off from the older age, in which Renaissance mariners sought the Indies, and Columbus, by accident, discovered the way to America. No

I

longer did men seek marvels and fear sea monsters and anthropophagi. Instead, a new rationalism, based upon mathematics
and empiricism, began to govern exploring activity, whose central focus became that of mapping terrestrial space. This included measuring the whole earth, charting the oceans, and,
with mathematical precision, the heavens, as an aid to mapping
the earth. It also meant locating patterns of terrestrial distribution for rocks, minerals, fossils, plants, animals, and men. Because of the seeming perfection of the Newtonian mechanistic
model and the Great Chain of Being, in which everything in nature had its proper place and nothing was superfluous; because
of the emergence of seemingly rational systems for biological
classification by John Ray and Carolus Linnaeus; because of the
assumption that the earth and the cosmos were somehow a finite
system; and because of a belief in the mechanistic empiricism of
John Locke, much of the Second Great Age of Discovery
seemed to depend upon a continual process of secular, scientific
system-building that replaced the certainties of medieval Christianity founded on the bedrock of Aristotle's vision of nature's
plan.

Men of learning, of various philosophical persuasions, soon
found, however, that neither globe nor cosmos seemed finite.
Explorers and expeditions from all nations proliferated and
bombarded the centers of learning with new discoveries almost
daily. The constant flood of new specimens, new data, and new
information eventually turned the static Newtonian world view
into an ever-changing, growing, cumulatively varied view of the
world in which science itself and its basic categories were continually being redefined. It was also clear, by the early eighteenth century, that science was rapidly emerging as a culture
unto itself with its own language, institutions, symbols, and recognized practitioners, and, in contrast to the age of Columbus,
its own nonreligious tests for truth. This was perhaps the most
momentous consequence of the Second Great Age of Discovery,
though the discovery of exotic, far-distant lands and peoples,
who seemingly stepped out of Eden itself, also turned the age

into one of feeling and romanticism. To quote only one example of this latter process, hear Professor J. C. Beaglehole describing the consequences of the British ship captain Samuel Wallis's discovery of Tahiti in 1768.

> Wallis had not merely come to a convenient port of call. He had stumbled on a foundation stone of the Romantic Movement. Not as continent, not as vast distances, was the ocean henceforth in common thought to be known. The unreal was to mingle with the real, the too dramatic with the undramatic; the shining light was to become a haze in which every island was the one island, and the one island a Tahitian dream.

Thus, the rapidly emerging culture of science took on a romantic as well as a methodological dimension, which became, as a result of ocean-spanning expeditions, still another influence that changed European, and eventually American, culture.

In countless instances, scientific institutions linked with exploration received acclaim and support from a public dazzled by real natural wonders brought from the ends of the earth. Every man became his own tastemaker, as South Sea wallpaper, complemented by chinoiserie bric-a-brac, Saracenic furniture, and parlor-table bird books, seemed perfectly appropriate in Moorish, Gothic, Egyptian, Palladian, or Tuscan villas. For many, still under the spell of the "Tahitian Dream," it became the height of fashion to visit George Catlin's Indian Gallery in Egyptian Hall, Piccadilly, and then ape the noble savage in all manner of life-styles. Thus, the "lost horizon" of the Second Great Age of Discovery emerged as a major force behind the Romantic Movement.

Explorers were, and still are, definitely part of the whole apparatus of the culture of science, though they are characteristically overlooked by historians of the "internal" history of science. One of the larger and, I hope, most obvious intents of this book is to describe just how explorers, even relatively crude, unlettered men, functioned as part of the emergent culture of science.

This objective, however, is secondary to that of providing a view of that "lost horizon," that varied landscape that constitutes the possibility of a whole new perspective in the writing of not only Euro-American but world history. It is in this second age that European values most directly impinged upon the whole world, including North America, and that the Americans so eagerly joined the western world's culture of science. The United States emerged as a new nation whose values and great state documents, like the Declaration of Independence and the Constitution, were based on the natural law assumptions of the culture of science, and its history has everywhere been bound up with the process of exploration—in the great West, on other continents, across the world's oceans, and to the poles at the ends of the earth. The culture of science and the attendant process of exploration in search of the new has set the values, tone, and rhythm of American culture from the eighteenth century to the present, when we are possibly experiencing a Third Great Age of Discovery delineated by the discovery of the relativity of times and spaces, streams of consciousness, a pluralistic universe and hence multiple perspectives, cultural relativism in anthropology, and the resurgence of systems thinking and equilibrium in geology and ecology. This "Third Great Age," like the second, has grown out of a scientific revolution, especially in physics, that has, in generating "modernism" as an intellectual mind set, overshadowed the continuing validity of the historically oriented sciences, such as those connected with biological evolution, that had been so crucial in giving shape to the Second Great Age of Discovery. Even the startling emergence of the theory of plate tectonics or continental drift in modern geology has curiously enough been seen in terms of systems, balances, and equilibrium, rather than in the historical terms it really represents. Thus the linear, history-oriented time-line worldview that emerged with the discovery of evolutionism in the Second Great Age of Discovery, though still valid, now appears to have lost its monopoly as a principle for organizing reality, but it nonetheless had its day.

The new Third Age of Discovery appears to be an age of *simultaneity*, in which primitive cultures must be equated with highly technological cultures. Times must be relative, and space conceptually altered—as in Cubism or the Dymaxion map projections of R. Buckminster Fuller, the twentieth-century Mercator. Highly experimental physical science, dealing with the sometimes "invisible" data of quantum mechanics, and affected by Heisenberg's uncertainty principle, rather than descriptive, inductive, and evolutionary science, has often characterized the thinking of a new twentieth-century age of discovery in which the explorers' domain has largely been connected with the relativism of outer space. Science as common-sense descriptive history, so characteristic of the Second Great Age of Discovery, has been eclipsed by the popularization of the ideas connected with modern physics and space age exploration. But living, as we are, in a bewildering Third Great Age of Discovery only makes the patterns of the First and Second Ages stand out more clearly as being intellectually dominated by religion as well as a desire for "trade and dominion" and an unfolding empiricism that highlighted emergent science as much as trade and imperialism respectively. In particular, we are able to see the history of the United States as it developed within the matrix of the culture of science and as one of the primary achievements of the Second Great Age of Discovery. America has indeed been "exploration's nation"—a culture of endless possibilities that, in the spirit of both science and its component, exploration, continually looks forward in the direction of the new.

ii

POSSIBLY if it had not been for Sir Joseph Banks's insistence in 1768 that Captain Cook carry with him on the *Endeavour* a complement of naturalists and artists, thus making a dramatic division with past practices, it could be argued that the First Great Age of Discovery would never really have ended. From the time of da Gama, who opened a route to the riches of the Indies, and Columbus, who discovered a New World en route to these riches, exploring activity on the part of the Portuguese and Spaniards continued for well over a century. After Magellan rounded South America and crossed the Pacific, he was followed by Mendaña and Quiros and Torres, who threaded their way through the Pacific Islands. Spanish explorer-conquistadors, beginning with Balboa and Cortez, spread out all over the New World, from the Seven Cities of Cibola in New Mexico to the Incan citadels in Andean South America. Orellana coursed down the Amazon, and legions of Spaniards trekked through South American jungles looking for the river of silver (somewhere at the headwaters of the Rio de la Plata) or for El Dorado—the golden king who presumably ruled over a domain somewhere in Guiana from a golden raft which perpetually sailed on a golden lake. By 1600, the Spanish had a world empire, and Manila galleons bound to and from the New World regularly crossed the Pacific.

Meanwhile, the Portuguese had not only explored but established themselves as traders in the Indies. Out from Goa, their chief trading port on the western coast of India, they sailed into the spice islands of Java and Sumatra. They crossed the South China Sea, put in at Formosa, and eventually reached Cipangu (Japan). In the sixteenth century the Portuguese were masters of the East, and in far-off Goa and Macao their exploits were celebrated by the poet Luís Vaz de Camoëns, whose *The Lusiads* remains the national epic of Portuguese discovery.

And then, around 1600, as Spanish and Portuguese energies began to wane, they were succeeded by the Dutch and the English, then the French and the Russians. In 1602, the Dutch formed the East India Company to consolidate gains already made by their explorer-traders in that remote part of the world. Men with unfamiliar names like Jantszoon, Hartogzoon, Thijszoon, Nuyts, and Tasman had discovered and circumnavigated Australia by the mid-seventeenth century. These and other Dutch navigators sailed to and fro among the Indies, sometimes discovering strange and remote places like Easter Island, found by Roggeveen in 1722. At other times they clashed with and extinguished the forces of Portugal in the Indies. Batavia, on the island of Java, became their trading capital. As early as 1609, they established a trading port at Hirado, in Japan, and became the only westerners to enjoy hospitality in that island kingdom until Matthew Calbraith Perry's ships appeared off Edo Bay in 1853. In the seventeenth century, too, the Dutch explored South America, sent Henry Hudson up the North American river that bears his name, and established trading footholds at New Amsterdam (New York), Albany, and the Cape of Good Hope in South Africa. It was an age of extremely practical exploration geared to trading rivalries and imperial designs on a global scale.

The interiors of the continents were likewise not neglected. During the seventeenth century the French, following Cartier and Champlain, coursed far up the St. Lawrence, establishing Quebec, Montreal, and Michilimackinac. They cruised the Great Lakes to Green Bay and the site of modern Duluth, and crossed over via the Fox and Illinois rivers to the Mississippi. In 1682 the Chevalier de La Salle sailed down that mighty river to its mouth in a country which he named Louisiana after his king. And while French explorers were roaming over the North American wilderness, the Russians were reaching out eastward across the vast stretches of what was to be their Asian empire. By 1643, Vasili Poyarkov had passed Lake Baikal and followed the Amur River to the Sea of Ohkotsk, which looked out on the Pacific. Russian explorers had crossed over three thousand miles of Siberian wasteland in less than fifty years. And to the north, Keghnev, Buldakov, and others had reached the Arctic coasts of Siberia by midcentury. Others had penetrated Central Asia to Afghanistan and Outer Mongolia.

In the seventeenth century, as the result of economic and imperial rivalries—even sometimes simple curiosity and accident, as in the case of the shanghaied pirate-explorer William Dampier—what the historian J. H. Parry has called the Age of Reconnaissance came to a climax.

At no point, it seems, was the western world free from the compulsion to explore, discover, and usually conquer. This is such a long and continuous process, and one so characteristic of occidental rather than oriental civilizations, that it must perforce be central to the nature of occidental man. From the cockpit of Europe—perhaps because of overpopulation and a surfeit of wars—there had been an immense energy directed toward searching out the remote places on the globe.

iii

AND YET, even given the existence of this continual process, one detects a sharp difference between the post-Renaissance "Age of Reconnaissance" and the new Second Great Age of Exploration. Europe had changed as the seventeenth-century Scientific Revolution and the Enlightenment dramatically changed men's minds and reason became the dominant human faculty. Men became more intensely interested in a systematic scientific examination of all parts of the globe in the hope of promoting universal progress, rather than the wars and crude religious rivalries of the past. The learned society, pretending to universal interests and the improvement of mankind, such as the British Royal Society and the French Académie des Sciences, replaced the *Wunderkammer* or individual cabinet of curiosities as the focus of information-gathering and learned analysis. This in turn greatly affected the nature of exploration, which became one of the most useful, if not spectacular, activities of the Enlightenment. Implicit in the methodology of eighteenth-century science was the idea of cumulative and linear progress in the field of knowledge. These twin objectives, science and progress, characterized the Second Great Age of Discovery. New techniques, new instruments, new forms of organizations, and new kinds of explorers developed rapidly, and the globe, once thought to be tolerably well known in the Renaissance *mappi-mundi*, was rediscovered once again in an entirely new way. Characterized by the rage for scientific discovery as a new excuse for adventure and more subtle imperial conquest, the eighteenth and nineteenth centuries stand on their own as the Second Great Age of Discovery.

Another hallmark of the Second Great Age of Discovery was a drive for precision. Since the days of Isaac Newton, mathematics and astronomy had come to the fore, and with the development of these disciplines arose the possibility of highly accurate mapping of the oceans and the continents. Indeed, the possibilities for new and precise mapping helped to focus so much attention upon charting the vast Pacific and its archipelagoes that some authorities, notably the late J. C. Beaglehole and J. H. Parry, have seen the exploration of the Pacific as the sole focus of a new age of discovery. Important as the Pacific was in the imagination of Europeans, however, the examination of the interiors of the continents, the search for a Northwest Passage across the Americas, and the investigation of the polar regions also occupied a more than equal amount of attention. Out of the investigation of the world's landmasses grew the new science of geography, chiefly promoted by the Prussian Alexander von Humboldt. He used the map as a device to stress interrelationships and the organic connection of everything in nature. Thus even teeming and varied life on earth could be pictured easily in mathematical relationships.

Mathematics was not the only form of precision characteristic of the new age of discovery, however. It was also an age of calculated empiricism. It harked back to Francis Bacon, who had declared, "Man, being the servant and interpreter of nature, can do and understand so much and so much only as he has observed in fact or in thought of the course of nature: beyond this he neither knows anything nor can do anything." Even more conscious of the views of John Locke and emerging Enlightenment figures in Scotland and France, the explorers of the Second Great Age of Discovery went out to see nature for themselves, armed with a desire for exceedingly close observation. They were no longer content with myths, marvels, or fables, or with confirming the truths of Aristotle's system of nature. What they saw, in fact, on their expeditions over oceans and continents forced a complete change in the field of natural history.

By 1735, Linnaeus, the Swedish botanist, had devised a new classification system based upon genus and species and derived from the actual observation of plants and animals. As more and more naturalists accompanied the expeditions, thousands of new genera and species were discovered, until the central organizing principle of all nature was severely threatened. So many new specimens were discovered that the Great Chain of Being, into which the whole of nature from insects to man had been fitted, began to disintegrate as an organizing principle of knowledge. No one suggested what was happening more clearly than Sir James Edward Smith, the first president of the British Linnaean Society. Writing of his work in Australia, he declared:

> When a botanist first enters on the investigation of so remote a country as New Holland, he finds himself, as it were, in a new world. He can scarcely meet with any fixed points from whence to draw his analogies and even those that appear more promising, are frequently in danger of misleading, instead of informing him. The whole tribe of plants which at first sight seem familiar to his acquaintance, as occupying links in Nature's chain, on which he is accustomed to depend, prove on nearer examination, total strangers, with other configurations, other oeconomys, and other qualities; not only the species themselves are new, but most of the genera, and even natural orders.

Like Sir James Edward Smith, literally thousands of naturalist explorers began to perceive so many anomalies in the Great Chain of Being that they first caused it to expand to the breaking point, and then by 1800 began looking for a whole new set of principles upon which to organize the natural history of the world. Whether on tropical islands, in the lush jungles of South America, or in the vast backcountry of North America, naturalists and the artists who accompanied them became aware of a teeming, variegated, proliferating world that was full of rich, qualitative sense impressions that seemed to grow and suggest change before their very eyes. Instruments like the microscope only enhanced these impressions. It was thus almost inevitable that the static world view governed by the Great Chain of Being eventually gave way to developmentalism, and a new organic metaphor, the tree of life, replaced the old mechanistic metaphor of the chain and its links. Following the dictates of Lockean empiricism, the natural historians had introduced a precise appreciation for the distinctive and the qualitative as well as the exotic in nature.

The shift toward a more organic principle was reinforced by the work of scientific artists—men such as Captain Cook's Sydney Parkinson and William Hodges, Humboldt's Aimé Bonpland, Mark Catesby, William Bartram, and even Captain Bligh, who, though remembered as a naval officer, was also an accomplished artist. These scientific illustrators not only stressed the brilliantly colored and exotic specimens of nature; they also portrayed ecological relationships. Very often these artists were well in advance of more specialized scientists in this area of endeavor. They depicted animals, plants, and people in their "natural surroundings" or "native habitats" in relationship to one another because they, like the mapmakers and geographers, were interested in the interrelationship of all terrestrial phenomena. Thus the artists and mapmakers, in collaboration with the explorer-scientists, helped make the growing, proliferating, changing tree of life the central metaphor of the age. By the latter quarter of the eighteenth century, even Peter Pallas, scientific explorer of the remotest reaches of Russia, had pictured a tree as representing all the species of plants and animals. Thus, in following Lockean or Baconian empiricism to its logical extreme on all fronts, both naturalists and artists found themselves in the protean world of the Romantic Age.

Profusely illustrated tomes and scientific reports became the vogue. In endless lists accompanied by engravings in varied hues and tints, they depicted everything from the golden bird of paradise and the strange pagodas of Japan to the gorillas of darkest Africa and the lost cities of Central America. Travel books, as well as accounts of expeditions, became the rage among the reading public. Periodicals like *The Gentleman's Magazine* and *The Illustrated London News* regularly carried features chronicling expeditions to the ends of the earth. And as far back as Daniel Defoe's *Robinson Crusoe*, the adventure novel tradition began, usually focused on a voyage or an expedition to an exotic place.

Thus, the explorers of the Second Great Age of Discovery rediscovered space, time, the cosmos, and a whole new imagination. They helped to create a revolution that affected virtually every form of cultural activity. And, though labeled explorers, they must certainly be counted as crucial members of a rapidly expanding scientific community—a community that, however indirectly, has come to dominate the modern world.

In all of this activity Americans were, for a variety of reasons, willing participants. From the earliest days of settlement—as the work of the British scientist Thomas Heriot and the artist John White and the writings of the adventurer Captain John Smith attest—what was to be America aroused intense curiosity. As the naturalist tradition grew in England and among the Jesuits of New France, North America became a vast, pristine collecting ground for men of scientific curiosity. For a time, virtually everything they found was new. America was a paradise for the scientific collector, no matter what his training or skill. Moreover, the country was wild enough so that every march through the backcountry could justly be called an adventure back in Europe.

A second phase of American participation in the new age of discovery was a product of the emulation of European scientists and scientific institutions. As the colonial settlements grew and men had more leisure, a number of them became serious naturalists and even explorers—like the great John Bartram of Philadelphia. They cooperated with British naturalists sent to the New World. They made collections of plants and animal specimens for English gentlemen just then (in the eighteenth century) turning to the cultivation of country estates with exotic gardens. They formed scientific societies like the American Philosophical Society for the Promotion of Useful Knowledge and the American Academy of Arts and Sciences, modeled after the British Royal Society and the French Académie des Sciences respectively. And they corresponded regularly with fellow naturalists and students of nature across the Atlantic. Recognition by European learned societies was a distinct mark of prestige for the American colonial.

A final stage in the American participation in the Second Great Age of Discovery came with independence. Since that great achievement, nationalism—or some form of national pride or a desire for national security—has played a great part in American exploring activity. This phenomenon has taken many forms throughout our history and is a complex theme in the whole narrative of American exploration.

It is of the greatest significance, however, that the United States began in the middle of a great age of exploration; one of the hallmarks of a great and emergent nation was that it, too, developed a culture adventuresome enough and sophisticated enough to join in the exploration of the globe and universe. America, beginning *in medias res*, responded well to the habits and rhythms of an age of exploration.

In the book that follows, I hope, by focusing upon explorers of all types who contributed to the growing body of knowledge, to see America and the Americans as part of the new cultural horizon—an intellectual landscape—that I have termed the Second Great Age of Discovery. The story begins with representative men and events, largely European, but very quickly turns to the theme of nationalism as explorers played their parts in what came to be called the Debate over the New World. Without real exploration, it was impossible to refute European savants who theorized that everything in the New World was inferior.

After this heated skirmish in the days of the early Republic, Americans then turned to the exploration of the sublime immensity of the continent. In the process, led by explorers, the

United States created a republican and democratic nation from
sea to sea. At the same time, recognizing that two oceans and the
Gulf of Mexico were to mark its borders and concerned with the
legitimate rights of a maritime nation, the United States also entered dramatically into the great era of maritime exploration.
Americans undertook their own investigation of remote islands
and landmasses in the world, in the course of which they discovered a new continent, Antarctica, and they began the process of
mapping the ocean floor. Indeed, an American, Matthew Fontaine Maury, pioneered in developing a whole new science—
oceanography. At no point was the United States exclusively
preoccupied with the great interior frontier of North America.
Thus studies of the exploration of the American frontier, about
which I have previously written, can now be seen in a larger
and, I hope, more meaningful context.

The sweep to the west, the ocean-spanning voyages, and the
penetration of other continents and remote islands immersed
American explorers and scientists in a spatial paradigm that was
centered in the science of geography. Organizing visual experience in relation to space became the first task of the age. New
visual tools, especially refinements in cartography and scientific
renditions of the landscape, had to be devised. Then, as explorers rediscovered lost cities or ancient forgotten cultures—as
geologists on expeditions, using fossil-dating techniques, greatly
extended the age of the earth, and as naturalists turned more and
more to developmentalism—the spatial paradigm for organizing
knowledge perforce had to take time into account. History on a
vast scale was rediscovered in the nineteenth century—natural
history and recorded human history, as well as the prehistory of
man, now known as archaeology, which was developed during
this era and in a sense joined the spatial paradigm as a means of
organizing knowledge. Thus, the age developed a peculiar bin-
ocular vision in which it saw both space and time at once. Indeed, thanks to the works of science-oriented explorers, artists,
philosophers, and theorists in laboratories, the age came to see
many "times" in many "spaces," until by the end of the nine-

teenth century, relativism and relativity had seemingly brought about the climax of the Second Great Age of Discovery—and the beginning of a new age that embraces the concept of a "chance universe" in a way that many of the followers of Darwin never could quite do without abandoning the teleology of a Divine Providence that controlled the destiny of nature.

All of this was not wrought solely by explorers in the traditional sense of the word, of course. But their efforts in discovering and gathering new information and the ways in which they presented and interpreted this information had a profound impact upon American and western culture—upon science, philosophy, and art, and also upon the popular imagination, which, after all, supported those other more esoteric realms. And yet, possibly because of its relationship to popular culture and adventure stories, exploration has most often been portrayed as a peripheral activity, a thing apart from the mainstream of serious (perhaps elitist) cultural development. It is the main burden of this book to show that this simply was not so in eighteenth- and nineteenth-century America.

And finally, from the above and what follows, it should be clear that large views of a nation's cultural and intellectual history can be conveyed in different metaphors or stories. In this account one will find few of the conventional figures discussed by previous historians of "the American Mind." On the other hand, the reader will, I hope, find abundant evidence of what the late Harvard historian Perry Miller called "the life of the mind in America."

BOOK ONE

THE BOOK OF THE CONTINENT

CHAPTER 1

The Cosmic Voyagers

THE CASE OF THE "OBLATE SPHEROID"

THE SECOND GREAT AGE OF DISCOVERY began on a global and even cosmic scale. Two questions of profound importance arose in the late seventeenth century with the publication of Sir Isaac Newton's *Principia Mathematica* in 1687. They agitated the best minds of Europe—particularly those affiliated with the recently formed British Royal Society and the French Académie des Sciences. The first was the scientific determination of the true shape of the earth. The second was the measurement of the sun's exact distance from the earth, which, if it could be calculated, would ultimately enable astronomers to map the whole solar system with accuracy. These questions, at first glance remote from the everyday practical concerns of men and nations, came to have a direct bearing upon the way in which all people looked at and adjusted to life.

Isaac Newton had argued that the earth was not a perfect sphere, as the ancients had maintained. Rather, because of the force of gravity, exerted principally by the sun and the moon, it was pulled out of shape. According to Newton, it bulged at the equator and was flattened at the poles. He did not prove this experimentally, but if it was true, then all the maps and charts of both land and sea, even those marvelous projections of Gerard Mercator, would have to be changed if men were to locate themselves with some precision on the globe. Ships at sea, the locations of capitals, the boundaries of nations, continents, mountains, lakes, rivers, not to mention landholdings of citizens, would all be affected significantly. Despite the efforts of chartmakers from Genoa to Amsterdam, it was well known by the early eighteenth century that existing maps were usually grossly inaccurate. The ocean-spanning voyages on which explorers searched diligently and fruitlessly for islands and continents recorded by previous captains brought this home more dramatically than anything else. The chief problem was the determination of longitude, particularly its determination at sea. But that was not to be solved until the mid-eighteenth century. Meanwhile, Newton's hypothesis spoke to the problem of latitude. If the earth varied in shape, what was to be the measurement of an arc of latitude?

Newton's assertion struck most directly at the savants of the French Académie. Most of them were devoted followers of one of Newton's great rivals, René Descartes, the French mathematician, who viewed the cosmos and, indeed, all matter as a dancing cluster of vortices or cones. Descartes and his followers accordingly saw the earth as a "prolate spheroid"—a football-shaped planet—rather than a waist-bulging "oblate spheroid." The French academicians were already acting on Descartes's principles. Under the leadership of Jacques Cassini de Thury, Astronomer Royal, and Jean Picard, they had made their own determination of an arc of latitude, based on the prolate spheroid theory, and they were busy establishing what they hoped would be the world's prime meridian of longitude running directly through Paris to the ends of the earth. They were also well along in creating the first truly scientific map of any nation—France, of course. Newton's assertions had to be rejected. The honor of France depended upon it.

In 1666, Christian Huygens, a Dutch natural philosopher, had arrived in Paris with a pendulum clock. Huygens's pendulum could be used to solve the problem, it came to be recognized by the French academicians; for if Newton was correct, the pendulum would swing more slowly at the equator than at higher latitudes because the pull of gravity would be less. Instantly grasping the logic of Huygens's experiment, Jacques Cassini de Thury sent one of his longtime associates, Jean Richter, to Cayenne near the equator in French Guiana to conduct the pendulum test. Richter returned with results that proved Newton, not Descartes, was right. National honor and personal reputation were dashed. Cassini denounced his onetime friend as *un hypocrite traître*, and refused to believe the results were conclusive.

The Newtonian forces were growing, however. Voltaire had visited England and had been captivated by the great mathematician and his vision of the cosmos. He, together with his mistress, Emilie du Châtelet, translated Newton's *Principia* into French lest those academicians who could not read Latin miss its message. Other rising scholars had also gone to England and come under the influence of Newton, and they insisted that objective truth, not national glory, was the goal of the Enlightenment and especially of its chief activity, science. The Académie decided to resolve the perplexing controversy in an eminently practical way. It dispatched two scientific expeditions, one to Lapland, or the north coast of Scandinavia, and one to Quito in Peru (now Ecuador), in the high, upland country near the equator. Each expedition was to measure an arc of latitude. The two could then be compared and the agitated community of scientific experts could then calmly determine whether the earth was oblate, prolate, or, as Aristotle said it was, perfectly spherical. The two expeditions were as much a test of Newton's theory of gravitation as they were of the Descartes-Cassini theory.

The first expedition left for South America in May 1735, under the leadership of thirty-four-year-old Charles Marie de La Condamine. He spent some fourteen years in the jungles and windswept highlands of South America, and it was not until March of 1743 that he and a colleague, Jean Godin, completed final measurements of the vital arc. Long before this, despite a shipwreck in the Baltic Sea, Pierre Maupertius had returned from Lapland in 1737 with *his* measurement of an arc for northern latitudes and convincing proof that Newton was right.

Cassini's great map of France had to be redone. Swallowing family pride, the Cassinis undertook this task, which consumed the energies of three generations and was eventually completed just on the eve of the French Revolution. But France and its scientific community salvaged more than honor as a result of the prolonged and dedicated labors of Charles Marie de La Condamine. Assisted by an intrepid team of French and Spanish scientists, most notably Pierre Bouguer, an experienced astronomer of the Cassini school; Louis and Jean Godin, mathematicians; Joseph de Jussieu, a botanist; Jean Seniergues, physician; Captain Jorge Juan y Santacilla and Captain Antonio de Ulloa, Spanish military engineers; and, not least, Pedro Maldonado, surveyor and governor of Esmeralda; and equipped with all of the latest scientific instruments, La Condamine's expedition— the first to include an international company of cooperating savants—formed a brilliant opening to the Second Great Age of Discovery.

La Condamine was the protégé of Voltaire. A young man of wealth and position, whose family had made a fortune in the "Mississippi Bubble" while others were ruined in this ill-founded speculation in Louisiana silver mines, La Condamine had been a soldier fighting in the Pyrenees when he became fascinated with South America. A Spanish prisoner had told him tales of the Andes and the Amazon, and thus had changed his life. Largely self-taught, he became, as was fashionable in France, a mathematician and geodesist (or earth measurer). At the age of twenty-nine, shortly after an expedition to the Barbary Coast, he was elected to the French Académie. His selection as leader of the South American expedition was largely due to two factors: he contributed 100,000 livres toward its expenses, and he was backed by Voltaire.

Leaving France in May of 1735, La Condamine penetrated the heart of the Spanish empire in America, including the rich ports of Cartagena and Puerto Bello in Panama, where both Drake and Hawkins had come to grief. After a long delay on the west coast of Panama, he and his party sailed for Manta, a dilapidated port on the coast of what is now Ecuador. Here his party split, with the main body sailing on to Guayaquil, and thence pushing on over the Andes to Quito. La Condamine and Bouguer remained behind and fell to work tracing out the arc, with La Condamine starting exactly on the equator at a point seventy miles north of Manta. When they had finished, Bouguer sailed off to join the others, while La Condamine, meeting Pedro Maldonado, pioneered, or rather rediscovered, a new route via the Esmeralda River to Quito.

There is no way to do justice to La Condamine's journey to Quito. Guided by the intrepid Maldonado, who was governor of the province, the French explorer plunged into the green jungle world. He traveled via dugout canoe up the Esmeralda River, confronted on every hand by lush vegetation, exotic birds—rainbow parrots, toucans, hummingbirds no bigger than a moth—monkeys, jaguars, huge frogs that climbed trees, crocodiles, tapirs, and lemurs, and all the sounds of a tropical world dominated by huge trees and arching vines which shut out the sky and the river. The boatmen were all blacks, survivors from the wreck of a slave ship. On the way, La Condamine also visited emerald mines, discovered a shining silver metal that became known to the world as platinum, and, most important of all, made the first effective scientific discovery of rubber and its many uses. He watched in fascination the natives tapping it from the trees and molding it into objects or fashioning it into waterproof bags. Entranced by the marvels of nature all around him, La Condamine, primarily an astronomer and mathematician, enthusiastically expanded his interests to include the rich, variegated world of natural history and a kind of primitive anthropology.

By this time, he had seen the natives of Panama, the blacks of Esmeralda, the diminutive Colorado Indians who came out of

the forests painted stark red from hair to toe, and the almond-
eyed, almost Mongolian peoples of the high Andean plateaus
as he and Maldonado made their way up out of the rain forest
to the ancient pre-Inca capital of Quito, a city whose backdrop
was formed by some of the highest mountains in the world,
from spectacular, volcanic Cotopaxi to mighty, towering Chimborazo. By the time he reached Quito, La Condamine, though
armed with barometers, thermometers, sextants, octants, theo-
dolites, and the *toise,* or French measuring stick, had become
more than a mathematician. He was a geographer and an ethnologist. It was the beginning of a pattern characteristic of the
age—one in which the new science, with all its intricate relationships among the terrain, the flora, the fauna, the peoples,
and the heavens, emerged as the synthesizing focus of the scientific explorer.

The whole expedition reassembled at Quito and began work
on the measurement of the arc. Their labors were immense, and
not completed until 1743, nearly eight years after they had
sailed from France. Essentially their work consisted first of
finding a large, flat plain where they could lay out a baseline determined by astronomical calculations. Then from this baseline,
they could triangulate their way across country, which they
eventually did to the extent of three exactly determined arcs of
latitude. These they connected up with the equator. Plagued by
politics and local superstition, which caused endless delays; dis-
consolate over the loss of five years' worth of botanical collections (an event which drove the expedition's botanist de Jussieu
irrevocably insane); confronted by sky-high mountains and active, erupting volcanoes atop which his surveying crews had to
work amid shriveling cold and lightning and fog, or barren deserts where the winds blew forever, furnace-hot in the day and
ice-cold at night, and where his men were always sick, La Condamine nonetheless held to his task. He held to it even after he
learned in June of 1739 that Maupertius had already proved
Newton's point, and in Voltaire's jubilant words, "flattened the

earth as well as the Cassinis." He even survived an international crisis over the stone pyramids he had erected to mark the spot of his arc measurements. At last, in March of 1743, his labors were over.

The party broke up, with some staying on in Peru and Ecuador, while La Condamine and Maldonado crossed over the Andes to the rain forest and began a three-thousand-mile descent of the Amazon. In the course of their journey, La Condamine and Maldonado made the first scientific map of the river and the region. They also located a spot where the natives said a canal joined the river with the Orinoco, thus providing a focus for a whole new generation of Amazon explorers. These explorers would have to face, however, still another phenomenon which La Condamine found highly interesting, the blowgun dart poison curare. He experimented with this and with quinine as a cure for tropical disease. He also became, as he emerged from the Amazon jungles, an advocate of smallpox vaccination. He had seen it and it worked in saving thousands of would-be doomed Amazonian natives.

When La Condamine arrived back in Paris in the spring of 1745, he came as a towering hero. His work inspired Voltaire's classic *Candide*, and he was voted into the Pantheon as one of France's forty "Immortals," an acclaim he richly deserved. He had helped, even more thoroughly than Maupertius, to determine the shape of the globe. And beyond this, his geodesy had led him from the heavens and the solar system into the immense possibilities of the new age of world geography with all its richness and wealth of detail.

ii

EYEING VENUS

THE SECOND great scientific enterprise of the age was stimulated by a rare celestial event. In 1761, and then again in 1769, the planet Venus, as observed from the earth, passed directly across the face of the sun. Such a pair of Venus "immersions" (and they always came in pairs) did not happen more than once in a century. These transits offered a matchless opportunity to men of science in the eighteenth century. Since the days of Johannes Kepler, who calculated the orbits of the inferior planets in 1627, early astronomers had speculated that it was theoretically possible to determine the distance of the sun from the earth by timing the transits of certain planets, namely Mercury and Venus, across the sun's face as they passed between the earth and the sun. Then, knowing the absolute distance of the sun from the earth, and the orbits of the planets, it might be possible to chart with precision the whole solar system.

As early as 1631, Pierre Gassendi, from a makeshift observatory in Paris, traced the paths of both Mercury and Venus across the sun, but his mathematical skills were insufficient to solve the basic problem. Then, in 1639, a twenty-two-year-old English astronomer, Jeremiah Horrocks, also observed a transit of Venus, but he too was unable to calculate with any precision what had come to be called the solar parallax. This was due chiefly to certain errors in Kepler's calculations of the planetary orbits, and the difficulty, given the instruments of the period, of timing exactly Venus's passage across the sun. Horrocks estimated that the passage had taken no more than fourteen seconds, but this was a very loose estimate, and even in the seventeenth century, astronomers and mathematicians were well aware that precise measurement and precise observation made all the difference in their experiments. However, there would be no second chance anytime soon. The transit of Venus across the sun would not take place again for 122 years, or until 1761.

Between 1639 and 1761, several astronomers made attempts to measure the sun's distance through the planet-parallax method. In 1672–73, Jean Dominique Cassini (Cassini I) and colleague, Jean Richter, sailed to Cayenne and attempted to use an immersion of Mars for the measurement. They failed. In 1677, Edmund Halley, observing from St. Helena in the South Atlantic, also failed when he attempted to use Mercury's transit for the same purpose. He came to realize that only a transit of

Venus would do, and speaking of that marvelous event, he wrote in 1691, "The sight which is by far the noblest astronomy affords, is denied to mortals for a whole century [sic], by the strict laws of motion. It will afterwards be shown that, by this observation alone, the distance of the sun, from the earth, might be determined. . . ." In 1716, he presented a paper to the Royal Society calling for preparations looking toward the transit of 1761 to begin immediately.

The impending transit of Venus preoccupied a great part of the western scientific world in the first half of the eighteenth century. It competed for attention, and then surpassed, the argument over the shape of the earth. In France, preparations were coordinated by Joseph Nicolas Delisle, whose whole family, like the Cassinis, was engaged in the mapmaking trade. Delisle, like many others in his day, was an indefatigable correspondent. He was also a great traveler and organizer. After he had met with failure in an observation of Mercury in 1723, he sailed to England and there met with Halley and Newton to discuss the whole transit problem. Then, accepting the invitation of Catherine I, he traveled to Russia, where he organized the astronomical activities of the Russian Academy. He supported Nicolas Louis de la Caille's expedition to the Cape of Good Hope to observe the transit of Mercury in 1753, which resulted in a failure to measure the sun's distance but did produce the first sky charts of the southern hemisphere. All of this was a buildup for the great undertaking of 1761. The French Académie engaged in endless discussions of the project. Mathematicians in both England and France pored over Edmund Halley's tables, and in 1760, Delisle published his famous *mappemonde*, or world map, showing the best places on the globe to observe Venus. In France, especially, all of this was followed step by step in the public press as a great national project.

In all, 120 observers from sixty-two separate stations around the world made observations of the Venus transit in 1761. This included a voyage made with great reluctance by the two immortal boundary surveyors Charles Mason and Jeremiah Dixon to the Cape of Good Hope, a trek by John Winthrop of Harvard

College to a remote mosquito-plagued station in Newfoundland, an expedition by Jean Chappe d'Auteroche to freezing Siberia, and elaborate voyages by Gui Pingre of France and Nevil Maskelyne, Astronomer Royal of England, to Isle Rodriguez in the Indian Ocean and St. Helena in the South Atlantic, respectively. All of these expeditions were guaranteed scientific immunity, despite the global skirmishes between England and France that constituted the Seven Years' War. These were among the most elaborate expeditions, but transit observations also came in from such widely scattered places as Peking, Calcutta, Tobolsk, Trondheim, Munich, Lisbon, Constantinople, and Rome. In an effort to gaze intently heavenward, a very considerable number of men trekked or voyaged over the earth.

Despite all the preparation, all the worldwide enthusiasm, the 1761 observations produced no agreement on the Venus parallax. In part this was due to the use of widely differing instruments, differences in the talents of the observers and the conditions for observing, faulty mathematical tables, and, most exasperating of all, the "black drop effect." This was an optical illusion that made it impossible to tell just the precise moment that Venus was in full internal placement on the sun. A strange umbilical linkage of Venus's black disk with the darkness of outer space remained before the eyes of viewers for some time after Venus had actually been immersed in the sun's bright disk. It was a phenomenon not unlike the difficulty of determining by eye the exact moment of disengagement between thumb and forefinger on the human hand.

Between 1761 and 1769, debate raged over the exact time of Venus's crossing. Ever-mounting public interest only made the expeditions planned for 1769 seem all the more urgent. Success seemed imminent—and who could wait another 122 years? In all there were 151 observers, many with better instruments, watching Venus from seventy-seven stations around the world. Under all sorts of conditions from bad weather and the decks of pitching ships on rolling seas to remote stations with primitive instruments, the scientific world watched the planet on its mysterious parade across the life-giving sun. Once again, skywatchers braved the remoteness of such places as the Malabar Coast, Cabo de San Luco at the trip of the California Peninsula, steamy Sainte Dominique in the West Indies, Lapland, Arctic Russia, and perhaps most noteworthy, newly discovered "Otahiti" in the South Pacific, where Captain James Cook was making his debut as an explorer.

Some idea of the intense American interest in the transit can be gained from the activities and reactions of David Rittenhouse of Philadelphia. The New World's foremost astronomer, Rittenhouse intercepted a lens destined for John Winthrop at Harvard, used it to make his own powerful telescope, and, working day and night, prepared for the great event. June 3, 1769, found him ready, lying prone on a muddy field just outside Philadelphia, propped up by an assistant, every muscle tense, his eye fastened to the telescope. Then, just as Venus made its fuzzy appearance on the edge of the sun's disk, he signaled contact and fell into a dead faint out of sheer excitement. The swoon lasted six minutes, so that he came to in time to record the planet's disappearance from the sun's face. Dr. Benjamin Rush, observing the scene, caught something of the age's and the American colonial's romantic faith in science: the transit "excited, in the instant of one of the contacts of the planet with the sun, an emotion of delight so exquisite and powerful as to induce fainting." Despite his swoon, Rittenhouse gained great fame in Europe on the strength of his observation of the transit. He had participated meaningfully in a ceremony that western man in the eighteenth century had come to regard as holy.

Once again, however, the results were inconclusive. More experience could not overcome the inherent optical difficulties of the "black drop effect," and the astronomers of the day had not yet learned that such phenomena as the constants of celestial progression and the gravity of the earth and the moon affected what they saw, and altered the precision of their observations. Still, scientific debate at the time obscured how very close the collective findings of the planet-watchers had come to real precision. When the nineteenth-century American astronomer Simon Newcomb went back over all the expedition calculations, he found an average immersion figure of 8.79 seconds, which was not far from the 1950 figure of 8.798. The Venus observers may have failed to measure the solar system in the eighteenth century, but they did not fail by much.

In a sense, the story of the observations of the eighteenth-century transits of Venus belongs properly to the internal history of astronomy. But the flurry of astronomical activity, the necessity of making observations from many points on the globe, had helped to generate two *anni mirabiles* of worldwide exploration. The entire episode illustrates the close connection between the mathematical breakthroughs of the scientific revolution, chiefly centered in cosmology, and the nature of exploration in the new age of discovery.

The importance of the work of this first generation of cosmic voyagers for the present story lies in the unprecedented number of scientific exploring expeditions that were generated all around the globe. Unlike the expeditions of an earlier age, these were indeed scientific rather than trading or plundering expeditions. They keynoted a new age in which, while trade, plunder, and imperial designs were still relevant to exploring activity, a new dimension had been added—the search for pure knowledge, scientific knowledge for the benefit of mankind in general. And if the scientific expedition was the dramatic manifestation of the Enlightenment, then no expedition stands out more clearly or has received more attention than that of Captain James Cook. His voyage on the *Endeavour* to Tahiti in 1769 and his subsequent Pacific voyages were (like the Andean labors of La Condamine) models of rigorous, exact exploration as he rediscovered, in the name of science, the oceanic world.

iii

PIRATES, PROMOTERS, AND CIRCUMNAVIGATORS

COOK'S VOYAGES, like the expedition of La Condamine and those of the 271 Venus-watchers of 1761 and 1769, stemmed from the global and celestial concerns of the scientific academicians, and from the popular and governmental concerns their academies generated. His primary mission in 1769 was, of course, to observe the transit of Venus from Tahiti, which Wallis had recently discovered on a circumnavigation in 1766–7. In addition, Cook was to search the far southern seas for the lost continent of Terra Australis Incognita, thought to have been sighted by Marco Polo, then by early Spanish and French voyagers, and somewhat more recently by the pirate Edward Davis. Terra Australis Incognita was said to be a vast southern continent equal to Europe or Asia or North America and incredibly rich in gold, jewels, and temples, and where the people rode elephants in lush tropical surroundings. The great Maupertius believed in the existence of a southern continent and urged Frederick the Great to mount a search for it. Then, too, a whole host of chroniclers and compilers of collections of voyages in the style of Hakluyt propagandized for the project. Charles de Brosses of Dijon, in his *Histoire des Navigations aux Terres Australes* (1756), laid out an elaborate argument for a search for the elusive continent, the most philosophical part of which was that such a continent was by nature a necessity; it had to be there—a large landmass to counterbalance the preponderance of land in the northern hemisphere; otherwise the earth itself would tumble over in space. De Brosses's sentiments were echoed by the Scotsman John Callander, whose *Terra Australis Cognita* (1766) was lifted largely from De Brosses's work. Both men shared the philosophical conviction that the southern continent was necessary for earthly balance; they also shared dreams of imperialism. De Brosses saw the great southern empire and control of the South Atlantic, the Pacific, and the Indian Ocean as the destiny of the French people, who would lead all mankind into a new era of progress and civilization. Callander saw it as Britain's destiny. His sentiments were reinforced by Alexander Dalrymple, formerly chief hydrographer to the British East India Company and then to the Admiralty itself. Dalrymple was probably the most knowledgeable man in Britain concerning the

South Seas. He alone, for example, had access to the manuscript
of Torres's voyage through the strait between New Guinea and
New Holland (Australia), and in 1767 he printed a small work,
*An Account of the Discoveries Made in the South Pacific
Ocean*, which included Torres's long-forgotten report. He, too,
espoused the global equilibrium theory and saw the southern
continent as one larger than Asia. According to his calculations,
it extended over 100° of longitude west of the coast of South
America in the latitude and direction of New Holland. It must
contain fifty million inhabitants and incredible wealth, and
would provide an immense market for British manufacturers
and traders—one that would dwarf the North American colonies that had begun to cause so much trouble. Dalrymple was
the best-informed and most experienced oceanic-exploring en-
thusiast of the age, and he longed to be the new Columbus who
would discover and conquer the last new world.

This was not to be, however, because Dalrymple was not a
naval officer and could not be given command of a ship. If he
could not command, he would not sail, and so the honor of commanding Britain's most climactic voyage of the eighteenth century went to plain Captain James Cook. Standing six feet tall
and of commanding presence, Cook was not given to flamboy-
ance or extravagant statements. Instead, he was the epitome of
the careful scientific observer. He had gained this skill through
extensive practical experience, first as second-in-command of
coaling vessels sailing the North Sea, then as an officer in the
British navy during the Seven Years' War. Here he had become
a surveyor and hydrographer. His charts of the St. Lawrence
River, Newfoundland, Nova Scotia, and Labrador were the
most painstakingly accurate of the entire century. In 1776, he
had observed and reported on an eclipse of the sun, which in-
gratiated him with the Royal Society. His skills as an astronomer as well as a hydrographer and sailor made him the ideal
choice to lead the Venus expedition to Tahiti and to lead the
search for the southern continent. Cook's secret instructions ordered him first to observe Venus from Tahiti, then to sail south,

locate Terra Australis Incognita, and report on its soil, products, and inhabitants. He was to make friends and alliances or, if the land was uninhabited, to proclaim British sovereignty over it. In fact, he was also to annex any other lands, such as the numerous islands of the Pacific, when he found it possible to do so. Upon his return, all logbooks, journals, calculations, etc. were to be immediately turned over to the Admiralty and his men were to maintain secrecy about where they had been. In Cook's voyages, science and imperialism went hand in hand.

This was not solely a British phenomenon. The whole age had begun to be fascinated by what Professor J. H. Parry has characterized as a scramble for "trade and dominion." This was not really unusual, however. What was unusual was the dedication and the contribution to science that emerged from the scramble.

Cook was not the first to explore purposefully the Pacific and the South Seas. That distinction in the "modern era" should perhaps be accorded to Abel Janszoon Tasman, whose work in nearly circumnavigating Australia and discovering New Zealand was not really appreciated by the Dutch East India Company, for which he sailed. The almost casual explorations by William Dampier, a sometime buccaneer, received vastly more attention. In 1687–88, a hostage to the piratical crew of the *Cygnet*, he had sailed across the Pacific from the west coast of Mexico to Mindanao in the Philippines, and then from island to island in the Indies. He was the first Englishman to land on New Holland's barren north coast—where his cohorts threatened to maroon him. In the course of his travels, Dampier became fascinated with the natural history and the peoples of the South Pacific. Under the most trying of circumstances, including storms, raiding ventures, and threats from his piratical colleagues, he kept a daily journal that eventually made his name. When he arrived back in England, he polished up the journal as best he could and published it in 1697 as *The New Voyage Around the World*. It was the most detailed and accurate account of its day, and made him famous—a friend to the great in the Royal Society and the Admiralty alike. In the book Dampier recounted the pirate Davis's story about the missing southern continent, and so went far in raising British enthusiasm for the quest for Terra Australis Incognita.

In 1699 the Admiralty sent him to the South Pacific in command of the *Roebuck,* which he took first to Brazil, then back across the South Atlantic past the Cape of Good Hope and directly on, running before the southern latitude westerlies, to the west coast of New Holland. Thus far he had followed an old Dutch route laid out by Tasman. Still following Tasman's charts, he sailed northeast along the Australian coast, then north to Timor, still farther north to New Guinea, around the northern end of that great, green island as far as New Ireland and New Britain, and just short of the long-sought Solomon Islands, before his ship's disrepair and his men's ill health forced him to take advantage of the monsoons and make for Batavia. There he had his worm-eaten vessel repaired as much as possible and headed for England via the Indian Ocean and the Cape of Good Hope. He made it as far as Ascension in the South Atlantic before the *Roebuck* literally fell apart. Rescued by a passing British ship, he returned to England not in triumph but to court-martial upon charges preferred by a rebellious lieutenant whom he had left to rot in a Portuguese prison in Bahia, Brazil.

Though censured by the Admiralty, Dampier was soon at sea again. As head of a privateering expedition, he captured at least three Spanish ships off the Pacific Coast of South America. But he was no leader of men, and subordinate captains ran off with two of the captured vessels. His command ship, the *St. George,* sank in the Pacific, and he sailed to the Indies aboard the smallest of the captured Spanish ships. When he reached the Indies, the Dutch seized his ship and all his goods. It was only with difficulty that he escaped imprisonment and made his way back to England. Still, this remarkable man was not through with the sea and the Indies. From 1708 to 1711, though now advanced in age, he sailed with Captain Woodes Rogers as pilot to a British round-the-world privateering expedition, which captured the annual great Manila silver galleon on its way across the Pacific from Mexico, and returned home in triumph. Dampier died in obscurity in 1715, still trying to gain his lawful share of the Spanish treasure. He had made three circumnavigations of the globe and knew the Pacific and the Indies as well as any man.

The fabulous success of Woodes Rogers's voyage had a profound effect upon the British imagination. More collections of voyages began to pour from the presses. Daniel Defoe seized upon the circumstances of Alexander Selkirk's lonely four years marooned on one of the Juan Fernández islands off the coast of Chile as the basis for his incredibly successful *Robinson Crusoe*. And even Jonathan Swift set Lemuel Gulliver's travels in the Pacific from Terra Australis Incognita to Japan. From 1741 to 1744 the British captain, later admiral, Lord George Anson sailed around the world and raided the whole west coast of Spanish South America. The famous voyage of Commodore John Byron, 1764–66, was made ostensibly to look for a shorter passage across America supposedly found by Drake. But Byron soon abandoned this and struck out for the Philippines (perhaps to catch another loaded galleon?), and then in search of the fabled Solomon Islands. On the heels of Byron's voyage, the Admiralty immediately sent out another expedition under captains Samuel Wallis and Philip Carteret. On June 18, 1767, Wallis discovered Tahiti and found it beauteous and ultimately friendly—in several respects the ideal place for a Venus observation. Then he, too, sailed far north to Guam, directly in the path of the Spanish treasure fleet. Failing to find such a fleet, he sailed north around the Philippines, thence to Batavia, and back to England, where he arrived in time to affect the destination of the Venus expedition of Captain Cook. Carteret, who sailed a more direct, westerly course, reached the Solomon Islands and even swung north to the Philippines, but his ship was in such wretched condition that he soon had to make for Batavia and home. He barely made it. Out in the Atlantic, north of Ascension Island, his leaky plodding ship was overtaken by a French vessel commanded by Louis Antoine de Bougainville. The two crews exchanged visits and supplies, but neither made mention of its circumnavigatory mission. Even during the years of international scientific cooperation and following the Peace of Paris ending the Seven Years' War, neither France nor England wished to share information as to "trade and dominion," or, for that matter, thinly disguised privateering in the Pacific.

With Louis Antoine de Bougainville's expedition, France had entered the race for the southern continent in earnest, but it had also not lost sight of the concerns of science. The French captain was the first of the great voyagers to include a scientific "corps" on his vessel. When he set sail from Nantes, France, in November 1766, he took with him Philibert de Commercon, a naturalist, and Pierre Veron, a young astronomer who was principally interested in the problem of determining longitude. Because of the contingent of scientists and Bougainville's own interest in geography and ethnology, his was to be the most important of the French voyages in the eighteenth century.

Bougainville was a short but elegant man of unusual intelligence. He had written a treatise on mathematics, had been secretary at the French embassy in London, and had served as an officer under General Montcalm in the great wilderness war in America. When he returned to France after the death of both Montcalm and the French North American empire on the heights of Quebec, he became an officer in the French navy and an ardent exponent of French control of the South Atlantic. Out of his own pocket he had financed a French colony in the Falkland Islands, which he had the painful duty of turning over to Spain on the outward leg of his voyage around the world—the first by any Frenchman.

Bougainville's course took him via the Falkland Islands and Rio de Janeiro to the Straits of Magellan, where he had a particularly stormy and difficult passage of some fifty-two days. Once around South America, he steered a west-northwest course designed to take him directly to Terra Australis Incognita. After nearly a month of searching out on the broad Pacific, he decided Davis's continent was merely a chimera, and he turned due west and eventually became the second European explorer to land at Tahiti's tropical paradise. He was welcomed more warmly than Wallis had been, especially by the native women, one of whom, dancing on the deck of his ship, dropped her sarong and overwhelmed the sailors. He named the island Nouvelle Cythère, and took a deep personal interest in its natural history and in the exchange of plants and animals and women and sailors. When he left the island, he took with him, at the insistence of the chief, the chief's brother Ahutoru, who was to create a sensation in Parisian society as the very embodiment of the "noble savage." Ahutoru himself became a devotee of French opera.

From Tahiti, Bougainville pressed westward, past the Samoan Islands to Espíritu Santo just north of the New Hebrides, to which he gave the poetic name Les Grandes Cyclades. Then he sailed still farther west through terrible weather and fog until he crossed the Coral Sea and confronted the Great Barrier Reef off the east coast of Australia. The Great Barrier Reef and lack of fresh water and provisions turned Bougainville north to New Guinea, which he noted for its lushness and "delicious smell." In turning north he, too, failed to pass through Torres Strait and thus failed to determine whether New Guinea and Australia were joined. Instead, on short rations, he passed through the tortuous shoals of the Louisiade Archipelago and made his way through the Solomon Islands unaware that he had gained one of the long-sought "prizes" of the Pacific—those islands thought to be the last refuge of the rich and legendary King Solomon. Finally, Bougainville made his way around New Britain, New Ireland, and the north coast of New Guinea to a Dutch settlement, Buru, in the Celebes, where his men had their first real food in months. From there he moved on to Batavia, and heard news of Carteret's voyage. He made haste to catch him, even though he stopped at Mauritius and the Cape of Good Hope. It was thus no accident when Bougainville, the French explorer, met Carteret, the struggling English circumnavigator, north of Ascension in the South Atlantic.

When he arrived back in France with only seven dead, despite
incredible hardships, Bougainville did not quite receive the
hero's welcome accorded La Condamine. A number of academicians refused to believe he had really circumnavigated the globe,
because he had not landed in China. Others must have been disappointed because he had not found the great southern continent. But Bougainville brought the South Pacific to France—in
his memoirs and collections and in the person of Ahutoru.
There would be other great French voyagers to follow him—La
Pérouse, tragically lost off the Santa Cruz Islands after actually
reaching Japan and Kamchatka; d'Urville, who actually landed
on Antarctica; and d'Entrecasteaux, whose search for La
Pérouse caused him to circumnavigate Australia (thus solving
the Torres Strait problem), discover the Trobriand Islands
(which, a little over a century later, made Malinowski and anthropology famous), and correctly identify the Solomon Islands
(thus debunking the ancient tales of gold and glory). None of
the French voyagers, however, brought the romanticism and
dreamlike vision of the South Seas to France quite so dramatically as Bougainville, who lived to a ripe old age in the nineteenth century, always willing to undertake another voyage
around the world.

iv

COOK'S FIRST VOYAGE

ALL OF THE EXPEDITIONS down through that of Bougainville
formed, in a sense, a prelude to the incredible work of Cook and
his men. When he embarked from Plymouth on August 26,
1768, bound for Tahiti, the southern continent, and all the islands in between, Cook carried a remarkable complement of
men. In addition to himself and Charles Green, who were to
serve as principal astronomers and Venus-watchers, Cook also
took with him young Joseph Banks and a retinue of eight persons who formed a natural history corps. Banks, a protégé of

Thomas Pennant, the explorer-artist of northern Canada, was rich, and a zealot for natural history. He personally employed every member of the natural history corps and purchased all the scientific supplies and equipment. His corps included Dr. Daniel Solander, a Swedish protégé of Linnaeus, who by 1753 had perfected his great system of classification in natural history and had collectors and agents all over the world. Solander was assisted by another Swede, George Dorllon. Other members of the corps who stood out were the artists Sydney Parkinson, Alexander Buchon, and Herman Sporing, a Finn. Parkinson was a landscape painter, while Buchon, who unfortunately died on the voyage, was an expert at drawing natives. Sporing drew natural history specimens and exquisitely precise renderings of native artifacts. Cook was not the first to take professional artists on a voyage of discovery, but he made the most effective use of them on all three of his voyages, and in so doing helped as much as Bougainville to create what Professor Bernard Smith has declared to be "the European vision of the South Pacific," an important paradigm in which science and art came together to change the thought of Europe.

Cook entered the Pacific by way of the Straits of Le Maire, or around the Horn. Once around the Horn, Cook headed directly for Tahiti, so as to be there for the June 3, 1769, Venus immersion. He arrived in Matavai Bay on April 13, and immediately began construction of an observatory. The great day, however, proved anticlimactic. Cook's journal entry is redolent with disappointment:

> Saturday 3rd. This day prov'd as favorable to our purpose as we could wish. Not a Clowd was to be seen the whole day and the Air was perfectly clear, so that we had every advantage we could desire in Observing the whole of the passage of the Planet Venus over the Suns disk: we very distinctly saw an Atmosphere or dusky shade round the body of the Planet which very much disturbed the times of the Contacts particularly the two internal ones. Dr. Solander observed as well as Mr. Green and my self, and we differed from one another in observing the times of the Contacts more than could be

expected. Mr. Green's Telescope and mine were of the same Magnifying power but that of the Dr. was greater than ours. It was nearly calm the whole day and the Thermometer expos'd to the Sun about the middle of the Day rose to a degree of heat (119) we have not before met with.

Cook, too, had fallen victim of the "black drop effect."

Meanwhile Cook, Banks, and the other naturalists made a complete survey of the island, and with much enjoyment and curiosity studied and perhaps cohabited with the native inhabitants. On July 13 they sailed away to the west with Tupaia, a chief, and his son, aboard as guides and interpreters. On the way west, Cook discovered, named, and claimed the seventy atolls that make up the Society Islands.

On August 9, 1769, Cook turned south in quest of the great southern continent. He did not find it, but he did sight New Zealand on October 6. Despite hostilities from the cannibal Maori, Cook delighted in New Zealand and made several landings there. On November 9, along with Green, he observed a transit of Mercury. But New Zealand was his real fascination. He sailed all around the northern island, sometimes in hurricane weather, making exact charts of its shorelines, while the naturalists probed inland. They met and made friends with the natives, who gave them a half-eaten human head. After a difficult circumnavigation of the southern island, Cook turned west toward New Holland. According to his biographer, Cook "had given New Zealand a sure and defined outline; in less than six months he had charted 2,400 miles of coast in a manner as accurate as it was unprecedented." This he had accomplished without the use of Harrison's new chronometer for determining longitude. Though it was in use after 1755, Cook had brought none along and depended entirely upon complicated lunar sightings for his very accurate determinations of longitude.

On April 19, 1770, Cook landed on the east coast of Australia at a barren spot disputed by miserable-looking aborigines smeared with white paint. In contrast to Tahiti and New Zealand, Australia did not appear to be paradise. The naturalists, however, had a dazzling time amid a whole new ecological system of completely different plants and animals. They named this spot Botany Bay.

The *Endeavour* then cruised north along the Australian east coast, noting the promise of Port Jackson as a harbor and passing the sight of present-day Brisbane. On the night of June 10, 1770, the *Endeavour* struck hard on the sharp coral of the Great Barrier Reef. The ship began to leak from a hole below the waterline and stuck fast; it was at the mercy of the crashing waves. The disastrous end to his voyage in sight, Cook remained cool while everyman, including the naturalists, worked furiously at the pumps. The ship was lightened as much as possible, and one Jonathan Monkhouse dove overboard with a sheet of oakum and dung-treated canvas and pulled over the hole a large patch which was held in place by ropes and the pressure of the water on the hull. The *Endeavour* was saved—at least temporarily. They made for land, and while the ship was being repaired, Cook fixed their longitude with great precision. While ashore collecting specimens in high excitement, the naturalists grew ecstatic over their first sight of kangaroos. They shot three. Despite this "triumph," they decided to name their landing place Cook's Harbor.

When at last they left the shore on August 6, they sailed up along the coast in constant fear of the Barrier Reef. Finally, however, they found an opening. If Cook had followed the course of previous voyagers, such as Bougainville, he would have headed directly north for the Louisiade Archipelago and New Guinea. Instead, in the face of great danger from the Barrier Reef and numerous shoals, he turned the tip of Australia and sailed through Torres Strait, proving that New Guinea and Australia were not joined, though he was still not sure that Australia was not a string of large islands. After a landing in New Guinea, where he was met by hostile natives, Cook and his officers decided to turn toward home. On October 10, they reached Batavia, to find that the ship was indeed in such poor condition that a complete overhaul was needed. The hull was scraped so thin, down to an eighth of an inch thickness, that it was a miracle that it had withstood the pressure of the heavy seas.

Cook's voyage has been justly celebrated as a model of preventive medicine. Thanks to a careful diet of fruits and other antiscorbutics, and a strict regimen of cleanliness, virtually no one had come down with scurvy, and not a man had died from disease caused by the voyage. But at Batavia, where disease thrived, virtually everyone fell sick with malaria and dysentery. Seven died, while Banks and Solander barely clung to their lives. As soon as possible, Cook sailed for Mauritius and the healthier climate of the Cape of Good Hope. On the way, twenty-two more men died. At last, however, on July 13, 1771, the *Endeavour* reached England.

Of his expedition Cook modestly concluded, "Altho' the discoveries made in this voyage are not great, yet I flatter my self that they are such as may merit the attention of their Lordships, and altho' I have failed in discovering that so much talked of southern continent (which perhaps do not exist) and which I my self had much at heart, yet . . . I presume this voyage will be found as compleat as any before made to the South Seas, on the same account." In some ways Cook was correct in his modest assessment. He was addressing men of great expectations, and he had found nothing spectacular, with the possible exception of Banks's remarkable natural history specimens. Cook had found no new continent, no rich islands, no templed cities, few new natives who were exploitable. But what he had done, with incredible diligence and skill, was to map with real accuracy for the first time an immense portion of the South Pacific, including New Zealand and the east coast of Australia. And he had confirmed that New Guinea was not part of Australia. His observations, and those of Banks and his men, bore the stamp of remarkable precision and insight into relatively new worlds of nature and men. "Geography is facts," Bougainville had asserted. Cook had presented, to the best of his ability, the facts about the South Pacific.

This does not begin to tell the whole story of the impact of

Cook's voyage, however. Banks and Solander, for example, had returned with seventeen thousand new species of plants. They also had collected hundreds of fishes, insects, and skins of birds and larger animals. Beyond this, the expedition's artists, particularly Parkinson and Sporing, since Buchon died early on the voyage, made more than fifteen hundred drawings of the tropical islands, the animals (such as the kangaroo), the fishes (most spectacularly the giant stingray seen off Australia), the birds, and the plants. They also recorded most carefully the many varieties of native inhabitants—fair Tahitians, black Melanesians, Australian aborigines, and the fiercely tattooed Maori of New Zealand. Parkinson's crayon portraits of the Maori are classics. They also pictured native structures such as the huts of the Patagonians and the strange elevated burial houses of the Tahitians. And both Parkinson and Sporing took great pains to record native artifacts, sometimes in diagrams of the great twin-hulled war canoes, sometimes in vivid paintings of the same elaborately carved canoes in action against the *Endeavour*, or at other times in very precise drawings of ceremonial masks, tattoo patterns, mourners' costumes, war clubs, or canoe ornaments. The quality of their botanical drawings alone has never really been matched.

Banks and Solander were presented at court, in demand at the finest clubs, given honorary degrees at Oxford, and eventually Banks was made the king's personal Royal Gardener; he made the Royal Botanic Gardens at Kew one of the wonders of the world of natural history, finally acquiring the immense collection of Linnaeus five years after the latter's death in 1778. Before he died, Linnaeus hailed Banks's collections from the *Endeavour* voyage as perhaps the greatest of all time. In a constant stream of letters, he fretted lest Banks be lost to science if he accompanied a planned second voyage by Cook.

He had no need to worry. The Admiralty indeed planned a second voyage for Cook, but Banks was not to accompany it. Inflated with glory, Banks insisted that the ships be tailored to his specifications. This the Admiralty refused, and Banks withdrew

from Cook's second venture—making a singularly unspectacular
trip to Iceland instead.

V

THE LOST CONTINENT AND THE DARK TRAGEDY

FOR COOK'S second voyage, he was furnished with two ships
very much like the stout *Endeavour*. They were the *Resolution*,
which Cook commanded, and the *Adventure*, captained by
Tobias Furneaux, who had sailed around the world with Wallis
in 1766–67. Once again Cook sailed under secret orders. His
main objective was to discover and explore the mysterious
southern continent, and specifically, to confirm the alleged discovery in 1739 by the French captain, Lozier Bouvet, of "Cape
Circumcision," reported to be in latitude 54° S, longitude
10°20', to see if it was the southern continent. In general, he was
to circumnavigate the globe at the highest possible latitude in
the southern hemisphere in search of Terra Australis Incognita,
establish British dominion over any newly discovered islands or
continents, look for new resources in the way of plants, animals,
and minerals, and make friends with the natives. Clearly, his
most important duty was to establish the British Empire on the
bottom side of the globe. Science was seen as being of primary
assistance in this imperial venture.

The *Resolution* and the *Adventure* sailed from Plymouth in
July 1772. They carried two first-rate astronomers, William
Wayles and William Bayly, and John Reinhold Forster and his
son, John George Adam Forster, as naturalists and artists, as
well as the important landscape painter William Hodges. Cook
was also supplied with four chronometers for determining longitude. One of these, designed by John Harrison, worked to
perfection throughout the voyage, and this proved to be a landmark in marine navigation and terrestrial mapmaking.

The voyage of 1772–75 was Cook's most extensive and perhaps most important, particularly in terms of marine navigation

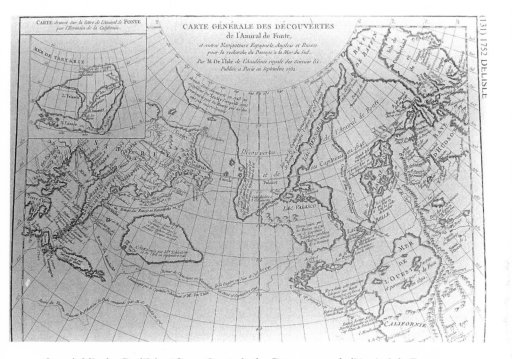

Joseph Nicolas De l'Isle, "Carte Générale des Découvertes de l'Amiral de Fonte, et autres Navigateurs Espagnols, Anglais et Russes pour la recherche du Passage à la Mer du Sud." Paris, 1752. From Carl I. Wheat, *Mapping the Trans-Mississippi,* vol. 1. This mid-eighteenth-century map is really a throwback to the fantasies of the sixteenth century. In 1577 Sir Francis Drake raided what he called "the backside of America" and sailed west around the world back to England. The French and Spanish, however, believed that Drake had found a northwest passage across North America. The French invented an Admiral Bartholomew de Fonte, who, they said, found a northern passage via lakes and rivers flowing west out of Hudson's Bay. Meanwhile, in 1592, the Spanish invented another admiral, Juan de Fuca, who had allegedly discovered the "Sea of the West," lying just north of California and reaching east across North America to a range of mountains out of which flowed the Missouri River. Today, what is left of this fantasy is known as the Straits of Juan de Fuca. However fantastic, De l'Isle's map was taken seriously in the eighteenth century, as Captain James Cook, on his second voyage, sailed north to Cook's Sound in Alaska in search of this northwest passage. The passage concept preoccupied—indeed doomed—maritime explorers for much of the nineteenth century, while de Fuca's "Sea of the West" became the "Rio Buenaventura," a mythical river that flowed west across the Great Basin to the Pacific. Many an American western explorer perished in the search for that chimera as well.

and terrestrial mapmaking. Following orders, he sailed to the Cape of Good Hope, then south in search of Cape Circumcision, into the frozen ice floes beyond the Antarctic Circle. From 52° onward, they saw on all sides immense ice fields and flotillas of icebergs, near one of which, protected by its gigantic mass, they celebrated Christmas of 1772. Finally, however, Cook turned north in search of the Kerguelen Islands, which he had heard about at the Cape. In so doing, he missed by about 10° of longitude the chance of discovering Antarctica at Enderby Land. About this time Cook became separated from Furneaux on the *Adventure,* and both ships made for New Zealand at latitudes between 50° and 60° south—far below Australia, but just north of Antarctica. They met again in New Zealand after Cook had made a voyage of over 10,900 nautical miles out of sight of land, while Furneaux had touched on Tasmania but failed to determine whether it was an extension of Australia.

From New Zealand, Cook and Furneaux turned north to refit at Tahiti. Then on their return south they became separated for the rest of the voyage. After touching at New Zealand again, Cook aboard the *Resolution* swung far south, once again beyond the Antarctic Circle. In February of 1774, he reached 71°10′ S, where, surrounded by "Ninety Seven Ice Hills or Mountains," he turned back. The *Resolution* had ventured farther south on the frozen ocean than any vessel in history. It remained for captains in the nineteenth century to reveal the secrets of Antarctica—the real southern continent.

Once again Cook swung back north across the Pacific to Easter Island, the Marquesas, Tahiti, the Friendly Islands, New Hebrides, New Caledonia (a discovery of a new island group populated by friendly natives), and New Zealand. In the fall of 1774, when the summer season in the southern hemisphere began, Cook headed directly for Cape Horn. He diligently searched the South Atlantic as far south as 60° for the southern continent. He found only the icy island of South Georgia, and a group of small islands which he named the South Sandwich Islands, after the Earl of Sandwich, First Lord of the Admiralty. Eventually, he made his way back to the Cape of Good Hope and thence upward through the Atlantic to England. He had sailed over seventy thousand miles in just over three years, much of it in the howling westerlies and icy currents at the bottom of the world, but he had found no continent. Furneaux, however, had preceded him home by a year and became the first captain to sail around the world from west to east. Nonetheless, the modest Cook became an even greater national hero. Among other things, he was made a member of the Royal Society and granted a formal audience with King George III.

Still, he was impatient for the sea, and the Admiralty was impatient for him to go. This time his mission was to search the western coasts of North America for a passage that led to the Atlantic. In short, he was to check out the ancient Spanish theory of a Northwest Passage from the Atlantic to the Pacific via the hypothetical "Strait of Anian," only from the Pacific side. Sir Francis Drake had engaged in the same sort of voyage along "the backside of America," as he termed it, in 1577–78. Thus, once again Cook set forth with two ships and a complement of excellent officers, including Charles Clerke, who had been around the world with both Byron and Cook, and William Bligh, who was later to gain fame as master of the ill-fated *Bounty.* He also took an even larger contingent of scientists and artists. The latter included John Webber and William Ellis, who, before the end of the expedition, had made more drawings than any previous artists.

On July 12, 1776, just before the momentous news of the American declaration of independence reached England, but after war with the colonies had definitely begun, Cook sailed from Plymouth on his last voyage. This one took him via the Cape of Good Hope, the barren Kerguelen Islands, and Tasmania to New Zealand once again. Then he swung north among the now familiar South Pacific archipelagoes to the Central Pacific, where he discovered the Hawaiian Islands, which he named the Sandwich Islands, again after the Earl of Sandwich. Here he found thousands of friendly Polynesians, causing him to speculate that this was indeed one of the great seafaring peoples. "How shall we account for this Nation spreading it self so

far over this Vast ocean?" he wrote. "We find them from New
Zealand to the South, to these islands to the North and from
Easter Island to the Hebrides; an extent of 60° of latitude or
twelve hundred leagues [3,600 nautical miles] north and south
and 83° of longitude or sixteen hundred and sixty leagues east
and west, how much farther is not known. . . ." In his three voyages, Cook had become a student of ethnology. He had calculated population statistics for most of the islands, like Tahiti,
with which he was familiar, and traced patterns of growth and
migration. He had also become familiar with the various island
customs and ceremonies. And though he was inclined to adopt
the Enlightenment view of the progress of races toward civilization (best represented, of course, in England), he also developed
such an appreciation for Pacific cultures as to virtually anticipate
certain aspects of modern cultural relativism. His awe at the vast
migrations and seamanship of the Polynesians was a case in
point.

From Hawaii he sailed east to the coast of Oregon, then north
to Vancouver Island and Nootka Sound, where he traded with
the Indians. All the way up the coast to Alaska, he saw no evidence of the Strait of Anian. June of 1778 found him threading
his way through the Aleutian Islands, where, turning north once
again, he passed through Bering Strait and reached 70°44N
across the Arctic Circle. Then ice in the Beaufort Sea turned
him back. Even more ice prevented him from coasting from
northern Siberia westward (on a new Northwest Passage), and
he stood south for Unalaska to repair his battered ships. During
this time he studied and admired the Siberian Chukchis and
compared notes with Russian fur traders who went back and
forth to Alaska. Then he headed south to a tumultuous welcome
in the Hawaiian Islands. Thousands greeted him in Kealakekua
Bay, and to his bewilderment he was made a god—something
slightly beyond the reach of the Royal Society. He and his men
stayed in Hawaii for three months, then they sailed away, to return after six days to repair their ships.

Upon their return, they found the natives strangely hostile.

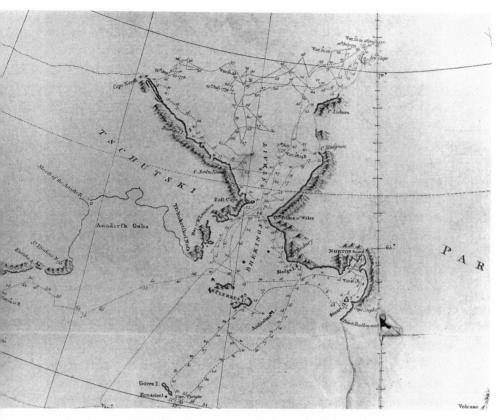

Captain James Cook, Map of the Pacific Ocean. 1772–1775. Published posthumously in Cook, *Voyage to the Pacific Ocean*, vol. 2, 1784, after p. 267. (*Harry Ransom Humanities Research Center, The University of Texas at Austin*) This is a section from Captain James Cook's map of the Bering Strait, made on his third voyage (1772–75), during which he sailed farther north than anyone before his time. The map indicates something of Cook's skill as a scientific explorer.

On the night of February 13, 1799, in a fight over a stolen cutter, Cook was stabbed, beaten to death, and cut into pieces by the aroused Hawaiians. It was a sudden incredible tragedy—realized as such by mariner and native alike, as the whole bay suddenly went silent. Some days later, saddened chieftains returned a piece of Cook's body (his thigh), which was buried in the sea. No one has explained the Hawaiians' sudden change of mood. Toward the end of Cook's three-month stopover, he had sensed that perhaps he was overstaying his time, but there were no overt hostilities when he left. So far as he knew, he was still a god. As we learn more about the complexities of prehistoric island politics, it seems plausible that he was murdered out of jealousy by a different faction from that which deified him. Or perhaps the deification ceremony was only for one who had returned from a mighty, extended voyage. In returning in just six days after his second departure, Cook had proved himself all too human, vulnerable, and a failure, boding no good future to Pacific voyagers. Perhaps they had deliberately slain a god of bad luck.

The great captain, like Magellan, was dead over a seemingly trivial incident. His men carried on. They sailed north to Petropavlovsk in a new attempt to penetrate the Bering Strait, but weather turned them back. Clerke, the second in command, died, and the ships of the expedition made for the shores of Japan, then Macao, the Strait of Sunda (not even touching at Batavia), the Cape of Good Hope, north through a storm around the British Isles, and finally home, which they reached on October 4, 1780. The news of Cook's death had already reached London on January 10, 1780. The next day the *London Gazette* published the news. All Britain, including the king, mourned. Men of all stations, including later his Polynesian friends, vied with one another in delivering eulogies. Statues were erected, portraits painted from memory, a Royal Society medal was commissioned and struck off. But perhaps the best eulogy was contained in a letter from young George Herbert, then traveling in Italy. He wrote quite to the point: "Poor Cooke [sic] is truly a great loss to the Universe." He had indeed been a cosmic voyager.

Cook's story illustrates the way in which the explorer and the exploring expedition had become a crucial part of the scientific revolution. In addition, his story and a reading of his journals indicate how far that revolution had progressed. Cook had begun his series of voyages in the role of mathematical astronomer and mapmaker, whose mission it was to observe the transit of Venus and accurately to map the archipelagoes of the Pacific and the continent of Terra Australis Incognita when he should locate it. Cook did not find the lost continent, but his maps and charts of the Pacific and those made under his supervision are monuments of astronomically based precision.

Cook's work has even more significance. Thanks to the initial influence of Banks, he realized that Newtonian science was only one aspect of his mission. Banks showed him the world of natural history, which became wider and more complex with every voyage he made, with every island he touched, with each strange new ecological system he encountered. He himself grew interested in the plants and the animals, the birds and strange fishes. And then he became a keen student of the native peoples he encountered and their cultures. On his third voyage, he even collected native vocabularies—Maori, Nootka, Unalaskan, Hawaiian. Songs such as Maori chants, religious rituals and folklore, sports, dances, sexual customs, the mysteries of human sacrifice and cannibalism—all these he probed into as deeply as he could. And what he could not set down in his journal, artists like Parkinson, Sporing, the Forsters, Hodges, Webber, and Ellis recorded in thousands of drawings and paintings which conveyed the visual quality of the exotic South Seas and cold polar life to European centers of civilization. They produced a documentary art that not only complemented Cook's written descriptions but suggested the idea of "natural habitat" and ecological relations. True, they did not develop these ideas to their ultimate Darwinian conclusions, but this was the age of induction, of information-gathering and the discovery of natural history data in space rather than time. Thus, little in the way of theory or even experiment derived from Cook's voyages. Instead, they represent the epitome of Baconian or Lockean empirical observation conducted over a huge portion of the globe. Cook's journals, maps, collections, and drawings represent an immense inventory, which forced savants back in the centers of learning to rethink fundamental premises about natural history and the richly varied peoples of the globe. Long before Herman Melville in *Typee* put his dilemma of evil in paradise, Cook had pondered human sacrifice in beautiful Tahiti and cannibalism in New Zealand. He had come from the abstract generalities of mathematical astronomy to the detailed complexities of the natural world. Still Cook remained ever the empiricist, the discerning, skeptical, even objective Lockean observer. His mental approach was matter-of-fact. His rhetoric was the rhetoric of understatement. He would have scorned, as he did on numerous occasions, mere speculation. His mission was to ascertain the facts, which he did in proving there was no Terra Australis Incognita and no Strait of Anian. Typical of the English and the Scots, he was not given to romantic enthusiasms and overarching theories of nature. Brave, cool and courageous, he had the curiosity of common sense.

vi

THE MAN WHO WOULD BE FAUST

IF COOK HAD BEEN supreme in oceanic discovery, Alexander von Humboldt of Prussia came to stand like a colossus over the scientific exploration and study of the continents. During the course of his long career (he lived to be eighty-nine) the scope of his work continually widened until it embraced the entire globe and even the universe.

Humboldt was born in 1769, the same year as Napoleon's birth and the transit of Venus, and died in 1859, the year of the publication of Darwin's *Origin of Species*. During that time, he managed to create the comprehensive science of modern geography. And, because it was a synthesizing discipline, it became the key scientific activity of the age. In his dramatic expeditions to the New World and Central Asia, and in his subsequent labors in Paris, where he wrote most of his books, Humboldt provided a model and a method for organizing all of the data that poured into Europe from the ever-increasing number of expeditions to all parts of the globe.

A romantic who, thanks to his friendship with young George Forster, artist-naturalist on Cook's second voyage, had dreams of being another Captain Cook, Humboldt nonetheless differed from the great Pacific explorer in profound ways. He was rich and could afford to finance his own expeditions independently of either the government or a scientific academy. He had been trained not in mathematics and astronomy (though he became a master of those sciences) but in geology and mineralogy, under the great geologist Abraham Gottlob Werner at the Freiburg School of Mines. He also had a boundless fascination with all aspects of natural history and became a prodigy in that field, while at the same time conducting advanced experiments in electricity patterned after those of Franklin, Galvani, and Volta. In short, from his very early years he was a virtuoso who was determined to inquire into every aspect of nature with an unchecked enthusiasm that contrasted significantly with the matter-of-fact, workmanlike approach of James Cook. He gained great stimulation from the Romantic Weimar-Jena school of Goethe, Schiller, and Schelling, who, as post-Kantian philosophers, were devising what the Germans called *Naturphilosophie*. They constantly looked for meaning in the form of universals that lie behind the appearances of nature. This point of view governed all of Humboldt's mighty labors. He constantly formulated large themes with potentially profound consequences, and he always looked for underlying patterns, unities, and laws which linked all parts of the globe and cosmos, practically, philosophically, aesthetically, and spiritually. A towering, Olympian figure, who was nonetheless extremely gregarious and intensely human, he made

"Humboldtian science" synonymous with "romantic science."
It was not in Germany but in Paris that Humboldt began to
see his dreams become realities. Bougainville, still vigorous at
seventy, offered to take him around the world. For a time it
seemed he might join Napoleon's armies in Egypt. Then, with
the botanist Aimé Bonpland, he was set to sail with Captain
Boudin to the South Pacific. But war intervened, and instead,
bearing passports from the King of Spain and the Council of the
Indies, he set sail in 1799 with his friend the intrepid Bonpland
for the green world of South America.

In all, Humboldt and Bonpland spent five years in South
America. They paddled up the mighty Orinoco, past its cataracts at Atures and Maipures to its source at Esmeralda in the
Cerro Duida mountain, a journey few, if any, men had undertaken in its entirety. Beset on every side by dense jungles,
clouds of malarial mosquitoes, strange and sometimes forbid-
ding wildlife—twenty-foot crocodiles, giant boas and ana-
condas, electric eels that could stun a horse, armies of peccaries
that crashed through the jungles like huge warrior ants, and the
ever-dangerous jaguars and panthers—Humboldt and Bonpland
were nonethelss exhilarated by the tropical world of the Orinoco. They collected thousands of plant and animal specimens,
studied the natives who came out of the rain forests with
curare-tipped blowguns and cannibalism on their minds, and
fixed the latitude and longitude of fifty-five positions in that
hitherto lost world. Their journey—one of the most celebrated
in history—covered fifteen hundred miles, and in the end they
found and explored the mysterious Casiquiare Canal that
formed the link, across the continental divide of South America,
between the northward-flowing Orinoco and the southward-
flowing Amazon. When they emerged on the northern coast of
Venezuela on June 13, 1800, they had succeeded in revealing the
mythical world of El Dorado that was eastern South America.

A subsequent journey was of even more heroic proportions.
Sometimes following the route of the conquistadors, sometimes
the still remaining roads of the Incas, they came up out of the

jungles to the high, windswept Andean plateaus. There, working out of Quito (where, over half a century before, La Condamine had laid out his arcs of longitude), they began to study Cotopaxi and the other great Andean volcanoes, some of which were still ablaze. Before they were through they had climbed, inspected, and studied them all. But their greatest feat was the ascent on June 23, 1802, of Mount Chimborazo, then believed to be the highest mountain in the world, at 20,700 feet. They made its ascent with little or no mountain-climbing equipment. At last they left South America behind and stood out upon the broad Pacific in what was eventually named the Humboldt Current, Humboldt's biographer notes that "Cotopaxi was in eruption then and two hundred miles out from land, above the slap of bow waves and creak of spar and timbers, he, Humboldt, could still hear the muffled boom of its thunderous farewell."

Humboldt and Bonpland then sailed on to Mexico, where they spent a year studying and compiling the first modern geography of that ancient province of Spain. In 1811, Humboldt published this work as the *Political Essay on the Kingdom of New Spain* in four volumes. Its economic data prompted a rush of European investments in the mines of Mexico. In 1814 he published his *Researches Concerning the Institutions and Monuments of the Ancient Inhabitants of America* in two volumes, relating the spectacular ruins he had seen in Mexico to those of the Incas in South America. This work sparked a renewed search for the antiquities of the New World, especially by the Frenchman Guillaume Dupaix and the American John Lloyd Stephens, who rediscovered the lost world of the Mayas.

As a conclusion to his expedition to the western hemisphere, in 1804 Humboldt sailed to Philadelphia, where he dazzled America's leading savants. Unfortunately he arrived too late to brief Meriwether Lewis, who, when Humboldt was holding forth before the American Philosophical Society, was somewhere out in the Rocky Mountains. Humboldt did meet President Jefferson, however, who was one of his heroes, both as scientist and as apostle of Enlightenment republicanism. He greatly admired, indeed even copied in literary form, though on a larger scale, Jefferson's *Notes on Virginia*, which the latter had published in Paris in 1784. The comprehensive, highly organized, yet romantic or picturesque style of Jefferson's treatise was exactly what Humboldt aimed for in his own work.

When he arrived back in Paris, Humboldt plunged immediately into the publication of his extensive findings in the New World. It was an ongoing project that lasted for twenty-five years, until 1839. Done in collaboration with Bonpland and a staff of scientists and artists, hence lavishly illustrated, it ran to thirty volumes and cost Humboldt his entire fortune. The narrative of his Orinoco expedition was published as *Voyage to the Equinoctial Regions of the New World, Made in 1799–1804*, in three volumes. It was a masterpiece that, however, curiously omitted his adventures in the Andes. Some of this was captured in a subsequent work, *Atlas pittoresque—Vues des Cordillères et monuments des peuple indigènes de l'Amérique*, in two volumes, in which the spare factual drawings of Bonpland became embellished and translated into the lush romantic paintings of F. G. Weitsch, E. Ender, and other followers of Claude Lorrain and Poussin. The epitome of this translation of Humboldt's South American vision into art, however, was the work of an American, Frederick Church, whose vast, rich panoramas of mountains and jungles were suffused with the warm, glowing light of the sublime. And yet, in true Humboldtian fashion, Church perfectly painted each detail of rock, bird, or leaf. His paintings were comprehensive and sweeping, but accurate in every detail. Thousands paid to see them when Church put them on exhibition in New York.

Humboldt would have approved of this artistic rendition of his work. In fact, he urged it. In *Aspects of Nature* (1808) he wrote, "It would be an enterprise worthy of a great artist to study the aspect and character of all these vegetable groups, not merely in hothouses or in the descriptions of botanists, but in their native grandeur in the tropic zone. How interesting and instructive to the landscape painter would be a work which should present to the eye, first separately, and then in combination and contrast, the leading forms which have been enumerated. . . ." Humboldt saw nothing wrong with including the emotions of the observer or perceiver as well. Science based on sensation, a mainstay of Enlightenment epistemology, had become the lens through which the romantic viewed the world. As epitomized by the work of Cook's artists from Hodges onward, and those who interpreted Humboldt's travels, extensive, first-hand experience in nature itself overthrew the canons of classical artificiality and made the concrete, the vivid, and the organic the focus of emotions, tastes, and whole constellations of new, highly individualistic ideas about the world. One of these was the concept of ecological reality, and another, in the case of Humboldt and his works in particular, was a kind of sublime vitalism that suffused the world and its creatures and made of ecology a dynamic rather than a static concept. Fundamentally, it was a version of the gospel according to Lamarck.

Visualization fascinated Humboldt. The map and the chart became primary tools for organizing all the multitudinous facts he discovered. The spare, precise, astronomically determined maps were necessarily included in his volumes, but he also delighted in charting geological formations, mineral layers, altitudes, weather, magnetic belts, isotherms, and the distribution of plants, animals, and people in relation to them. He also devised cross-sectional diagrams which showed the relationship of plants and animals to altitude and topography. These maps, charts, and diagrams were different, somewhat more abstract ways of showing the complete interdependence of nature's ecological reality. Sometimes he drew startling conclusions from these correlations. In taking note of the similarity between American and European rocks in the context of his studies of volcanoes, earthquakes, and terrestrial magnetism, Humboldt in some ways anticipated present-day theories of continental drift. On several occasions, his tendency toward geographical determinism overreached itself. In one of his most famous conclusions, he posited the existence of an "isothermic zodiacal

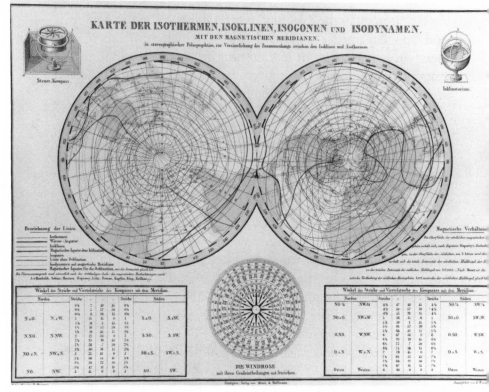

Alexander von Humboldt, "Karte der Isothermen, Isoklinen, Isogonen und Isodynamen, mit den Magnetischen Meridianen." From *Atlas zu Alexander von Humboldt: Kosmos*. 1859, plate 14. (*Harry Ransom Humanities Research Center, The University of Texas at Austin*) Alexander von Humboldt saw the map as a device for relating different kinds of terrestrial phenomena, as well as information concerning them, on one organizing image. On this polar projection map, Humboldt is correlating four different phenomena, including isogons, the earth's magnetic fields, and isotherms, the climatic zones of the globe. The latter, he felt, formed a climatic zone around the earth that channeled the migrations of peoples and animals. American proponents of Manifest Destiny borrowed this concept from Humboldt and saw the Anglo-Saxon people destined to migrate across North America and the Pacific Ocean to the Orient along a climatically preordained "Isothermal-Zodiacal Belt."

belt"—a climatic belt that stretched around the earth and determined the migratory course of the world's peoples and empires. Many an American expansionist in the nineteenth century made use of this theory as if to support a destiny that was, according to Humboldt, scientifically "manifest."

Through all his work, however, Humboldt had a master plan, an objective that was never swayed by European wars, court intrigue, revolution, changes of government, or even his trip, at an advanced age, across Siberia and into Central Asia. He wanted to encompass the whole cosmos in his work. It is unclear just when the idea came to him, because he wrote about it on several occasions. Perhaps the first was in a letter written from high up in the Andes in which he said:

> The ultimate aim of physical geography is . . . to recognize unity in the vast diversity of phenomena. . . . I have conceived the mad notion of representing in a graphic and attractive manner, the whole of the physical aspect of the universe in one work, which is to include all that is at present known of celestial and terrestrial phenomena, from the nature of the nebula down to the geography of the mosses clinging to a granite rock. . . .

When he was past seventy, he finally commenced his modest work as the capstone of his career. *Cosmos* followed his earlier plan exactly and lucidly, ranging from a discussion of Laplace's nebular hypotheses about the origins of the earth and the solar system to the relationship of plants, animals, weather, soil, topography, and terrestrial magnetism as they formed a unified "field" over the whole earth. When he died in 1859, Humboldt had only reached the fifth volume of this Faustian work.

Probability theory tells us today that man cannot completely "know" the cosmos—certainly no one man, however erudite—but in the eighteenth century, and for much of the early nineteenth century, this seemed theoretically possible. Newton and Linnaeus and Werner and Hutton and Laplace and Buffon and Cuvier had shown the way; but so, too, had the explorers whose cornucopia of discoveries in natural history and ethnology, carefully drawn maps of the earth and the heavens, and even the thousands of drawings and paintings derived from the expeditions had, as much as anything else, allowed science to take a central position in western civilization.

CHAPTER II

The North American Adventure

FOR NEARLY a century, while a significant number of the best minds of Europe grappled with the cosmos, an equal number turned their attention to the Americas. The New World represented a whole new environment, and since the onset of the Scientific Revolution, environment had come to play a crucial causative role in the formation of human society in the minds of European thinkers. The climactic formulation of this theory was Montesquieu's enormously influential treatise *The Spirit of the Laws* (1748). In this magisterial work, the Bordeaux philosopher argued that societies, governments, and laws survive only when they are appropriate to the geographical environment. If this was the case, then the outlook for the New World, at least in the view of certain eighteenth-century savants, was not promising—or at best was uncertain and puzzling because North America was not a promising environment.

In one sense, the debate was of a piece with the Tahiti question, or the New Holland and New Zealand questions. When explorers first beheld Tahiti, they thought it a kind of Eden.

Then later observations suggested that it was not Eden—the practice of cannibalism, infanticide, and promiscuous sexual relations suggested rather that Tahiti either represented an underdeveloped, infantile culture, or a sad reversion to degeneration and loss of innocence. The crude aborigines and the strange flora and fauna of New Holland (Australia) strongly suggested that it was a primitive world virtually forgotten by the Almighty; and the violent cannibalism, the barbaric native tattoos, and the remnants of even older cultures in New Zealand meant that it was in a stage of degeneration. The New World, complex and various, with tropical rain forests, deserts, swamps, strange beasts, cannibal tribes, and lost, idolatrous civilizations, encompassed all of these possibilities and more for the speculative philosophers of the Enlightenment.

What the *philosophes* were debating was the nature of Nature and New World prehistory. If inferior environment was the cause of either retardation and primitivism or degeneration, then what did the future hold for those who chose to live as colonists in America? However one might be tempted to agree that the Indian was an inferior breed—a savage—one was then forced to conclude that nature produced him and that he prefigured the future of the New World colonist and frontiersman. For in the New World, particularly in North America, the frontier—that vast continent of uncharted wilderness composed of forest, lakes, mountains, deserts, swamps, and savannas—was the future.

Interestingly enough, it was the French (if we discount the irascible Dr. Johnson) who were most pessimistic about America. They took their cue from the Comte de Buffon, the greatest naturalist of the eighteenth century. He declared the Americas literally a new world—that part of the globe that had remained inundated longest and thus had emerged most recently from the waters of the Great Noachian Deluge. As he put it, "All the evidence seems to point toward the greater part of the American continent being a new land, still untouched by men, in which nature had not had time to carry out all her plans, to develop herself to the full. . . ." Because the waters had so recently receded, America was still a swamp. And because it was a swamp, the air was cold and miasmal. It followed then, of course, that the natives were cold, the animals small, and the vegetation monotonous and primitive. But Buffon was charitable and an evolutionist as well. His own researches, which he thought well concealed in the massive tomes of his endless work on the whole of nature, led him to believe that the world was really millions of years old instead of the biblical 4004. It was only that America had emerged recently—he could not explain why. And someday, in the distant future, when the climate and hence the environment improved, it would evolve into "the most fruitful, healthy," and "richest land of all."

Voltaire and the Abbé Raynal were not so generous, though in some ways they were more amusing. Voltaire dubbed America the land of the beardless Indian and the cowardly lion. Americans, at least native Americans, lacked the amative powers of the Europeans, as was evident from their lack of facial hair. Likewise, the lions of America had no manes, and the cognoscenti of Europe must know what this meant. The Abbé Raynal, who should possibly have been concerned with less erotic matters, could not control himself:

> The men there are less strong, less courageous, without beard or hair; degenerate in all the signs of manhood.... The indifference the male takes towards the other sex to which Nature has entrusted the place of reproduction suggests an organic imperfection, a sort of infancy of the people of America similar to that of individuals of our continent who have not reached the age of puberty. It is a deep-rooted failing of that other hemisphere, a sort of impotence that reveals clearly how new the continent is.

Immature, prepubescent, or ... degenerate? The Abbé de Pauw, a stern Prussian, opted for the last. In his formidable *Recherches philosophiques sur les Américains ou Mémoires intéressants pour servir à l'histoire de l'espèce humaine* (1768), de Pauw found everything in the New World, from the quadrupeds to the crocodiles, from the natives to the immigrants, weaker, smaller, feebler in every way and getting worse. It was a clear case of degeneration, not underdevelopment. With de Pauw's *Recherches*, the assault of European savants reached a kind of absurd climax.

Though the sober Scottish historian William Robertson, in his vastly influential *History of the Americas* (1777), reached the same conclusion, it is difficult to take these assaults seriously. One suspects that it was all an elaborate jest. Certainly the wise Dr. Franklin caught something of this spirit. He blithely quoted the incredible reproduction statistics for American colonials (population doubled every twenty years in Pennsylvania, for example); and on one famous occasion at a French banquet for American diplomats, he slyly proposed to settle the question of size immediately. Would everyone please rise? Yes, the comparison between the diminutive French hosts and the towering American guests would do nicely.

Most Americans, however, took the assault seriously, none more apparently so than Thomas Jefferson. He made much of fossil finds in America, especially "The Great Claw of Megalonyx," the toenail of a giant sloth that was nearly six times larger than that of the largest lion, found at Big Bone Lick in Kentucky. There too, in 1767, the scout George Croghan, the mapmaker Thomas Hutchins, and a Philadelphia trader, George Morgan, found mastodon remains which dwarfed anything in Europe. Jefferson found this discovery conclusive, and refused to admit that such beasts were not still roaming about in the western wilderness of America. He wrote in 1781:

It may be asked why I [list] the mammoth as if it still existed? I ask in return, why I should omit it, as if it did not exist? Such is the economy of nature, that no instance can be produced of her having permitted any one race of her animals to become extinct; of her having formed any link in her great work so weak as to be broken. To add to this, the traditional testimony of the Indians that this animal still exists in the northern and western parts of America would be adding the light of a taper to that of the meridian sun.

Just to drive his point home, he sent General Sullivan to ransack the Maine woods for a moose to send to Paris so that France could see that America had large animals. And in 1784, in response to questions put to him by French tormenters, he published his classic *Notes on Virginia*, among the most systematic and scientifically detailed works on America written up to that time.

Only a nationalistic spirit can explain Jefferson's extreme reaction. As a man of science, he knew full well that for more than one hundred years, explorers and naturalists had been roaming the North American wilderness, seeing for themselves its rich and variegated wonders. Moreover, they had been drawing maps, compiling ethnographies, collecting Indian vocabularies, and sending whole shiploads of seeds, plants, and animal specimens to European capitals and centers of learning. And by the time of the Great Debate, in the late eighteenth and early nineteenth centuries, nobody knew more about America than the French. For example, the annual *Jesuit Relations*, or reports from North America chronicling the French achievements from Champlain onward, contained a wealth of information.

In a very real sense, the new age of discovery had begun in North America some time in the seventeenth century. Every year, more and more explorers penetrated, scrutinized, charted, and classified wilderness America. And the more they explored the wilderness of immense forests and billowing lakes, the more they grew enthusiastic, even greedy, about its future. Debate about the Great Deluge, the amativeness of the Indian, the size of crocodiles, or the manes of lions might be foolish—even embarrassing for the beardless, balding Voltaire—but the real debate was over the New World environment and what it promised for the future of human development. If it were not for the fact that the scientific controversy was in reality the outward sign of genuine political, ideological, and social combat between the Old World and the New, it would be a supreme irony. For in overlooking the tremendous amounts of information about America they had at hand, the leading European men of the Enlightenment were proving to be scarcely enlightened at all.

ii

A RUDIMENTARY SCIENCE OF SPACE

SINCE the days of Aristotle, science had been regarded as the accumulation of organized knowledge. But also since the days of Aristotle, men had debated the nature of true knowledge and its proper form of organization. Thus, down through the ages, science as an activity had continuously evolved. It had evolved not only in response to philosophical structures and assumptions, but also in response to the accumulation of new facts. This made its evolution uneven. Some ages saw great strides in cosmology, others in medicine, anatomy, chemistry, and natural history. The polymaths of the Enlightenment on both sides of the Atlantic attempted to leap forward in all fields at once. In so doing, they pared away superstition and replaced it with reason. They tossed aside the fabulous and replaced it with critical observation. The spirit of the age was at once a spirit of faith in reason, science, and progress on this earth, and yet one of the criticism and skepticism that we now see does indeed lie at the heart of modern scientific endeavor.

Thus the *philosophes* had long since passed the time when they could believe in anthropophagi, whose one-eyed heads hung from their chests, or one-legged men who hopped like rabbits and were called Skraellings, or Patagonian giants or even El Dorado or the Seven Cities of Cibola. They would not believe every tale out of the newfound land. Buffon, especially, since he had read almost exclusively in South American missionary accounts, had run into repeated fables. Thus he and other "moderns" were not ready to accept the vast literature of the *Jesuit Relations* and the startling tales of explorers in North America. Much of Europe had been dazzled by the sly Recollect Fr. Louis Hennepin, whose books, especially *Description de la Loui-*

siane (1683), *Nouvelle découverte d'un pais plus grand que l'Europe* (1698), and the English version, *A New Discovery of a Vast Country in America.* .... (1698), were widely read accounts of America's wonders. Not the *philosophes*, however. They and most members of the Académie des Sciences, not to mention the Office de Marine, knew that Hennepin had lied about his role as a discoverer. They knew, for instance, that the great, but possibly mad, La Salle had sailed down the mighty Mississippi to its mouth, not Louis Hennepin, as he claimed. He might have discovered St. Anthony's Falls and roamed over Minnesota as a prisoner of the Chippewa until rescued by Daniel Duluth, but he had not sailed down the Mississippi. Therefore, all his statements were suspect.

Likewise, everyone knew better than to take seriously the work of the discredited renegade and vagabond Baron Lahontan. Who could believe that fabulous section of *New Voyages to North America* (1703) in which he told tales of discovering Welsh Indians—descendants of Prince Madoc—on the River Longue that flowed west from the Mississippi through the country of strange tribes to a great inland sea where dwelt the Gnicsatares in Tibetan splendor? In short, there was really no way for armchair members of the Académie des Sciences—philosophers and theorists—to determine the veracity of accounts that poured into Europe from America for more than a century. And while they were interested in the shape of the earth and the cosmos, they were far less interested in the Strait of Anian, the River Longue, or any Northwest Passage across America. That information was primarily of use to imperial agents of the king and the church or those strange ragged men of the woods, the *coureurs des bois*, like those renegades Radisson and Groseilliers, who, after discovering the Mississippi, had turned north to Hudson Bay and sold out to the English king, Charles II, who promptly established France's great rival in Canada, the Hudson's Bay Company, in 1670.

Considering the fate of France, which lost her American empire to England in 1763, the *philosophes*, especially those who

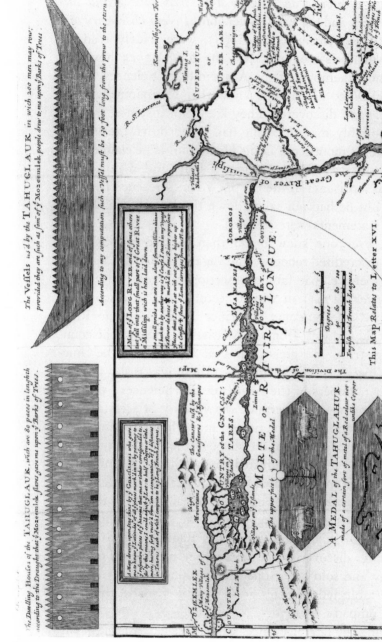

Baron de Lahontan, "Map of the Long River." From *New Voyages*. 1703. (*Library of Congress*) Lahontan's was an imaginary map of the West. By indicating the "River Longue" crossing the whole West and emptying into the Pacific, Lahontan started the myth of the Rio Buenaventura that was not refuted until Frémont's expedition of 1843–44.

had influence with the king, should have listened more intently
to that host of crude practitioners of "the rudimentary science of
space." At the very least they could have done wonders to encourage French immigration to North America, had they only
pondered and then publicized such statements of unbounded
enthusiasm for the North American backwoods as Radisson's:

> We embarked ourselves on the delightfulest lake of the world. . . .
> the country was so pleasant, so beautiful and fruitful that it grieved
> me to see that the world could not discover such inticing countrys to
> live in. . . . those kingdoms are so delicious and under so tempered a
> climate, plentiful of all things, the earth bringing forth its fruit twice
> a year, the people live long and lusty and wise in their way.

"The people" were, of course, the Indians whom the French explorers, traders, and missionaries came to know so well. Had the
elite of France listened and learned from the explorers, North
America might still be French or French-Indian, since the
coureurs des bois never looked down on the red men and inter-
married with the native Americans as a matter of course.

No, by the time of the great scientific debate over the New
World, there was no lack of information about the country in
France. Nearly a hundred volumes of the *Jesuit Rélations* had
been compiled. The findings of a century of work by intrepid
explorers who braved the frozen winters, hostile tribes, and
seemingly endless wilderness were also reasonably well known.
In 1664, François du Creux had already published *Histoire
Canadensis*, a summary of the explorers' knowledge of North
America that was a kind of French version of the voyages of
Hakluyt or de Brosses. And virtually every year, beginning with
Champlain's works published in 1632, new French maps of
North America appeared. Some of the classics were Nicholas
Sanson d'Abbeville's *Amérique Septemtrionale* (1650) and *La
Canada ou Nouvelle France* (1656), L. B. J. Franquelin's *Carte
de l'Amérique Septemtrionale* (1685), and the works of Guil-
laume Delisle, especially his *Carte de la Louisiane et du Cours
du Mississippi* (1703).

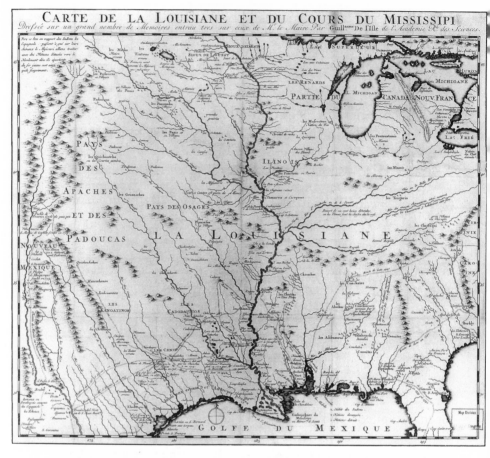

Guillaume De l'Isle, "Carte de la Louisiane et du Cours du Mississipi." 1718–55. *(Library of Congress)* De l'Isle's map, which remained the basic French map of North America until the mid-eighteenth century, pushed Louisiana as far east as the Allegheny Mountains and New France as far south as the Ohio. It was a major salvo in the war of maps.

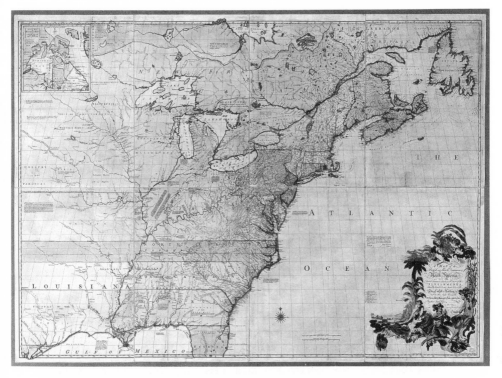

John Mitchell, "Map of the British and French Dominions in North America."
1755. *(The University of Texas at Arlington)* Dr. Mitchell's map was the most complete map of colonial America. It pushed the British colonies to the Mississippi in response to aggressive claims represented on French maps. It took a series of wars to resolve the conflict symbolized on this and De l'Isle's map.

Mitchell's map was also used as the base map for the Treaty of Paris, which marked the end of the American Revolution.

The Delisle family, like the Cassinis, were cartographers to the king, and this map of 1703 not only represented a detailed summary of all French knowledge about the interior of North America, including the correct course of the Mississippi, but also claimed cartographically the known North American interior from the Rio Grande on the west to the Alleghenies on the east and from the Gulf of Mexico to the Arctic circle. Delisle made many corrected versions of this map down to 1735, when his last version was published to refute the English arrogance of Henry Popple, who in 1732 had published his *Map of the British Empire in America with the French and Spanish Settlements Adjacent Thereto*, in which he pushed British America all the way to the Mississippi, using much of Delisle's earlier data to do so.

Europe's savants came to know of the French discoveries in the heart of North America. In 1702, Johann Baptist Homann, a German ex-monk, began his career as a cartographer in Nuremberg. He became cartographer to Emperor Charles of Germany and Peter the Great of Russia, and some two hundred maps later was still charting North America. His sons followed in his footsteps. Then there were the great Nicholas de Fer of Belgium and Gerard van Keulen of Amsterdam, and still more Frenchmen, notably Nicholas Belling, Philippe Bauche, and J. B. d'Anville. The latter succeeded Delisle as the leading French authority on North American space, especially with his map *Canada, Louisiane et les Terres anglaises* (1756), accompanied by an extensive explanatory *mémoire*. The publication of this map and *mémoire* was intended to more than match the work of the great English botanist John Mitchell, for many years a resident of Virginia, whose huge *Map of the British Colonies in North America, with the Roads, Distances, Limits, and Extent of Settlements* was published in 1755, shortly followed by his imperialistic polemic, *A New and Complete History of the British Empire in America* (1756), a three-volume work. Mitchell's map, drawing upon all the available French information, plus that of hundreds of British explorers, traders, and surveyors, was the climactic map of North America in the eighteenth century. It contained more information and was more accurate than all those that preceded it, and many that followed it. Along with Popple's map, it hung in the "war room" of George Washington's revolutionary headquarters, and the treaty ending the American Revolution was based upon it.

But "the rudimentary science of space" did not come as easily, or at least as quickly, to the English as it had to the French, who had soon penetrated to the heart of the continent via the St. Lawrence, the Great Lakes, and the Mississippi. The English colonies faced the great barrier of the Alleghenies or "Endless Mountains," as the Indians called them. The first successes of English explorers were to the south around the end of the great Appalachian barrier. First came the young German immigrant John Lederer, who in 1669–70 explored the upper James River, then the Roanoke, and finally found a way around the mountains in northern Georgia. He was followed by a whole host of would-be fur traders, most notably Abraham Woods, Thomas Batts, and Robert Fallam. One "bright but illiterate" boy, Gabriel Arthur, managed to get himself captured by the Indians. As their prisoner, he roamed all over the country beyond the mountains—as far as the Tennessee, the Ohio, and possibly the Mississippi, and the Chattahoochee and Savannah to the south and southeast—but he could make little geographical sense of where he had been. Abraham Woods was only guessing when he wrote to a cartographer friend in England, John Richards, who promptly put Arthur's travels on his map. This important information also appeared on Joel Gascoyne's *A New Map of the Country of Carolina* (1682), termed "the most accurate map of the region until well into the eighteenth century."

The Virginia traders were soon outstripped by adventurers from South Carolina. They worked at first out of Charles Town, located between the Ashley and the Cooper rivers (so named by the philosopher John Locke on his map of 1671, made for his speculator patrons, one of whom was Anthony Ashley, the philosophical Earl of Shaftesbury). The Carolina explorers encompassed a great range of interests that motivated their expeditions. Most were interested in the fur trade, but a number of others sought to collect Indian slaves for shipment to Jamaica. Still others went out filled with dreams of imperial glory and plain scientific curiosity. Dr. Henry Woodword led the cavalcade. Pronouncing the country a "second paradize," he reached the Westo Indians on the Savannah River by 1674, and established a thriving fur trade. Other traders provoked the Westo War, thus destroying the Westos as middlemen and opening the way into the Cherokee, Choctaw, and Chickasaw country of western Georgia, Alabama, and Mississippi. By the end of the century they were challenging the Spanish in Florida and the French, who clung precariously to settlements established at Biloxi and near the critical mouth of the Mississippi. In 1698, Captain Thomas Welch had reached the Mississippi, and crossed it near the juncture with the Arkansas at almost the same spot reached by Hernán de Soto in 1541. Welch made friends and alliances with the Quapaw Indians living there, and also with Jean Couture, a survivor of either La Salle's or Tonti's Mississippi expeditions. By his alliances with the Quapaws and the powerful Chickasaw near Natchez, Welch threatened to cut the French Mississippi artery in half. Couture also showed him a route up the Mississippi, along the Tennessee, and over the mountains to Charles Town. By 1700, Bienville, the French founder of Louisiana, had declared his own war on the British infiltrators.

But the British trader-explorers were too many, and they kept coming. They eventually dominated the southeastern tribes— until the day nearly 150 years later when Andrew Jackson broke their hold in the Battle of Horseshoe Bend. Some of the Carolina explorers were colorful and highly enterprising, like Sir Alexander Cuming, who in 1730 won the hearts of the Cherokee by taking seven of their chiefs to London and safely returning them. Others were sinister slave hunters, like Thomas Nairne, who discovered the Everglades, produced a map and a "memorial" of the country in 1711, and then perished appropriately by hideous death at the hands of his intended red victims. Still others were scientific men like John Lawson, who regularly sent natural history specimens back to the famous London apothecary James Petiver, an agent of the Royal Society. Lawson managed to publish an important treatise on his peregrinations entitled *New Voyage to Carolina* in 1709, including an early picture of a buffalo, before he, too, perished at the hands of outraged red men. In this case, a survivor reported that poor Lawson was stuck full of pitch pine splinters, which were then lighted, making him a human torch.

In contrast to the rapid thrusts into the interior from the south, British colonials made relatively little progress in the north, where they were blocked not only by the Alleghenies and the French coming down from the Great Lakes, but also by the Iroquois. The domain of the Six Nations of the Iroquois extended from the Great Lakes to the upper Ohio, and even down into the lower valleys of the Susquehanna and its tributaries. They had conquered a great number of lesser tribes, like the Delaware and the Mohicans, and hence as a confederation held control over a vast hinterland, much like the Aztecs in Mexico. Nominally friendly to the English and hostile to the French and their Huron allies, the Iroquois nonetheless played both European nations off against each other most skillfully all during the imperial struggle for North America. As long as the struggle lasted, they were the great and powerful middlemen.

In dealing with the Indians, early Americans learned most of what they knew about the continental interior. They also gained a detailed knowledge of the red men. For the frontiersman, life depended upon knowing the difference between a Seneca and a Shawnee, and life also depended upon knowing the detailed customs of each of the tribes. At first, the English settlers knew very little, and what they did know came from contacts with these nations at Albany, far up the Hudson River, or from French sources. The latter were what Governor Cadwallader Colden depended upon when he wrote the first systematic treatise on the Iroquois, *The History of the Five Indian Nations*

Depending on the Province of New York, in 1727, long before any Englishman had penetrated their country. In fact, Colden, impatient with superior French knowledge, wrote his book as a guide and encouragement to future British frontiersmen to enter the Iroquois territory. Shortly afterward, subjects of Britain did enter the Iroquois country in great numbers, the beginning of a flood tide of settlement that either washed the tribes away or pushed them far to the west. In this process, early Americans amassed an amazing amount of information on the tribes to the west, which rests today in colonial archives. And with the work of Colden and then the Moravian missionary John Heckewelder, whose *Account of the History, Manners, and Customs of the Indian Nations, Who Once Inhabited Pennsylvania and the Neighboring States* was published by the American Philosophical Society in 1819, systematic study of the red men began. It was never true that, like Columbus, white Americans considered all red men simply as Indians. It was, for example, the white man's knowledge of the finer distinctions of Indian life and politics that helped bring about the downfall of the mighty League of the Iroquois.

iii

GOD AND MAN ON THE SUSQUEHANNA

THE FIRST great explorer to penetrate the northern Alleghenies was not an Englishman at all but a Palatine German immigrant, Conrad Weiser. His family had moved from Württemberg, Germany, to the Schoharie Valley of New York. There, when he was seventeen years old, Conrad Weiser had been sent to live with Chief Quagnant of the Mohawks. He learned the language and customs of the Six Nations, received an Indian name, and remained fast friends with them for the rest of his life. Indeed, he became the chief interpreter and diplomat between the British and the Six Nations. He also became a leader of his own people as he led them into Pennsylvania to settlements just east of the Alleghenies from Easton on the Delaware to Harrisburg on the Susquehanna. He settled his own family, which eventually included fifteen children, at Tulpehocken on a beautiful and strategic pass over the mountains that led to Shamokin, the southern capital of the Iroquois. There lived Shikellamy, the great subchief of the Six Nations, who was Weiser's steadfast friend for most of their lives.

A strange, remarkable man, Weiser set the pattern for the frontiersman a generation before Daniel Boone made his appearance. Weiser was equally at home with the red sachems and painted warriors of the wilderness, the pietistic, learned Germans from the Palatine, and the scholars and statesmen of Philadelphia, most notably James Logan, Benjamin Franklin, and John Bartram. At his bucolic farm at Tulpehocken, he might have served as a model for Crèvecoeur's famous "new man, the American," who carved his own free estate out of the wilderness on the road west from Philadelphia.

But Weiser had another side, too. For a long interlude of perhaps six years, he deserted his devout Lutheranism to become a cowled and bearded monk in the wild Utopian colony of Johann Conrad Beissel, who thought he was a second Christ. Weiser helped Beissel establish a communitarian settlement at Ephrata on the Cocalico River, in which strict celibacy was the rule. Separate quarters using no metal were built for men and women, together with a stone meeting hall and sanctuary three stories high, where Beissel held weird Rosicrucian ceremonies in a chapter room with four small windows that looked out foursquare to a world readying itself for the millennium. In the meantime, "the Second Christ," or "Friedsam Gottrecht," as Beissel called himself, composed strange mystical hymns and called his brethren out at all hours of the night to sing them as they marched through winter snows in solemn cowled processions. He called the collected hymns *Godly Chants of Love and Praise*, and they were published by Benjamin Franklin, along with the master's *Ninety-nine Mystical Sentences*, which gave ultimate direction to his community.

Though still a religious mystic, Weiser eventually broke with
Beissel, however. The issue was sexual. Beissel censured Weiser
for fathering four children while under his vow of celibacy, and
Weiser led the brethren in an attack on Beissel for his obvious
sexual assaults on the women's cloister. Though Ephrata proved
to be the longest-lived community in America, lasting until
1920, Weiser had little to do with it after 1745. The relationship
of Weiser with Ephrata was significant, however. It was symbolic of the frontier experience in western Pennsylvania, where
hordes of German pietists coped with the Indians and the wilderness, while at the same time participating in a strange communitarian way in what came to be known as the Great
Awakening.

So many such communities sprang up on the Pennsylvania
frontier that the famous Count Zinzendorf came to America to
coordinate them. Weiser saved his life from the Indians. He also
guided Bishop Augustus Spangenberg on the way through
Pennsylvania to North Carolina, where he established the Wa-
chovia community. In his contact with these German immigrants, Weiser, the frontiersman, exchanged learning and
knowledge with men of Heidelberg, Bonn, Halle, and other
great continental universities, where knowledge was far ahead of
that in England and France. It was only fitting that Weiser's
son-in-law should be the famous Bishop Henry Muhlenberg,
who at Bethlehem on the Pennsylvania frontier established one
of the great German centers of scientific learning in early
America.

Weiser's work as an explorer really began in the winter of
1736. In 1731 and 1736 he had convinced his friend Shikellamy
to visit James Logan in Philadelphia. These visits culminated in
a treaty between the Pennsylvanians and the Iroquois, which
had to be ratified before the grand council at Onondaga. Accordingly, Weiser and Shikellamy set out via Shamokin, deep
into the backcountry along the upper Susquehanna to Onondaga, far up north in western New York. Weiser kept two journals, one in English and one in German, which recorded the

incredible march through snow and rain, across rushing rivers and over uncharted and precipitous mountains. Exhaustion, sickness, and starvation plagued the party until, finally, at one point on April 8, Weiser sat down by a tree to die. His Indian friend persuaded him to continue, however, and at last, two days later, in a pouring rainstorm, they came to Onondaga, where Weiser successfully concluded his treaty with the mighty Six Nations. His journals are the first recorded description of the unknown wilderness along the upper Susquehanna. Part of their route later became a well-traveled trail.

Thereafter, nearly every year Weiser was in the Indian country. In 1743, on the eve of King George's War with the French, he led another expedition to Onondaga. This time he was accompanied by Lewis Evans, a surveyor and mapmaker, and the great American naturalist John Bartram. This expedition provided Evans information for his important map of 1749, which, when published in 1755, became the most accurate map of the western country. It also provided Bartram with the opportunity to collect natural history specimens for the first time beyond the Alleghenies. Bartram, whose journal was published in London in 1751, reported on "the inhabitants, climate, soil, rivers, productions, animals, and other matters worthy of notice." Among the last were his remarks on the Great Deluge. He wrote, from atop the Gooseberry Mountains, above the forks of the Susquehanna, "the Waters at the flood gradually ebbed and flooded several times. The shelf-like shore lines indicated that." As for the Indians, he believed them to be from Japan or Tartary, but they could also have been Norsemen, Prince Madoc's Welsh refugees, Egyptians, Phoenicians, or Carthaginians. In short, he didn't know. Nonetheless, Bartram's little journal was widely read in Europe, and made its contribution to the debate over the New World.

Weiser had thus introduced natural history to backcountry America. In 1748, together with George Croghan, another notable frontiersman, and William Franklin, the son of the great Benjamin, he opened up the Ohio Country to the Pennsylvan-

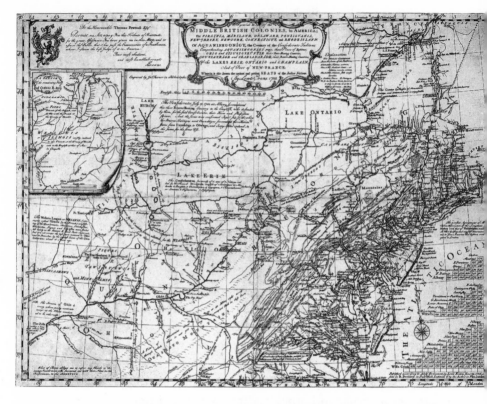

Lewis Evans, "A General Map of the Middle British Colonies in America." 1755.
(Library of Congress) This was in part the work of the frontier scout. Evans accompanied Conrad Weiser and John Bartram to Onondaga in 1743. He later worked closely with other frontier scouts, such as George Croghan and Christian Post.

ians. In that year, he followed the so-called Allegheny Trail due west into Shawnee country, to Logstown on the Monongahela. There they concluded a treaty that kept the western Indians from joining the French in the coming great war. In his private notes he wrote, "Erecting of a good Correspondents and a Regular trade with the Indians on Ohio would Secure that fine and large Country to the English nation. . . ."

The treaty of Logstown proved to be of not much consequence, however, as soon after, when war broke out with the French, the Ohio Indians descended upon Pennsylvania. Braddock's defeat terrified friendly Indians and settlers alike, and consequently much of Weiser's time was spent rallying a frontier defense of the Alleghenies, rather than in exploration. His last important contribution to the opening of the West was in providing assistance to General John Forbes, who in November 1758 captured Fort Duquesne from the French. Conrad Weiser had been the first, and perhaps the greatest, of the explorer frontiersmen who opened up the interior of North America to England.

iv

THE MYSTERIES OF THE OHIO

WEISER, though the archetypal frontiersman, was not the only noteworthy explorer of his time, but he, along with the Irish fur trader George Croghan, had done much to turn British attention to the Ohio country on the far western flank of the Six Nations. They were, of course, not the first Europeans to come in contact with "the mysteries of the Ohio." French fur traders and missionaries coming down from the lakes via the Miami, the Wabash, and the Monongahela had visited its shores often. French maps, however inaccurately, charted its course and gave it the name La Belle Rivière. In 1729, de Lery, the chief engineer of Canada, made a careful survey of the Allegheny and upper Ohio. As a result, the French were the first to recognize the strategic importance of the "golden triangle," where Pittsburgh

now stands. Also, in response to the Croghan-Weiser expedition
to Logstown in 1748, white-coated Captain Céleron de Blainville
trooped through the wilderness at the head of two hundred
French regulars, planting lead plates denoting France's possession of the country—which, of course, belonged to the Indians—and warned the English off the Ohio.

That the French were serious about the Ohio even before
Céleron de Blainville planted his lead plates was clear from the
fate of John Howard and his men. In 1742, as head of a party of
land scouts commissioned by the governor of Virginia, he had
set off across the Alleghenies from a rendezvous at the Great
Natural Bridge. Howard and his men, floating down Wood
River on a "bull boat" made of buffalo hides, reached the Great
Kanawha and headed down it into the Ohio. They made their
way down the Ohio, around the Great Falls, to the Mississippi,
which they reached on June 7, 1742. At this point, they did not
turn back, but instead set off down the Mississippi on a reconnaissance of the French inland empire. Near the end of their
journey, they were captured by the French and imprisoned in
New Orleans awaiting transport as slaves to the mines of Mexico. But the French moved slowly; after two years in prison, two
of the men, John Salley and one Baudran, escaped. Using ox
hides, they made another bull boat and paddled across Lake
Pontchartrain to freedom. Aided by the Choctaws and other
tribes trading with the Carolinans, they made their way across
Mississippi, Alabama, and Georgia to Charles Town. Salley's
adventure was not over, however. He elected to sail home to
Virginia, and just out of sight of Charles Town harbor he was
captured by French pirates. After much negotiation, he was released, and he finally reached home on May 17, 1745. Salley had
kept a journal of his travels, but it was confiscated by the
French, so he wrote out his story from memory and gave it to
the British authorities. A copy of Salley's "Brief Account" was
secured by Peter Jefferson (Thomas Jefferson's father), and he
used it in the making of his *Map of Virginia*, done in collaboration with his friend Joshua Fry and published in 1751.

Meanwhile, to the north, shortly after de Blainville passed Logstown, two British expeditions converged on the spot and quickly neutralized the Frenchman's influence. The first one was led by Christopher Gist of Maryland, a surveyor as well as a wilderness scout, perhaps best known to history for having saved George Washington's life on his first wilderness campaign. Gist was employed by the Ohio Company of Virginia, a group of land speculators with large imaginations. His mission was to explore and map the Ohio country as far as the Great Falls (present Louisville). In October 1756, he left his friend and neighbor Daniel Boone and set out from Old Town at the head of the Potomac loaded with instructions from company officials. He swung north to the Juniata River, and then west along an Indian trail to Logstown, where he arrived just after the French had departed. He found the Indians hostile, and started back for Virginia. On the Scioto River, however, he met the veteran George Croghan, and together they returned to the lower Ohio. At Togwotee Town on the Miami River, they turned the tide of Indian allegiance and swung the western tribes behind Britain.

Two years later, in 1758, together with Croghan, Gist returned to Logstown and there concluded a treaty that granted the English colonists and land speculators settlement rights east of the Ohio River. Gist then crossed the Ohio and made his way across Kentucky to his home in Yadkin, North Carolina. He preceded Daniel Boone into this country by eighteen years. In so doing, he provided the first important information on that country to British mapmakers. Gist's relatively careful field maps were used by Joshua Fry to update his maps of 1751.

In the meantime, Dr. Thomas Walker, another Virginia land speculator, after many misadventures, had, in the winter and spring of 1749–50, followed the Clinch and Powell rivers through the Cumberland Gap into Kentucky. He had found one of the continent's crucial mountain passageways. In a few years, led by Daniel Boone and James Henderson, a cavalcade of settlers would march through the gap into Kentucky's forests and savannahs. Joshua Fry put Cumberland Gap on his map, too.

Though in 1748 one war between France and England—King George's War—had ended, this turned out to be merely an armistice. Soon, too, the French realized that the juncture of the Ohio and the Allegheny was the "prime meridian" for control of the strategic Ohio River. They built a fort near there, named Fort Le Boeuf, about the time that Dr. Walker was describing the merits of Kentucky to his neighbors. This was too much for the Virginians, who had unlimited expansionist dreams in that direction. Never mind Pennsylvania's claims. So in 1753, they sent Major George Washington, accompanied by Christopher Gist and a small army, to demand that the French evacuate the fort. Along the march from Virginia to the Ohio, Washington defeated a force under Jumonville, but not only did the French at Fort Le Boeuf reject Washington's demands; they also defeated him at Great Meadows on July 4, 1754. The French and Indian War had begun.

Washington and Gist had made careful maps of the strategic country, and when in 1755 General George Braddock took the field at the head of an army of British regulars, they were with him. George Croghan, made a captain, commanded Braddock's Indian allies. With such experienced talent to assist him, it is one of the great military marvels that the stubborn Braddock suffered his disastrous defeat on Turtle Creek and plunged the whole British frontier into terror at the advance of hostile French and Indians.

The English were too numerous for the French, however, and after George Croghan journeyed north to Albany and negotiated a peace with the Six Nations, General John Forbes was able to march an army straight across the Alleghenies, with no skirmishes, and take Fort Le Boeuf, or Fort Duquesne, as it had recently been named. The British called it Fort Pitt. By 1761, General Wolfe had conquered General Montcalm on the Plains of Abraham, near Quebec, where the future great explorer Bougainville served as Montcalm's second-in-command. Shortly thereafter, Montreal fell; the French and Indian War was over.

By the end of the war, however, both Britain and France knew a great deal about the Ohio country.

If they had not learned enough, the British learned infinitely more as a result of the Illinois chief Pontiac's brief conspiracy in 1764 aimed at attacking Fort Detroit and Fort Pitt in a grand effort to push the white men out of the Ohio country. In that year, Pontiac was surprisingly successful in organizing the western Indians in an effort to drive the English back beyond the Allegheny Mountains. But the settlers held at Fort Pitt and Fort Detroit, while a force under Colonel Henry Bouquet defeated Pontiac's Indian forces at the battle of Bushy Run. Shortly afterward, two expeditions were sent to survey and map the Ohio River and its northern tributaries. One of the expeditions included, in addition to the great naturalist John Bartram, Thomas Hutchins, Bouquet's official cartographer. Hutchins surveyed not only the Ohio country, but the Mississippi and Gulf Coast as well. He eventually became geographer to George Washington's Revolutionary Army, then the first Geographer of the United States, and ended his career laying out the Seven Ranges of the Ohio in pursuance of the Northwest Ordinance of 1787. Though he died before work on the Seven Ranges was completed, Hutchins's work there created the basic grid-pattern land division system that eventually made it possible to parcel out the vast western domain of the new United States as its people relentlessly marched across the continent.

To the south, in 1769 Daniel Boone entered Kentucky, said by John Finley, his brother-in-law, to be a veritable Eden. Thus began a decade dominated by Boone, Finlay, Simon Kenton, and other long-hunter explorers in Kentucky, which a forlorn Cherokee chief, Dragging Canoe, dubbed "the dark and bloody ground" at the signing of the Treaty of Sycamore Shoals in 1775. By that treaty the Cherokees ceded the Cumberland and Kentucky river valleys, or what is now virtually the whole state of Kentucky, to white speculators.

Kentucky was the scene of long and epic struggles between frontiersmen and Indians that did not terminate until the defeat of Chief Tecumseh's forces, led by his brother the Prophet at the Battle of Tippecanoe in 1811. Two books made Kentucky famous. The first was published in 1784 by John Filson, a comparatively recent resident of Kentucky. It was entitled *The Discovery, Settlement and Present State of Kentucke and an Essay Towards the Topography, and Natural History of That Important Country.* The title promised more than the very brief book presented, but Filson also included the first accurate map of Kentucky, which was of the greatest interest to settlers and land speculators. He also added an appendix, "The Adventures of Col. Daniel Boon," which was of interest to incipient American and European romantics, and hence made the book famous. Filson had created the first American backwoods literary hero.

The description of Kentucky itself was interesting, however. Filson was very systematic. He covered such topics as "Situation and Boundaries," "Rivers," "Nature of the Soil," "Air and Climate," "Soil and Produce," "Quadrupeds," "Trade," and "Curiosities." Besides touting the "loose, deep, black" and fertile soil of Kentucky, he also described the abundance of wild game, including a herd of a thousand buffalo a hunter had claimed to have seen, and the bones of a prehistoric creature (the mastodon) found in Big Bone Lick near Lexington. Though inferior to Jefferson's *Notes on Virginia*, published in the same year, Filson's book, in structure, coverage, and general approach, is a companion piece of Jefferson's great contribution to the debate over the New World. And in Boone, Filson had elucidated what Crèvecoeur meant when he described "this new man, this American." The courts of Europe could never produce such a man of the wilderness—nature's nobleman as epic hero.

The other book was Gilbert Imlay's *A Topographical Description of the Western Territory of North America*, published in 1792. Imlay, who was an adventurer and speculator, had acquired land in Kentucky as a result of being a lieutenant in Washington's army. In all, he spent only two years in Kentucky, however, before being driven out by the sheriff and the courts. An incredibly romantic figure, Imlay soon turned up in Paris with Mary Wollstonecraft as his friend and mistress. Written to attract settlers to his Kentucky lands, Imlay's vivid descriptions caught the attention of the French romantics. Ascending from the Ohio River, he wrote, the would-be settler finds land where

> an eternal verdure reigns, and the brilliant sun of lat. 39°, piercing through the azure heavens, produced in this prolific soil, an early maturity which is truly astonishing. Flowers full and perfect, as if they had been cultivated by the hand of a florist, with all their captivating odours, and with all the variegated charms that colour and nature can produce, here, in the lap of elegance and beauty, decorate the smiling groves. Soft zephyrs gently breathe on sweets, and the inhaled air gives a voluptuous glow of health and vigour, that seems to ravish the intoxicated senses.... Every thing here gives delight....

Imlay, indeed, had delved into the mysteries of the Ohio and found Eden. Nonetheless, by the turn of the century, the debate over the New World had swung sharply in America's favor. Buffon recanted. Only Raynal and the surly de Pauw held out. America had become an Eden of the future, the home of natural man blessed by the Creator in all things.

V

THE DISCOVERY OF PLENTITUDE

THE WORKS of Filson, and particularly Imlay, were impressionistic and romantic, but they also reflected what could be found in every literate explorer's account of North America and virtually every volume of the *Jesuit Relations*. In addition, they reflected the findings of a long line of European and colonial naturalists, whose serious labors began as long ago as the late seventeenth century. They all shared a vision of nature's plenitude in America. As far back as 1679, John Banister, one of the earliest English naturalists to visit America, stood in awe of the flights of passenger pigeons that "darken the sky," and wild turkeys and swans and geese and ducks in abundance. He wrote of the "multitudes of vegetables, many of them unknown to me," of trees that have strange fruit and of curious plants like the *"Phalloidea sive Penis Caninus"* or "dog's prick mushroom," which "stunk egregiously." When he thought of the incredible task of describing and drawing such wonders in the name of science, he declared that what he had seen was "so strange and monstrous that I am afraid that they may be thought chimeras to be found no where but in his brains that drew them."

Nonetheless, Banister, set down in the wilds of Virginia, intended to persist in his duty. He was part of a new scientific network that was beginning to span the globe—the naturalist's network. Thanks to the work of Continental scholars like Boerhaave, Gronovius, de Jussieu, Buffon, Ray, Lister, and ultimately Linnaeus; thanks to the interest of institutions like the Royal Society, the French Académie, and even the Temple House Coffee Club (which by 1691 numbered some forty-one enthusiastic naturalists); thanks to gardeners like Peter Miller and Capability Brown; thanks to the enthusiasm of men like Sir Hans Sloan and Bishop Henry Compton, whose gardens and collections were the envy of Europe; and thanks most of all, perhaps, to the new urge for scientific discovery around the globe, the study of natural history began to develop dramatically in tandem with the study of the cosmos in the late seventeenth century. North America shared in this development as a great natural laboratory and hunting ground for naturalists, who never failed to find something new and wonderful to add to the Great Chain of Being.

Consider the line that begins with Banister, probably sent by John Ray and Bishop Henry Compton to Virginia, where he was largely supported by William Byrd I. This genealogy of naturalists would include Hugh Jones, also of Virginia; poor John Lawson, who first went to the New World on impulse, yet made extraordinary and accurate comments on the richness of

America before he was burned to death by the Tuscaroras, a tribe he admired; two John Claytons from Virginia; Dr. John Mitchell, whose map and jingoistic diatribes overshadowed his considerable contributions as a naturalist; Paul Dudley and Cotton Mather, breeders of hybrid corn in Massachusetts; Cadwallader Colden in New York; and Mark Catesby.

Pause at Mark Catesby, for it was he who best dramatized the work of the naturalist and the abundance of America. A friend and neighbor of John Ray, who was struggling mightily to bring the new science to bear on the chaos of classically oriented natural history, Catesby first sailed to America in 1712 with his sister on her honeymoon. She had married a man named Cocke who lived in Virginia. Through him, Catesby met William Byrd II and other colonial patrons, and he spent seven years botanizing in the tidewater region and deep into Virginia's mountains. He also went to Bermuda and Jamaica. By 1719 he was back in England with boxes of American plants, one of which he presented to Samuel Dale, a powerful figure in the naturalists' world. Catesby's gift bore fruit. By the end of 1720, he was commissioned by the Royal Society to go to America "to Observe the Rarities of that Country for the uses and purposes of the Society."

On May 3, 1722, Catesby arrived at Charles Town. For the next three years, he traveled up and down the Carolinas from the tidewater to the backcountry. His journey took him into Georgia and as far south as Florida. He often traversed the same area in different seasons to observe the changing plant life. In so doing, he became perhaps America's first ecologist. He was enormously interested in the relation of plant and animal life to the terrain (in terms of altitude and soil) and the climate as well as the seasons. On all this he kept careful notes, while at the same time making meticulous descriptions of the hundreds of plants, animals, birds, fishes, and Indians that he saw. The collections that he sent back to England were staggering, especially since most of the specimens were new. Each shipment was eagerly awaited by his backers, who proudly distributed dupli-

cates to their correspondents in Europe. As a collector, he had
no peer up to his time. In late 1725, he sailed to the Bahamas,
where he studied the fish. Then he returned to England in 1726
with a plan. He wanted to produce an illustrated natural history
of North America. Funds were short, however, and this was not
to be. Instead, with the aid of a French artisan, Joseph Goupy,
he taught himself engraving and began to work on a more modest book. It was 1743 before he completed *A Natural History of
Carolina, Florida and the Bahama Islands*, in two volumes and
an appendix. Catesby's *Natural History* included some two
hundred colored plates of plants, insects, birds, fishes, amphibi-
ans, and quadrupeds to complement his extensive text. They
were surely the most beautiful drawings of North American
phenomena in the eighteenth century, rivaled only by the work
of William Bartram and of Thomas Pennant, who worked almost exclusively in Canada and the Arctic.

In Catesby's work, there stood the bison scratching himself
on a pink-flowering magnolia tree; there stood the blacksnake
coiled against a red lily; there stood the mockingbird on the limb
of a lavender-flowered dogwood tree; there stood brilliantly colored cardinals and finches and varieties of woodpeckers; there
darted the bald eagle after his prey—immensely out-of-scale in
comparison to a tiny Indian in a canoe, suggesting that Catesby
had long ago picked out the national bird; there, in 171 plates,
spread the flowers of the New World in shimmering colors,
from the yellow of the jasmine to the red of the trumpet tree.
Nothing in print suggested the dazzling plentitude of America
half so much as Catesby's *Natural History of Carolina, Florida
and the Bahama Islands*, though the work of another naturalist,
William Bartram, would come close.

John and William Bartram became America's best home-
grown explorer-naturalists. John, the father, was born in 1699,
was orphaned early, and became a farmer on Kingsessing Creek,
a few miles outside of Philadelphia. Like his friend Conrad
Weiser, he had a large family, nine children in all. About 1730,
Bartram went to Philadelphia, bought some books on botany,

and learned a rudimentary Latin so that he could correspond with other botanists. Gradually, he gained a circle of friends, including the great James Logan, who not only had the largest library in the colonies, but also was a considerable horticulturist himself. He lent Bartram a microscope and all the standard English books on botany, including Linnaeus's *Systema Naturae*, when it came out in 1735. Through Logan also, and through Benjamin Franklin, he was put in touch with the London merchant Peter Collinson. Collinson was a Quaker, like Bartram, but that was not what they had most in common. Natural history commanded their mutual attention. For a number of years, Collinson had acted as agent for the Royal Society in securing natural history specimens from America. He found in Bartram the ideal collector and correspondent. Though the two men never met, they exchanged so many letters over the years, full of professional and personal worries, that they became lifelong friends.

Each year when his family chores were over, Bartram would venture into the mountains and along the rivers of western Pennsylvania, gathering new specimens. Many of these he planted in his own natural, and to the untutored eye unkempt, garden, which became a famous sight for all travelers to see. Most of the specimens he shipped to Collinson, however. And so successful was he at supplying the naturalists' network that Linnaeus was moved to call him out of pure joy "the finest natural botanist in the world." His protégé Peter Kalm, who traveled through America and met Bartram, could confirm this.

Once he had absorbed the knowledge from James Logan and other Philadelphia savants, and once he started getting orders from Collinson, Bartram began to range widely over America. In 1738 he made a twelve-hundred-mile overland trip into Virginia. In 1743 he went up the Susquehanna with Conrad Weiser and Lewis Evans. He also worked the rich Catskills, where he found "the greatest variety of uncommon trees and shrubs I ever saw in such a compass of ground." In 1754 he visited Governor Cadwallader Colden, the squire of Coldringham, up the Hudson

near Newburgh, New York. There he met Alexander Garden of
Charles Town, and perhaps the three greatest American botanists of the day shared their knowledge and experience. In 1760
he was in Charles Town again, swapping information with Dr.
Garden. Shortly afterward, he accompanied Colonel Henry
Bouquet, conqueror of Fort Duquesne, down the Ohio. Then he
was in the Carolinas in 1762. And on one last trip, at the request
of Bouquet, who had become governor of Georgia, he went as
far south as the St. Johns River in Florida. On this trip he was
accompanied by his son William. The result of what turned out
to be a grueling field expedition, aside from the collections, was
John Bartram's last book, *A Description of East Florida with a
Journal Kept by John Bartram of Philadelphia*, published in
London in 1767. So great was English interest in the author and
the region he traversed that it went through three editions. Bartram came to be designated "the King's Botanist," and he gained
a special fame in the eyes of European scientists; he represented,
somewhat like Conrad Weiser and the better-known Benjamin
Franklin, the rustic, noble, intelligent man of nature—a wilderness savant whom even the testy Linnaeus admired, and who
believed devoutly that his main work was observing the hand of
God in the variegated patterns of nature.

William Bartram shared many of these same qualities and be-
liefs, but in contrast to his father, who traveled incessantly for
most of his middle and later years, William made his name on
the strength of one expedition, hundreds of brilliantly executed
drawings, and one immortal book that provided key inspiration
for the European Romantic Movement. In 1768 Peter Collinson
died, but not before he helped to set William on the naturalist
path. The good Quaker was succeeded by Dr. John Fothergill,
who became William's English patron. With Fothergill's encouragement, William undertook a four-year expedition, from
1773 to 1777, through the Carolinas, Georgia, Florida, Alabama,
and as far west as the Mississippi, up which he sailed as far as
Baton Rouge, where he met William Dunbar, who was to be one
of the first to carry science beyond the Great River.

William Bartram's book, published in 1791, was entitled *Travels Through North and South Carolina, Georgia, East and West Florida, the Cherokee Country, the Extensive Territories of the Muscogulges, or Creek Confederacy, and the Country of the Choctaws, Containing an Account of the Soil and Natural Productions of Those Regions, Together with Observations on the Manners of the Indians.* It enjoyed incredible popularity in its time, especially abroad, where it went through nine editions. Anyone who subscribed to the theory that America was a cold, monotonous country had to be disabused of this notion by Bartram's book. He had the romantic's eye for variety in nature. He remarked upon clouds of delicate insects—*Ephemera*—who were "as complicated as . . . the most perfect human being" and "well worth a few moments' contemplation." He heard the morning calls of the wild turkeys and remarked on pink flamingos etched against the sky. He described the dreaded Okefenokee swamp and revisited the St. Johns River. He wrote vividly of the "subtle and greedy alligator" in a kind of adventure tale designed to show people like Buffon that America bred monsters as well as any other part of the world. "Behold him rushing forth from the snags and reeds," William wrote passionately of the alligator. "His enormous body swells. His plaited tail, brandished high, floats upon the lake. The waters like a cataract descend from his opening jaws. Clouds of smoke issue from his dilated nostrils. The earth trembles with his thunder." He also made a vivid drawing of the swamp leviathans bellowing, snorting fire, thrashing their tails.

But Bartram didn't need drawings to embellish his prose. He saw the snake bird in colors, cream, black, and silvery white, like a Japanese print; he saw the savanna cranes soaring high in squadrons upon "their light elastic sail." He saw fish shimmering beneath the water's sunlit surface—red, russet, silver, blue, green, and orange. He saw trees and bushes and flowers, milkwhite, golden yellow, brownish purple, scarlet. And in one notable passage he put the whole ensemble together. In an orange grove, interspersed with palm trees and magnolias, he came

upon an "enchanting and amazing crystal fountain, which incessantly threw up, from dark rocky caverns below, tons of
water every minute." He saw "whole armies" of brilliantly colored fish descending into the abyss, "into the mouth of the bub-
bling fountain." In some anxiety he looked into the abyss, and
there he beheld them

> as it were emerging from the blue ether of another world, ap-
> parently at a vast distance, at their first appearance no bigger than
> flies or minnows, now gradually enlarging, their brilliant colors
> [beginning] to paint the fluid.
>
> Now they come forward rapidly, and instantly emerge, with the
> elastic expanding columns of crystalline waters, into the circular
> basin or funnel; see now how gently they rise, some upright, others
> obliquely, or seem to lay as it were on their sides, suffering them-
> selves to be gently lifted or borne up by the expanding fluid towards
> the surface, sailing or floating like butterflies in the cerulean ether.

Upon such passages the English poet Coleridge built his reputation, and other striking scenes stimulated Wordsworth, but
that was not the important thing. What William Bartram had
succeeded in doing was pointing up in endless profusion the
richly varied beauties of America. Using words, he painted
plentitude in Technicolor. No one else ever quite matched him
in presenting the case.

By the time William Bartram published his book, the new
United States had developed its own network of naturalists, its
own learned centers, collections, gardens, and learned journals.
Out from these learned centers departed a new wave of naturalists who would cross the Mississippi and reach to the far Pacific.
The principal American center was, appropriately, Philadelphia. There William Bartram stayed at home tending his garden
and became legendary. But there too, at the behest of Benjamin
Franklin, in 1743, was founded the American Philosophical Society for the Promotion of Useful Knowledge. The Philosophical Society became a focal point for the discovery of
America—its geography, its flora, its fauna, and its Indian lore.

To the north, in Boston, John Adams founded another learned society, the American Academy of Arts and Sciences, modeled after the French Académie, but despite the presence of Harvard faculty members and an impressive band of "scientifics," it never matched the American Philosophical Society as a power in American science and discovery.

Philadelphia for nearly one hundred years became the prime center of the new, or Enlightened, learning in America. And, as if to stand as the symbol of national pride in discovering and making knowledge useful to the masses, flanking Independence Hall stood Peale's Museum. Charles Willson Peale, perhaps as much as anyone, symbolized the Second Great Age of Discovery. He was first of all an artist who gained fame painting numerous portraits of George Washington. Then in 1786 in his house on Lombard Street he established a natural history museum whose principal novelty was the remains of a Kentucky mastodon lent to Peale by Dr. John Morgan of Philadelphia, brother of the discoverer of the bones. Peale's Museum grew until it occupied both Philosophical Hall and the Long Room on the second floor of Independence Hall. The extensive museum became Philadelphia's premier attraction. In addition to a collection of portraits painted by Peale, the museum featured all manner of curiosities, alive and dead, from a six-legged cow to an Egyptian mummy. Literally hundreds of stuffed specimens of birds and animals appeared in lifelike poses. All of these items were classified according to the principles of Linnaeus, then arranged in the Great Chain of Being, and finally, when possible, presented in ecologically accurate situations that resembled dioramas. The climax of Peale's labors came when he, himself, was able to "exhume" two mastodons from a site in upstate New York (his famous painting depicts the event), assemble the bones, and set one of them up for display in his museum, thereby demonstrating not only the cunning of American science, but also the new continent's great antiquity. On Christmas Eve of 1801, he held a banquet under the skeletal belly of one of the huge beasts. While the diners drank toasts in French champagne, a pianist, also seated under the mastodon, played choruses of "Yankee Doodle." As one writer has correctly pointed out, Peale was pure showman, but his museum and its popularity also signified the mass American interest and national pride in discovery and science, the twin processes out of which their country had been born and which would set the rhythm for its future.

In 1801, Thomas Jefferson was President of the United States, but he was also president of the American Philosophical Society, to him possibly a much more important honor. In his dual presidential capacities, he was forming plans for further discoveries beyond the Mississippi. Like most Americans, exploration and discovery were part of his heritage. He had spent his youth on the Virginia frontier following the labors of his father, the mapmaker Peter Jefferson, who in turn had followed the labors of those "rudimentary conquerors of space" George Croghan, Christopher Gist, and Lewis Evans. Jefferson, the polymath, the politician, the cosmopolite, but also the product of the frontier, would lead America's sweep to the west and add immense treasures to the storehouse of human knowledge in the bargain. Standing at the vanguard of the American adventure into the vast continent, Jefferson had already won the debate over the New World.

CHAPTER III

A Continental Consciousness

i
THE STAKES OF HYPOTHETICAL GEOGRAPHY

NOT THE French and Indian War, not the American Revolution, not even the tide of American settlers who poured over the Alleghenies into the valleys of the Ohio and the Mississippi stilled the clash of imperial energies over the North American continent. By the late eighteenth century any geopolitical thinker knew that the stakes to be won in that part of the New World were vast—but no one knew just how vast. England, France, Spain, and even Russia knew more about the Pacific than they knew about North America despite the great struggles of the recent imperial wars. In an emerging age of scientific mapmaking, North America remained in large measure a construct of myth. For the entire seventeenth century, and on some maps of the eighteenth century, California was still an island. Then there was the Strait of Anian. Though it was actually invented by the Venetian mapmaker Giacomo Gastaldi in 1546, the Spaniards believed that in 1578–79 the English pirate Francis Drake had found a Northwest Passage across the top of the world. They called it, following Gastaldi, the Strait of

97

Anian. They were sure, too, that a certain Admiral de Fonte had
rediscovered the passage. He had been preceded by an equally
mysterious Captain Maldonado in 1588. Another mythical
Spaniard, Juan de Fuca, had confirmed that it lay somewhere
about 48° north latitude and that it was part of a great inland
sea. And thanks to rumors filtering out of Russia by way of the
cartographic Delisle family, a good many European geopolitical
thinkers were not so sure that Vitus Bering, the mysterious
Swedish explorer in the service of Russia, or his lieutenant,
Alexei Chirikov, had not, by right of discovery, made the strategic strait the personal domain of the imperial Russian sovereign.
All this meant that despite their knowledge of the potential
riches of North America, for a long time Europeans and Americans alike regarded the passage to India or China as being of primary importance. It was a mercantile age. As such, the linkage
between discoveries on the North American continent with
those in the Pacific, the Far East, and the Arctic were of the
most critical significance. Straits and inlets and bays and es-
tuaries were discoveries beyond price, despite the fact that
Henry Hudson's great find had proved a frustration for more
than two centuries. Rivers, too, took on unimaginable significance, especially if they emptied into the Pacific. But even if
they could not yet be proved to empty into the Pacific, they
were important so long as they flowed to the west. If a broad
Strait of Anian could not be found, a river passage would do
nearly as well.

This was the obsession of the Irish geopolitical fanatic Arthur
Dobbs, who at first refused to believe that a great river did not
flow west from Hudson Bay. So certain was he of this fact that
he badgered Parliament into sending two expeditions to the
western shore of the bay in the 1740s. One, commanded by
Captain Christopher Middleton, proved conclusively that no
such river existed. Dobbs, a powerful political figure, insisted
that Middleton was lying to cover up for the deficiencies of the
Hudson's Bay Company, whose charter he tried to have re-
voked. He succeeded at least in convincing the Admiralty to

offer a reward of twenty thousand pounds for the discovery of the Northwest Passage that he was sure was there. The standing reward did much to alert Captain Cook's officers when they cruised the Northwest Coast nearly thirty years later.

But Dobbs was not through. In 1744 he published *An Account of the Countries Adjoining Hudson's Bay*, which was a compendium, a tract really, made up of all the Northwest Passage hints or clues that he could assemble. Admiral de Fonte loomed large over the work, but the "factual" accounts of one Daniel Coxe in *A Description of the English Province of Carolina* (1727) and of the Baron Lahontan with his River Longue piercing the west to a linkage with another river flowing into the Pacific proved most inspirational to Dobbs.

By 1761 Dobbs was governor of North Carolina. In this role he somehow persuaded Robert Rogers to undertake his search for the Northwest Passage. Rogers, the victor at Fort Francis, leader of the most heroic forced march of the French and Indian War, prime antagonist of Pontiac, and most recently a celebrated London author and playwright, was easily persuaded to use his base at Detroit as the takeoff site on the dash for glory. But his administrative duties chained him to the Great Lakes outposts, so instead he sent Jonathan Carver, a young colonial mapmaker. Carver was to proceed from Lake Superior to the head of the Mississippi and thence via a short portage to a river called by the Indians the Ouragan, which flowed into a broad bay on the Pacific. In 1766–67 Carver moved west on his great journey. But he got no farther than the Sioux encampments on the Minnesota River. This, however, stimulated him to write a book which purported to solve all the problems of continental geography, *Travels in the Interior Parts of North America* (1778).

Carver's vision still included a great river flowing westward out of Hudson Bay, but he really concentrated on another geographical phenomenon of critical importance. Somewhere just west of the Minnesota River, he confirmed, lay the "Shining Mountains," discovered by the French explorer Pierre Vérendrye and his sons in 1740. The Shining Mountains were the highest point of land in North America. According to Carver, down from these mountains flowed the Bourbon River into Hudson Bay, the Mississippi into the Gulf of Mexico, the St. Lawrence into the Atlantic, and the Oregon some two thousand miles into the Pacific. He had located, he believed, the Continental Divide, but more important, the strategic hub of the continent. So powerful and so plausible was Carver's concept that even after Lewis and Clark's journey and the incredible marches of the Canadians Mackenzie, Fraser, and Thompson, even as late as 1810, Zebulon Pike and other western geographers believed in a single mountainous source for all of the great rivers of the West.

Ironically, in view of the fact that the new age of discovery was committed to scientific exactness, hypothetical geography had taken on a kind of religious urgency by the 1770s. Pseudoscience in the guise of the new learning was almost as persuasive as real science, especially when men wished to believe what would serve them best. This was particularly evident in the traders' versions of North American geography. Not only was there competition among nations as to who would first discover the Northwest Passage, and hence dominate the continental road to India, but an intense rivalry developed between commercial factions in Canada. The Hudson's Bay Company, with its chartered monopoly, attempted to control all exploration into the interior, but free-lance traders working west over the old French Great Lakes–Saskatchewan route far outstripped the Hudson's Bay men, and a virtual war began. One result was the important expedition of the Hudson's Bay Company explorer Samuel Hearne up the Coppermine River to the Arctic Sea in 1771. Hearne's difficult trek, which ended in a massacre of some Arctic Indians, should have laid to rest all thoughts of a passage to the Pacific flowing out of Hudson Bay, because his route lay athwart all such possible passages north of Fort Churchill. But others still saw (and quite correctly) a linkage of the Churchill River with the Saskatchewan, and thence a viable route deep into new beaver country to the west.

Alexander Henry reached this vital linkage before the Hudson's Bay Company, and established posts that controlled the route west to the Saskatchewan and north as far as Lake Athabaska, on the edge of the great northern tundra. By 1779 the "outlaw" traders had formed the Northwest Company and were bidding fair to dominate all the trade of far northern and far western Canada, though none of them was fully aware of the immense Rocky Mountain barrier. By 1778, an American from Connecticut, Peter Pond, who together with Alexander Henry, another American, had allied himself with the Northwesters (members of the Northwest Company), established a trading post near Lake Athabaska. As the years went by, Pond spent much of his time speculating on the Northwest Passage problem. In 1781 he and Alexander Henry petitioned Sir Joseph Banks and the Royal Society to finance an expedition to the west aimed at recently discovered Cook Inlet on the south Alaskan coast. He was refused. But in 1789 Pond was instrumental in launching another explorer, Alexander Mackenzie, on an expedition north and west out of Great Slave Lake toward what they both thought was the Pacific.

Mackenzie was then only twenty-five years old, but already a masterful leader and a full partner in the Northwest Company. He needed all his leadership skills on this, his first great expedition, as he crossed a thousand miles of tundra coursing down what is now called the Mackenzie River, in the shadow of the towering Mackenzie Mountains, only to reach, not the Pacific, but the Arctic Ocean. Along the way, at the head of a grumbling and near mutinous party of half-breeds and Indians, he passed from one suspicious tribe to another, preventing each from attempting massacre on its northern neighbors. But in the end he found no Northwest Passage, only ice floes, a huge tidal estuary, and white whales. He named his river Disappointment.

But Mackenzie, like Pond, was a thinking man. When he returned from his journey, he determined to sail to England to secure proper instruments and the training to use them so that on his next expedition he would know precisely where he was and could chart his position with the same precision as Cook and his men. While in England, he picked up knowledge in the form of maps and accounts of the sea explorers of the Pacific coast from Captain Cook onward. He put this together with his own vast knowledge of western Canada, and formulated a plan. In the spring of 1793, he set out from Lake Athabaska west along the Peace River and into the Canadian Rockies. No trip was ever more arduous or terrifying. The great rushing gorge of the Peace River made his birchbark canoes virtually useless. Portages around rapids were endless. The ascent of the Rockies was strange and terrifying, and all along the way, Indians daily threatened their lives. But Mackenzie was a consummate wilderness diplomat. He secured their aid, instead of their hostility, and managed to pass safely from one menacing tribe to another without seriously offending any of them. His men, nonetheless, lived in constant terror.

Slowly, however, they crossed the mountains, descended the Finlay River, passed the ghastly Prince George rapids, and were seemingly on their way to the Pacific at last via the Fraser River when suddenly it became impassable. Vetoing the pleas of his men to turn back for home, and ignoring the warnings of his Indian guides, who feared the coastal savages (who were indeed fierce and hostile), he retraced his steps, portaged to the Bella Coola River, and, in a large coastal Indian war canoe, sailed out onto Dean's Channel and the far Pacific on July 20, 1793. He and his men were the first white men to really cross the entire North American continent. Acutely conscious of this fact, he took two days making careful celestial observations to determine his exact position. Then he paused to paint in huge vermilion letters on a rock: "Alexander Mackenzie, from Canada, by land, the twenty-second of July, one thousand seven hundred and ninety-three." In more ways than one he had made a mark to shoot at. His account of his two incredible journeys appeared in 1801 as *Voyage from Montreal, on the River St. Lawrence Through the Continent of North America, to the Frozen and Pacific Oceans; in the Years 1789 and 1793*. It was a masterpiece of exploration literature, and perhaps the most influential North

American explorer's account ever published, in that it set afoot not only a whole series of new Canadian expeditions to the West, but also Lewis and Clark's expedition as an American answer to the imperial struggle for North America.

It is important to see the Canadian and later the American thrust to the west in the context of a worldwide commercial and imperial struggle in which exploration and emerging science played a vital part. While Rogers, Carver, Hearne, Pond, Mackenzie, and others were reaching out across the continent, eventually disproving the Northwest Passage myth, the great European powers increasingly focused their attention on the Northwest Coast of America. Because of Spanish lethargy after the voyage of Sebastián Vizcaíno up the coast of California in 1602, the initiative passed to imperial Russia. The voyages of Bering and Chirikov to Alaska and the Aleutian Islands in 1741 opened the way to a horde of *promyshlenniki*, or free-lance traders from Siberia. The *promyshlenniki* were descendants of the tough cossacks who had forged across Asian Russia in less than fifty years. They were ruthless with regard to the seal, the sea otter, and the Alaskan Indians, whose women they abducted en masse and whose men they slaughtered in equal measure. By 1770 the Russian fur hunters were swarming all over the Aleutians and the Alaskan mainland, and by the end of the decade they had succeeded in establishing two outposts at Cook Inlet and Prince William Sound in Alaska proper. More would follow with the creation of the Russian American Company in 1799. The imperial monopoly was eventually headed by Alexander Baranov and Nikolas Rezanov. Its operations reached as far south as Fort Ross on the Russian River just north of San Francisco Bay by the early nineteenth century.

During this time various scientific expeditions were sent out from Okhotsk and Kamchatka. In 1764 Lieutenant Ivan Synd sailed from Okhotsk into the Bering Sea, sighted the Alaskan mainland somewhere between 64° and 66°, landed briefly, and then returned to port. In the same year Captain Peter Krenitsyn in the *St. Catherine* and Lieutenant Mikhail Levasher in the *St.*

Paul, with a well-equipped expedition, sailed to Alaska, wintered at False Pass near Unimak Island, and returned home with very little information. Then at the instigation of the formidable scientist Peter Pallas, and with the blessing of the Empress Catherine, an English captain, Joseph Billings, who had sailed with Cook, departed from Okhotsk in 1790. He cruised to Alaska, and then in a series of voyages lasting to 1792 he thrust north through Bering Strait looking for an all-weather route to Russia's Arctic ports. He failed, and his scientific results were meager. Thus on the Northwest Coast during the eighteenth century, Russia forged ahead in commercial ventures but failed markedly in scientific endeavors, principally because of scant maritime experience and the fact that her scientific establishment was largely imported from France and Prussia and hence was continually distrusted by powerful figures in the Russian court.

Nonetheless, all of this frightened the Spanish, whose long-neglected Pacific Coast empire suddenly seemed of great value to them. In 1769 the vistador, José de Gálvez, began a series of maneuvers to counter Russian and expected British incursions into Spain's Alta California empire. Perhaps what touched off alarm more than anything else was Captain Anson's raids on the west coast of South America and his capture of a Manila galleon in 1764. Gálvez's first move was to establish a mission and garrison at Monterey along the northern California coast in 1769–70. In the course of the search for Monterey Bay, Sergeant Francisco de Ortega first sighted magnificent San Francisco Bay. By 1776, due to Juan Bautista de Anza's march overland from Primeria Alta (Arizona), the garrison at Monterey was strongly reinforced and firm control was established over San Francisco Bay.

The Spaniards also undertook a series of harrowing voyages far up the coast. In 1773, departing from a newly established naval base at San Blas on Mexico's west coast, Juan Pérez sailed as far north as the Queen Charlotte Islands, claiming all the land he saw for Spain. Scurvy plagued his crew, however, and he had to turn back. On his southward voyage he discovered Nootka Sound, which he named San Lorenzo. This rather insignificant inlet on the northern reaches of Vancouver Island was to become the eighteenth-century focal point of controversy over control of the Northwest Coast.

Two years later, with Pérez now demoted to chief pilot, another expedition sailed north commanded by Bruno Hezeta and Juan Francisco de la Bodega y Quadra. This was an important expedition. As the two captains coursed north aboard the Mexican-built *Santiago* and the *Sonora* respectively, they had very different adventures. Both ships encountered hostile Indians wherever they landed on the coast, but Hezeta turned back, because of the illness of his crew, relatively soon after passing Nootka. In sailing south he completely missed the Strait of Juan de Fuca, but he did discover a great river flowing into the sea— the Columbia. He called the estuary Assumpcion Bay, fixed its position exactly at 46° 17′, and noted in his log that the "currents and eddies of water cause me to believe that the place is the mouth of some great river, or of some passage to another sea. . . ." Also, the currents were too strong to sail up into the river, and he could not land because he and his men were too weak to pull up the anchor should they let it down. So he sailed away, leaving the mighty Columbia to be rediscovered and claimed for the United States by Captain John Gray in 1792.

In the meantime, Bodega y Quadra, aboard the *Sonora*, encountered difficulties with the Indians near present-day Grenville Harbor on the Washington coast. A crew sent ashore to refill water casks was set upon and hacked to pieces before the eyes of the captain and his men. The next day, Bodega y Quadra and the scurvy-ridden men of the *Sonora* beat off an attack by Indian war canoes and headed north, intent upon completing their mission to Alaska despite all difficulties. They made it as far as 58° 30′ north latitude before they had to turn back, since nearly everyone was down with scurvy. Before turning back, however, they reached today's Mount Edgecumbe at 57° north and Bucareli Sound at 55° 14′, at both of which they landed and, with crosses erected, claimed the country for Spain. The intrepid Bodega y Quadra had completed his mission in the face of great difficulties that he believed could be alleviated by the establishment of a Spanish provisioning outpost farther north at Bucareli Sound.

These voyages and discoveries convinced the Spaniards more than ever that the Northwest Coast was an essential part of their empire. In addition, the rich sea otter trade beckoned. A monopoly, the Philippine Company, was established to exploit the trade in 1786. In the same year the Spaniards were alarmed by the fact that a French scientific expedition led by Jean François de Galaup, Comte de La Pérouse, commanding the *Astrolabe* and the *Boussole*, had not only landed all along the west coast of South America, but also reached Alaska's Lituya Bay and claimed it for France. La Pérouse made his actions known to Spanish officials at Monterey, where he landed to seek supplies before sailing off to the South Pacific and disaster off New Guinea.

La Pérouse was, of course, not the first rival to sail into Spanish coastal territory. As has already been related, in 1778 Captain Cook made a detailed inspection of the coast, rediscovering Nootka Sound and naming Cook's Inlet in Alaska after himself. Three major results emerged from Cook's Northwest Coast expedition. He established a British claim to Nootka; he thought he had proved no Northwest Passage existed, since he sailed to a point well north of Alaska (though Mackenzie on his trek headed up the Peace River, believing it discharged into Cook's Inlet); and his men discovered that fifteen hundred sea otter pelts that they casually traded from the Indians brought incredible wealth when sold in Asia. When the account of Cook's last voyage was published in 1784, this episode plunged the British into the trade and dominion game on the Northwest Coast.

As early as 1785, Captain James Hanna sailed the *Harmon* from China to Nootka, where he fought off a fierce Indian attack. His voyage was successful, however, and he sold his furs in China for twenty thousand Spanish dollars. The next year he was back again along with six other British vessels, all of which were licensed by both the East India Company and the South Sea Company. One Captain James Strange landed on Vancouver Island, laid claim to it, and left Dr. John Mackey to winter with the Indians. Each year more English captains sailed for the Northwest Coast. One of them, Captain Francis Barkley, aboard the *Imperial Eagle*, discovered the Strait of Juan de Fuca in 1787.

In the meantime, the Spaniards grew apprehensive. Esteban José Martínez and López de Haro set sail for Alaska in 1788, principally to scout out the Russian encroachments on Spanish territory. In a drunken, quarrelsome voyage, the two captains managed to reach Prince William Sound and Kodiak Island, where they established friendly contact with Evstrat Delarov, the representative of Russia's Shelikov-Golikov Company. Then they cruised as far north as Dutch Harbor, another Russian outpost, where the Russian trader Potop Zaikov frightened them with stories of an imminent Russian expedition to Nootka. Upon his return, Martínez's report galvanized Viceroy Manuel Antonio Flores into immediate action. In 1789 he sent Martínez to Nootka Sound to estabish what was to look like a Spanish outpost at that strategic place. Martínez did so in 1789, but took his task rather more seriously then his superiors intended. He did build a settlement at Nootka, and he captured the captains and crews of two British vessels, sending them as prisoners to San Blas. One of the British captains, John Meares, with some justice, laid claim to having built a small post at Nootka in 1788, predating the Spanish occupation. The rash actions of Martínez resulted in the Nootka Sound Controversy that brought Britain to the brink of war with Spain. Spain, weakened by the debilitation of her ally France, whose king had his hands full with a revolution at the time, in humiliating fashion broke down and withdrew all its exclusive claims to the Northwest Coast above San Francisco Bay. Britain appeared to have won the imperial struggle.

But this was not necessarily so. In the crucial years 1788–89, two American captains, John Kendrick and Robert Gray, with their ships the *Lady Washington* and the *Columbia*, rendezvoused at Nootka. They had made a profitable haul of furs, and Gray soon sailed off to Canton and thence around the world, the first Yankee skipper to do so. In 1792 he was back on the Northwest Coast again. By that time the area was positively crowded. Spain had sent Commander Alejandro Malespina with the *Descubierta* and the *Atrevida* on its most ambitious scientific undertaking to date. Both ships, loaded with scientific men, cruised the coast for five years (1789–94) in a futile effort to eclipse the great work of Cook. Grand as Malespina's expedition was, it was actually overshadowed by that of Britain's Captain George Vancouver, who carefully mapped the huge island that bears his name and the Strait of Juan de Fuca, and rediscovered Puget Sound. But Vancouver, great cartographer and navigator that he was, was himself upstaged by plain old Robert Gray on the *Columbia*, who rediscovered Hezeta's great river and renamed it the Columbia. Gray had located the real key to the control of western North America, and by virtue of his landing in the Columbia's estuary on May 12, 1792, he established for all time an American claim to that mighty river system. At this point Americans lagged far behind the Enlightenment-inspired exploring expeditions mounted by Europe, but they knew their way around the world's seaways and, as in the case of Gray, they kept a sharp eye out for the "main chance." In a futile gesture, Vancouver sent Lieutenant W. R. Broughton to the Columbia in 1793. He ascended it for one hundred miles, compiling the first map of the river, which did not, however, establish a valid British claim to it, nor did it appear to be the Northwest Passage.

No one had discovered a Northwest Passage; not the daring Canadian Northwesters, not the Russian, Spanish, French, or English navigators, not even Padre Vélez de Escalante, who in an epic journey in 1776 penetrated the Great Basin in the heart of the American West, gazed down upon Utah Lake, and claimed to have seen a Río Timpanogos flowing westward to the

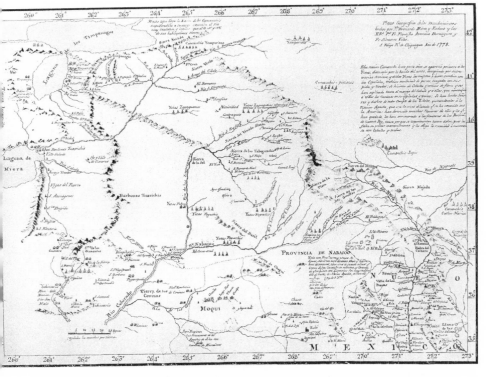

Captain Bernardo Miera y Pacheca, "Plano Geografico de los Descubrimientos hechos por Captain Bernardo Miera y Pacheco y los RR.ˢ P.ˢ Fr. Silvestre Vélez [de Escalente]." *(Beinecke Library, Western Americana Collection, Yale University)* This Spanish map indicates the discoveries in the Southwest made by an expedition led by Padres Escalante and Dominguez as far north as Utah Lake in 1776. Note how the Spanish seem more interested in Indian tribes (reservoirs of heathen souls) than in landforms.

ocean. The nearest thing to a Northwest Passage had been discovered by Captain Gray, and his discovery was soon to be followed up by the first official United States scientific exploring
expedition led by Captains Meriwether Lewis and William
Clark at the behest of the scientist-President Thomas Jefferson.

ii

FROM THE NORTHWEST PASSAGE TO THE GREAT WEST—A
SHIFT OF FOCUS

THOMAS JEFFERSON was an avid reader of scientific treatises, a
collector of Indian vocabularies, a geographer and surveyor, a
romantic devotee of the great travel literature of the eighteenth
century best typified by the reports of Captain Cook's magnificent voyages, and, perhaps most of all, a shrewd geopolitical
thinker. Long before he became president, Jefferson was thinking in transcontinental terms. In 1786 he enthusiastically en-
dorsed the visionary plan of one John Ledyard, a Connecticut
Yankee who had sailed to the Northwest Coast with Captain
Cook. At Secretary of State Jefferson's behest, and with support
from Sir Joseph Banks of the Royal Society, Ledyard set out
across Europe and the Empire of Russia in an effort to approach
the Northwest Passage and the Northwest Coast, with its rich
sea otter preserves, from the mysterious East via Siberia.
Though for a time Russian authorities helped him—got him as a
lone traveler all the way to Yakutsk in Siberia—they eventually
recognized that he represented a potential Yankee threat to the
exploitation by Russian companies of their private hunting
grounds in Alaska. The Empress Catherine had him apprehended at Yakutsk, brought back across Russia, and deported.
Ledyard never returned to the United States. Instead, on a mission for Sir Joseph Banks, he died on the Upper Nile trying to
locate a sub-Saharan passage to the Niger. Ledyard's career
demonstrates in a dramatic way the ambivalence of the explorer
in the Second Great Age of Discovery. He was first and fore-

most a man of science, an adventurer-explorer for whom climactic discoveries were more important than imperial or national interests. Thus he could change allegiances at will in the interests of discovery.

Something of this same spirit of ambivalence as to the interests of science versus national interests seems to have motivated Jefferson when he commissioned the French citizen André Michaux to journey via the Ohio and the Missouri to the Pacific in 1795. In many ways Michaux was an excellent choice for the mission. A dedicated naturalist, he had botanized in France as far south as the Pyrenees and had spent three years on similar activities in exotic Persia before he was sent by his government to America in 1785. Michaux's early years in North America rivaled in the breadth of his travels even the mighty John Bartram. Operating from a base in Charles Town, he virtually retraveled Bartram's route through the Carolina mountains and into Florida. He sailed to the Bahamas and in 1794 trekked through the vast wilderness west of Hudson Bay, where he learned of Mackenzie's recent transcontinental expedition. Upon his return he proposed that the American Philosophical Society support him in a venture that would duplicate Mackenzie's feat, only via the Ohio and Missouri rivers. With Jefferson's endorsement, he set out for the Ohio country, ostensibly on a nonpolitical scientific mission. But, unfortunately in his case, the French ambassador, Edmond Genêt, persuaded him to act as an agent among the trans-Appalachian settlers in an effort to turn them against both Spanish America and the United States. Thus Michaux's mission was aborted in the wake of the Genêt affair. Something of the extent of his western travels is evident from the journal published by his son who accompanied him, *Travels to the West of the Allegheny Mountains in the States of Ohio, Kentucky, and Tennessee, and Back to Charleston by the Upper Carolinas . . . Undertaken in the Year 1802.*

Spurred on by his knowledge of Mackenzie's crossing, Gray's discovery of the Columbia, the increasingly accurate western data appearing on the English cartographer Aaron Arrowsmith's maps, and the almost daily news of Spanish-sponsored ventures up the Missouri, Jefferson determined at all costs to launch an American scientific expedition to the Pacific. For this mission he chose his own neighbor and personal secretary, Meriwether Lewis, who in turn chose as his partner the bluff frontier soldier William Clark, also of Virginia. In 1802, Jefferson presented his plan to Congress as a commercial venture. Congress approved an appropriation for this aim, since it was consistent with the views of the majority of its members, who considered the federal government's powers limited to those specifically enumerated in the Constitution. At the same time Jefferson presented the Lewis and Clark expedition to the Spanish minister Casa Yrujo as a "literary" or scientific mission. Clearly, Jefferson had multiple motives for the Lewis and Clark expedition. Indeed, the breadth of his objectives was to characterize almost all future American exploration, in contrast to the limited-objective expeditions of Britain and Spain in North America. Jefferson was after much more than trade in beaver skins, and much more than a defense of the holy faith and the mines of Mexico. He wished to project, through discovery, the future of the continent.

The extensive scientific training in all branches of knowledge given Meriwether Lewis by the members of the American Philosophical Society in Philadelphia attested to this. If that were not sufficient indication of the scope of his objectives, Jefferson's very detailed instructions, based on those given to the early western trader John Evans by a previous trader-explorer, James Mackay, when he ascended the Missouri River as far as the Mandan Indian villages in 1796, certainly were. Lewis and Clark were to explore the Missouri River, cross over the mountains to the Columbia, and thus locate "the most direct and practicable water communication across this continent for purposes of commerce." Jefferson meant not only commerce with far-off Canton, but also commerce with the Indians in the heart of the continent. Accordingly, he ordered Lewis and Clark to produce an accurate map of the country they traversed; they were to study the Indians carefully, especially their numbers and intertribal

alliances and animosities, as well as their customs, their econo-
mies, and the possibilities of trade with them; they were, in addition, to note the "soil and face of the country," its vegetables,
animals, minerals, volcanoes, and weather, and even its fossils.
In short, they were to take note of everything that would be of
use to future settlers, rather than simply fur traders. Moreover,
their line of march and the influence that they might bring to
bear on the Indians, whom they were enjoined to treat very
well, would automatically form a kind of border or boundary
between the United States and British Canada. Never mind that
they would technically be in Spanish territory. The latter point
was remedied, of course, by Spain's retrocession of Louisiana to
France and Jefferson's purchase of Louisiana in 1803 just before
Lewis and Clark got started on their epic trek.

From a scientific point of view, by the time they started up
the Missouri on May 14, 1804, Lewis and Clark were exceedingly well informed. In addition to Lewis's scientific training in
Philadelphia, they had access to Jefferson's own vast archive of
information about the West, especially the latest maps. When
they reached St. Louis, they could also study the Missouri River
maps of the Spaniard Antoine Soulard, and those of John Evans
and James Mackay. Not only had the latter two men been to the
Mandan villages near present-day Bismarck, North Dakota, but
Mackay, a former Northwester, had come down upon the Missouri from the north. Through the work of his former associate
Antoine Larocque, he knew of the Yellowstone and its tributaries, the Big Horn and Powder rivers. So Lewis and Clark
knew what to expect far above the great bend of the Missouri.
Beyond that, the territory was completely unknown until they
reached the Columbia River system.

There is no need here to trace their famous journey in detail.
Day after day, they struggled up the broad reaches of the Missouri, sometimes sailing, sometimes pulling their heavy keel-
boat. They encountered surprisingly little trouble with Indians,
and they were almost daily dazzled by the teeming wildlife that
abounded over the northern plains. On December 7, 1805, a bit-

ter cold day, Sergeant Patrick Gass recorded in his journal, "Captain Lewis and eleven more of us went out . . . and saw the prairie covered with buffalo and the Indians on horseback killing them. They killed thirty or forty, and we killed eleven of them." Gass, who seems fixated on the plentitude of game, nearly every day recorded hunters returning with staggering loads of deer, elk, bear, buffalo, mountain sheep, wild turkeys, badger, beaver, and even porcupine. Fish, too, were abundant, as in one day the men netted over two hundred catfish.

The journey to the Mandan villages took seven months. There Lewis and Clark established quarters for the winter of 1804–1805 and sent a party back down the river with their preliminary reports in the early spring. The rest of the party continued upriver in homemade canoes. They made their way up around the Great Bend, past the Yellowstone and the Great Falls to the Three Forks, which mark the source of the Missouri. Then, with the help of Sacajawea, a Shoshone Indian woman who accompanied them, and a number of other Indians they met along the way, they found their way over the difficult mountains of Idaho via Lemhi Pass to the Salmon River and the Bitterroot Valley. From a point which they called Traveller's Rest, near present-day Missoula, Montana, they crossed, via Lolo Pass, over to the Clearwater, which flows into the Columbia. On November 7, 1805, they at last reached the shores of the Pacific. As a counter to Mackenzie's pointed message, far to the north on the Bella Coola, Clark carved on a tree near the mouth of the Columbia, "William Clark, December 3rd 1805. By Land from the U. States in 1804 and 1805." Despite Clark's scientific dedication, imperial rivalries were not far from his mind.

After wintering in a cluster of huts near the mouth of the Columbia, they returned home in two parties. Lewis led one group overland via Lolo Pass and the Sun River to the Great Falls, while Clark coursed southward along the outward route, then crossed over below the Great Falls to the Yellowstone River, where the two parties linked up again for the final voyage back down the Missouri. They arrived in St. Louis on September 26,

1806. A small group of citizens assembled on the bank to cheer them.

To the men of the West, Lewis and Clark's expedition had immense importance. It opened up the whole rich upper Missouri and Rocky Mountain country to fur traders and hunters. Before their main party even reached St. Louis, fur traders, hearing of their feat, had already launched expeditions up the Missouri and into the mountains. Some of these parties were aided by veterans of the expedition like George Drouillard and John Colter, who made spectacular explorations in their own right. And for the nation's future as a whole, the Lewis and Clark expedition had immense importance. They had measured the width of the continent and described its incredibly rich potential, and in their rugged journey they had laid out a crude Northwest Passage that underscored the importance of the Missouri and Columbia rivers, to which the United States now had the best claim. Most of all, they focused the attention of Americans upon the continent itself rather than the passage to India. With certain exceptions this was to preoccupy American explorers for much of the early nineteenth century. It certainly commanded a full measure of the attention of her geopolitical thinkers, whose theories of Manifest Destiny were dimly foreshadowed by William Clark's bold mockery of the Canadian Alexander Mackenzie's vermilion paint message back on the Bella Coola too far to the north.

Significantly, the United States had launched its sweep to the west with a government-sponsored scientific expedition. Unlike the findings of the fur trade monopolists of Canada, or those of the secretive Spanish bureaucracy, Lewis and Clark's important and broad-ranging discoveries belonged to the people of the new democracy. In the first decades of the nineteenth century, with certain exceptions this became a conscious American policy. Jefferson, for example, understandably concerned with the boundaries of the Louisiana Purchase, was responsible for several federal expeditions to determine the southwest boundary of the new American domain. In these ventures he turned to men

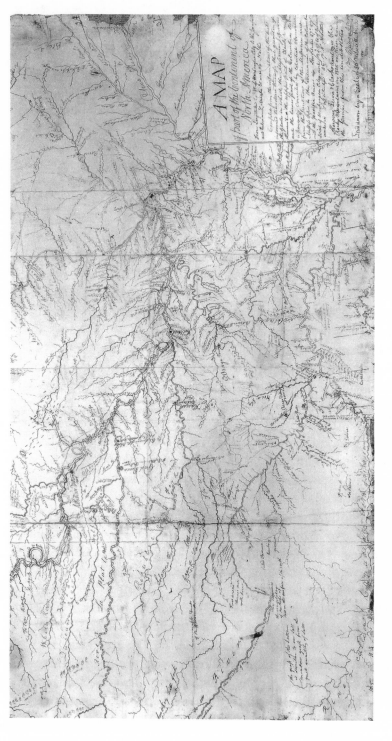

Meriwether Lewis and William Clark, "A Map of part of the Continent of North America." 1809. (*Yale University*) This is a master map of the whole trans-Mississippi West north and west of St. Louis. Governor William Clark kept it in his office in St. Louis and added data from fur traders who passed through the city from out of the West. Notice, however, that what is now Colorado is missing from the map, making the Upper Missouri country almost adjoining New Mexico and the Spanish settlements.

of science. In 1804, Dr. George Hunter and William Dunbar, lately of Philadelphia and friends of William Bartram, headed up the Red River, which was the assumed boundary of the Purchase. They were turned aside by Indians and explored the Ozark Plateau instead. Jefferson duly reported the results of their expedition to Congress, along with the preliminary information sent down from Fort Mandan by Lewis and Clark.

In the spring of 1805, Jefferson secured $5,000 from Congress to send Captain Thomas Sparks and the naturalist Peter Custis up the Red River boundary. They marched nearly seven hundred miles upriver, conducting the first ecological survey of the southern reaches of the still-disputed Louisiana Territory. Intercepted by a detachment of belligerent Spanish cavalrymen, following Jefferson's instructions they meekly turned back downriver. Because it nearly precipitated a border war with Spain, this expedition was only casually mentioned in Jefferson's report to Congress, and its scientific results were never published. But as of 1806, the federal probes of the Louisiana frontier had produced nothing like a clear idea as to what President Jefferson and the American people had purchased. Regretting the permission granted to Lewis and Clark's "literary" venture, Spain had suddenly grown secretive and defensive.

This posture was not without cause. Michaux and the French had repeatedly intrigued against Spain's vulnerable northern provinces. And in 1796, General Collot had been allowed by Jefferson to make a meticulous survey of the Ohio and the Mississippi with an obvious eye to a campaign against New Spain. Already humiliated by the Nootka Sound incident and panicked over the possibility of losing New Orleans, St. Louis, the Mississippi, and the Californias, Spanish officials spent the first decades of the nineteenth century constantly on their guard.

In such an atmosphere of intrigue was conceived the prairie expedition of Lieutenant Zebulon Pike. Basically it was the brainchild of General James Wilkinson, the U.S. governor of Louisiana. Wilkinson, appointed in what must have been an oversight by Jefferson, was a master of intrigue. A friend of

Aaron Burr, and a double agent in the pay of Spain, Wilkinson seems to have harbored thoughts of carving out a Louisiana empire for himself, or at least in partnership with Burr. Ruling this empire, as Burr put it in a coded letter to Wilkinson of July 29, 1806, "will be a host of choice spirits. Wilkinson shall be second to Burr only; Wilkinson shall dictate the rank and promotion of his officers. Burr will proceed westward never to return. . . ." But Wilkinson was even more devious than Burr. He managed to detach himself from that clumsy freebooter and, with Pike's scientific exploring expedition, to gain credit for one of the most successful espionage operations in American history.

In the summer of 1806, Wilkinson ordered Pike to venture out across the prairies and locate the source of the Red River—a project which he knew to be dear to Jefferson's heart. At the same time he sent along Dr. John Robinson, who intended to collect a debt in Santa Fe, which was nowhere near the Red River. This clearly suggests that Pike's real mission was not the Red River but a Santa Fe spying venture. But then with incredible duplicity Wilkinson warned the authorities in Santa Fe of Pike's mission and at the same time informed them of Burr's grandiose filibustering plan, possibly through Dr. Robinson, who also gained enough information about New Spain to compile his own important map of 1819.

How much Pike knew of this when he set out from Belle Fontaine, near St. Louis, on his prairie expedition perhaps no one will ever know. He seems everywhere to have done his duty with determination and courageous devotion, even when he knew the Spanish cavalry, under Don Falcundo Malgares, was pursuing him. Instead of being alarmed, he merely used Malgares's trail as a road along the front range of the Rockies toward Santa Fe. When he reached the Arkansas River, he sent his adjutant, Lieutenant James Wilkinson (the intriguer's son), downriver with maps and reports for the general. Then he turned west toward the Rockies, which he first sighted on November 15, 1806, "looking like a small blue cloud." For the next two months he explored the southern Rockies, and climbed not

Pikes but Cheyenne Peak. From this vantage point he believed he could see the whole of the Rockies. This led him into accepting Jonathan Carver's erroneous belief that all the great rivers of the West had a single source. It also ironically led him, in effect, to leave out Colorado on his map, since he believed that just north of Cheyenne Peak lay the Yellowstone and other tributaries of the upper Missouri. This was perhaps due to the fact that when he drew his map of the western country back in Washington, Pike copied Humboldt's map of New Spain, which the baron had recently presented to Jefferson. Thus, except for the Texas portion, Pike based the cartographical description of his expedition on the work of a savant who had never seen the country at all.

Eventually, Pike took his men on a difficult winter climb over a pass in the Sangre de Cristo mountains to a bleak encampment on the upper Rio Grande. Though he declared he was lost, Pike certainly knew just where he was, since Dr. Robinson had headed south to Sante Fe just a few days before a detachment of Spanish soldiers arrived to arrest Pike and the remaining men of his party. Pike's famous statement "What! Is this not the Red River?" was disingenuous to say the least.

Pike's capture by the Spanish afforded him a chance to reconnoiter the whole of New Mexico, much of Chihuahua, and the Camino Real across Texas. The information, geographical, economic, and military, was thorough and comprehensive—ideal for anyone contemplating a venture against Spain's northern provinces. That such a venture was not forthcoming might actually have been due to Pike's scientific reports. After traveling many days over the dry endless prairies, he concluded that the whole high plains region was a "Great American Desert" where nothing but nomads could live. In so doing, he stamped a geographical image upon the minds of Americans that persisted for much of the nineteenth century and greatly affected public policy.

But for all his efforts, neither Pike nor any other American had yet traced out the course of the Red River boundary of Louisiana. This duty was eventually assigned to another scientist-explorer, Major Stephen H. Long. Long was a graduate of Dartmouth College and a member of the newly created United States Army Corps of Topographical Engineers. By the time he embarked on his Great Plains expedition, Long had already served as terrain adviser to the Baltimore and Ohio Railroad and had traveled from Minnesota to Louisiana, locating sites for a ring of frontier forts. His original mission in 1819 was to ascend the Missouri River as head of the scientific contingent of General Henry Rice Atkinson's little army designed to frighten the British fur traders entirely out of the Missouri River country. Atkinson's men all came down sick, however, near Council Bluffs, and Secretary of War John C. Calhoun changed Long's orders. At the head of a seasoned group of scientific naturalists and artists from Philadelphia, including Edwin James, Thomas Say, Samuel Seymour, and Titian Peale, he headed out across the prairies for the front range of the Rockies determined to locate the source of the Red River. Long and his men made a careful survey of the high plains and Seymour made the first-known drawings of the Rockies, an accurate but hardly dramatic representation of that towering range.

Seymour, British-born but trained in Philadelphia, was essentially a topographical artist. Nothing in his previous experience, however, prepared him for the scenery of the vast western prairies and the dramatic front range of the Rockies. Thus his small, carefully made watercolors (painted over pencil sketches) hardly seem to do justice to the incredible country that he was paid to picture for the first time. Seymour was cautious. His two most dramatic paintings were *Distant View of the Rocky Mountains*, a panorama from about fifty miles out on the high plains, and *View of James* [Pikes] *Peak in the Rain*. These two works, though small, suggested something of the sweep and majesty of the country. Unfortunately, only one of them was printed as a plate in the Long expedition report. Seymour's other pictures were exact renditions of very specific places—sandstone formations at the foothills of the Rockies, the spot where the Platte entered the mountains, and a strange formation since known as Elephant Rock. Seymour took his duty as a documentary artist very narrowly; consequently those Americans who viewed his lithographs in the Long expedition reports saw, as their first views of the Great West, only fragments of its sublime, endless immensity. Seymour's fellow artist Titian Peale likewise afforded little help to those curious about the West. Except for one striking watercolor of the fire-belching steamboat that took them up the Missouri to Fort Atkinson and a romantic view of a sunset on the river, Peale concentrated on making exact renditions of the animals and plants. It was as if both artists, operating under military command, stuck to the exact letter of their instructions. In later years, Peale appears to have regretted doing so, because from the 1850s through the early 1870s he repeatedly repainted Seymour's landscapes in a more dramatic scale and fashion and populated them with groups of his animal drawings. And yet, just as one cannot dismiss the Long expedition for its faults and errors, one cannot dismiss these early works of Seymour and Peale. They represent the first visualization of the West—an important aspect of the scientific and imaginative understanding or lack of understanding of the still-to-be-discovered sweep of the continent. For almost ten years, between 1822 and 1832, these pictures, Long's map, and Dr. Edwin James's report on the expedition officially defined the West.

Long's men climbed Pikes Peak, measured its altitude above the plain, and in general conducted a significant reconnaissance of the whole plains and front range region. Then Long divided his party, sending Captain John R. Bell down the Arkansas River, where his men deserted with most of the expedition's maps and notes to date. Major Long compounded the disaster when he mistook the Canadian for the Red River and sailed back down it to what he expected to be glory. Great was his mortification to find that he had chosen the wrong river and that the Red River still lay in unknown territory. His was an important oversight, because Secretary of State John Quincy Adams in

1819 had just concluded the Transcontinental Boundary Treaty with Spain, in which the elusive Red River figured most importantly.

Nonetheless, Long's expedition did produce, after Lewis and Clark's map of 1814, the most important and comprehensive view of the West. His map of 1821 remains a landmark of American cartography. So prominent was it that most geographers adopted it immediately and gave him instead of Pike the dubious honor of naming the Great Plains "the Great American Desert." Seymour's illustrations and the scientific descriptions in the report did little to dispel this impression. Captain Bell, Long's second-in-command, described the plains region as "a dusty plain of sand and gravel, barren as the deserts of Arabia." Edwin James, chronicler of the expedition and its chief geologist, saw the western portion of the plains as an extension of "the Mexican Desert" and its eastern portion bore "a manifest resemblance to the deserts of Siberia." He apparently liked the Russian comparison because he elsewhere described the upper Canadian River region as "sandy wastes and inhospitable steppes."

But James's geological account of the plains and Rockies went far beyond mere descriptions of a desert region. He reconstructed the geological history of the region in a way that was both uncommonly perceptive and very daring for its time. Most significantly, in looking at the vast plains and Rockies region, James assumed it was formed over an exceedingly long span of time. He was not speaking of a few thousand years when he described the upthrusting of the Rocky Mountains, their gradual erosion, and the deposition of the various levels of strata that made up the Great Plains. He was thinking in terms of eons of time. In a striking passage he declared, "The sandstones being entirely mechanical aggregates, consisting of rounded fragments of rocks formerly constituting a part of the primitive mountains, would seem to have been deposited at a very remote period, when the waters of the primeval ocean covered the level of the great plain and the lower regions of the granitic rocks." This vision was influenced by the great German geologist Abraham Gottlob Werner, who saw the entire earth as being the product of sediment formed from a primeval ocean. But James went beyond this, seeing a "primitive" layer of rocks beneath the surface sedimentary rocks, and more important, he grasped the fact that the Rockies were formed by a massive upthrust and the Great Plains themselves were also uplifted "by some cause equally unknown." As this happened, a great interior sea that covered the heart of the continent retreated toward the Gulf of Mexico. In an era that generally calculated the age of the earth biblically at 4004 years and that rejected the long time span needed to make the evolutionism of Erasmus Darwin and Robert Chambers plausible, Edwin James's dramatic reconstruction of plains and Rockies geologic history was indeed daring. This perhaps accounts for the neglect of his geological report on the part of contemporary reviewers.

Long's expedition, as its most recent historians have tried to point out, had a significant scientific impact, despite the fact that Long and his colleagues had to have their report privately printed by Carey, Lea and Carey of Philadelphia. John C. Calhoun, as Secretary of War, would only authorize the purchase of a few dozen copies, though the War Department paid for the printing of Long's important map. Despite the lack of federal support for its publication, the report of Long's expedition did appear in 1822 as a handsome work in two printed volumes and an atlas that included a small fraction of the artwork of Seymour and Peale. It was also reprinted in 1823 in an English edition of three volumes that did not include a separate atlas.

Long himself supervised the production of the report, though Edwin James, working along with Long and Thomas Say in an office in Philadelphia, appears to have done most of the writing, particularly the narrative and the long geological section. A number of Captain Bell's notebooks had been stolen on his trip down the Arkansas River, and James's notebook seems to have been the most extensive surviving account, so perhaps this is why he was selected as the expedition's chronicler. The report itself, however, contained much more than a narrative. There were extensive notes by Say, Peale, and Baldwin on the fauna and flora of the plains, and a number of animal species, such as the coyote, were named by their first scientific discoverer, Say. The plant specimens were used by John Torrey, America's foremost botanist, to work up a new "American System" of classification that was an attempt to replace that of Linnaeus. Museums and lyceums all up and down the East Coast of America benefited from the expedition—either through the reception of parts of its collections, or in hearing lectures delivered by members of the scientific corps.

Future explorers also were in Long's debt. They used his map and his personal advice, as well as that of members of his company, such as Titian Peale. But, in addition, they mined his work for specific information on the many plains Indian tribes that the expedition had encountered. And not the least useful appendix to Long's report was the first "dictionary" of trans-Mississippi Indian sign language—a seventeen-page treatise entitled *Indian Language of Signs*. This was the pioneer attempt at a systematic understanding of the universal plains language. It was not really replaced until the publication of Captain Garrick Mallory's work in the late nineteenth century.

Of all those who exploited Long's report, America's foremost novelist, James Fenimore Cooper, perhaps did so to the utmost. His elegiac Leatherstocking novel *The Prairie*, written in Paris and published in 1827, derives most of its details, if not its inspiration, from Long's report. In Cooper's novel the prairie itself becomes almost a character with its bleak wastelands and its gloomy landmarks like Scotts Bluff and Courthouse Rock. But just as later historians have impugned the Long expedition for falsely labeling the plains "the Great American Desert," later critics, like Mark Twain, failed to see the underlying geographical accuracy of Cooper's novel.

As for Pike and Long and those subsequent American explorers who followed them in labeling the plains a "Great American Desert," who is to say after the "Dust Bowl" of the 1930s that

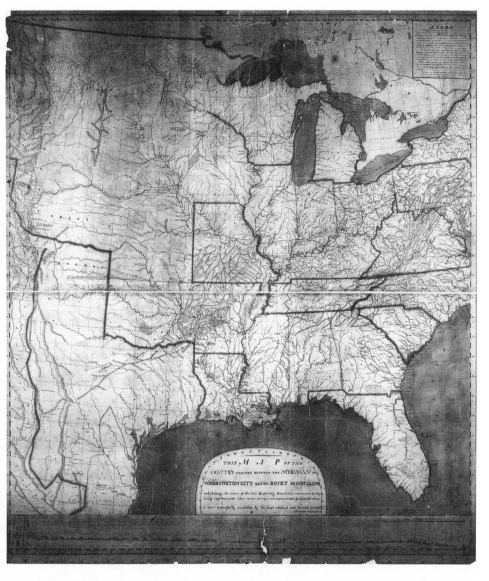

Major Stephen H. Long, "Map of the Country situated between the Meridian of Washington City and the Rocky Mountains." 1821. *(The National Archives)* Note that Long has printed "Great Desert" across the Great Plains.

they were entirely wrong? Clearly given the pre-windmill, pre-artesian well, pre–dry-farming era in which they lived, no one possessed the technology to farm the plains successfully. Generations of discouraged sod-house pioneers could well attest to their wisdom.

These early military-scientific expeditions into the West, chiefly Jeffersonian in inspiration, were obviously important to the history of the United States and to science in general. Lewis and Clark spanned the continent, mapping the Missouri-Columbia routes remarkably well, given their crude instruments, while Pike and Long began another sort of venture into the interior and initiated more professional scientific mapping and analysis of the West. But their most important contributions were twofold. They turned the country's focus from the far Pacific to the West itself, and by the very Enlightenment-naturalist range of their inquiry they set the pattern for flexibility in American exploration. Their labors were meant to be the vanguard of the central adventure of nineteenth-century America: the settlement of the West.

CHAPTER IV

The Fur Trader as Explorer

THE ROCKY MOUNTAIN COLLEGE

LIKE the Empire of Russia, the United States, also on the periphery of western civilization, in the early days of the Republic had few scientific institutions such as the Royal Society that could support extensive scientific exploring expeditions. Jefferson did what he could, using the American Philosophical Society and the resources of a minuscule post-Revolution military establishment. But the major thrust that established a "continental consciousness" beyond the Rocky Mountains came from the enterprise and vision of the American and British fur traders of the Far West. Like the cossacks and the *promyshlenniki* thrusting eastward across Siberia to the remote shores of Alaska, American fur traders and hunters pushed the interests of the United States westward to the shores of the Pacific.

These fur traders and hunters, or mountain men, as they came to be called, were not scientific explorers. Sometimes they were businessmen and far-seeing entrepreneurs who established a network of outposts in the wilderness—up the Missouri River, in the Columbia River Basin system, at the headwaters of the

Platte, or even along the rivers of the Southwest out of old Santa
Fe. Other men were adventurers who in small companies or as
free trappers penetrated the heart of the Rockies and spread out
all over the West. These adventurers, the heirs of Daniel Boone,
Simon Kenton, and others of the Kentucky long-hunter tradition, were dependent upon the Indians whose homelands they
were invading. Like Lewis and Clark, they learned the intricate
courses of great river systems and the location of critical passes
over the mountains from local Indian guides, who shared their
knowledge for useful trade goods and fascinating trinkets. And
beyond the larger aspects of geographical information, the
mountain men learned from the Indians how to live off and live
with the land as well as the dangers of a vast wilderness. On first
thought, one could hardly call this "science" or the Indian and
the mountain men "scientists." Yet they were seriously engaged
in the process of empirical information-gathering, and their very
lives depended upon the testing of geographical hypotheses
formed for very practical reasons. If passes were frozen during
the winter, or game was scarce in regions where one might suppose it to be abundant, men froze or starved. Thus, perforce, the
mountain men learned not only the geography but the ecology
of the West. And in learning it, they also established a crude
communications network that passed on the information. The
annual fur trade rendezvous in the heart of the Rockies was one
place where they exchanged such information; around the winter campfires in Indian villages was another. But the most obvious information-gathering institutions were the forts or trading
posts scattered along the rivers. Thus, the Missouri became a
virtual telegraph line for information about the West. For a
time, the territorial governor, William Clark, collected all this
information and incorporated it in a master map that he kept in
his office in St. Louis. Later the large fur companies and the St.
Louis newspapers also became prime sources whose facts and
opinions reached the very halls of Congress and the mapmakers
of Philadelphia. Much has been written in derision about the ignorance of the mountain men in their "Rocky Mountain

College," and tales passed down about the "discovery" of Shakespeare's works by Jim Bridger. But the importance of the Rocky Mountain fur trade lies in the fact that it was a very different kind of college, whose subjects were not Shakespeare and Walter Scott, but the multifaceted physical aspects of the Great West and its widely varied Indian inhabitants. This was no trivial curriculum.

And beyond all this, the fur trade and the federal Indian agents attendant to it, as well as the small military detachments sent to protect it, were the means whereby the West of the Indian first became visualized for an American and European public. This, too, was no small achievement when thousands of Americans were already contemplating a brave new life in a land they could picture less than they could the face of the moon and the midnight constellations in the skies above them.

ii

ASTOR'S GLOBAL ADVENTURE

THE MOST GRANDIOSE, if not most sophisticated, of American fur-hunting ventures was undertaken by John Jacob Astor, an enterprising fur merchant from New York who was soon to become the richest man in the United States. With the aid and encouragement of Jefferson himself, now retired from the presidency, Astor launched what could only be called a global venture to the Northwest Coast. Inspired by the Canadian Northwesters, particularly Alexander Henry, who had reached the Mandan Indian villages on the upper Missouri in July of 1806, he formed the Pacific Fur Company and sent a party overland via the Missouri, the Snake, and the Columbia to the Pacific. This party left St. Louis in 1810, at first intent upon ascending the Missouri along the Lewis and Clark route. Meanwhile, in September of that year, Astor also sent a ship, the *Tonquin*, loaded with trade goods, around the Horn to rendezvous with the overland explorers at the mouth of the Columbia.

His plan was to tap the fur trade of the Northwest and ship it to China aboard the *Tonquin*. This scheme was perhaps too intricate and grandiose, but it achieved several important results.

Astor's attempt, led by the New Yorker Wilson Price Hunt, to ascend the Missouri River was stopped by the fierce Arikara seven hundred miles up the river. Hunt, perhaps out of naiveté as to the distances and terrain involved, decided to switch to horses, and set out across the Dakota prairies along the Grand River in July of 1811. In so doing, he and his men broke a new trail across the West. From the junction of the Grand and Missouri rivers, they negotiated the Dakota Badlands and passed north of the Black Hills and south of the Big Horn Mountains until they reached the Wind River Valley. Following that valley in the heart of Crow Indian country, they crossed the Continental Divide at Union Pass near the head of the Wind River Range. Then they passed through beautiful Jackson's Hole and its desolate counterpart, Pierre's Hole, thence across the wastelands of southern Idaho to the Snake River, which they followed with great difficulty to the Columbia. When they reached the mouth of the Columbia they established Fort Astoria on the south bank of the river. It represented still another claim, besides those of Gray and of Lewis and Clark, to the Northwest Territory, though not, as it turned out, a permanent claim.

In the meantime, Hunt and his men experienced extreme hardships on the overland crossing. Game was scarce along their route; the Snake River proved not to be navigable; the morale of the party suffered; they became split and lost. The southern Idaho country through which they passed seemed a mountainous desert rather than a western paradise. Not until the following spring did the final elements of the party reach Astoria. They had discovered an overland route south of that taken by Lewis and Clark.

While Hunt and his inexperienced band struggled overland, the *Tonquin* and its crew had reached the Columbia, passed over its difficult bar, and set up Fort Astoria. This part of the operation seemed to go well, and the *Tonquin* sailed north to trade with the exotic tribes of Vancouver Island. Here, however, trouble with the Indians developed because of the cruelty of Captain Thorne. A band of Salish, seeking revenge, overwhelmed the ship, killing its entire crew, save one. A mortally wounded able seaman named Thomas Lewis managed to fire the powder magazine while the whole tribe was aboard and blew the *Tonquin* and several hundred Salish Indians to smithereens. The Astorians' main link to the outside world was gone.

But Astoria was not destined to be isolated for long. In the spring of 1813, the British fur trader John George McTavish led a ragged band of Northwest Company men up to the gates of the fort, informed its inhabitants that war existed between Britain and the United States, and demanded its surrender. McTavish and his men were soon backed up by the British man-of-war H.M.S. *Raccoon*, but such force was not necessary. Astor's men quickly agreed to haul down the flag and sell out to the British. Some, like the able Donald McKenzie, even joined them. It was clear that Astor's objectives were economic rather than political, and Jefferson himself was known to favor only the establishment of "sister republics" in the Far West, rather than an imperial extension of the United States. To a large extent, Astoria was an outpost, a caravanserai on the long road to the riches of the Indies.

Before Astoria surrendered, however, Robert Stuart and six men (one of whom went insane from the hardships and returned to Astoria) set out eastward across the mountains to St. Louis. Their march, too, was full of hardships, and the possibility of starvation always confronted them. The Blue Mountains and the Snake River country proved especially difficult, and a winter detour for fear of the Indians far north to Jackson Hole nearly destroyed them through cold and starvation. But they finally prevailed, arriving in St. Louis on April 30, 1813. They had conquered the Rockies in the dead of winter, but more important, with the exception of the detour to Jackson Hole, they had located and traversed what became the Oregon Trail. The most important features they had discovered were the South

Pass across the mountains around the southeast end of the Wind
River Mountains, and the Sweetwater River route to the Platte,
which they followed across the plains. The South Pass became
the "great gate" through which hundreds of thousands of immigrants poured on their way west.

iii

INTO THE UNKNOWN BEYOND THE FRONT RANGE

MEANWHILE, a new breed of western explorer had begun to appear on the scene—the mountain man. Part romantic adventurer, part self-made entrepreneur, the mountain man was a
characteristically American figure who had no counterpart in
Europe or anywhere else in the world. The mountain man was
essentially a long-hunter who roamed the Rockies for years at a
time, exploiting their bounty in beaver furs, enjoying the life of
the great outdoors while at the same time hoping to make his
fortune. Some did, like William Ashley, Robert Campbell, and
William Sublette, all of whom eventually entered first the outfitting and supply business and then banking, with the profits
gained in their quest for Rocky Mountain beaver. Most did not
quite realize their American Dream, however. The life of the
mountain man, armed only with his Hawken rifle, a knife,
maybe a hatchet, and a small "possibles sack," plus a dangling
chain of Oneida beaver traps, was rugged and dangerous. If the
perils of nature, starvation, or wild animals did not get him, hostile Indians did their best to remedy the situation. Nonetheless,
the mountain man loved the grand freedom of the Rockies, the
adventure and the questing after the new. This, along with his
sensitivity to the wilderness, was what made him an explorer.
And his life so close to the Indians, so attuned to their knowledge, so adapted to their ways, made him an expert explorer.

The first mountain men were members of Lewis and Clark's
Corps of Discovery. Private John Colter left the expedition on
the way home, far up the Missouri, to join two outward-bound

hunters in a season of beaver trapping. George Drouillard of Lewis and Clark's band also became a famous mountain man a short while afterward. Both men worked for Manuel Lisa, a wily Spaniard who had come to St. Louis from New Orleans, and of whom it was said that "rascality sat on every aspect of his dark-complexioned Mexican face." So hated by his men that he dared not turn his back on them, Lisa was nonetheless a very successful fur trade entrepreneur.

Lisa had immediately grasped the potential of Lewis and Clark's discoveries. As early as April of 1807 he launched an expedition of forty-two men up the Missouri. Making his way past the now hostile river tribes, he established a fort in the heart of the Rocky Mountain Indian country at the junction of the Big Horn and Yellowstone rivers in present-day Montana. From there he sent out small parties of men in all directions. John Colter joined Lisa's company, and in the winter of 1807, armed with only a pistol and a pack of trade goods, he set off westward to trade with the Crow Indians in the Big Horn Valley. On his incredible journey, he passed the site of present-day Cody, Wyoming, where he discovered an extensive geyser basin forever after dubbed in derision Colter's Hell. More important, he passed around the south end of the Absaroka Mountains into the Wind River Valley, and soon found himself in the wintry beauty of Jackson Hole. He was out of Crow country now, but among Sacajawea's Shoshones, who must have guided him past the towering Tetons to Pierre's Hole on the west side of that range. In this swing to the south and west, he appears to have been looking for some way of linking up with the Spaniards to the south. After wintering in Pierre's Hole, Colter turned for home, which was Lisa's fort. On the way back, he discovered the wonders of what is now Yellowstone Park. Few, however, would believe his stories about what he had seen.

While Colter had been adventuring to the southwest toward Pierre's Hole, Drouillard had explored the entire Tonque River and Big Horn basins. He had drawn a crude map of where he had been, alluding to the existence of Spanish outposts a "few days" march south on the Green River. He, too, had looked for a transmontane passage southward to the Spanish settlements, but, for some strange reason, he could not get over the relatively low Owl Creek Range into the Wind River Valley, which, followed southeastward, would have led him to the South Pass. From there he could have crossed westward to the Green River and the area which Spanish traders from Taos actually visited on a regular basis to trade with the Indians. Nonetheless, Drouillard possessed great knowledge of the northern beaver country, which did not die with him when he was killed on an unfortunate expedition to the Three Forks of the Missouri in 1810. His information, along with that of Lisa and Colter, was recorded on Governor William Clark's large manuscript map of the West. Thus, what might have been the obscure information of the mountain men became public knowledge.

In August of 1811, another band of twenty trappers, led by Jean Baptiste Champlain, headed south from Manuel's Fort on the Yellowstone, intent upon linking up with Spanish traders from Santa Fe who were reputed to be among the Arapahoe in what is now Colorado. In sending out this expedition, Lisa hoped to make further contact with the Spaniards beyond the reach of United States authorities, who had forbidden him to trade directly with Santa Fe. Champlain's band of trappers did indeed reach the Arapahoes, but hardly intact. Three were killed by hostile Blackfeet, about seven turned back to the Big Horn Valley in discouragement, four made contact with the Spanish and were escorted via Santa Fe to prison in Chihuahua, while Champlain and five other trappers made their way along the front range of the Rockies to the Arkansas River. Eventually, they were forced back to the Arapahoe villages on the Platte, where three more were killed. Finally, Champlain and a companion named Porteau elected to stay with the Arapahoe and were never heard from again. One intrepid man survived this disastrous expedition—Ezekial Williams, whose story forms the centerpiece of David Coyner's semifictionalized book *The Lost Trappers*. Williams was determined to reach St. Louis with the fortune in furs that he had taken during his harrowing two winters in the mountains. In June of 1813, he set off down the Arkansas with a canoe full of furs, but was captured by the Konsa Indians. Eventually in August he was released and he made his way down the Arkansas and then to Arrow Rock Trading Post on the lower Missouri River. There a U.S. Indian agent, George C. Sibley, helped him retrieve some of his furs from the Konsa village. A year later, despite the fact that he was under suspicion of murdering his leader, Champlain, Williams persuaded two Missouri friends to journey back up the Arkansas with him, where they retrieved a very large cache of furs. Williams was never tried for the murder of Champlain. Instead, the recounting of his exploits made clear for the first time the errors of Pike's map and the immense distance between the Yellowstone country and the Spanish settlements in New Mexico. He and his cohorts had discovered Colorado. More than that, they had managed to link Lisa's outpost, far up on the Yellowstone, with Spanish Santa Fe. Jean Baptiste Laforgue and three members of that party who reached Santa Fe were undoubtedly the first Euro-Americans to link the upper Missouri with the far-off Rio Grande. If their story had been preserved, it would have been one of the great tales of early western exploration.

While Lisa's men were exploring the tributaries of the upper Missouri and looking for a transmontane route to the Spanish settlements at Taos and Santa Fe, his secret partner, Jacques Clamorgan, had made his way in 1807, across the plains and into Santa Fe hard on the heels of Zebulon Pike's ill-fated expedition. There he awaited the arrival of Lisa's men from the north in vain. In the fall of 1812, he was joined by another of Lisa's agents, Charles Sanguinet, who was searching for the lost trapper Jean Baptiste Champlain—and his expected bonanza in furs.

During the next decade, increasing numbers of American adventurers made their way across the Southwest and into the Spanish capital. Most were humiliated and ejected or imprisoned by the wary Spaniards. In 1821, however, the trader William Becknell led a party into Santa Fe and was welcomed. Mexico had just become independent of Spain. The people of the northern province were eager for trade with the Americans, and the trade was so rich that Becknell hurried back to St. Louis in time to return in the same year with another caravan. In so doing, he laid out the Santa Fe Trail, over which thousands of wagons and American emigrants and soldiers would pass. The Santa Fe Trail had many variations because of grazing possibilities, Indian problems, etc., but the main routes lie either over Raton Pass on the border of Colorado and New Mexico and then into Taos, or else far to the east via the Cimarron River and Las Vegas and into Santa Fe.

Almost from the beginning, hard-bitten mountain men filtered into Santa Fe and Taos, looking for a good time and new beaver streams in the mountains of the Southwest. In 1822, William Wolfskill trapped both the lower and upper Rio Grande. And in 1823, he ascended the Rio Grande, crossed over the Continental Divide, and explored the San Juan River country of northwestern New Mexico and southern Colorado. He brought back a fortune in furs, and by 1824 at least four other parties had rushed to the San Juan country in his footsteps. Though the Spaniards had long ago preceded them in the person of Padre Sylvestre Vélez de Escalante, these were fresh discoveries for the Americans. They went by two routes. One took them from Taos through the San Luis Valley and along the Uncompahgre and Gunnison rivers in western Colorado to the Green River as far as the Uinta Mountains. Another took them via the Chama, the San Juan, and the Dolores rivers to the Green, which teemed with beaver. One of these parties, led by a large, rotund mountain man, Etienne Provost, circled around the Uinta mountain barrier in northeastern Utah and made its way down Weber River Canyon through the Wasatch Range to become among the first Americans to see the Great Salt Lake. No Spaniard, not even Escalante, had stumbled upon it before the American trappers coming up from the south and down from the north. The year of its discovery was 1825.

Other bands of southwestern trapper-explorers struck off to the west. In 1825 Sylvestre Pattie and his son, James Ohio, trapped the Gila River. Then in late 1826, Pattie joined a party led by Ewing Young that traveled west along the Gila, then north to the rim of the Grand Canyon. Largely ignoring this marvel, which they were the first Americans to see, they headed northeast via the Little Colorado to the Grand River, which they followed to its source in the Colorado Rockies. Pattie's account of the journey asserts that they then marched north via the parks of Colorado to the Big Horn and the Yellowstone, but it seems more likely that Ewing Young and his men reached only as far north as the Sweetwater and Upper Platte rivers before they returned to Santa Fe. At any rate, theirs had been among the most incredible western journeys to date, for they had traversed the West diagonally from the far Southwest at the junction of the Gila and the Colorado to the central ranges of the Rockies, linking up with the country that Jean Baptiste Champlain and Ezekial Williams had explored in 1811–13. Along the way they had seen the Grand Canyon and the majestic country of the Colorado River Plateau.

The other achievement of the southwestern mountain men was the opening of a route from Santa Fe to the Pacific. In 1827 Sylvestre and James Ohio Pattie followed the Gila to the Colorado and the Colorado to its mouth in the Gulf of California, and then turned north across the desert. Guided by Yuma Indians, on March 18, 1828, nearly dead from thirst and starvation, they reached Santa Catalina Mission in California. They were taken to San Diego and clapped into prison, where Sylvestre died. Only James Ohio survived to tell the tale of their continental crossing. But they had been preceded by Jedediah Smith in 1826, and by Richard Campbell, who had crossed directly from the junction of the Gila and the Colorado to San Diego. In 1829, a Mexican mule trader, Manuel Armijo, laid out the "Old Spanish Trail" to California, largely following Escalante's route north of the Grand Canyon and then coursing south to a site near present-day Las Vegas, Nevada, and thence across the Mojave Desert, over Cajon Pass, and into Los Angeles. By 1832, there were at least three trails that crossed the Great Southwest from Santa Fe to California.

Far to the northwest, Canadian fur traders also began the exploration of the interior. In the continental United States, Cana-

dian exploration really began with the Falstaffian Donald
McKenzie, who weighed nearly three hundred pounds. After
his return from Astoria, McKenzie was rebuffed for disloyalty
by John Jacob Astor, so he sought employment with the Northwest Company. In 1816, he returned to Astoria, or Fort George
as it was called under British occupation. At first, because of his
physical appearance, he was not taken seriously, but in one year
he revitalized all of the company's posts in the Northwest—primarily by constantly making friends with the Indians. Ever
since his overland trek with the Astorians, however, McKenzie
was struck by the possibilities of the Snake River country. He
saw that it led straight to the heart of the Rocky Mountain beaver country. Therefore, in 1818 he led the first of the Northwest
Company's Snake River brigades to the junction of the Snake
and the Columbia, where he built a trading fort. Then he set off
across the Blue Mountains toward the Skamnaugh or Boise
River in western Idaho. He continued east, trapping the tributaries of the Snake until he reached the country between the
Snake and the Green rivers. He also marched north to Jackson
Hole.

The next year, 1819, in experimenting with supplying his
field parties by water, McKenzie became the first to traverse
Hell's Canyon of the Snake River. In addition to this feat,
McKenzie also managed to hold off a Shoshone war party by
holding a match to a keg of powder and threatening to blow
himself and the war party into the next world. Undaunted by
this flirtation with disaster, he then led his men as far east as
Bear Lake in eastern Utah, but he never troubled to follow Bear
River, which flows out of Bear Lake into Great Salt Lake; hence
he never saw that great inland sea.

After he left the Northwest in 1821, McKenzie had several
successors, but only one could match him—Peter Skene Ogden.
The son of a Revolutionary War Loyalist, Ogden was known as
a troublemaker and hellion in the Northwest Company. On one
occasion, his fiery temper caused him to chase a rival up a tall
pine, to which he promptly set fire in high glee. In 1824, a re-
formed Ogden led his men southeast into the Bear River coun-

try, where in December they first glimpsed Great Salt Lake. Ogden believed that a great river flowed westward from the lake to the Pacific. He had seen it. It was the Umpqua of Oregon. Thus the myth of the Buenaventura or River of the West flowing out of a great inland sea to the Pacific, first promulgated by the Baron de Lahontan in his fictional *New Voyages to North America* (1703), lived on.

In the spring of 1825, Ogden made contact with American mountain men at Mountain Green just east of the Great Salt Lake. Most of his men deserted to the Americans, and Ogden, threatening revenge, made his way back to Fort Nez Perce only with difficulty. All told, Ogden made five trips into the western interior. He marched south into California via the Willamette Valley and opened up a new route to Spanish territory. He also discovered the Humboldt River, which flows across northern Nevada. This became a vital link in the trail to California, followed by American emigrants a decade later. He explored the northern shores of Great Salt Lake. And he made a remarkable journey south from the Humboldt Sinks in Nevada to the Colorado River near Needles, California, and thence to the mouth of the Colorado in the Gulf of California. On this occasion, in 1827, he engaged in a pitched battle with the Mojave Indians, leaving twenty-six of them dead or, as he put it, "made to lick the dust." He had crossed the Great Basin from north to south. By 1830, he knew more about the West beyond the Wasatch Mountains than any other man except Jedediah Smith. His knowledge was represented on French and British maps by A. H. Brué of Paris and Aaron Arrowsmith of London. Their maps were immediately acquired by American fur traders and ironically helped to speed the demise of the British in the Northwest.

iv
THE ENTERPRISING YOUNG MEN

AFTER the Astorians' abortive adventures and the daring forays of Lisa's parties, the major American inroads into the West were made by men of the Rocky Mountain Fur Company. In February of 1822, William Ashley of St. Louis placed an advertisement in the *St. Louis Gazette and Public Advertiser* calling for "Enterprising Young Men . . . to ascend the Missouri to its source, there to be employed for one, two or three years." Ashley's call was answered by some who became the greatest of all mountain men–explorers—Jedediah Smith, Thomas Fitzpatrick, David Jackson, William Sublette, James Clyman, Edward Rose, Hugh Glass, and Jim Bridger. Ashley himself was an adventuresome, imaginative man who had great flair—and ambition. A Virginian of aristocratic mien, he aspired to great and sudden wealth and then a political career. These he hoped to achieve with the help of his seasoned partner, Andrew Henry (one of Lisa's old engagees), and the "Enterprising Young Men."

At first Ashley's expeditions came to disaster. One of his large bateaux sank in the Missouri with all the trade goods aboard. A second expedition was pinned down and all but destroyed by the fierce Arikara on a sandbar in the river opposite their village. With the Indians all along the Missouri aroused, there was no chance of moving in the wake of Lewis and Clark by 1824. Ashley thus determined to take his parties overland. Andrew Henry led one band by land to the Yellowstone, eventually establishing a post at the confluence of the Yellowstone and Powder rivers. From there he sent John H. Weber and a party that included Jim Bridger across into the Wind River Valley to winter with the friendly Crow Indians.

The other party was led by Jedediah Strong Smith. Smith was only twenty-four years old, but he had been a woodsman all his life as his family moved west from New York State to Illinois. He had been struck with exploring fever ever since a family friend back in Pennsylvania, Dr. Titus Simons, gave him a copy of Nicholas Biddle and Paul Allen's 1814 account of the Lewis and Clark expedition. Smith was also a religious man, which perhaps accounts for his great courage. He was to become famed among the mountain men for his Bible and his courage.

On that first expedition, Smith took his men out across the Dakota Badlands to a spur of the Rockies called the Black Hills (not the famed Black Hills of South Dakota). At this point, he was attacked by a grizzly bear that seized his whole head within its jaws, ripping off his scalp and one of his ears. His men killed the bear, but they held out little hope for Smith. However, under Smith's calm direction, they sewed his scalp and ear back on. Ten days later he was ready to take to the trail—hardly a handsome specimen with a patched-on ear and a squinted, sewed-up eye, but nonetheless in one tough piece.

Soon they made the Powder River, crossed over the Big Horn Mountains via Granite Pass, and descended into the Big Horn Basin. Though it was a beautiful spot, they did not tarry there, but joined Weber's band in a bleak, bitter-cold winter encampment with the Crows in the Wind River Valley. There, despite the cold, they joined the Indians in hunting the buffalo that were seeking shelter in the mountains. Together they killed over a thousand.

At the end of February, Smith and his men attempted to get out of the Wind River Valley via the upper end—Union Pass, used by the outward-bound Astorians. Deep snows blocked their path, however, and they returned to the Crow village. There the Crows, using a deerskin and piles of sand for the mountains, showed them a route around the southeastern end of the Wind River Mountains. So, still in bitter cold, they followed the Popo Agie to the Sweetwater. Blizzards engulfed them. The wind blew so hard they could not light a campfire. Game was scarce, and they almost starved, but somehow they turned the flank of the Wind River Mountains. In so doing, they crossed over the Continental Divide at the South Pass, rediscovering, once and for all, that great emigrant gateway to the West. Ever afterward, the South Pass was used by most overland parties.

On March 19, Smith and his men reached the Green River, called by the Indians the Seedskeedee. There they split up into beaver-trapping parties. Smith followed the Green as far south as the Uinta Mountains, on the other side of which Etienne Provost and his men, all unbeknownst, were struggling toward the Wasatch Mountains and Salt Lake. That same season, Smith and his men made contact with a brigade of Northwest Company men under Alexander Ross on the Blackfoot Fork of the Snake.

Meanwhile, Weber and his men had followed Smith's trail out of the Wind River Valley and across South Pass to the Green River. From there, they trekked north to Bear Lake and the Bear River. In the early spring of 1825 one of their number, Jim Bridger, on a bet, sailed down Bear River in a bull boat and came out in Great Salt Lake. He became its official discoverer. According to a member of the party, Robert Campbell, "He went to its margin and tasted the water, and on his return reported his discovery. The fact of the water being salt induced the belief that it was an arm of the Pacific Ocean...." Old myths, like that of the Rio Buenaventura or the Timpanogos, died hard.

In 1826, Jedediah Smith became Ashley's field leader, and in the same year he conducted one of the great exploring expeditions in the annals of the West. On August 22, Smith set out from Great Salt Lake "for the purpose of exploring the country S.W. which was entirely unknown to me, and of which I could collect no satisfactory information from the Indians who inhabited this country on its N.W. borders." Smith's route took him southwest past the Sevier River and Utah Lake, then down along what became the "Mormon Corridor" to the Vergin River (which he called the Adams River after the current President) and through the wonders of present-day Zion National Park. When he reached the Colorado River far below the Grand Canyon, Smith instantly recognized it as the same Seedskeedee or Green River which he had left at last year's rendezvous. He took his men across the Colorado and into the villages of the grass-skirted Mojave Indians. There he learned from the Indians of an ancient Indian trading trail across the Mojave Desert. His men rested, Smith led them along this trail and into the Spanish settlement at San Gabriel (Los Angeles). His was the first American party to cross the Southwest into California.

After tarrying for nearly a month in San Gabriel, in part because of the hostility of the Spanish authorities, the intrepid Smith led his men north to the American River. Here they tried to cross over the Sierras to the east, but were thwarted by heavy snows. Smith was determined to explore the country between California and Great Salt Lake, however. Like Ashley and others before him, he believed that there was a Rio Buenaventura, and he hoped to find it. So he took only two men with him up the Stanislaus River into the snowy Sierras. After eight grueling days, they made their way over the mountains via Ebbetts Pass. The most difficult part of the trek—across the arid wastes of the Great Basin—had only begun. Before them stretched a thousand miles of alkali desert, little game, no friendly Indians to guide them, and no landmarks. Following a route that took them along the south shore of Walker Lake, which they were the first Americans to discover, they passed by the future sites of Manhattan, Tonopah, Ham Springs, and Ely, Nevada. Then they turned north, through Connors and Sacramento passes, but still the endless desert lay before them. On the 25th of June, one of the men gave out. Smith and his remaining partner had to leave him and push on. Three miles ahead they came to an isolated mountain and water. They rushed back to rescue their marooned comrade, then they all struggled on until, on June 27, they saw before them Great Salt Lake. Smith and his two companions had done what no white man, nor probably even a red man, had ever done before. They had crossed over the towering Sierras and traversed the Great Basin from west to east. It should have been clear from their trek that no Rio Buenaventura, or anything like it, existed in the form of a water passage to the Pacific. Smith was laconic about the whole trip: "My arrival caused considerable bustle in camp, for myself and party had been given up as lost."

As soon as he could, Smith and another band of trappers set out over the southwest corridor route to reinforce or rescue the men he had left in California. This time, however, disaster dogged his footsteps. The Mojaves had been turned into enemies by marauding white men, and they massacred ten of his men. Smith and the rest were driven into the desert and only with the greatest difficulty reached California. There the authorities were distinctly hostile, and Smith fled by ship to San Francisco Bay, where he rejoined his men out of reach of Spanish soldiers. The trappers then turned north toward Oregon, enjoying great success. But on the Umpqua River, the entire party was wiped out, except for two men and Jedediah Smith himself, who was away from camp on a lone scouting expedition. Eventually he made his way north via the Willamette Valley to the Hudson's Bay post at Fort Vancouver, where he was well received. But his entire band of brave men lay dead back on the Umpqua—testimony to the dangers of a trapper's life.

After recuperating at Fort Vancouver, Smith went up the river to the company's post at Fort Colvile, near the Kettle Falls of the Columbia. While in the company of the Canadians, Smith noted the rich possibilities for American settlement in the Willamette and Columbia river valleys. Upon his return, he drafted a letter to the Secretary of War to this effect, signed by his partners David Jackson and William Sublette. In the letter, Smith described the dangers of allowing the prosperous British settlement at Fort Vancouver on the Columbia to expand, and the ease with which a wagon train of settlers could make its way via the South Pass all the way to the Oregon country, where bumper crops could be expected by farmers. "The object of this communication," Smith stated, "being to state *facts* to the Government, and to show the facility of crossing the continent to the Great Falls of the Columbia with wagons, the ease of supporting any number of men by driving cattle to supply them where there was no buffalo, and also to show the true nature of the British establishments on the Columbia, and the unequal operation of the convention of 1818." It was a geopolitical letter, indicating something of the sophistication and intense patriotism of the mountain man–explorer as it called for the extinction of the convention of 1818, which allowed the United States and Britain to occupy the Columbia River Basin jointly. Long before the campaign slogan "Fifty-four forty or fight" came into promi-

nence in the presidential campaign of 1844, Smith and his partners were urging the American occupation of the Columbia
region and its settlement by American farmers, who would
cross the continent on trails blazed by the mountain men. This
letter gained national prominence, and was published by Congress. It aroused intense enthusiasm on the part of Americans
for emigration to Oregon. Nothing conveyed the sentiments of
the mountain men regarding the Oregon country better than the
doggerel of one Moses "Black" Harris, who wanted to sweep
the Columbia River country "clear of the British and the Indians."
He wrote:

> Here lies the bones of old Black Harris
> who often traveled beyond the far west
> and for the freedom of equal rights.
> He crossed the snowy mountain Heights
> was free and easy kind of soul.
> Especially with a belly full.

It aroused intense enthusiasm on the part of Americans for emigration to Oregon.

Meanwhile, Smith was not through exploring. From Fort
Colville, he journeyed all the way to the Canadian border. Then,
joining his partner, David Jackson, at Flathead Lake, he moved
south down the Bitterroot Valley into Pierre's Hole for the
summer rendezvous. In the late summer, he and his men passed
north through the Yellowstone Park area, but curiously they did
not tarry there. Instead, they moved on to the Big Horn Basin,
crossed over into the Wind River Valley, and then swung north
to a winter encampment on the Powder River, just east of the
Big Horn Mountains. The following year (1830), Smith continued to explore the upper Missouri region, but that was his last
year. He went downriver into retirement. However, the curiosity of the explorer would not let him rest. He had never traversed the Santa Fe Trail. In 1831 he did so—and was killed by
Comanches on the Cimarron River.

Without question, Jedediah Smith was one of the greatest explorers America ever produced. He had traversed every part of

the West from the upper Missouri to the deserts of the Far
Southwest. He knew the heart of the Rockies, the Great Plains,
California and Oregon, the Columbia and the Great Basin,
which he was the first man to cross. He had pioneered in the rediscovery of the central route across the Rockies via the South
Pass, and he had personally informed the United States govern-
ment of the rich possibilities for settlement in Oregon and Cali-
fornia. He even left a map behind—the so-called Frémont-
Gibbs-Smith map. On a Frémont map of 1845, Dr. George
Gibbs of Oregon, apparently using a manuscript map given him
by Smith, had sketched in all of Smith's vast geographical
knowledge, including copies of notes made by Smith. Moreover,
Smith's knowledge in less detailed form even reached the aging
Albert Gallatin in time for inclusion in his *Map of the Indian
Tribes of North America*, published by the American Antiquarian Society in 1836. Gallatin's ethnographic map, reinforced by Smith's data, became the standard such map of the
country until the 1850s.

There were, of course, many other mountain man–explorers.
Some of them were important because they were trailblazers for
the emigrants who moved west starting in 1832. One of these
trailblazers was Joseph Rutherford Walker, who had exploring
in his blood, and came to know more of the West than any man
save Jedediah Smith and possibly Peter Skene Ogden. A tall,
handsome fellow, Walker was a Tennessean who had gravitated
to the Missouri frontier by the time he was in his early twenties.
By 1822 he had already made two trips to Santa Fe and subsequently aided the official government survey party in laying out
the Santa Fe Trail. He also helped found the outfitting center
for the southwestern expeditions in Independence, Missouri,
and served as the sheriff of that rough, brawling town. His exploring days began when he met Captain Benjamin Louis Eula-
lie Bonneville at Fort Gibson in Oklahoma. Bonneville was
ostensibly on leave from the United States Army to conduct a
fur trading expedition to the Rocky Mountains. It seems clear,
however, that his mission was more than that. He was spying
out the central Rockies for the United States government and

searching for a route to California. Though he proved to be a very bad fur trader, Bonneville, thanks to Walker's help, accomplished both of these governmental objectives admirably.

In the spring of 1832, with Walker as his field lieutenant, Bonneville set out from Fort Osage for the mountains. He followed the now familiar path via the Platte, the Sweetwater, and the South Pass to the Green River. Eventually, he built a fur trading post on a tributary of the Green near the favorite site of the mountain men's annual rendezvous. To fur trade veterans, it seemed a poor location, but it was an ideal spot to monitor the British relations with the Indians. Later, as British interests receded farther west, he followed, building another post on the Salmon River much farther north and west in present-day Idaho. At the Green River rendezvous of 1833, Bonneville organized a party under Walker to march north around Great Salt Lake and cross westward to the Pacific. The plan was well known to all. According to Zenas Leonard, clerk and chief chronicler of the expedition, "I was anxious to go to the coast of the Pacific, and for that purpose hired with Mr. Walker as clerk for a certain sum per year." Thus, Walker and his men intentionally struck out for California, through what was still Spanish territory, as unofficial agents of the United States government. They coursed westward from the Great Salt Lake across burning stretches of desert to the Humboldt River. Then they followed that river as it curved southwestward to the Humboldt sinks at the base of the Sierras. Here they found themselves in starving condition and forced to fight a battle with the Indians. Almost in desperation they struck out into the Sierras via a southern branch of what is now known as the East Walker River. They soon found themselves crossing the mountains over a kind of pass between the watersheds of the Merced and Tuolumne rivers. In the course of their struggles they became the first men to sight the misty falls and breathtaking chasms of Yosemite. They also came upon the "Big Trees" or redwood forests at the foot of Yosemite as they descended into California.

On Walker's return journey he moved south in California,

and, aided by Indian guides, located a pass around the southern end of the Sierras which was very practical for wagons and immigrants. This was Walker's Pass—for a long time a primary immigrant gateway into California. Walker himself clearly realized what he had done and subsequently led wagon trains back over the route he had laid out. For in the course of his return journey to Salt Lake, Walker had located the main trail to California. Maps based on Walker's work were published in Washington Irving's two classic works on the west, *Astoria* (1836) and *The Adventures of Captain Bonneville* (1837).

For the rest of his long life (1798–1876) Walker wandered all over the West, making countless trips back and forth to California. He guided wagon trains; he herded horses along the Old Spanish Trail. He twice guided Frémont, and was in at the beginning of the Bear Flag Revolt that helped touch off the Mexican War in California. His dream was, however, to explore the Green River down its course through the Uintas and the high plateaus of Utah. He was never able to do so, and that feat brought immortality to Major John Wesley Powell nearly twenty-five years later. Instead, in the 1860s, while advanced in age, Walker, after an extraordinary series of adventures in central Arizona, found gold. On the site of his gold strike, the town of Prescott grew and became the territorial capital. Walker, as explorer, had spanned the age from the mountain man to the prospector. Along the way he had been a U. S. Army scout, horse trader, and rancher. His career encompassed most of the activities of the frontier West.

Though seemingly remote from the organized development of world science, the mountain men made both Europeans and Americans alike conscious of, and to a remarkable degree knowledgeable about, the continent west of the Mississippi. Primarily fur hunters, they nevertheless themselves were conscious of a national mission. They gathered a great deal of geographical information and passed it on to governmental officials like William Clark and the Secretary of War. They made crude maps. They guided government explorers. They presented accounts of their travels in countless newspapers, as-told-to books, and personally written reminiscences. They also contributed an incredible oral tradition as to what the West was really like—a tradition that has fortunately been reconstructed by the patient labors of many historians. The story of the mountain man's hard-won and gradually accumulated knowledge thus becomes an integral part, not only of the emergence of a continental consciousness, but also of the nonelitist aspect of the way in which geography itself developed in the United States. The mountain men were not sent out by a Royal Society, nor even by an American Philosophical Society. Nevertheless, their discoveries became part of the nation's and the world's accumulated information, reaching the excited meetings of the American Ethnographic Society and even the drafting rooms of Europe's outstanding cartographers. In a democracy, it was difficult to keep important information secret, especially if it was directly relevant to the aims of continental expansion and settlement. In this sense, they contributed mightily, if rudimentarily, to continental consciousness.

This laurel fits all of that courageous band of men who entered the Rockies in the first decades of the century and succeeded so well at their task of opening up the country that by 1850 their great day was at an end. Much has been made of the decline of the fur trade—the changing fashion in fur hats in Europe, and the trapping out of once-teeming beaver streams—but another factor in the passing of the mountain man's era was the great flow of emigrants to the West beginning in the 1830s. With parties of would-be farmers, miners, railroaders, and storekeepers roaming all over the West along the trails blazed by the mountain men, the life of the solitary trapper became less and less feasible. There were other, more exciting tasks to turn to. And Walker's career, along with those of a notable collection of other fur hunters—Jim Bridger, Kit Carson, and Tom Fitzpatrick, to name but a few—illustrates that they did just that. But before the mountain man's era was over he had made a place for himself in the annals of world exploration that can never be forgotten.

CHAPTER V

Humboldt's Children

i

THE ROMANTIC WEST

THE ADVENTURES of the American mountain men and the exploration of the plains and Rockies attracted worldwide attention. To Europeans, the American West was a wild and exotic country full of strange animals and strange people. Though mountain men and U.S. government expeditions were exploring the region in practical terms, Europeans wished to fit it into a romantic horizon in the manner of the great Alexander von Humboldt. In the early decades of the nineteenth century, literally dozens of European explorers—many of them his disciples—came to see the American West with their own eyes, prepared to be dazzled with its wonders. Theirs was a different kind of exploration and theirs were different discoveries.

They were in search of new experiences in a remote and faraway place—as if knowledge of the remote land and its mysterious peoples would annex it in mind and spirit to the ever-widening domain of the emergent culture of pure science, which the mighty Humboldt in his vast researches personified. They were also in search of adventure and the unknown as a kind of refuge from the stifling world of the industrial revolution with its cities and its burgeoning bourgeois population of expectant capitalists. Something of this feeling seems to have prevailed, whatever the social status of the explorer. Dukes and princes journeyed west, but so did penniless naturalists and artists who saw themselves rising above the mundane concerns of everyday life. They all belonged to a self-designated class of dedicated romantic adventurers who felt they had a mission to contribute something to the world in the largest, one might say cosmic, sense.

And the rivers that ran out of the West, the Mississippi and especially the long rolling tide of the Missouri, were their first gateways to the land of adventure and romance in the interests of mankind. The Missouri, for example, was like the Nile. One could take a boat over two thousand miles up its muddy current into a country that dazzled the mind fully as much as the Sudan or ancient Nubia. Such a voyage, full of scenic wonders and exotic peoples, also took one back in time, just as it did in Egypt, to the origins of man, except that the Indians of the upper Missouri seemed to take one back to the very creation. They were Ur men. And even the Rockies, when the explorers reached them, seemed commensurate with Africa's "Mountains of the Moon," while the Mandan Indians, reputed to be descendants of the legendary Prince Madoc of Wales, offered a challenge to early romantic anthropologists fully as exciting as the search for the vestiges of the fabled kingdom of Prester John somewhere in the wilds of Ethiopia.

This sense of romantic adventure was epitomized, if not caricatured, by the expedition of the Venetian dilettante Giacomo Beltrami to the source of the Mississippi. A political outcast from his native Italy, Beltrami seemed doomed to wander forever through Europe and over the globe in what he jauntily called his "pilgrimage." In 1823, however, he found himself in St. Louis with Major Lawrence Talliaferro, the Indian agent for Fort St. Anthony in the Minnesota Territory. Beltrami had planned to head down the Mississippi and embark for Mexico. Instead, for reasons now obscure, Talliaferro persuaded him to journey north with him aboard the first steamboat to ascend the

river to the Falls of St. Anthony, site of the present-day Twin
Cities in Minnesota. Beltrami agreed to go because he wished to
view the mysterious Indian tribes whose "extraordinary character had, from infancy, excited my astonishment and incredu-
lity." He had already connected in his mind the Cahokia Indian
mounds near St. Louis with Mithraic temples and the pyramids
of Giza.

At Fort St. Anthony (now Fort Snelling), Beltrami attached
himself to Major Stephen H. Long's expedition assigned to survey the border between the United States and Canada. Long, a
no-nonsense, scientific person, disliked the arrangement, but
Beltrami tagged along. When they reached Pembina on the Red
River of the north, or "Bloody River" as Beltrami called it,
the Venetian realized that Long had taken him far north of the
sources of the Mississippi. Indignantly he struck off from the government expedition on one of his own. With a cowardly interpreter and two Chippewa Indians, he turned south up the
"Bloody River" into what he believed to be a country filled with
"ferocious savages." This proved to be partially true. His small
party was ambushed by Sioux, and the Chippewa as well as the
interpreter ran off, leaving Beltrami sitting disconsolately alone
in the forest gloom with his "kit" and a birchbark canoe, which
he had not the faintest idea how to paddle. At first he imagined
himself Robinson Crusoe, deserted and alone. But then, with visions of the intrepid heroes of Roman and Greek legend before
him, he pushed on into the wilderness, towing the canoe with
his supplies. Atop the supplies, like the Knight of La Mancha,
he raised his standard—a red silk umbrella—and struggled eastward through the rain and the swampy country of western
Minnesota. The glittering prize of being the first to discover the
sources of the mighty Mississippi lay always before him. To
him it was as important as the search for the sources of the Nile
which was to attract a host of British explorers some years later.
In a manner of speaking, he was rescued in the nick of time by
some Red Lake Chippewa, who first thought him crazy, then ultimately guided him to his destination—a lake which he named
Julia after his lost paramour. He saw, or thought he saw, streams

flowing outward from the lake in two directions—one forming the source of "Bloody River" and the other the source of the Mississippi. Sitting on the shore of Lake Julia, Beltrami was overcome with elation. "Oh! What were the thoughts which passed through my mind at this most happy and brilliant moment of my life!" he wrote. "The shades of Marco Polo, of Columbus, of Americus Vespucius, of the Cabots, of Verazini [sic], of the Zenos . . . appeared present . . . at this high and solemn ceremony. . . ." Beltrami eventually descended from this sublime mountain of glory and, after a series of terrifying misadventures, reached Fort St. Anthony and civilization only to meet disdain. No one believed him. No one cared. The source of the river was clearly in American territory and thus was diplomatically insignificant. In New Orleans he published an account of his expedition as high romance in the form of letters to his beloved, the Countess Giulia Medici-Spada, with a somewhat anticlimactic title, *A Pilgrimage in Europe and America, Leading to the Discovery of the Sources of the Mississippi and the Bloody River, with a Description of the Whole Course of the Former, and of the Ohio.* Ironically, Beltrami did not even discover the true source of the Mississippi. In 1832, Henry Rowe Schoolcraft, Indian agent for the Minnesota Territory, rather matter-of-factly discovered the true source of the river, not in Lake Julia but in Lake Itasca. But Beltrami's quest, despite its farcical episodes, partook of the same vision that made the West an endless source of fascination for many European and American explorers alike in the early part of the nineteenth century.

Thomas Nuttall was still another species of exploring visionary. He was a British naturalist who had arrived in Philadelphia in 1808. In 1811, he found himself headed up the Missouri River into Indian country in the company of Wilson Price Hunt and the Astorians. Originally sent by America's most eminent botanist, Benjamin Smith Barton, to collect plant specimens around Winnipeg, Nuttall had met Hunt at the great fur trading post of Michilimackinac. The veteran fur trader convinced him that Barton's plan was impractical and offered to take him along on his expedition up the Missouri in the wake of Lewis and Clark. This meant that he could collect plants in country no other trained botanist had seen. So, in the spring of 1811, Nuttall found himself heading upriver into the heart of the West. Along the way he met John Bradbury, another English naturalist, and the amateur collector Henry Marie Brackenridge, a St. Louis lawyer. He also met Sacajawea, who had guided Lewis and Clark, and Manuel Lisa, who befriended him.

Nuttall always needed a friend with experience and judgment. In love with botany and the adventure of collecting out in the unknown, he often forgot himself. Washington Irving described him in *Astoria*:

> Mr. Nuttall was a zealous botanist, and all his enthusiasm was awakened at beholding a new world, opening upon him in the boundless prairies, clad in the variegated robe of unknown flowers. Delighted with the treasures, he went groping and stumbling along among a wilderness of sweets, forgetful of everything but his immediate pursuit. The Canadian voyagers used to make merry at his expense, regarding him as some kind of madman.

He was dubbed *le fou*, and this mad, unworldly image probably saved his life. The Indians regarded him as a medicine or mystery man. They not only avoided attacking him, but saved his life whenever he became lost on the prairies far up the Missouri near what Nuttall called "the Northern Andes." Somehow the English botanist made it back alive from Lisa's post near the Big Horn and Missouri rivers. He arrived in New Orleans with a large collection of plants, animal skins, rocks, and Indian artifacts and took ship immediately for England, thereby missing the blockades of the War of 1812.

He was not always destiny's child, however. Most of his American plant discoveries were pirated by Frederick Pursh and published in his *Flora America Septentrionalis* in 1818. When Nuttall returned to America in 1817, he became a founder of the Philadelphia Academy of Natural Sciences. He later became lecturer in botany at Harvard and a legend as well, because of the fact that he entered his second-floor study by means of a trapdoor and rope ladder, which he pulled up behind him. But Nuttall, with his interest in plants and geology and birds (in 1818 he published *Genera of North American Plants and a Catalogue of Species to the year 1817*, and in 1832 his famous *Manual of the Ornithology of the United States and Canada*), was primarily an explorer and collector.

In 1819, he set off on an expedition to the Arkansas country which took him through the Ozarks and the Arkansas River bottoms—among rude Indian villages and gangs of cutthroats and river pirates. Ill with malaria, he pushed on up the Arkansas halfway to the Rockies before he gave up and headed back to "civilization." But perhaps his grandest expedition came in 1834, when he accompanied the Boston ice dealer Nathaniel Wyeth up along the Oregon Trail all the way to the Pacific. On this trek he and Wyeth were accompanied by another naturalist, John Kirk Townsend, and the famous missionaries Henry Spaulding, Jason Lee, and Marcus Whitman. Townsend's diary is replete with references to Nuttall's hardy if otherworldly dedication to natural science. And when he reached the Pacific, Nuttall did not stop. He went to Hawaii and then down the California coast as far as San Diego, where he was spotted, thin and spindly with his trousers rolled, collecting in the Pacific tide pools, by one of his former students, Richard Henry Dana. In fact, Nuttall returned to Boston around the Horn with Dana aboard the *Pilgrim* (of *Two Years Before the Mast* fame). Dana remembered that as they rounded the Horn in furious gales, Nuttall wanted to stop and collect specimens on the remote Patagonian shores. The captain pushed on for home.

ii

THE MAD DUKE AND THE SUFFERING ARTIST

THE most widely traveled European explorer was Frederick Paul Wilhelm, Duke of Württemberg. Educated as a scientist by

a student of Cuvier's at the Stuttgart Gymnasium, Duke Paul
was inspired by the work of Humboldt and wished to follow in
his footsteps. By 1822 when he left on his first trip to America,
the duke was already an experienced geographer and naturalist.
He had traveled in the Near East, North Africa, and Russia. In
addition, he was a member of the most prestigious European scientific societies. Moreover, he was abreast of the most recent
works on the American West. Before he left on his voyage he
had carefully studied the first two volumes of Dr. Edwin James's
report on Major Stephen H. Long's expedition of 1819–21.

The duke made seven excursions into the United States between 1822 and 1860, when he died suddenly at his castle at Bad
Mergentheim. Five of these trips were expeditions into the
West. The first of these took him up the Missouri nearly a thousand miles, where he was turned back by fur trade agent Joshua
Pilcher, who brought news of the Arikara battle with General
Ashley's mountain men. The only published account of the
duke's travels—that of his 1822 expedition—indicates that he
was a careful observer of nature and a great admirer of the Indians. When he left for Europe, he brought back extensive collections in natural history and Indian artifacts.

In 1827 the duke married Princess Sophie of Thurn and
Taxis, and the following year a son was born. Shortly afterward
Duke Paul left for the West once again. This time he traveled far
up the Missouri and lived among the Sioux, the Blackfeet, and
the Assiniboin. He reached the Yellowstone and the Three
Forks of the Missouri and managed to get himself rescued from
the Blackfeet by the Sioux Indians. One of these Sioux he
brought to his castle in Germany, hoping to civilize him. Instead, during a sporting contest at arms, the Sioux attempted to
brain him with a tomahawk. Shortly afterward the Indian was
returned to his native hunting grounds.

For the most of the 1830s and 1840s the duke turned his attention to Egypt, the upper Nile, and other exotic parts of the
world. But in 1849 he returned to the American West for an extended trip. He visited Texas, especially the settlements at New

Braunfels, then Sutter's Mill and the Gold Rush sites in California, and of course the Rockies.

During this extended excursion he met a fellow countryman, Heinrich Balduin Möllhausen, who was later to become another of Humboldt's protégés and a famous explorer in his own right. In 1851 Duke Paul employed Möllhausen, who was something of an artist, to accompany him on a dash across the plains to Fort Laramie. Despite the fact that Möllhausen was sick most of the time, they made their way with difficulty across the swollen fords of the Platte to the famous Rocky Mountain fur trade bastion and then started back for St. Louis. Their return trip was beset by calamity. The wagon broke down, Indians stole their horses, Möllhausen remained desperately ill, and the duke nurtured a monumentally ill temper. Ultimately, he abandoned Möllhausen out on the praries of Kansas as winter snows set in. But Möllhausen, cold, starving, fearful of Indians, and armed to the teeth, survived to be rescued by friendly Oto Indians. Meanwhile, the duke explored the West and Mexico until July of 1856, during which time he also visited most of South America. His last trip to the West was in 1857, on the way around the world via Australia, the South Pacific, China, and the Middle East. By the time he returned to Bad Mergentheim and Princess Sophie, the duke had run out of money entirely, but he had assembled one of the finest ethnographic and natural history collections in the world, of which his specimens from the American West formed a major part. But when the duke died shortly after his return, his collections had to be sold to pay his debts. Only the castle and a few paintings remain at Bad Mergentheim to memorialize the duke's Humboldtian dream of a cosmos of knowledge.

The duke's artist, Heinrich Balduin Möllhausen, went on to a productive career of his own. In 1853, having returned to Germany and studied with Humboldt himself, he returned and accompanied Lieutenant Amiel Weeks Whipple's army expedition in search of a railroad route to the Pacific. And in 1857, he accompanied Lieutenant Joseph Christmas Ives's expedition up the Colorado and into the Grand Canyon. He was among the first white men ever to set foot on the floor of the Grand Canyon. For both of these expeditions' reports, Möllhausen supplied strange moonscape drawings that in comparison with the actual sites proved to be remarkably accurate. Then he published his own accounts of the trips. Beyond that, inspired by the creator of Leatherstocking, he became one of the most famous and prolific writers in nineteenth-century Germany. He wrote some forty-five novels in 157 volumes and eighty short stories, most of them dealing in authentic terms with the American West. To some he became known as the German Fenimore Cooper. But others remembered him in old age wandering about Berlin still dressed in mountain man garb, and fondly referred to him as *der alte Trapper*. He was a survivor, and like the other German writers who visited the West, Friedrich Gerstäcker and Charles Sealsfield, he made the Far West of the plains and Rockies vivid and exciting to would-be German immigrants.

iii

THE PRINCE AND THE PAINTER

STILL another German explorer in the Humboldtian tradition made it possible for Continental Europeans to see the upper Missouri country and its mysterious people for the first time. Maximilian, Prince of Wied Neuwied, near Coblenz on the Rhine, journeyed to America in 1833, intent upon exploring, studying, and recording the West. He took with him a young Swiss landscape painter, Karl Bodmer, whose five hundred stunning watercolors and aquatints did indeed reveal the landscapes and the Indians of the West for the first time to European audiences. He produced perhaps the best, most accurate, yet haunting ethnographic drawings and paintings ever done in America. And beyond that Bodmer also caught, long before George Caleb Bingham and Mark Twain, the romance of early life on the Mississippi, as steamboats plying that great artery of inland commerce fascinated him as well as the whole process of the advance of American civilization into the wilderness during the era of Andrew Jackson.

By 1833, when he came to America, Maximilian was a veteran explorer and close student of both geography and anthropology. His principal teacher had been J. J. Blumenbach of Göttingen, the greatest German naturalist of his day and the founder of scientific anthropology. His book *On the Natural Variety of Mankind* was the great classic in the field. It was Blumenbach who inspired his student, Humboldt, to carry on his mighty labors, and it was, in turn, Humboldt, whom he met in Paris, who launched Prince Maximilian on his active career as an explorer. Between 1815 and 1819, Maximilian and two other German naturalists had tramped through the jungles of eastern Brazil between latitudes 13° and 23°. The prince concentrated his energies on studying the primitive natives who lived deep in the jungle gloom. Following the major question posed by Blumenbach, he wished to find out whether primitive man was at an early stage of cultural evolution or in a last stage of degeneration. His expedition to North America was designed to pursue the same question and further to learn whether the Indian was really a descendant of the Mongols of Asia, thereby confirming Blumenbach's theories of epigenesis and racial diffusion over the globe. Almost the first time he studied Indians closely—at Jefferson Barracks outside St. Louis—Maximilian concluded that they were not Tartars or Mongols, but an entirely indigenous race whose customs had grown up in isolation from Asia from the very beginning of human history. The thought that he was studying original peoples whose lineage went back almost to the beginnings of nature itself fascinated Maximilian and gave to his careful researches an inevitable coloring of high romanticism.

After wintering in the Utopian colony at New Harmony, Indiana, the prince, accompanied by his personal hunter Dreidoppel and the artist Karl Bodmer, ascended the Missouri River aboard the steamboat *Yellowstone* on April 10, 1833. This was

the same American Fur Company vessel that had taken the
painter George Catlin up the long river the year before. Maximilian's little expedition ascended the Missouri finally as far as
Fort McKenzie, nearly three thousand miles upriver in the heart
of the Blackfoot country. There they spent over a month in the
tiny outpost founded precariously only three years before. Maximilian had intended to proceed onward to the sources of the
Missouri and thence to the Pacific, but the whole country was in
the midst of a series of Indian wars, so the prince and Bodmer
contented themselves with studying the warlike Blackfeet at the
height of their power. During the course of their stay at Fort
McKenzie, the Assinboin attacked a Blackfoot encampment outside the fort and an Indian war swirled all around them for almost a week. Bodmer was able to execute a painting of this
Indian battle, which is very probably the only eyewitness
recording by a European or American of such an event. Equally
important, Bodmer was able to paint portraits of the leading
men of the Blackfoot confederacy—Distant Bear, a medicine
man; Buffalo Bull's Back Fat, whom the American George Catlin had also painted; Middle Bull of the haunting blue-painted
face; and the fierce blackened visage of the war chief Iron Shirt.
Though they were ethnological types, they emerged as real, un-
forgettable people under Bodmer's precise pencil and vivid but
exact watercolors. Despite the Indian danger, Bodmer also
climbed the hills around Fort McKenzie and painted the vast
horizons of the upper Missouri with the Highwood Range of the
Rocky Mountains in the distance. He also painted a series of incredibly beautiful views of the Mauvais Terres or eroded Badlands of the Upper Missouri employing the techniques of the
north German Romantic school, though with much more imaginative use of light and color. Far surpassing the crude work of
Samuel Seymour in 1819–20, Bodmer portrayed the immensi-
ties and vast scale of the western landscape as well as its amazing
curiosities with what the novelist F. Scott Fitzgerald was later to
call "something commensurate with man's capacity for wonder."

Maximilian and Bodmer wintered in a crude cabin at Fort Clark between the clay hut villages of the Mandan and Hidatsa tribes. They were somewhere just south of present-day Bismarck, North Dakota, and the weather reached 46° below zero, but Bodmer kept painting the noble personages—Chief Mah-to-tope of the Mandans and Periska Ruhpa the Dog Dance warrior, chief of the Hidatsa. The latter painting of the dancing chief with fan-shaped feather headdress has often been called the greatest of all Indian portraits. Bodmer also paid attention to the Indian ceremonies—the scalp dance and the buffalo dance—investing them on canvas with all the mystery and power they possessed in actual life. And despite the below-zero weather that froze his paints and numbed his fingers, Bodmer also captured the bleak Dakota landscape in a way that no one except modern cinematographers has since. His masterpiece—a view of Indian women struggling across the ice from the village to collect wood under a leaden sky in midwinter—conjured up the age-old "Song of the the Volga Boatmen."

Meanwhile Maximilian had made careful ethnological studies of the Mandan and Hidatsa to go along with those he made of the Blackfeet. When the once-mighty Mandan were reduced to 120 survivors after the devastating smallpox epidemic of 1837, and half of the Blackfeet were wiped out in the same epidemic, Maximilian's researches and Bodmer's paintings became, along with the systematic studies of Catlin, the only significant graphic records of those almost destroyed cultures at the height of their powers.

In the spring of 1834, the prince and Bodmer descended the Missouri and made their way back to Europe. There Bodmer set to work on a monumental atlas of aquatint views of the exotic sights that they had seen while Maximilian polished his extensive journals for publication in two volumes. In 1836, Bodmer exhibited a number of his watercolors in Paris—five years before George Catlin. He also published some of his more spectacular works in a Swiss family magazine, but it was almost a decade before the monumental aquatint *Atlas* appeared in 1841, together with the prince's narrative. It was, however, a sublime moment in the revelation of the mysteries of the New World to the Old. Maximilian and Bodmer's great report, which almost bankrupted the prince and sent Bodmer off to Barbizon and obscurity for the rest of his life, was perhaps the finest work ever executed in the Humboldtian tradition.

The British were also not to be outdone. Sir George Gore hunted the Yellowstone. Captain Frederick Ruxton emerged from Mexico and tramped all over the West with the mountain men. His classic work *Life in the Far West* (1849) told the story of real trappers under the fictionalized names of Killbuck and La Bonte in such a way as to rival Washington Irving's *Astoria* and *The Adventures of Captain Bonneville* for both English and American readers.

iv

FAR FROM BIRNAM WOOD

BY FAR the most flamboyant European explorer of the American West was a Scottish baronet, Sir William Drummond Stewart of Murthley Castle, which stood on the Tay between Shakespeare's Birnam Wood and Dunsinane Peak. The second son of his family line, Stewart looked forward to no great inheritance and so became a soldier, a wanderer, and a sportsman. He had served with Wellington in his Peninsula Campaign and blunted the French cavalry charge at Waterloo. In 1833, after an inconvenient marriage to a servant girl and a bitter fight with his older brother, who controlled the family estate, he came to America, where he intended to spend the rest of his life hunting and roaming in the wild West with the mountain men. In all, Captain Stewart spent seven seasons in the West and saw most of its wonders. His first trip out was over the Oregon Trail to the Green River rendezvous in the company of mountain man William Sublette. From the beginning Stewart loved every moment of it—the sky-high mountains, the gaudily painted Indians, the nubile squaws, the trading, the tall tales, the legendary trappers, and most of all the thrilling chase over the rolling prairie on horseback after the buffalo. Nothing in the world could match the wild free life of the mountain men out on the Seedskeedee. Stewart had discovered a romantic landscape and a romantic life-style.

In the course of his years spent with the mountain men from 1833 to 1838, Stewart traveled north into the Big Horn and Yellowstone River country; he trekked south along the front range of the Rockies to spend a winter of revelry in Taos; he traversed the beautiful interior parks of Colorado and made his way over the Oregon Trail to Fort Vancouver; he spent a season high atop the Wind River Mountains; he gazed awestruck at the sublime beauty of Jackson Hole; and finally on one last expedition upon his return to America in 1843, he stood amid the wonders of the Yellowstone geyser basins. He had explored and experienced the Rocky Mountain West during a period of momentous transition. Despite the high spirits at the annual rendezvous he could see that the fur trade was in decline. (In fact, he made an American fortune by speculating in New Orleans cotton himself.) He could also see the gradual growth of traffic on the Oregon Trail beginning with missionaries, continuing with entrepreneurs, and culminating with a cavalcade of farmers who went west in the late 1830s.

By 1836 he had decided to capture some of his wilderness experiences on paper, so he began writing novels, first *Altowan* and then *Edward Warren,* which were thinly disguised accounts of his romantic adventures with the mountain men and Indian girls. He also discovered in New Orleans the young Baltimore painter Alfred Jacob Miller. Miller went west with Stewart in 1837 and captured in countless sketches, watercolors, and gouaches the rich sights of Rocky Mountain life. He recorded the wild hunts, escapes from Indians, the trapper at work and at leisure. He pictured the rendezvous in all its gaudy splendor on canvas, and he stood like some early Gauguin recording naked Indian girls bathing in a cool mountain stream.

The butchering of the buffalo, the yell of triumph, the sight of panic and stampede, all of these he painted with a romantic freshness that somehow represented discovery as it impressed upon the imagination of his mentor Sir William Drummond Stewart. It was a kind of exploration that neither Miller nor Stewart would ever forget—not even after Sir William was eventually forced to return to Murthley Castle to assume the duties of a lordship upon the death of his hated brother. Few men had seen and remembered more of the West than Stewart, and none save Karl Bodmer and George Catlin had recorded its wild, pristine life so well as Alfred Jacob Miller.

V

THE RED MAN'S HEROIC HISTORIAN

QUITE possibly the grandest, most heroic person to survey the West as romantic horizon did not at first carry Humboldt's ideas in his knapsack. He was not a European but an American—plain George Catlin from Wilkes Barre, Pennsylvania. Trained as a lawyer, he had become a self-taught portrait painter. But from the time that he first saw a group of western Indian chiefs en route to Washington he was inspired to a whole new career. He remembered the chiefs as "lords of the forest" strutting in "silent and stoic dignity" about the city, "wrapped in their pictured robes, with their brows plumed with the quills of the war eagle, attracting the gaze and admiration of all who beheld them." "The history and customs of such a people," he declared, "preserved by pictorial illustrations, are themes worthy the lifetime of one man, and nothing short of the loss of my life, shall prevent me from visiting their country, and of becoming their historian." And their historian he became. In an age when the romantic multivolume histories of writers like William Hickling Prescott, John Lothrop Motley, and Francis Parkman were most admired, the work of George Catlin topped them all, for his was a moral mission. He intended to record "a correct account" of the treatment accorded the original inhabitants of the continent and to delineate "the courses which have led to their rapid destruction." He hoped, somehow, to arrest the "juggernaut of civilization" and restore justice to the Indian, but everything he observed in his travels through the West made him pessimistic. He proposed "a nation's *Park* containing man and beast, all in the wild and freshness of their nature's beauty." As a last resort, he assembled an "Indian Gallery" of some 310 paintings and numerous artifacts which he displayed up and down the East Coast of America, hoping to persuade the goverment to purchase it as a memorial to the fast-vanishing original inhabitants of the continent. Failing this, in 1841 he took his Indian Gallery to London and then to Paris, where it created a sensation. It appears that Catlin never intended to sell his Indian scenes and portraits individually as might a professional artist. Rather he saw himself as a new kind of historian who transcended the printed medium to tell the sad tale of a people "who had no voice to speak for themselves."

In pursuit of his mission, in 1832 Catlin steamed up the Missouri with the help of the American Fur Company aboard the first voyage of the *Yellowstone*. When he passed the last vestiges of civilization, Catlin was dazzled by the "enamelled prairies" and the flocks and herds of game roaming free, often as far as the eye could see. When he reached Fort Union, he set up a studio in one of the tower bastions of the fur trade fort. There, day after day, he painted portraits of the principal chiefs of the plains Indian tribes. His studio became a neutral ground, a sacred den of mystery where hereditary enemies such as the Crow and the Blackfeet sat side by side waiting their turn to pose for one of his portraits. His "medicine" was powerful, since he caught their likenesses as if they were alive, laughing and scowling as their moods struck them.

In addition Catlin collected all the Indian costumes and other artifacts that he could in order to preserve an exact record of the red man's exotic dress. His prize was an elaborate Blackfoot medicine man's costume with the complete head of the almost extinct golden bear. Catlin also recorded the language and customs of the plains people. His most spectacular feat in this respect was his recording of the secret Mandan Okipa ceremony—a four-day experience in which wild sexual abandon alternated with grim torture ceremonies. Men in buffalo skins tried to dance the bison in from the plains while they engaged in mock copulation with a comic personage who also chased the village women with a huge spotted penis. In days following, brave young men of the tribe volunteered to hang by skewers through their breasts until they lost consciousness. Aided by the resident trader, James Kipp, Catlin was the only student of Indians to witness this strange, wild ceremony, and when he published his account, buttressed by abundant testimonials, his veracity was challenged in Henry Rowe Schoolcraft's six-volume official account of the North American Indian tribes. This challenge became part of the official record that plagued Catlin for the rest of his life. All that he had recounted in picture and print was true. Indeed, his detailed account of the Mandans, together with that of Prince Maximilian, are the primary record of the life and customs of that almost vanished tribe.

In 1835, Catlin accompanied a contingent of U.S. dragoons on a reconnaissance across the southern prairies to Comanche country in the Wichita Mountains of what is now extreme southwestern Oklahoma. Despite the fact that he was deathly ill with a fever that killed nearly half the dragoons, including their commander, Colonel Henry Leavenworth, Catlin carried on and survived. He survived to learn the secret of the source of the plains Indians' ubiquitous red pipestone—a closely guarded mystery. He was taken by the Indians to the pipestone quarry in western Minnesota in 1836. Today the distinctive red pipestone is known as Catlinite. By the time he took his Indian gallery to London, Catlin could sum up his considerable achievements. In his monumental work *Letters and Notes on the Manners, Customs, and Conditions of the North American Indians*, he proudly declared:

I have visited forty-eight different tribes, the greater part of which I found speaking different languages, and containing in all 400,000 souls. I have brought home safe, and in good order, 310 portraits in oil, all painted in their villages—their wigwams—their games and religious ceremonies—their dances—their ball plays—their buffalo hunting and other amusements (containing in all over 3000 full length figures); and the landscapes of the country they live in, as well as a very extensive collection of their costumes, and all their other manufacturies from the size of a wigwam down to the size of a quill or a rattle.

Catlin had some interesting theories about the Indians. He was convinced that the Mandans were descendants of Prince Madoc and the Welsh who sailed to America in the twelfth century. Most authorities viewed this as quixotic, but they had to take seriously his argument that except for the Welsh Indians, all the other tribes or linguistic groups were indigenous to North America and very ancient. They were not the result of epigenesis but rather of separate creation.

Catlin did best when he was among the wild and untamed. The civilized white men only brought him misfortune. His Indian Gallery had to be sold for debt in London. His wife and son died in Paris, and he narrowly escaped imprisonment for debt. But undaunted, Catlin started all over again. Encouraged by the great Humboldt himself, he sailed to South America and painted its numerous Indian tribes more extensively than anyone had ever done before. Then he traveled up the coast of California and beyond the Oregon country, incorporating his adventures in still another work, *Last Rambles Amongst the Indians of the Rocky Mountains and the Andes*, published in 1863. Prior to his "last ramble," Catlin, though nearly penniless and living with mice as his only friends in Brussels, recreated his entire Indian Gallery in drawings and paintings made from memory. Today this is called his "cartoon collection." It caused the Secretary of the Smithsonian, Joseph Henry, to call Catlin home and afford him rooms in the sandstone castle on the Mall to complete his work. Of course, so great was Catlin's enthusiasm for the Indian and his culture that his work was not complete when he died in 1872. Catlin's work, profoundly moral in intent, full of the romance of the wild and the primitive, yet as meticulous as he could make it, emerged as more than the product of one of Humboldt's children. If, as Walt Whitman once wrote, "the United States is the best poem," then Catlin's incredible body of work is perhaps its best monument to that unspoiled romantic horizon that lay before us in the mid-nineteenth century.

vi

GEOPOLITICS AND THE GREAT SCIENTIFIC
RECONNAISSANCE

THE TRANS-MISSISSIPPI country was clearly changing about the time that Catlin left for Europe in 1841 and Stewart made his last hunt in 1843. A new kind of explorer had entered the West. In 1842, Lieutenant John C. Frémont of the United States Corps of Topographical Engineers led an expedition to South Pass, the Seedskeedee, and the Wind River Mountains to map the whole area scientifically. And though Frémont was romantic enough to climb the highest peak in the Wind Rivers and unfurl an eagle flag symbolizing America's "Manifest Destiny," he was also reducing exploration to a science. For the next two decades, Frémont and others like him from the Corps of Topographical Engineers brought the hand of government and the skills of science to the exploration of the West. Through the acquisition of knowledge they began to assume control of the West. In so doing, they became servants of a rapidly growing America whose citizens echoed the cry "Westward the course of empire takes its way."

By 1840, Oregon had become a focus of American aspirations. Frémont's mission in 1842 had been to map the South Pass, a key point on the Oregon Trail. But even as he was carrying out that assignment, another expedition had returned to Washington with a report on that remote territory. Captain Charles

Wilkes of the United States Exploring Expedition, a naval enterprise, had made a thorough investigation of the country as part of his great global exploring expedition of the Pacific islands and the Oregon coast. On the Northwest Coast he divided his forces. Wilkes led one group of ships in an exploration of Vancouver Island, the Strait of Juan de Fuca, and Puget Sound. He also examined Gray's Harbor at the base of the Olympic Peninsula. The captain and his men found the beautiful coastline every bit as exotic as the South Pacific. It was a land of fur-caped Indians who danced in hideous transformation masks, sailed their carved fifty-foot-long war canoes far out into the ocean, and studded their villages with mysterious totem poles that harked back in some ways to the pre-Christian villages of the barbarians in the Danube Valley. Wilkes's scientists and ethnographers had a field day on the Northwest Coast.

Wilkes, however, was primarily interested, like so many navigators of the Northwest Coast, in global policy and safe harbors on the Pacific shores, which is why he searched the entire coastline north of the Columbia very carefully. He also sent out extensive inland expeditions: one from Puget Sound south to the Columbia, one up the Columbia past the Dalles or rapids to the Hudson's Bay post at Fort Colvile near the junction of the Snake and the Columbia, and one south through the Willamette Valley to California's San Francisco Bay. The last expedition determined that there were no good harbors south of the Columbia and no great rivers leading into the interior.

Meanwhile Captain Hudson, in charge of the other half of Wilkes's fleet, had come to disaster off the mouth of the Columbia. He lost his flagship, the *Peacock*, to the treacherous currents and sandbars at the mouth of the river. It thus became clear to both Hudson and Wilkes that the Columbia estuary was not safe harbor. The only such harbors lay far north of the Columbia in or around Puget Sound. Thus American diplomatic efforts should be aimed at securing territory at least that far north.

The expansionist Senator Thomas Hart Benton of Missouri

was not unmindful of Wilkes's information. On what he always insisted was his own initiative, he sent his son-in-law, Lieutenant John C. Frémont, on a "secret" mission to Oregon in 1843. When Frémont set out from Independence in 1843, he was part of a cavalcade of would-be settlers heading west over the Oregon Trail. J. B. Chiles's party had departed for California ahead of him, as had Elijah White's caravan bound for Oregon. Sir William Drummond Stewart headed a large entourage bound for one last hunt on the Green River, while William Gilpin was traveling across the mountains with visions of a transcontinental railroad dancing in his head. Frémont's party was guided by the veteran mountain man Tom "Broken Hand" Fitzpatrick, and he was soon joined by two other giants of the fur trade, Kit Carson and Alexis Godey. In an effort to locate a new trail, Frémont marched out along the Kansas rather than the Platte River, crossed over the front range at the head of the Cache la Poudre River, then trekked over the barren Laramie Plain to the Sweetwater and the South Pass. From there he and his men crossed the Wasatch Mountains and gazed upon Great Salt Lake as it lay before them in "still and solitary grandeur." "The Pathfinder" described the Salt Lake Valley in such glowing terms that his report inspired Brigham Young to take his beleaguered Mormons out of Nauvoo, Illinois, and settle in the deserts of Utah.

Then Frémont pushed on, past the British outpost at Fort Hall in Idaho, to the Columbia River, where he paused at the Dalles. He sent a party on to the mouth of the Columbia and thus technically linked up with the Wilkes Expedition, but his mind was really set on turning southward in search of the oft reported Buenaventura River. On November 23, 1843, he did just that. He and his men followed the Des Chutes River and after a few days came out on the northern edge of what Frémont was the first to recognize as the Great Basin. In fact he gave it that name. The rest of his journey took him south along the Sierras, and in the middle of winter, in despair of their lives as they plunged through deep snow in the confusing mountain passes, he and his men crossed over the Sierras above Lake Tahoe. When, frostbitten and exhausted, they finally struggled down from the snowbound peaks, they followed the American River to Johann Sutter's new ranch, which J. B. Chiles's emigrant party had already reached before them over an easier route. In crossing the Sierras and descending the American River, Frémont and his men had, of course, walked right over California's main gold region, which in six years would be crowded with fortune hunters of every description. But the Pathfinder and his men were not exploring for gold. They had Manifest Destiny on their minds, and in particular California's possibilities for agricultural settlement by Americans. On this account Frémont wrote glowing reports about California as a pastoral paradise. He did not, however, locate a Rio Buenaventura or any other easy way of reaching this paradise.

His return march took him across Tehachapi Pass and over the Old Spanish Trail across the Great Basin desert to the site of present-day Las Vegas. There he was joined by Joseph Rutherford Walker, who showed him a shortcut across the Colorado River plateau; then Frémont took his men via the White and Duchesne rivers just below the Uinta Mountains, which straddle the Green River, to the Bayou Salade or great central park of Colorado. This stretch included some of the wildest and least-known parts of the western wilderness.

From the parks of Colorado the return journey was over a familiar route via the Pueblo at the head of the Arkansas River and Bent's Fort on the Arkansas near the junction of the Purgatory River. On his expedition of 1843–44, Frémont had, in effect, circumnavigated the whole West. Clearly he had not really been a pathfinder, but rather a political and scientific explorer. He was searching out the possibilities for an American occupation of the West. With this in mind, and with the substantial aid of Charles Preuss, his Prussian cartographer, he made the first overall map of the West based on relatively accurate astronomical sightings. He also refused to include portions of the West he had not seen, though, in an exception to his rule, he made an error in connecting Great Salt Lake with the freshwater Utah Lake. He did, however, correctly define and label the immense Great Basin for the first time. This was perhaps his greatest geographical achievement. He also followed up his large comprehensive map with an emigrant map drawn in seven sections by Charles Preuss. This became one of the most important of all maps of the Oregon and California trails because it gave precise distances and detailed information on landmarks, river crossings, grazing lands, and Indian tribes. When Frémont submitted his report and maps to Congress, they created a sensation and were reprinted and widely distributed by proponents of continental Manifest Destiny. He was the explorer as propagandist *par excellence*.

Frémont did not rest on these achievements, however. In the spring of 1845, he headed west again, ostensibly to explore the U.S.-Mexican border country at the headwaters of the Arkansas and Red rivers. After journeying to the upper Arkansas, he sent his second-in-command, Lieutenant James W. Abert, down the Canadian River with his report. Then, with a tough crew of seasoned mountain men, he headed west across the mountains and Salt Lake desert to California. Once in California he bid defiance to the Mexican authorities and put his men to the service of the Bear Flag Revolution—the opening gun of the war with Mexico. The geopolitics of Manifest Destiny seem to have fired his imagination and directed his efforts at exploration. Even his scientific and cartographic work seems bent to this end. And it is quite clear that he did succeed more than anyone else in dramatizing the desirability of California's affiliation with the United States. His emigrant map made the road to the Pacific look easy, and his dispatches from California in 1845 declared, "By the route I explored, I can ride in thirty-five days from the Fontaine-qui-Bouille River [just above Bent's Fort on the Arkansas] to Captain Sutter's; and for wagons the road is decidedly better."

For his series of reports, Frémont received a letter of congratulations from none other than Baron von Humboldt himself.

vii

GREAT RECONNAISSANCE

THE WAR with Mexico in 1846 introduced a greatly increased number of Army explorers into the West. Virtually all of these military explorers were commissioned officers in the Corps of Topographical Engineers, commanded by Colonel John James Abert. These men formed an elite corps, for the most part specially trained at West Point (John C. Frémont and Stephen H. Long being conspicuous exceptions) to draw accurate maps and make careful sketches of terrain in which the Army might operate. Some of their most outstanding projects, however, were done in peacetime. Among these were Captain H. H. Humphreys and Lieutenant H. L. Abbott's survey of the physics and hydraulics of the Mississippi River, the Great Lakes Survey, and the Pacific Railroad Surveys of 1853.

In the Mexican War, however, every main element of the invading armies under Generals Taylor, Wool, Kearney, and Scott carried a complement of Topographical Engineers. The most spectacular work to come out of the war was Lieutenant William H. Emory's march with General Stephen Watts Kearny's command to Santa Fe and then west via the Gila River and the Mojave Desert to California. Emory published a detailed report of the march complete with the first accurate map of the Southwest and a series of remarkable illustrations by the artist John Mix Stanley, who, after recently living among the Comanches of Texas, accompanied his expedition. Stanley's illustrations were the first real views of the Far Southwest made by an artist who had actually seen that exotic, beautiful desert country. Emory's *Notes of a Military Reconnaissance from Fort Leavenworth in Missouri to San Diego in California, including Parts of the Arkansas, Del Norte, and Gila Rivers* (1848) is a classic of western exploration. In it he made two observations that were to have major importance in western and American history. First he observed that much of the Southwest was too arid for individualistic settlement. No enterprise could survive without cooperation in the distribution of water. Secondly he declared, "No one who has ever visited this country and who is acquainted with the character and value of slave labor in the United States would ever think of bringing his slaves here with any view to profit. . . ." The latter, since Emory was a fellow Whig, undoubtedly influenced Daniel Webster's speech on the Compromise of 1850, concerning "the imaginary Negro in an impossible place" in which he spoke out for expansion to the West while denying that slavery could ever prosper in its wake.

Emory, as a result of his vast experience, became perhaps the country's leading expert on the Southwest. Between 1848 and 1855, except for a brief interlude, he supervised the demarcation of the U.S.-Mexican boundary line from Brownsville on the Rio Grande to San Diego on the Pacific. In his work he introduced a new kind of exploration—regional exploration on a vast scale undertaken by teams of surveyor-explorers. The Mexican Boundary Survey was one of the major undertakings of the period. It resulted in a diplomatic crisis over the accuracy of Disturnell's map, upon which the borders of the two countries were actually laid down in the 1848 treaty with Mexico. To resolve the dispute, the United States made the Gadsden Purchase from Mexico—a large slice of what is now southern Arizona—in 1853. The survey required the actual laying down of the astronomically determined boundary upon the earth, a very sophisticated scientific achievement that placed Emory among the first rank of the world's geodesists. And most important, it resulted in a series of maps and a tremendous regional survey of the geology, flora, fauna, archaeology, and Indian tribes, plus an all-important consideration of the proper transcontinental railroad route across the Southwest to the Pacific. Emory was a pathfinder for a new age of locomotion and steam.

The most extensive Army exploration of the period had to do

with this latter subject. In 1853, Secretary of War Jefferson Davis ordered the Topographical Corps into the field to conduct a series of explorations and surveys across the West to determine the most "practicable and economical" location for a transcontinental railroad. Isaac I. Stevens, seconded by Captain George B. McClellan, led a northern survey between the 47th and 49th parallels seeking to connect the Great Lakes with the Pacific Coast. Lieutenant John W. Gunnison led another party out along the 38th parallel below the Uinta Mountains and far south of the Great Salt Lake. Lieutenant Amiel Weeks Whipple traversed the 35th parallel west from Santa Fe. And Lieutenants John G. Parke and John B. Pope worked from each end of a southwestern, or 32nd parallel route. Parke and Lieutenant H. L. Abbott also explored north and south along the Pacific Coast for a route that would link up the coastal ports with whatever railroads might be built. There were also other parties in the field. John C. Frémont, now resigned from the Army, led an expedition along a line close to his march of 1845, and his party almost perished in the deep snows of the southern Rockies. Also the Texas engineer Andrew B. Gray led a state-sponsored expedition out across the Pecos River that he hoped would connect with any line moving west from El Paso del Norte.

Only one great tragedy occurred on the federal railroad surveys. Lieutenant Gunnison and most of his men were massacred by the Ute Indians on the Sevier River in Utah. Lieutenant J. G. Beckwith assumed command and traced out a route from Great Salt Lake across to California. He was aided by Captain Howard Stansbury's careful survey and map of Great Salt Lake in 1849–50. The result of the Pacific Railroad Surveys in practical terms was nil. Each of the expedition leaders proclaimed his route the "most practicable" to the Pacific, which left the whole question deadlocked by sectional politics in Congress. Jefferson Davis clearly favored the southern route in his final report, but factions split the South and would-be eastern railroad terminal cities all up and down the Mississippi. It was not until the summer of 1866 that James T. Evans, working under the command of Colonel Grenville M. Dodge, discovered Lone Tree Pass over the Rocky Mountains, which made the Union Pacific portion of a transcontinental railroad possible. A Republican-Unionist administration under Abraham Lincoln had long since decreed that the route would be a northern one with its eastern terminus at Omaha across the Mississippi from Council Bluffs. As early as 1860, Californians had determined that Donner and Truckee passes were suitable for a railroad over the Sierras heading east.

Throughout the 1840s and 1850s, Army explorers conducted what amounted to a "great reconnaissance" of the American West. In 1849, Lieutenant James Hervey Simpson led the first expedition since the days of the Spaniards into the Navajo stronghold at Canyon de Chelly. High up on the canyon walls he and his men discovered the lost cliff dwellings of the ancient Anasazi culture. In 1851, Captain Lorenzo Sitgreaves trekked across the Southwest just below the Grand Canyon in an early search for a wagon or railroad route. Both Simpson and Sitgreaves were accompanied by the artist Richard Kern, who visualized for the first time the vast Anasazi ruins at Chaco Canyon and Canyon de Chelly. He also recorded the first interior view of the mysterious, closely guarded pueblo kivas and the sacred dances at Zuñi. Six years later, aboard a prefabricated steamboat, Lieutenant Joseph Christmas Ives chugged up the Colorado River to the Grand Canyon at its juncture with Diamond Creek. He and his party were the first white men ever to reach the floor of the canyon. The artists of his party, Heinrich Balduin Möllhausen and F. W. von Egloffstein, were the first men to picture the stupendous canyon, which they did in highly dramatic views. Also along with this party was the geologist John Strong Newberry, who saw the possibilities of such a deep descent into the earth and traced out the first important stratigraphic column in the West. His description of the different layers of earth that he could observe from the canyon floor provided a measuring stick for all future geologists in the West. Ives's report on the expedition was a masterpiece in both literary and scientific terms. Not the least of its contributions, besides Newberry's column, was the first relief map of the West, drawn by the Prussian F. W. von Egloffstein. Hardly had Ives finished his expedition at the Hopi villages at Oraibi and Moenkopi when Captain John N. Macomb, also accompanied by the geologist Newberry, discovered and described the junction of the Green and the Grand rivers in western Colorado, thus fitting a key piece into the puzzle of western geography. Macomb and his men also saw abundant remains of the lost Anasazi civilization as they marched along the San Juan River, though they missed the grandest ruin of them all—Mesa Verde.

Farther north, Lieutenant Simpson crossed the Great Basin once again in search of a railroad route, while Lieutenant Governor Kemble Warren explored the Dakota Badlands and the upper Missouri. In 1859–60, Captain W. F. Raynolds explored the upper Missouri, the Big Horn Basin, and the Wind River Mountains, and marched all around but did not penetrate the Yellowstone Park region. Along with Raynolds were two paleontologists, Fielding Bradford Meek and Ferdinand V. Hayden. Together, and with data from the Warren expeditions as well, they worked out the cretaceous geological horizon of the Dakota country and a stratigraphic column for the upper Missouri region, and discovered great caches of extinct animal bones. When they brought their collections back to Philadelphia they provided Dr. Joseph Leidy with the material for the first accurate book on prehistoric American zoology, *The Ancient Fauna of Nebraska*. Leidy also found the remains of tiny primitive horses among the collections and published a paper showing how the horse had evolved through time. This came out in 1859, just before Charles Darwin published his *On the Origin of Species*. And finally, as if to close out exploration in the continental United States, just on the eve of the Civil War, Lieutenant John G. Parke, working with the Royal Engineers, laid out the last boundary through the northwestern wilderness between the United States and Canada.

All of these expeditions were described in lavishly illustrated reports published by Congress. Taken together they represent the most comprehensive dissemination of scientific information about the West ever undertaken up to that time.

Between 1840 and 1860, Congress published in all some sixty works dealing with the exploration of the West. Many of these were lavishly printed series replete with esoteric reports by scientists who accompanied the expeditions and lithographs illustrating the virtually unknown western landscapes and aboriginal inhabitants. In a period usually decried as parsimonious with regard to the sciences and the arts this represented an incredible federal subsidy to those pursuits, which was critical in the professionalization of science in America and at the same time launched the careers of artists like Edward, Richard, and Benjamin Kern. It also made the mapmaking and printing as well as engraving and lithography industries for the first time independent of Europe. One must also add to these sixty subsidized western ventures in the period fifteen naval expeditions and their reports of activities around the globe, as well as the reports of the very large Coast and Geodetic Survey, the Naval Observatory, Schoolcraft's lavish six-volume *Historical and Statistical Information Respecting the History, Condition, and Prospects of the Indian Tribes of the United States* (1851–57), the reports of the Great Lakes Survey, Humphreys and Abbott's extensive studies of the Mississippi, and the *Annual Reports* of the Patent Office, which reported on scientific agriculture. And when one considers that the annual federal income fluctuated between a low of $8,302,702 in 1843 and $74,056,699 in 1856, this subsidy of the sciences and the arts (exclusive of federal buildings and the Smithsonian) must, at times, have represented perhaps one-quarter to one-third of the federal budget. At no time since in the history of the United States has anything like that ratio been reached.

The capstone of all the reports on Army exploring activity in the Era of the Great Reconnaissance was the extraordinary set of thirteen volumes generated by the Pacific Railroad Surveys.

They represented "an encyclopedia of western experience," and their publication cost amounted to over $1 million alone—almost twice as much as the actual surveys. In addition to the narrative accounts of the individual expeditions, the *Railroad Survey Reports* also included volumes on geology complete with geologic maps of vast regions and volumes on plants, animals, birds, and fishes as well as an ethnographic report that covered most of the Indian tribes of the West. Dozens of artists and scientific illustrators worked to enhance the large quarto volumes, presenting for the first time a comprehensive vision of the West to the public. In scientific terms the *Railroad Survey Reports* dramatically illustrated the advent of specialization and teamwork in the study of a region. In that they were also aimed at determining the possibilities of the whole West for settlement, they represented a very early ecological study, monumental in scope. And finally they represented a cartographic milestone. Each expedition leader had drawn a detailed map of the country he traversed. All these were published in the *Reports*; in addition, Lieutenant G. K. Warren compiled the data from these maps and those of all the other Army expeditions into the first scientifically accurate comprehensive map of the West. After the pioneering work of Lewis and Clark it was perhaps the most important map of the West ever drawn.

The era of Army exploration represented a strange phenomenon in a sense. As Professor Daniel Boorstin has put it, during this period part of the West was "settled before it was explored." But what this meant, of course, was that each age sought different things from the West, and the development of science and technology refined the questions that explorers sought to answer as each decade passed. Dramatically during the era of Army exploration, questions shifted from those of the fur trader and farmer to those of the gold seeker, townbuilder, and railroad entrepreneur as California suddenly filled with 300,000 people and Colorado threatened to do the same in 1859. The fact that the questions shifted and each age produced explorers bent on different missions merely underscores the fact that exploration is a

Lieutenant Gouverneur Kemble Warren, "Map of the Territory of the United States from the Mississippi to the Pacific Ocean, to accompany the Reports of the Explorations for a Railroad Route." 1857. *(The National Archives)* This is the first scientifically based comprehensive map of the American West.

social process of seeking—not necessarily and finally discovering.

viii
HUMBOLDT'S HERITAGE AND THE PARADOX OF PROGRESS

HUMBOLDTIAN science came to a dramatic climax in pre–Civil War America. The emergence of a continental consciousness and the extensive scientific reconnaissance of the American West placed maximum emphasis upon the organization of concepts concerning space. Mapping was the first chore—mapping on a scale more extensive and more complex than any yet attempted in the world up to that time. The making of surface charts at sea was relatively simple compared to mapping the vast and varied terrain of North America with many different purposes in mind. Not only did the scientific explorers outline the West and chart the courses of its many rivers, they also laid down the mountains, deserts, high plains, interior valleys, and incredible complexities of the canyon country of the Southwest, the Dakota Badlands, and the Snake River to the northwest. The Army Topographical Engineers brought the making of landform maps to a high art. But even then their task did not end. Following the principles of Humboldt, they stressed the correlation between landforms and ecology and between landforms and some of the deeper secrets of the earth, such as the lines of terrestrial magnetism as they emanated from the poles. Weather, soil types, vegetation, and characteristic forms of animal life were either incorporated into the maps or directly related to them in the engineer-explorers' reports. In one striking imitation of Humboldtian technique, J. M. Bigelow fashioned a cross-sectional chart or diagram graphically showing the relationship of plant growth, particularly trees, to altitude, from the plains to the mountaintops. Humboldt had done just such a thing for the Andes, though with less precision. In addition, the mapmaker-explorers also recorded, in a fashion similar to Lewis and Clark's carrying out of Jefferson's instructions, the location and extent of the Indian tribal domains as well as evidences of the archaeological remains of ancient civilizations. The data from the early western expeditions had resulted in Albert Gallatin's first important ethnological map of the continent, published in the *Transactions* of the American Antiquarian Society in 1836. Gallatin's map accompanied his ambitious work "A Synopsis of the Indian Tribes of North America," which, though it included extensive material on linguistics, was basically organized geographically. Some of Gallatin's data was derived from Jefferson's early studies, but much more of it came from mountain men like Jedediah Smith, whose route of 1826–27 first appears on this map, and the data accumulated by Governor William Clark from fur hunters as they passed through his headquarters in St. Louis. By the end of the Great Reconnaissance period, the huge blank spaces to the Far West and Southwest in Gallatin's map had nearly all been filled in. Knowledge of the location, habits, and languages of the red man had grown exponentially, though relative to later researches it was still at a rudimentary stage.

Beyond mapping and correlating the phenomena visible on the earth's surface, however, the Great Reconnaissance explorers also traced geological formations over immense distances in the West. The Pacific Railroad Surveys alone produced three such maps. One was by the Swiss geologist Jules Marcou and one by the Yale geologist W. P. Blake, both of whom had gone on the western expeditions. A third geological map was drawn by James Hall, of Albany, New York, the doyen of American geologists in the period. The maps differed markedly and caused bitter controversy among the three geologists, with Marcou getting the worst of it because he was a foreigner and nationalism was running at high tide, even in science, during the heady period of Manifest Destiny. But in fact all three geological maps were rash, premature, grandiose conjectures about one of the most complex geological situations in the world. Despite the stratigraphic work of Newberry in and above the Grand Canyon and the subtle examination of the cretaceous horizon in the Dakotas and Montana by Hayden and Meek, the three major geological maps of the West in the period were woefully inadequate guesses about the spatial extentions of subterranean formations. The sense of time and geological sequences that made James Hall's earlier classic, *The Paleontology of New York State*, a landmark in American geology was relatively absent in his conjectures about the western extent of geological formations. This was to be the glory of the great post–Civil War geological surveys of the American West that gave the United States world predominance in that science.

The comprehensive survey of a vast region was characteristic of Humboldt's approach to the study of the earth, and he went out of his way to particularly applaud the Pacific Railroad Surveys and especially the work of Frémont, who responded by naming rivers, mountain chains, and even deserts after him. All American earth scientists were eager for Humboldt's approbation, not only because of his mighty labors and his colossal preeminence in science, but also because he seemed to grasp the profound unity in nature—to be master of some overarching, transcendent, romantic secret about the whole earth and the cosmos that seemed to give a final meaning and direction to those efforts that began in the eighteenth century to know the mind of God through knowledge of His every manifestation in nature. The scientist and the religious leader alike could agree on this point—often in the period they were one and the same person. Endless empirical observation, classification, relation, and correlation in maps, reports, drawings, and catalogues would yield, so the men of the time believed, "the thoughts of the Creator," as the great Harvard naturalist Louis Agassiz put it. As such, among "Humboldt's children," scientific exploration took on a religious or at least post-Kantian romantic dimension. As Arnold Guyot, the author of *The Earth and Man*, put it, "a science of the globe which excludes the spirit world, is a beautiful body without a soul." These sentiments were echoed by Captain James Hervey Simpson away out west in central Utah as in the midst of his survey of a mountain range he paused to write in his notebook that "these distant views have, at least to my mind, a decidedly moral and religious effect. . . ."

Humboldtian science was thus the science of space, but in its potential completeness it was also the science of the romantic and the sublime. It fit an age where everything came to have a symbolic meaning to the religious, the philosophical, and the learned and even to many of the common people, who were continually caught up in religious revivals and the spawning of mysterious new fads and religions, of which Mormonism became the great exemplar. And yet, because Humboldtian science focused on space, on the exquisite beauty of the harmonious universe from the macrocosm to the microcosm, it tended to ignore a new reality that was fast dawning upon the nineteenth century—the dimension of time. Great as he was, Humboldt was nonetheless limited in his perspective. His geography proved to be a mighty intellectual tool for relating the multitudinous facts of nature as explorers and scientists were discovering them all over the globe, but it was fundamentally descriptive and static. Unlike the earlier concept of the Great Chain of Being, Humboldt's system was infinitely expandable, in theory at least. New facts could be continuously worked into the system, and even if they multiplied so rapidly as to outrun the immense synthesizing powers of Humboldt himself, no matter, because, as the Pacific Railroad Surveys demonstrated, *teams* of scientist-explorers could work together and integrate the new data faster and more efficiently. Indeed, the whole global exploring enterprise of the period did as much to make possible the professionalization of science as all the academies and universities in the western world, if not more. In providing employment for teams and legions of would-be scientific men who gathered the world's data at an ever-increasing rate, the scientific exploring expeditions of the Second Great Age of Discovery, especially those in the American West, professionalized science. They turned the amateur naturalist into the recognized man of science whose full-time job was collecting and organizing and understanding the secrets of nature and sometimes God. It is no accident that as religions became disestablished state by state in America during the 1820s, many ministers, without guaranteed state support, turned to science and either became professionals in the field, like the Rev. Edward Hitchcock, head of the Massachusetts Geological Survey, or at least earned professional respect in the fast-growing scientific community.

But it was the static and quasi-religious quality of Humboldtian science that appealed as much as anything to the philosophically and theologically minded of Romantic America. Trained, either formally or informally, in the same Scottish Enlightenment tradition that had produced Thomas Jefferson, American thinkers of the emergent Romantic Age believed fundamentally in the ordered harmonious world of Newton and in the existence of laws governing everything in nature. Humboldt, himself a product of the Enlightenment, simply enlarged their vision, gave it mathematical precision, but also mystery and meaning and a sublime profundity. On a much larger scale he echoed the cosmos of Emerson's *Nature*, in which one, perceiving the utility, beauty, and fundamental discipline of nature, is immediately made aware of its spiritual content. Moreover, in striving for completeness of knowledge of the cosmos, Humboldt struck a familiar chord in the minds of Emerson's followers. "Nothing is quite beautiful alone; nothing but is beautiful in the whole," declared Emerson. He, like most American romantics, wished to see nature as one vision of wholeness or completeness. As a towering figure in world science, Humboldt seemed to prove that this could be done—proved it even to the most empirical, Baconian-minded thinker as well as to the transcendental and romantic thinker. But to all of them nature never really changed. Humboldtian science implied a vast continuous present. It was a world museum filled full of exotic specimens each related, but also with an intense quality that stamped itself vividly on the mind, especially of the explorer who discovered it for the first time. These exotic images were translated into best-selling travelers' accounts and explorers' narratives, vivid lithographs of faraway sublime landscapes, hand-painted bird and animal books, mass-distributed views of previously unknown cultures and peoples, of lost cities with strange architectural configurations in jungles or atop sky-high mesas way out west over a limitless horizon. Whether through mass media or in direct confrontation with George Catlin's countless paintings and Indian wild West show, Americans in this period suddenly found themselves immersed in the vivid, vast, exotic eclecticism that was the continuous present of the Humboldtian world museum. Exploration and science shaped American taste and lifestyles at every level of society.

And yet, while for the philosophically minded and the American connoisseurs in the world museum everything stood still in a single moment of awesome beauty, for other Americans scientific exploration meant progress and change. The Pacific Railroad Surveys were sent west, after all, to bring about practical change. They were aimed at locating transportation routes over which emigrants could move into and settle and populate the West. They were aimed at locating exploitable resources— particularly mineral resources after the great California gold strike of 1848. To a practical-minded Congress, maps were simply guides to silver mountains, immense tracts of homesteading land, timber and water resources, or at least caravan and transportation routes leading to the Pacific Coast and the infinite potential of the China trade.

From the 1820s onward, while the United States was acquiring a "continental consciousness," virtually every state began mounting a geological or "natural history" survey aimed at locating and assessing natural resources that could be exploited. In 1823, for example, Denison Olmsted, a Yale graduate, made a geologial and mineralogical survey of North Carolina, following up on rumored gold strikes in that state. His report and map located gold and other mineral deposits of real value. It was the first such state report of its kind and became a model for others.

The most extensive of the state surveys was that of New York. This project began when Stephen Van Rensselaer, impressed by Amos Eaton's determination of rock strata along the cuts for the Erie Canal, commissioned him to survey his own holdings for possible coal-bearing formations. Soon the people of the state, feeling that such special knowledge should not be the privilege of a rich man only, authorized through the legislature a New York State Natural History Survey. The state was divided up into four regions and thoroughly examined by independent teams of naturalists and geologists. So extensive were their operations that the New York Survey, which lasted from 1836 to 1843, became a training ground for a whole generation of geologists and naturalists just as the Erie Canal had been a nursery for self-taught engineers.

Meanwhile, out west, more and more prospecting expeditions were mounted. Attracted by the discovery of rich lead deposits in Missouri, young Henry Rowe Schoolcraft, soon to be one of America's most famous ethnologists, made an extensive trip through the Missouri and Arkansas mineral region in 1817–18. His first published work, *A View of the Lead Mines of Missouri* (1819), attracted great attention and started a mineral rush to the region. One of those who sought his fortune in Missouri mines was Moses Austin of Durham, Connecticut, who later shifted his vision to Texas.

The possibility of immense resources occupied not only the attention of the people of Missouri but the federal government as well. In 1824 the commissioner of the General Land Office dispatched David Dale Owen, son of the famous Utopian socialist Robert Dale Owen, to the western regions adjoining Missouri. In one season, using 139 assistants, he surveyed eleven thousand square miles in Wisconsin, Iowa, and Illinois and concluded that "the district surveyed is one of the richest mineral regions, compared to extent, yet known in the world." Later Owen, in company with Senator Lewis Cass, made an extensive survey of Michigan that located its rich copper deposits, putting it on the way to becoming a seat of industry in the West.

When he sent the geologist George W. Featherstonehaugh west to explore the Ozark Mountains in 1834, Colonel John

James Abert, chief of the Topographical Engineer Corps, caught perfectly the tensions that governed American exploration and scientific endeavor during the period. He informed Congress:

> It is not merely questions of abstract science which are involved in his [Featherstonehaugh's] observations; it is not merely the additional light which will be thrown by his researchers upon various subjects which now agitate and occupy the learned of the world, which are to give interest to this duty . . . but it is the development of immense and hitherto unknown sources of wealth and active inland trade, the exposing of various deposits of coal, iron, lead and the precious metals, and the encouragement of these who will furnish to industry the profitable employment of capital.

It was the age of Humboldt; it was also the age of Jacksonian expectant capitalism. Exploration and science had to serve two ends in America. Results from far-flung expeditions into the wilderness frontier, in the view of the emerging cadre of professional scientists, had to make significant contributions to the world's body of knowledge, whose outlines had already been determined by Humboldt and other European savants. On the other hand, expectant capitalists and the legislatures which supplied the funds for expeditions saw them purely as instruments for practical material progress. There was nothing "transcendent" about them unless one viewed unrestrained capitalism, as some did, with something approaching religious awe.

While Governor John Floyd of Virginia pointed to the "great wealth that lies buried in the earth" and called for men of science "to bring before this country and make known its value and usefulness to capitalists," Senator Weller of California was even more impatient. His constituents could find the gold, but urgently needed wagon roads and railroads to bring it out of the hills. The elite military scientific corps would not do. Instead what was needed were "practical men . . . who instead of taking instruments to ascertain the altitude of mountains take their shovels and spades and go to work . . . while an engineer, perhaps, is surveying the altitude of a neighboring hill."

Thus, for Americans exploration had begun to be a paradoxical if not ambiguous experience. It led to imperial ambitions and a headlong rush to exploit the resources of the continent as fast as they could be discovered. In many cases measured, careful scientific expeditions were outrun by prospectors and land-hungry farmers. At the same time, almost from the beginning of the rush across the continent, other men began to pause and consider the consequences. James Fenimore Cooper, for example, devoted his Leatherstocking series to a consideration of these consequences. Civilized America had a mission to move forward into the wilderness, led by pathfinders like Leatherstocking, but in so doing it inevitably destroyed the pristine beauty of America's nature which was its greatest spiritual resource. Any number of nineteenth-century spokesmen echoed these sentiments to the extent of being skeptical of science itself, not to mention the value of progress. Perhaps the most eloquent of these was the painter-explorer George Catlin. Speaking on behalf of the fast-vanishing Indian, he movingly declared:

> I have viewed man in the innocent simplicity of nature . . . and I have seen as often the approach of the bustling, busy, talking, elated, and exultant white man, with the first clip of the plough share, making sacrilegious trespass on the bones of the dead. . . . I have seen the grand and irresistible march of civilization . . . this splendid juggernaut rolling on and beheld its sweeping desolation.

All he could do was record the demise of the Indian in thousands of drawings and paintings and register feeble protests to the government in Washington.

Humboldt and his children in America, as in Europe, had opened up a world to science and human knowledge, but often they did not foresee the consequences. To them it was a grand, romantic adventure in discovery in a world that they assumed would essentially remain the same—forever exotic, forever mysterious, forever symbolic of transcendent spirit. Science itself was neutral, since it was essentially only an inquiry into the im-

mediate nature of reality. Humboldtian scientist-explorers in
the main put their emphasis on description and classification for
its own sake. Essentially they were adventurers and connoisseurs and metaphysicians. As such they helped to raise standards and professionalize science. Humboldt's children in
America, imbued with a strong nationalistic spirit, soon imitated
their European counterparts and moved out into the world museum carrying their scientific mission beyond North America's
shores literally to the ends of the earth. They created an atmosphere out of which emerged the greatest naturalist-explorer of
the age, Charles Darwin, who in turn rendered Humboldtian
science obsolete.

ix

PAINTER OF HUMBOLDTIAN GRANDEUR

THE AMERICAN who most epitomized these Humboldtian visions at midcentury was Frederick Edwin Church of Hartford,
Connecticut. A pupil of Thomas Cole, whose Hudson River
paintings were an anthem to the American landscape, Church
carried his own vision far beyond Cole's. His true mentor was
Alexander von Humboldt. In his library one could find virtually
all of the great Prussian's works—*Aspects of Nature, Views of
Nature*, the *Personal Narrative*, and *Cosmos*—and he took to
heart Humboldt's call for a painter who would capture with "a
new and hitherto unknown brilliancy" the incredible views that
he had witnessed in the Andes and the Tropics. In 1853, Church
set out for the remotest reaches of South America, intent upon
following in the great explorer's footsteps with pencil and brush.
He was accompanied by a friend from the newly created
American Geographical and Statistical Society of New York,
Cyrus W. Field, who in a few short years would be engaged in
laying the great Atlantic telegraph cable. They arrived at the
mouth of the Magdalena River in Colombia at the end of April
1853 and traveled up that river to its head of navigation. Then

they made their way over the mountains to Bogotá. Following in the footsteps of Humboldt and La Condamine, they passed through Colombia and on to Quito in Ecuador, where at last they could see the two mighty mountains celebrated by Humboldt—towering Chimborazo and the volcanic, spuming Cotopaxi. From this initial trip Church painted *The Cordilleras* and *The Andes of Ecuador*—the first of what one critic has called Church's vast "earthscapes." *The Andes of Ecuador* represented a fifty-mile vista that captured the whole natural ensemble of a continent from the contours of its Cordilleran spine to the tiniest details of the leafy vegetation of its tropics. It was a pictorial version of Humboldt's *Cosmos*, an "epic of the Tropics."

In 1857, now also influenced by the spirituality of John Ruskin, Church returned directly to Ecuador to sketch Chimborazo and Cotopaxi. In point of fact, he spent more time making sketch after sketch of the "black, rugged peaks" of Sangay as it was alternately covered by fleecy white clouds and then columns of smoke from its eruptions. Given the Huttonian geology of the time, in which the earth was pictured as being the product of gradual cooling of a molten ball of lava and concomitant thunderous volcanic eruptions, Church must have thought himself at the dawn of creation even more than those artists who studied the Ur men far up the Missouri. The result of Church's second excursion to South America was two more "earthscape" masterpieces, *The Heart of the Andes* and *Cotopaxi*. Again, they were vast brilliant panoramas that seemed to capture the very beginnings of the earth itself and to include even the minutest details of this fact. *Cotopaxi* was especially dramatic with its portrayal of a volcano in eruption and its alternate vision of the dark and light side of nature's grandeur. The American public as well as the critics were fascinated with his works, and thousands stood in line to pay for a glimpse of the mighty canvases. In 1864, Church's *Heart of the Andes* was exhibited along with Albert Bierstadt's *Heart of the Rockies* to raise money for the Civil War Sanitary Commission. Many in the viewing audience saw it as a contest between the natural grandeur of the United States and that of South America, but that was not precisely the point. Both paintings represented a kind of capstone to the idea of Manifest Destiny. Even to its remotest recesses and places of secret grandeur, the whole hemisphere was ours. The intense symbolic meaning in both pictures, painted by American explorers who had been there, was not only convincing of this fact, but overwhelming evidence that thanks to the Almighty the power of the Americans knew no limits. Church and Bierstadt had penetrated to the hearts of both continents and figuratively captured them.

But Church was imbued with the spirit of modern science as well as the role of the explorer. He avidly read Lieutenant Matthew Fontaine Maury's important work, *The Physical Geography of the Sea*, and he realized there was a new domain to conquer. At the top of the world, Maury had written, was an "open polar sea" that generated the warm currents that sent the mammoth icebergs floating down like gigantic crystal palaces into the Atlantic. This seemed to be confirmed by the vivid account of Dr. Elisha Kent Kane, who spent two years, 1853–55, frozen in the Arctic looking for the remains of the lost British explorer Sir John Franklin, and by the writing as well as the conversations of his friend Dr. Isaac Hayes. The doctor had lost his foot to gangrene on Kane's expedition, but he longed to mount another to search out that last of the earth's secrets—the open polar sea. In the summer of 1859, just as Hayes was mounting his expedition north, Church and a clergyman friend, Louis Le Grande Noble, sailed for Newfoundland. Church had decided to paint the mighty iceberg that symbolized the last of nature's secrets. The result of his trip was *The Iceberg* (1861), one of his greatest masterpieces, which did indeed reveal a mighty iceberg from the perspective of an interior lagoon that seemed almost warm and tropical while surrounded with mountains of ice shining in the sun. Here symbolically was the "open polar sea" at the ends of the earth. And as he shipped the painting to England, Church added the wreckage of a ship's mast in the foreground as a symbolic, cruciform memorial to the lost

Arctic explorer Sir John Franklin and to all of mankind who might be present at this cradle of death and regeneration.

Thus Church, in some ways, was the most spiritual of Humboldt's children. He added the religious sublime to the romantic visions that shined before Americans at midcentury. In his activities as an explorer and as a painter, Church also symbolized the growing American interest in the whole globe, including the oceans as well as the continents. The spirit of Manifest Destiny did not stop at the water's edge on this or any other continent. It traveled with Americans for most of the nineteenth century as they explored the great oceans and frozen wastes of the world from pole to pole.

PORTFOLIO I

New Lands

ONE OF the important characteristics of the Second Great Age of Discovery was the addition of artists as well as naturalists on exploring expeditions. The role of the artist was to document the appearance of new lands, new peoples and even lost cities for scientists back home and for the general public. The result of the artists' excursions over vast oceans and uncharted continents was the creation of a whole new focus in art and even in science. The fixed categories of Aristotelean science were abandoned with the profusion of new data, but likewise so, too, were the traditional subjects commonly painted by artists. Though still to a certain extent "programmed" by European artistic conventions, the expedition artists presented a whole new horizon of subject matter. Like the emergent eighteenth-century scientist, the artist focused on an empirical understanding of nature as "a world out there," instead of employing internalized Platonic conventions as a way of seeing. Because their mission was to document, they perforce began to render copies of nature. As Barbara Stafford has recently noted, the artist John Constable argued that "the painting of natural phenomena might legitimately be regarded as experimental science." Constable declared that the artist was involved with "a constant process of learning through close observation of the phenomena in nature." This was the mission of expedition artists, and to the extent that they opened European and American eyes to a wider subject matter, even to the possibilities inherent in landscape paintings, as opposed to the then fashionable history painting that featured scenes from ancient classical times or Christian icons featured in Renaissance art, they created a revolution in art. They went beyond mere transfer of natural scenes onto paper and canvas. They often substituted nature for God, or dramatically represented God in nature. His "spirit was made flesh" or reified in mountains and prairies, rivers and oceans. Nature, however accurately portrayed, became a symbol for something transcendental and sublime. Artistic spokesmen from Edmund Burke to John Ruskin realized this, and articulated it in lectures and books. In addition, men of science—like Humboldt and Agassiz, two giants of the age, saw nature in symbolic terms. As Emerson put it in his most important work, "nature is the symbol of spirit." Thus, more than any other artistic productions, expedition art formed a main current in the Romantic Movement. It was created in the interests of science, but it was infused with new emotions of wonder and awe at the handiwork of the Supreme Artificer. Beaglehole was certainly correct when he wrote of Samuel Wallis on first landing at Tahiti in 1786:

> Wallis had not merely come to a convenient port of call. He had stumbled on a foundation stone of the Romantic Movement. Not as a continent, not as vast distances, was the ocean henceforth thought to be known. The unreal was to mingle with the real, the too dramatic with the undramatic; the shining light was to become a haze in which every island was the one island, and the one island a Tahitian dream.

Art, as well as science, entered a new age of discovery. The whole world had become an inspiration.

The ocean-spanning voyages, the exploration of tropic isles where cannibals dwelt, the trek across continents like North America with its great West, and the penetration of the weirdly beautiful polar regions was also a grand adventure for artists. As Barbara Novak has put it, "The artist became a hero of his own journey." His own struggle with nature altered his way of seeing it and "replaced the heroic themes of mythology." Thus, the environment itself became an actor in the artist's heroic drama of the self. Against all odds he would overcome natural obstacles, unimaginable dangers, and capture nature—wondrous, but also dangerous, nature—on his canvas. Expedition art, therefore, whether of landscapes or of peoples, or even animals and fishes, was in every sense an art of adventure. Despite its scientific intent, it was an art infused with emotion—perhaps even more than reason. And this sense of emotion—grand, sublime, even terrifying—can be seen in all the artistic productions from the work of Sydney Parkinson and William Hodges on Captain James Cook's first expeditions in the late eighteenth century, to the works of the mammoth camera photographers of the Great West in the latter days of the nineteenth century. The very adventure involved in observing and capturing the far away and the exotic in a work of art—or for that matter in any scientific experiment, as Werner Heisenberg has told us—invariably incorporates the feelings of the observer in the results of his work. This was never more true than in the science and art of the Second Great Age of Discovery, where nature became the awesome face of God.

i

LANDSCAPE OF ADVENTURE

CAPTAIN COOK and Sir Joseph Banks set the precedent in 1768 when they took artists Sydney Parkinson and Alexander Buchan along on the voyage to Tahiti to observe the transit of Venus across the sun. The most famous of Cook's artists, however, was William Hodges, who accompanied the great navigator on his epic second voyage to the Pacific and the polar regions from 1772–75.

Hodges, who was one of the first to experiment with capturing true atmospheric effects on canvas, produced the very archetype of the exotic when he painted Tahiti bathed in a clear glow of romantic light. The day was always bright in Hodges's Tahiti, and the water, "soft and caressing" as it met the towering green mountains. Perhaps Hodges had already fashioned this point of view before his voyage with Cook. From June 1764 to November 1766, he accompanied an expedition to the sunny isles of Greece and Asia Minor, sponsored by the Society of Dilettanti, and led by the antiquary Richard Chandler.

The following two paintings by Hodges are suffused with the tranquillity he associated with Tahiti. In effect, he is creating the Tahitian dreamscape. Yet in these works he managed to fashion the exotic through the use of color, light, and, in the first instances, the portrayal of strange native craft. The composition of the pictures, however, followed the time-honored principles of Claude Lorrain. Both pictures are committed to a balanced composition with diagonals leading the eye to the mountains in the background. *The* Resolution *and* Adventure *in Metavai Bay* concentrates on the ships from Europe contrasted with the Tahitian vessels, with Cook's ships being the focal point of the picture. In *Tahiti Revisited*, Hodges includes a classical Renaissance bather in the right foreground suggesting that he was not entirely quits with artistic convention.

William Hodges, "The *Resolution* and *Adventure* in Matavai Bay, Tahiti." 1776. Oil on canvas. *(National Maritime Museum, London)*

198

William Hodges, "Tahiti Revisited." 1776. Oil on canvas. *(National Maritime Museum, London. On loan from Ministry of Defense—Navy)*

HUMBOLDT AND HIS FOLLOWERS

WHILE EXPLORING South America, Humboldt called for artists to follow him in depicting the grand ensemble that was nature. His own no-frills work suggested the majesty of the sights he had seen. Mount Chimborazo, then thought to be the highest mountain in the world, stands out boldly against the high Andean plain. In a second picture, Humboldt manages even more drama by making a diagram featuring the distribution of plants according to altitude, as well as the atmospheric conditions surrounding the volcanic mountain. Humboldt thought of this as scientific art.

Alexander von Humboldt, "Chimborazo." Aquatint. From *Vue des Cordilleras.*
(Harry Ransom Humanities Research Center, University of Texas, Austin)

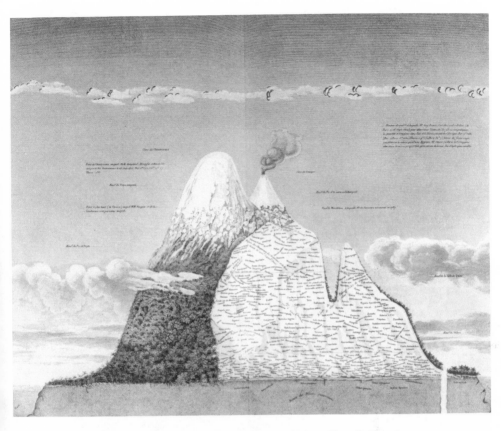

Alexander von Humboldt, "Chimborazo and Plant Chart." Aquatint.
From *Essai sur la Géographie des Plantes*
(Paris, 1805; reprint. New York: DaCapo Press, 1973, frontispiece).
(Harry Ransom Humanities Research Center, University of Texas, Austin)

Frederick Church, "Cotopaxi." 1862. Oil on canvas. *(Detroit Institute of Arts)*

In 1853 and again in 1857 the American artist Frederick Church journeyed to South America, following Humboldt's routes. With pictures like
this, Church, the most famous American painter of his day, embodied
Humboldt's geographical philosophy. Church painted a huge, very dramatic and colorful earthscape, featuring a gigantic smoking volcano that
yet had every detail of plant, leaf, even the minuscule birds perfectly
painted in the picture. He captured both the macrocosm and the microcosm in this fusion of science and art.

Titian Ramsay Peale, "West Crater 'Kaluea Pele' from the 'Black Ledge,'
November 22, 1840." Oil on canvas. *(American Museum of Natural History)*

The outer caldron wall, inner ledge, and main "fire pit" Halemaumau are
well illustrated. *(Department Library Services, American Museum of Natural
History)* From Herman J. Viola and Carolyn Margolis, *Magnificent
Voyagers*.

Even before Church became fascinated with volcanoes, Captain Charles
Wilkes and the scientists of the Great United States Exploring Expedition, particularly James Dwight Dana of Yale, made a thorough study of
them. Here, in a painting by Titian Peale, Wilkes and his men are seen
down in the crater of Hawaii's Kaluea Pele.

George Catlin, "A Fight with Peccaries. Rio Trombutas." Oil on canvas. The author and a Carib Indian are coming to the rescue of Smythe, who is treed, and his powder expended. *(National Gallery of Art)*

In 1852, the famous painter of Indians, George Catlin, made the first of three journeys to South America. After his first journey, made in search of gold, Catlin met and fell under the spell of Humboldt. In his second and third journeys, Catlin concentrated on portraying *all* of the natives of the western hemisphere, as well as specimen pictures of the environment. In this picture Catlin is coming to the rescue of his friend Smythe, who is besieged by an army of angry peccaries deep in a forest of northern South America.

WONDERS AT THE BOTTOM OF THE WORLD

THE ANTARCTIC fascinated explorers first as a myth, then as fact, after its discovery by the Stonington, Connecticut, sealer, Nathaniel Palmer. In a few years' time, American and British sealers decimated the seal population on the islands off Antarctica. This illustration by Captain Edmund Fanning shows the sealers in action.

Edmund Fanning, "View of a Seal Rookery at Beaucheene Island, South Seas." Lithograph. From Fanning, *Voyages Round the World Between the Years 1792–1832.* (*The Peabody Museum of Salem*)

Captain Charles Wilkes, "U.S.S. *Vincennes* in Disappointment Bay."
Oil on canvas. *(The Peabody Museum of Salem)*

Captain Wilkes, whose expedition proved the frozen wastes of Antarctica constituted a continent, painted this majestic picture of his flagship standing off the southern continent.

Wilkes also painted this more informal view of himself and crew on an "ice island" off Antarctica. Wilkes is in the left foreground sliding down the ice, while his dog Sydney looks on approvingly. This is the only recorded instance where Wilkes seemed to have had a sense of humor.

Titian Ramsay Peale, "The *Vincennes* anchored near an 'ice island' in Antarctica."
Oil on canvas. From a sketch by Captain Charles Wilkes.
One of the few depicting the seamen of the Exploring Expedition.
The dog is Sydney, a pet Wilkes obtained while in Australia.
(Yale Western Americana Collection, Beinecke Rare Book Library, Yale University)

THE ARCTIC seemed grand and terrifying to explorer-artists. In 1853 and 1854, Dr. Elisha Kent Kane tried to reach what was believed to be an open polar sea beyond the ice barrier in the Kennedy Channel between Baffin Island and Greenland. His ship was caught in the ice. As a result, Dr. Kane spent two winters marooned in the Arctic. This does not seem to have affected his eye for its weird beauty, as his drawings for these engravings indicate. The first shows his ship entrapped in the ice. The second is a very important picture showing Kane's crewman William Morton gazing out upon the legendary "open" polar sea.

Kane's second-in-command, Dr. Isaac Hayes, despite losing a foot on the first expedition in 1853–55, tried again to push through to the polar sea. As the illustration on top of page 208 indicates, he had a stirring adventure.

Elisha Kent Kane, "The Nip off Cape Cornelius Grinnell, Force Bay." Steel engraving. From Kane, *Arctic Explorer*, vol. 1.
(William H. Goetzmann Collection)

Elisha Kent Kane, "The Open Water from Cape Jefferson." Steel engraving.
From Kane, *Arctic Explorations*, 1853, 1854, 1855 (published 1856), vol. 1.
(William H. Goetzmann Collection)

Isaac Hayes, "Adrift on an Ice Raft." Woodcut.
From *An Arctic Boat Journey* 1860.

Frederick Church, "Aurora Borealis." 1865. Oil on canvas. *(National Museum of American Art, Smithsonian Institution. Gift of Eleanor Blodgett)*

Frederick Church, who had only cruised among icebergs off Newfoundland, portrayed the Far North as an eerie, almost religious adventure lit by the lights of God.

Alfred T. Agate, untitled oil depicting the *Flying Fish* in heavy seas off the coast of Antarctica. *(Alfred T. Agate Collection, Naval Historical Foundation)*

Alfred T. Agate, one of the artists on the Wilkes Expedition, painted nearly 150 scenes. Here he records the drama of the small schooner, *Flying Fish*, amid heavy seas off the coast of the Antarctic.

William Heine, "The Mississippi in a Typhoon." Lithograph. From Francis L.
Hawks, *Narrative of the Expedition of an American Squadron to the China Seas and
Japan . . . under the Command of Commodore M. C. Perry, United States Navy*
(New York, 1851) *(Perry Castañeda Library, The University of Texas)*

By 1853 the ships were bigger and steam-powered side-wheelers, but the
sea was still a frightening environment. This is Commodore Matthew
Calbraith Perry's flagship caught in a typhoon in the China Sea. The artist, Heine, was undoubtedly on the ship, not gazing from a distance.

HUNTING IN TWO ENVIRONMENTS

THESE TWO pictures show man and beast struggling to survive from "Greenland's Icy Mountains to Africa's Sunny Clime."

Elisha Kent Kane, "Walrus Hunt off Pihantlik." Engraving. From Kane,
Arctic Explorations. 1853, 1854, 1855, vol. 2.
(William H. Goetzmann Collection)

Paul Du Chaillu, "Elephant-Battle Among the Fans." Woodcut.
From Paul Du Chaillu, *Explorations and Adventures in Equatorial Africa.*
(William H. Goetzmann Collection)

THE AMERICAN WEST

IN THE NINETEENTH century, the American West seemed just as exotic and exciting as the South Seas and the polar regions. In part this was because of its Indian inhabitants. But also, the vast horizons, the endless rivers, the mountains, and the stupendous canyons struck the explorer artists with awe, from George Catlin in 1832 to Thomas Moran in 1872. Sometimes this awe was touched with thoughts of home and mother, as well as of God.

George Catlin, "Big Bend on the Upper Missouri above St. Louis."
Oil on canvas. *(Gilcrease Institute, Tulsa, Oklahoma)*

Karl Bodmer, "Rock Formations on the Upper Missouri." Watercolor on paper.
(The InterNorth Art Foundation, Joslyn Art Museum, Omaha, Nebraska)

Karl Bodmer, "Mih-Tutta-Hang-Kusch, Mandan Village."
Watercolor on paper. *(Northern Natural Gas Company collection,*
Joslyn Art Museum, Omaha, Nebraska)

Here Mandan Indian women cross the ice from their village in forty-six degrees below zero weather in search of firewood. Karl Bodmer, a young Swiss artist who accompanied Prince Maximilian of Wied Neu Wied on an expedition up the Missouri River in 1833–34, painted the vast wintery horizon of the Dakotas like The Steppes of Russia.

Alfred Jacob Miller, "Lake Scene, Wind River Mountains." Oil on canvas.
(Walters Art Gallery, Baltimore, Maryland)

The archromantic Alfred Jacob Miller liked to paint the Wind River Mountains and the high glacial lakes bathed in moonlight.

John Mix Stanley, "Herd of Bison Near Lake Jessie." Lithograph.
From *Pacific Railroad Reports*, 1853.

The artist John Mix Stanley, on one of the Pacific Railroad Surveys of 1853, saw the Dakota prairies as an abundant land of flocks and herds.

Albert Bierstadt, "Dawn at Donner Lake." Oil on canvas.
(InterNorth Foundation, Joslyn Art Museum, Omaha, Nebraska)

The artist Albert Bierstadt painted this view of Donner Pass in California's Sierras. He makes it a pastoral scene, whereas the pass was marked with horror as members of the Donner immigrant party of 1846 perished in its snows after indulging in cannibalism. The pass was also the location of the Central Pacific Railroad, completed before Bierstadt painted this bucolic picture.

Thomas Moran, "The Grand Canyon of the Yellowstone." Oil on canvas. *(National Museum of American Art, Smithsonian Institution. Lent by the U.S. Department of the Interior, National Park Service)*

Moran painted this enormous canvas in 1872–73 and sold it to the United States government. He presents us with an awesome view of what lies beneath the geysers and paint pots of present-day Yellowstone Park.

James McNeill Whistler, "Portrait of the Artist's Mother"
on copper plate illustrating the coast of Boston Bay, November 1854.
*(William A. Stanley, National Ocean and Atmospheric Survey,
Coast Survey No. 2, Anacopa Island, Coast and Geodetic Survey)*

For a few months, from November 1854 to February 1855, James
McNeill Whistler was employed by the U.S. Coast Survey to draw profiles of the shorelines in California. Here while sketching Boston Bay, he
dreamed of home, and made the first recorded sketch of "Portrait of the
Artist's Mother."

In 1873 the photographer William H. Jackson discovered a mountain with
a snowy cross shining on its face. His friend Thomas Moran embellished
on the scene in this woodcut of 1874.

218

Woodcut after Thomas Moran's painting, "Mountain of the Holy Cross."
(William H. Goetzmann Collection)

Heinrich B. Möllhausen, "First View of the Grand Canyon," 1857. Lithograph.
From Möllhausen, *Reisen in die Felsengebirge Nord-Amerikas* (Leipzig, 1860).
(Barker Texas History Center, The University of Texas, Austin)

William H. Holmes, "Grand Canyon from the Foot of Toroweap."
1882. Lithograph. From "Atlas" to Captain Clarence Dutton,
Tertiary History of the Grand Canyon District. (William H. Goetzmann Collection)

William H. Jackson, "Near the Foot of Toroweap." Photograph.
(The National Archives)

A photo taken near the spot depicted by Holmes in the previous picture.

William H. Holmes drew this dramatic picture (OPPOSITE) of the Grand Canyon in 1881 to illustrate the majestic power of erosion. It is perhaps the most accurate picture of the canyon ever drawn, yet it is also composed with drama and awe-inspiring feeling.

DRAMA AT THE CRESTS OF CREATION

William H. Jackson, "Self-Portrait on Ledge at the Top of Yosemite." Photograph. In this self-portrait at the top of Yosemite, William H. Jackson takes a photograph. *(Western History Department, Denver Public Library)*

William H. Jackson, "Harry Yount, Mountain Man and Yellowstone Park Ranger, Poses at Berthoud Pass." Photograph. *(The National Archives)*

In the striking photo below, Eric Hegg portrays gold seekers struggling over Chilkoot Pass above Skagway on their way to the Klondike in 1898.

Eric Hegg, "Above Sheep Camp, Chilkoot Pass, Alaska." Photograph.
(Special Collections Division, University of Washington Libraries)

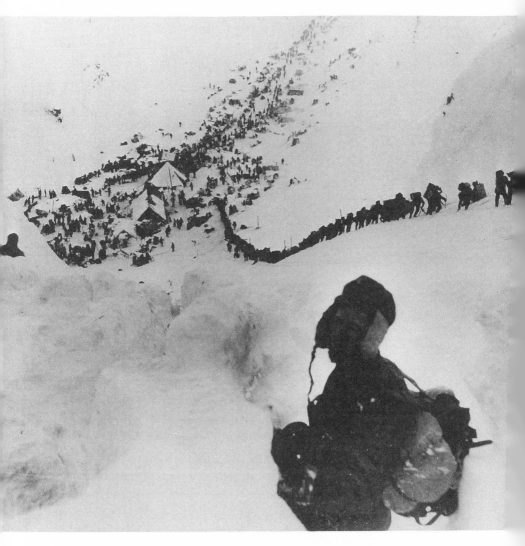

Edward S. Curtis, "The Muir . . . from the West." 1899. Photograph.
Harriman Expedition, 1899. *(Bancroft Library)*

In 1899 the soon-to-be-great photographer of Indians, Edward S. Curtis, accompanied railroad magnate Edward S. Harriman and a party of scientists on an expedition to Alaska. Here Curtis could not resist making this dramatic view of his friend John Muir's very own glacier. Muir was pleased.

Robert E. Peary, "April 7, 1909, at the North Pole." Photograph.
(Edward P. Stafford, National Geographic Society)

At the North Pole, Matthew Henson *(center)* and four Eskimos displayed
flags while Robert Peary snapped this photograph. Henson was holding
the polar flag made by Mrs. Peary.

B O O K   T W O

THE BOOK OF
THE
OCEANS

CHAPTER VI

"The Whole World Is an America, a New World"

i
THOREAU'S TRAVELS

EXPLORATION, scientific exploration that was making known the remote, exotic places of the earth as well as its vast watery spaces, fascinated an astonishing variety of Americans. One of those fascinated was, paradoxically enough, the stay-at-home sage Henry David Thoreau of Concord, Massachusetts. Famous for his writings on the microcosmic world of Walden Pond, Thoreau nonetheless traveled to the ends of the earth regularly—through books. "The whole world is an America, a New World," he wrote in his journal for 1854, the same year he published *Walden*. For most of his life, Thoreau regularly read explorers' accounts, gleaning from them not only a vicarious spirit of adventure but also a feeling for the authentic observation of different forms of nature in ecologies at widely scattered points around the globe. In his quiet study at Concord, in his cabin at Walden Pond, or stretched out under a poplar tree in his backyard behind the family pencil factory on Concord's Main Street, Thoreau voraciously and eclectically absorbed all the information he could about a wide world which, to the explorer, was indeed as unknown as the heart of the Rockies. Thoreau was another of Humboldt's children.

Between 1852 and 1854, as the United States Army was conducting its great Pacific Railroad Surveys across the West, Thoreau read his way through all three volumes of Humboldt's *Personal Narrative of Travels to the Equinoctial Regions of the New Continent . . .* , Captain Cook's *Voyages,* and Darwin's *Voyage of a Naturalist Round the World.* But Thoreau, like most people of his time, was not just interested in the "giants" of exploration; he read everything. Sometimes he traveled through Canada and witnessed the ghastly martyrdom of the fur hunters with Alexander Henry (one of his favorites); sometimes he trekked across Tartary with Thomas W. Akinson, entered Indian captivity and turned savage with John Dunn Hunter, penetrated the mysteries of Central Africa with Barth and Clapperton and Livingstone, had adventures in the frozen Arctic with Isaac Hayes and Elisha Kent Kane, toured the Chinese Empire with Evariste Régis Huc, journeyed to Mount Ararat with Frederick Parrot, accompanied the adventuress Ida Pfeiffer on *A Lady's Voyage Round the World,* stood with Beltrami, then Schoolcraft at the source of the Mississippi, followed Lieutenants Herndon and Gibbon down the Amazon and Orinoco.

On certain days he was with Bayard Taylor in California's Eldorado or suffering on the Mosquito Coast with Ephraim George Squier, Mrs. Frank Leslie's first husband. He avidly read the boys' books of Captain Mayne Reid, experiencing the *Perils of a Peruvian Family amid the Wilds of the Amazon* or *Adventures in Search of a White Buffalo.* He also read the entire five-volume account of Captain Charles Wilkes's Great United States Exploring Expedition to the Antarctic Coast, Oregon, the South Seas, and around the world. And with Herman Melville, he also took "a peep at Polynesian life" as exemplified in the latter's "true" account of Nuka Hiva's cannibal Typees. One of the great romantic American writers, unique in that many of his impressions "imploded" into the microcosmic symbolism of Concord and Walden Pond, Thoreau nonetheless paradoxically reflected the romantic horizon of his time—an infinite global horizon that in the nineteenth century became American as much as that of any other nation.

ii

THE MOUNTAIN MEN OF THE SEA: EDUCATION AND
SIGNIFICANCE

IF THOREAU in his enthusiasms could be numbered among "Humboldt's Children," an even greater impetus to American exploration derived from the voyages of Captain Cook. John Ledyard, from Groton, Massachusetts, had sailed as a corporal of marines with the great navigator on his third and ill-fated voyage to the Northwest Coast of America. More important to Ledyard than the tragedy of Cook's death in Hawaii was the fact that members of the expedition had managed to trade sea otter pelts obtained on the Northwest Coast for a fabulous return in Canton, China. When he returned to America, Ledyard tramped up and down the Eastern Seaboard trying to sell financiers and Yankee skippers on the value of a triangular trade between the Northwest Coast, Canton, and America. He even published an account of his voyage with Cook, *A Journal of Captain Cook's Last Voyage to the Pacific* (1783), to drum up enthusiasm for his visionary venture. But though he got some encouragement from Robert Morris, "the fancier of the Revolution," and always remained Jefferson's "kindred spirit," Ledyard never himself received backing for a Northwest Coast venture.

Nonetheless, Cook and other British navigators commanded great attention in a nationalistic post-Revolutionary America that was disposed to dispute Britain not only for the continent, but for the oceans and the trade of the exotic East as well. Even while Ledyard was touting his fur trade schemes, the *Empress of China* left New York harbor in 1783 bound for Canton, where it arrived in August of 1784. The ship carried as supercargo Major Samuel Shaw of Boston, whose duty it was to report back to the new Confederation government the prospects for success in trade with China. The report issued upon his return stimulated other merchants to follow the success of the *Empress of China.* By 1796 the *Experiment,* the *Grand Turk,* and the *Hope* had all sailed for China. On the latter vessel Shaw returned to Canton, there to remain as "United States Consul" before the Constitution of 1787 had even been written.

All of this merely underscores the intense and continuing interest that Americans had in the oceanic frontier. The transatlantic trade with colonial America and the West Indies had been vital to the British Empire, and its transformation in the Navigation Acts of 1760 and subsequent Parliamentary proclamations had been one cause of the Revolution. And even while the struggle for independence was taking place, the pacifistic Quakers of Nantucket under the leadership of Francis Rotch formed the earliest American "multinational" company devoted to continued whaling ventures on a broad scale, at various times sailing under American, British, and French flags. They worked the North Atlantic, the coasts of Africa, and the Brazil Banks and even sailed as far south as the Cape of Good Hope and the Falkland Islands.

Not only Nantucketers, who were a special breed, but merchants and sea captains all up and down the Atlantic Coast looked to the sea frontier; they were far more interested in that as the future of America than they were in the vast and dangerous wilderness at their back. Much of the exploratory work, especially in the days of the early Republic, was not done by the great merchants or the government, which was weak and feeble during the entire Federalist Period. Rather it was done by whaling men and sealers in relatively small ships backed by small groups of investors who hoped to gain their fortunes on just one or two ventures out onto the unknown seas, very much like the early fur traders of the Far West. Even the structures of the ventures were much the same—a small amount of capital was raised to procure basic equipment, in this case the ship and supplies, and the captain and crew of the vessel worked on shares from the return. Thus organized, these small expeditions sailed out across the world in the days of the early Republic in direct competition with mighty Britain, whose ports were all closed to American ships. They succeeded very well, and in Melville's words, penetrated "into the remotest secret drawers and lockers of the world." The whalers and the sealers were the mountain men of the sea. They blazed trails across the world's vast oceans and into the frozen polar regions that had eluded the great navigators of Cook's generation. And in so doing, they added a great deal to the world's body of knowledge. As a consequence, they must perforce be counted as a significant factor in the development of modern science.

At first their methods were as crude as those of the fur trapper in the Rockies, and they had no Indians to guide them. Only the great European navigators were equipped with the latest sextants and Harrison's wonderful chronometers. The whalers and the sealers depended upon lunar observations with crude instruments for determining longitude at sea, and the compass and log line for charting direction and rate of speed. They had no way of correcting for magnetic deviations of the compass. Indeed, it would take many years of sophisticated work before anyone could confidently do this—something Humboldt realized from the outset of his career as a scientific explorer. But the seaborne trailblazers were able to determine latitude by the sun's or the north star's angle with the horizon, and they eagerly learned as much of the practical aspects of seamanship as they could. When Nathaniel Bowditch, already well known as a mathematician and navigator, made his several ocean voyages between 1795 and 1803, officers and crew alike quizzed him with fascination. As Stackpole has put it so eloquently:

Each ship was a nautical school room, with the foremast hand as anxious to learn as the officers. In the search and discovery of new whaling grounds, new conditions had to be thoroughly learned— the prevailing winds and currents of that section of the sea or coastal region, the type of headlands or shore line, the holding or anchorage ground, the seasons of the year when the whales came into this part of the watery world. This was a training which had been acquired in regular habit down through the years. The whalemen had developed into natural explorers of the sea. They were America's first oceanographers.

Thus those were not idle words that Melville wrote when he declared that "a whaleship was my Yale College and my Harvard."

The whole "practitioner" aspect of early American science as it related to the sea is often overlooked amid tales of hair-raising adventure, though the heavy freight, the incredible detail of whaling lore in *Moby Dick*, should certainly have given us a clue to the substantial body of knowledge amassed by these oceangoing explorers in every phase of science from geography and navigation to exceedingly close observations of natural history. To read Melville's works is also to gain insight into the vast anthropological experience of the oceanic explorers and to gain the first glimmerings of what came to be known by the end of the nineteenth century as "cultural relativism." Melville's tolerance for and fascination with native customs, as instanced for example in *Typee* and the Queequeg episodes in *Moby Dick*, are by now well known, but one finds the same insights countless times in the journals of the other oceanic explorers of the day. Just as the mountain man had to know intimately the habits and customs of the red men, often had to live with them, depend upon them, empathize with their culture, so too did the sealers and whalers who sailed among the islands of the vast Pacific. Some, like David Whippey of Nantucket, who "went native" in the Fiji Islands, became content to be adopted members of cannibal cultures. Everywhere they went, from Patagonia to Kamchatka, from Nuka Hiva to Sunda, the sea explorers confronted, experienced, contended with, and came to understand in great detail alien cultures around the world. Ishmael's friend Queequeg in *Moby Dick* was no figment of Melville's imagination. Queequeg was fact to countless whalers and sealers. And the anthropological information they brought back, including the alien men themselves, who walked the cobbled streets of New Bedford and Nantucket, helped to prepare the way for the whole science of anthropology by raising profound questions as to the nature, classification, and origin of man.

Perhaps the most dramatic insight into the practitioner scientific atmosphere that prevailed in the ports from which the sea explorers departed can be gained from looking at the career of America's foremost navigator, Nathaniel Bowditch of Salem, Massachusetts. The son of a retired drunken sea captain, Bowditch was a mathematical prodigy. He had little formal schooling, and instead began to work at the age of ten in his father's cooperage shop. At twelve he became a clerk in a ship chandlery, where he became thoroughly familiar with the great sea ventures that left Salem harbor for the Indies. In the meantime, encouraged by Rev. William Bently and others, he studied mathematics and navigation assiduously. His earliest exposure to broad information was *Chambers' Cyclopaedia*, part of a library salvaged from an English privateer wrecked off Salem harbor. Then he devoured the many volumes of the *Transactions of the Royal Society*, placed at his disposal by the town's elders when he was made a member of the Salem Philosophical Library. And finally, teaching himself Latin, he mastered Newton's *Principia*, a copy of which had been given to him by the Rev. Bently. In analyzing the *Principia*, he found an error in Newton's calculations, which was promptly and unfairly discounted by the great Samuel Webber, Hollis Professor of Mathematics at Harvard. Nonetheless, the young, locally taught mathematician became a celebrity in New England, where he became president of the American Academy of Arts and Sciences and received an honorary degree from Harvard.

Because he was a prodigy it is misleading to think of Bowditch as "typical" of the practitioner scientist of early New England, but certain aspects of his associations reveal the common atmosphere in which he worked. He had access to a good local philosophical library; he regularly conversed with sea cap-

tains and navigators; he became familiar with sea charts, surveying techniques, and the use of navigational instruments; and he
could participate in the activities of Salem's East India Marine
Society. The society was a clearinghouse for information gained
by East Indiamen as they returned from their long voyages, and
where they regularly deposited logbooks for one another's reference (unlike the sealers, who were more secretive). Nearly
every seaport had an equivalent 'of the East India Marine Society, so the exchange of information concerning the sea quickly
became institutionalized. And when Bowditch discovered a new
method for determining longitude at sea by means of lunar observations, he freely passed on his findings. When he took to sea
on each of his five voyages to the East Indies, he made a point of
educating all aboard in the intricacies of navigation. Perhaps the
climax to this came on one voyage to the Philippines when a
Scottish captain, skeptical of American navigational abilities,
soon discovered that every man aboard Bowditch's ship could
perform all the tasks of the navigator, including the difficult
lunar-longitude determination. Later the great Salem merchant
George Crowninshield proudly demonstrated just how wide-
spread this knowledge had become in Salem, thanks to Bowditch, by having his Negro cook perform lunar observations for
the European scientist Baron Branz von Zack. "How does it
happen," the baron later wrote, "that commanders of French
vessels, with thirty-four schools of hydrography established in
the kingdom, either know not, or do not wish to know, how to
calculate lunar distances, while even the cooks and Negroes of
American vessels understand it?"

Bowditch's most famous work, *The New American Practical
Navigator*, was simply an extension of his work in the practical
instruction of his fellow seamen. Approached in 1799 by Edmund Blunt, the Newburyport bookseller and publisher of
Captain Lawrence Furling's *American Coast Pilot*, Bowditch
agreed to correct and update John Hamilton Moore's standard
work, *The Practical Navigator*. During the course of his East
Indies voyages, Bowditch worked steadily away at the project.

He corrected two editions of the work, finding eight thousand errors in Moore's calculations. By 1800 it was evident that Bowditch should publish a completely new work under his own name, which he did in 1802, entitled *The New American Practical Navigator*. It became standard immediately and has remained ever since the oceangoing skipper's bible. It is now published regularly along with the *Coast Pilot* by the United States government. In 1802 it was a great expression of emergent American national achievement, as was Bowditch's complete revision of Laplace's *Mécanique Céleste* in 1818, which Bowditch finally published in 1829–30. If Laplace had seemingly filled in all the blanks in Newton's cosmos and propounded a climactic theory of the universe, the practical scholar from Salem more than doubled the information in Laplace's great work while modestly correcting the Frenchman's many errors. As oceanic and even as cosmic voyager, Bowditch played a significant part in the debate over the quality to be expected from "the New World."

iii

THE MOUNTAIN MEN OF THE SEA: DEEDS, ADVENTURES, AND ACCOMPLISHMENTS

IN 1788, within four years after the publication of the sad account of Cook's third voyage, American fur hunters rounded the Horn and headed for the Northwest Coast and eventually China. These first American ventures were commanded by Captain John Kendrick aboard the *Columbia* and Captain Robert Gray aboard the *Lady Washington*. Upon reaching the Northwest Coast, they anchored at Nootka, where they were somewhat smug observers of that famous controversy between Britain and Spain. While the two "superpowers" were confronting each other, the Americans quietly loaded their ships with furs and established an unobtrusive base at Nootka. In 1789, Kendrick remained at Nootka while Gray, with the *Co-*

lumbia loaded with furs, sailed for China and thence via the Cape of Good Hope back to Boston. The *Columbia* was the first American vessel to sail around the world, and the news of her success soon brought other sea otter hunters to the backside of America. The *Hope* sailed in 1790, as did the *Hancock*, and Gray himself departed on another run in September of that year. All of these voyages, though exposed to great danger in rounding the Horn and from attacks by the fierce Indians of the Northwest Coast, were fabulously successful. By 1792, as Samuel Eliot Morison puts it, "the trade route Boston–Northwest Coast–Canton–Boston was fairly established." In the meantime, on his second voyage aboard the *Columbia*, Captain Gray discovered the mighty and important river that bears his ship's name.

By 1792 also, American whalers had rounded Cape Horn and were coursing out in all directions across the infinite Pacific. The first of these was the *Beaver* out of Nantucket; then came the *Rebecca* out of New Bedford. These were accompanied by four of Francis Rotch's American "multinational" whalers sailing out of Dunkirk. Meanwhile a sizable number of American whale ships took the East Indiamen's route via South Africa and the Indian Ocean. In that *annus mirabilis* 1792, three ships from the fleet headed in that direction, the *Asia*, the *Alliance*, and the *Hunter*, and they rediscovered the remote snow-covered Kerguelen Islands far south in the Indian Ocean, not far from Antarctica. They had braved a smallpox epidemic on Madagascar, French hostility, and fog, sleet, and snow as well as the "roaring forties." Other vessels rediscovered the South Georgia Islands eight hundred miles southeast of the Falklands and then the South Sandwich Islands some 450 miles closer to the South Pole. Three sealers started stations at Tristan da Cunha and then on the Juan Fernández Islands off the Pacific coast of South America. In 1792 there were at least thirty-nine whaleships in the Pacific. Tierra del Fuego became such familiar terrain that one beach used for drying seal skins was known as "the New Haven Green." Thus whalers and sealers alike swarmed into

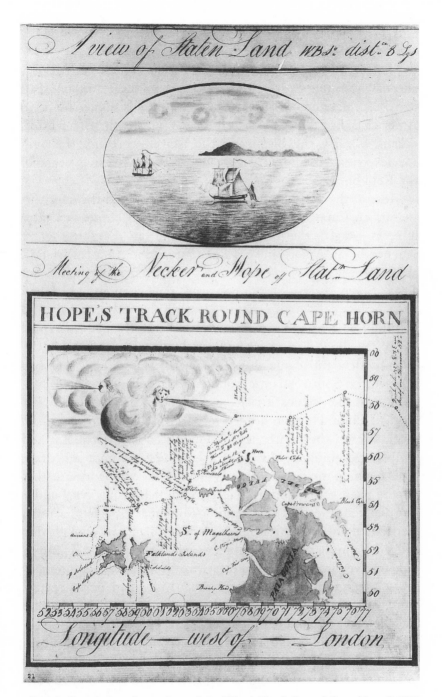

Captain Joseph Ingraham, chart of the "*Hope*'s Track Round Cape Horn," 1790–1792. The *Hope* was the first American ship to sail around the world.

the Pacific in the years from 1790 to 1800. By the second decade of the nineteenth century more than three million seals had been slaughtered in the southern islands alone; by 1920 Americans had killed a record 53,877 whales in the world's oceans. Clearly the bison and the beaver were not the only species endangered by Americans in the expansive years of the Republic.

Most of the early sealing expeditions exploited the southern islands off Cape Horn and the Cape of Good Hope. Sea otter hunters ranged the Northwest Coast from California, first touched by an American vessel in 1796, to the Aleutian Islands, already ruthlessly worked over by the Russians and their Aleut allies. Some sealing ships, however, ranged more widely on more or less deliberate exploring expeditions. Captain Edmund Fanning, who was to circumnavigate the world five times and live to tell about it in a stirring book, in 1798 loaded his ship the *Betsy* with a full cargo of seal skins at Más Afuera. He had coursed the South Atlantic, rounded the Horn with some difficulty, and then struck it rich on the lonely islands off the west coast of Chile. He then headed for China, weaving through the exotic isles of the South Pacific. He visited the Marquesas and then La Dominique (Hiva Oa), where he came upon a bedraggled, terrified missionary, one William P. Crook, landed at that remote place some months before by the whaleship *Duff* under the pious auspices of the London Missionary Society. Crook, menaced daily by the tattooed islanders, had had enough. He begged Fanning to rescue him, which the captain did just in time to save him from the irate natives. Crook guided Fanning to the Washington Islands, where the natives had never seen a white man's ship. They attacked it in war canoes, but Fanning and the *Betsy* escaped. Fanning later learned that Captain Ingraham aboard the *Hope* bound for the Northwest Coast had previously sighted those islands from a distance, claiming them for the United States and naming them for the "father of the country."

The *Betsy* cruised on northward to Nuka Hiva, as yet unspoiled, and named its broad harbor Massachusetts Bay. Still farther north, Fanning discovered a series of low-lying atolls which he named after himself. On the 14th of July, 1798, the *Betsy* reached Tinian Island in the Marianas. Here they found the survivors of a wrecked British Indiaman, including the captain's widow, his child, and twenty-one men, about half of whom were Malays. Fanning took aboard the widow, the child, and the surviving Englishmen, but he left the Malays behind to guard the wrecked ship's cargo. He reached Canton about the first week in August. There he deposited the survivors and spent two months haggling with Canton traders. Finally, on October 30, 1798, he sailed out of Canton in company with a large vessel from Philadelphia for mutual protection against Malay pirates, who infested the waters of Sunda Strait. Off Sumatra they were attacked by a fleet of proas and gaudily dressed Malay pirates. The Philadelphia ship put on full sail and disappeared over the horizon, but the *Betsy* was not so lucky. She bore the brunt of the attack.

The fleet of proas bore down on the *Betsy* in three squadrons, their occupants yelling hideous threats. Just then the wind died, slowing the *Betsy* to one and one-half knots. Fanning steeled the resolve of his small crew by telling them that should there be "any flinching, death by the scimitar or poisoned kris as usually dealt out by these villains, was certainly in store for us." Then in a brilliant naval maneuver, he "crossed the enemy's T" in a manner worthy of the great Admiral Horatio Nelson himself. First Fanning concentrated on the pirate captain's flotilla coming up fast astern. He suddenly tacked so that his four eight-pound cannon and two brass six-pounders could rake the pirate captain's ships, which they did. And each time the pirates turned to escape the shot, Fanning tacked and let fly again with his cannon and a raking musket fire. The pirate vessels were dismasted almost immediately, and the pirates tried to escape by rowing. Fanning, ignoring the other two enemy fleets, pursued the crippled central fleet. At last he grappled the chief's proa and swarmed aboard with his men. The pirates surrendered, with the Malay chief turning in his wicked-looking curved kris and placing his head beneath Fanning's foot. All weapons and supplies destroyed, Fanning let the pirates depart in peace.

Meanwhile the other two fleets, seeing the fate of their leader, disappeared into the bays and jungle rivers of Sumatra. Fanning sailed the *Betsy* on to Krakatoa, where he was met by a Dutch naval vessel hunting the pirates. Fortunately Fanning arrived at Krakatoa as early as 1798; that picturesque volcanic island blew up in 1883 in perhaps the greatest natural disaster in recorded history. After Krakatoa, however, the *Betsy* encountered little difficulty as she crossed the Indian Ocean, rounded the Cape of Good Hope, and sailed up the Atlantic into New York harbor on April 26, 1799. She was the first New York vessel to circumnavigate the world. Profit: $52,300.

The *Betsy*'s was a famous voyage, but American whalers and sealers as they roamed the Pacific encountered "a thousand Patagonian sights." In 1808, Captain Matthew Folger aboard the *Topaz* rediscovered remote Pitcairn Island and was greeted by the sole survivor and descendants of the *Bounty* mutineers. For the first time the world learned of the tragic fate of Fletcher Christian and his men after they left Tahiti. A gauge of Captain Folger's sympathies can be gained by noting that after returning the surviving mutineer Alexander Smith to America, he proudly handed over the *Bounty*'s azimuth compass to Rear Admiral Hotham, R.N., whose fleet was conducting an informal blockade of Nantucket Island.

Perhaps the most harrowing experience of all, however, was that of the crew of the whaleship *Essex*. On November 20, 1820, somewhere between the Galápagos and the Marquesas in the vast reaches of the central Pacific, the whaler *Essex* was rammed and sunk by a sperm whale eighty-five feet long. The enraged whale made two runs at the *Essex*, completely stoving in the bow of the ship. Owen Chase, the first mate, who survived to tell the tale of the whole calamity, remembered, "The shock to our feelings was such as I am sure none can have an adequate conception. We were dejected by a sudden most mysterious and overwhelming calamity.... We were more than a thousand miles from the nearest land, and with nothing but a light open boat, as the resource of safety for myself and companions." Chase and the survivors climbed into the small boats and sailed off south-southeast in the wrong direction. Had they sailed due south they would have hit the Marquesas, but they were afraid of cannibals. Had they sailed or drifted northwestward they would have reached Hawaii, but they worried about the hurricane season. Instead they headed directly across the open Pacific for Valparaiso, Chile, over three thousand miles away. They soon made Henderson Island, a mere sand spit in the ocean, and reorganized, completely unaware that friendly Pitcairn Island was just a few miles away over the horizon. But the captain was relentlessly bent on South America, so, leaving three men behind on the island, the longboats sailed on, through gales, sharks, starvation, lack of water, madness, and death. One boat was completely lost. Eventually the near-crazed sailors turned to cannibalizing their deceased mates. Owen Chase described the fate of Isaac Cole:

> We separated his limbs from his body, and cut all the flesh from the bones, after which, we opened up the body, took out the heart, and then closed it up again—sewed it up as decently as we could and committed it to the sea. We now first commenced to satisfy the immediate cravings of nature from the heart, which we eagerly devoured....

The next day Cole's remaining flesh had "turned of a greenish colour," wrote Chase, "upon which we concluded to make a fire and cook it."

Captain Pollard's boat was in even worse straits. It had run out of natural corpses! On February 1, 1821, the four survivors in his boat decided to draw lots to see who would die for the benefit of the rest. Owen Coffin, the captain's young nephew, drew the death lot. Charles Ramsdell, also in his teens, drew the executioner's lot. Then each man took turns volunteering to die. Coffin was finally killed by Ramsdell and eaten by the survivors, one of whom died ten days later. But the last two men, Captain Pollard and Ramsdell, survived. Chase and two men had survived in the other boat, so, in all, five men out of sixteen emerged from the awful voyage of three months and thirty-seven hundred miles. The three men who remained on Henderson Island were rescued after 102 days. And William Bond, a black whaleman, who seems to have deserted the longboats early on at "Ticmas Island," was never heard from again. The story of the *Essex*, of course, became a Pacific legend. Owen Chase wrote a vivid account of their sufferings. Jeremiah N. Reynolds published "Mocha Dick, or The White Whale of the Pacific" in the *Knickerbocker Magazine* for May 1839. And out of all this Melville created *Moby Dick*, though he left out more than half of the terrible story.

By the time of the *Essex* tragedy, whalers were spreading out all over the Pacific. In 1818, Captain George Washington Gardner, commanding the *Globe* out of Nantucket, had originally discovered the "offshore grounds" of the central Pacific upon which the *Essex* was hunting. In the years 1819, 1820, and 1821, whaling reached its first great peak in the Pacific. The first American whalers landed at Hawaii in 1819. In 1820, Captain Jonathan Winship, aboard the *Maro* in company with the British ship *Syren* of London, discovered the Japan whaling banks, or "on Japan" as the whalemen called them. In 1821 the first American missionaries were landed in Hawaii by Captain Oriah Coffin of New Haven. Hiram Bingham, also of New Haven, who was to become the most famous, if not most troublesome, of all the South Seas missionaries, was among their number. "Civilization" had come at last. In the course of their whale, seal, and sea otter hunting, American mariners had scoured the Atlantic, the Indian Ocean, and the vast reaches of the Pacific discovering and rediscovering countless islands and reefs from Iwo Jima in the Bonins to Deception Island in the South Shetlands. In a report to the Secretary of the Navy in 1828, Jeremiah N. Reynolds, who toured New England's ports interviewing captains, mates, and sailors and inspecting logbooks and charts, reported that some 233 islands, reefs, and oceanic rock clusters had been located or discovered by the New England whalers and sealers. Many of these duplicated earlier discoveries, but it was nonetheless significant that the New England captains recorded and charted them. They were building up a science of the sea that in informational terms far outran the data provided by the standard Pacific map of the day, that of Aaron Arrowsmith of London.

In effect, noting the habits and migratory seasons of the whales, the New England whale hunters had blazed trails in the sea much as had the fur hunters in the Rocky Mountains. They had located major whaling grounds along the coast of Chile, then the "offshore grounds" of the mid-Pacific, the equatorial grounds which wound through the hundreds of islands from the Galápagos to New Guinea, Hawaii, the Japan Banks, the Indian Ocean, and, after 1835, the whaling grounds of Kodiak Island and Kamchatka. In a typical season they would round the Horn in late October or early November, work the inshore Chilean grounds, then make their way via the Galápagos, the Marquesas, and the Society Islands across the "offshore grounds" or the "equatorial grounds." Gradually they worked north to the "on Japan" grounds. Hawaii and Nuka Hiva in the Marquesas were common rendezvous points. Other whalers cruised from the Chilean grounds to the Galápagos grounds and the equator to California, then across to Hawaii and Japan. Dr. Charles Townsend's careful study of 1935, however, indicates that by far the greatest number of whales taken by Americans in the Pacific were clustered within 5° north and south of the equator from the Galápagos to New Guinea. The whalers, however, ranged all over the Pacific in search of the leviathans. And in so doing they contributed mightily to world exploration. As Jeremiah N. Reynolds put it:

In these untried paths, new reefs, new islands, and dangers were constantly encountered, and their situations noted down in the logbooks and journals of vessels as they chanced to fall in their way. On

their return to the United States, these discoveries generally formed
a paragraph, which went the rounds of the press, and then sank into
oblivion. Often, however, it was seized upon by some European
constructor of maps, and placed in the charts as an important acquisition to geography, but without mentioning the names or alluding
to the nation of the discoverers.

In Reynolds's report, nationalism had surfaced in an overt way,
as regards the honor and the glory of discovery.

iv

THE PACIFIC SQUADRON

IT HAD already surfaced, however, during the War of 1812. In
November of 1812, Captain David Porter, a veteran of the war
with the Barbary pirates, set sail in the United States frigate
Essex bound for the Pacific. His mission was to protect American whalers and sealers and to destroy British commerce. The
Essex was the first American warship to enter the Pacific, and
Porter's naval campaign was remarkable. Assisted by Lieutenant
John Downes, also a veteran of the Tripoli engagements, he
succeeded in capturing twelve British vessels, all the while provisioning his ship far from home from stores captured from the
enemy. Lieutenant Downes turned two of the captured whaleships into men-of-war, and for more than a year Porter and
Downes wreaked havoc among the British Pacific whaling fleet.
In the course of his cruising, Porter landed at Nuka Hiva and
took possession of it for the United States. He christened it
Madison Island and established a short-lived fort there. In the
case of Porter's venture, the flag followed trade, and the whaling
interests appear to have been responsible for America's first
overseas venture into imperialism. It may also have been something in Porter's aggressive personality as well, because as early
as 1815 he proposed the expedition to Japan that was later carried out by Commodore Matthew Calbraith Perry.

Porter's adventures aboard the *Essex* came to an abrupt end on March 28, 1813, when, in a bitter battle in Valparaiso harbor, his ship was disabled by the British warships *Phoebe* and *Cherub*. He was taken prisoner and eventually paroled, so that he was once again on active duty with the U.S. Navy by the end of the War of 1812. His exploits became all the more famous when he published in 1815 *Journal of a Cruise Made to the Pacific Ocean*, in two volumes.

After the War of 1812, beginning in the 1820s, the United States Navy began to maintain a regular Pacific Squadron commanded by Commodore Isaac Hull and headquartered in Valparaiso. Since in part the war had been fought over freedom of the seas, United States policy was aimed at maintaining just that as a service to the whaling, sealing, and emerging sandalwood industries. Some of the ships of the Pacific Squadron conducted spectacular missions. In August of 1825 the schooner *Dolphin* commanded by Lieutenant John "Mad Jack" Percival set out from Chorillos in Peru to apprehend mutineers who had taken over the whaleship *Globe* near Fanning Island. He was also ordered to make a general reconnaissance of the South Pacific, checking out islands reported to have been discovered by whaling ships. A long list of these islands was furnished by Commodore Hull to Lieutenant Percival before his departure. His cruise took him to the Galápagos, Charles Island, the Marquesas (especially Nuka Hiva), the Carolines, the Union Islands, and the Gilberts, where a pitched battle with the natives ensued in which Mad Jack nearly lost his life while stranded on the beach in the face of a horde of angry stone-throwing Gilbertese natives. He survived, however, and the *Dolphin* cruised on to Mili Island in the Marshalls, where, again in a great struggle, the mutineers William Lay and Cyrus Hussey were apprehended. Then Percival headed for Hawaii via Maloelap Island and Aur Island. Finally on January 19, 1826, the *Dolphin* entered Honolulu, the first U.S. warship to land at Hawaii. Mad Jack and the *Dolphin*'s stay at Hawaii was not without incident—even legendary implication. By 1826, the "Connecticut Band" of missionaries had virtually taken over the island, controlling eleven-year-old King Kamehameha III and the Queen Regent Kauhu-manu as well as the "prime minister," "Billy Pitt" Kalimimoku. The missionaries backed the local rulers in their refusal to pay $300,000 in debts owed to American merchants which the *Dolphin* had been sent to collect. Percival forced the chiefs to pay up. This made for bad blood, but feelings ran even higher over the missionaries' refusal to let the native women, following long custom, swim out to cohabit with the sailors aboard the ship. The crew rowed ashore, broke into the prime minister's residence, and nearly mobbed the trouble-making American missionary Hiram Bingham to death as he flailed vainly about with his flopping umbrella. Only the queen regent's sister saved him from death as she flung her substantial body across his frail frame. Percival at last quelled the riot as the chiefs agreed to let the *wahines* visit the ship. So successful was Mad Jack's diplomacy that it became a legend, even a custom; to this day the U.S. Navy celebrates Mad Jack Percival Day once a year in Hawaii.

On his return from Hawaii, Percival sailed through the Society Islands, the Austral group, Rimatara, Tubai, Rapa, Moratiri, and the Corones, after which he sailed thirty-five hundred miles straight across the ocean to Valparaiso. The cruise of the *Dolphin* was thus more than a colorful incident in naval history. It marked the real beginning of systematic exploration of the Pacific islands by the United States Navy.

In addition, in the Pacific the Navy was slowly but surely assuming the role of "policeman" much as the British were doing off the coast of Africa. The policeman role was further exemplified by Captain John Downes's expedition aboard the *Potomac* to chastise the Malay pirates at Quallah Battoo, Sumatra. In February of 1832, sailors and marines stormed Quallah Battoo and, in a battle lasting two and a half hours, destroyed the pirate stronghold. The United States, following the track of the whalers, sealers, and Indiamen, had established an official "presence" in the Pacific which was to last, perhaps for good. The flag had indeed followed trade for better or for worse, and the activities of the Pacific Squadron might well form a case study in the nature and cause of imperialism. Certainly its assumption of massive if not pretentious responsibility suggested that the Pacific Squadron symbolized a rampant American nationalism that was to characterize the rest of the century. But even before the days of "Mad Jack" Percival and "Bloody John" Downes, imperial rivalries had come to focus in a most unlikely place in the world's oceans—the Antarctic.

v

THE SEA LIONS AND THE SOUTHERN CONTINENT

ON his epic voyage aboard the *Resolution* in 1774–76, Captain Cook had pushed far south of the Antarctic Circle, discovering and naming the South Sandwich Islands and South Georgia Islands, but he missed the great continent itself. Despite the high interest in Terra Australis Incognita, this subject was obscured by Cook's death on his third voyage and by the opportunities offered by the Northwest Coast sea otter trade with China. Thus, though by 1792 British and American whalers, sealers, and China traders were regularly rounding the Horn and cruising the Pacific, few skippers were inclined to push south into the frozen Antarctic seas on voyages of discovery. The first great breakthrough was an accident. Blown off course, the British sealer Captain William Smith, aboard the brig *William*, discovered the South Shetland Islands, just off the tip of Antarctica in 62° 40′ south latitude in February of 1819. Though the weather in the South Shetlands is some of the foulest in the world, he found them to be covered with seals, and he sent his men, despite the conditions, to kill them for their furs. Taking on his large cargo of sealskins, he sailed to Montevideo and made ready for another voyage. This he undertook in October and claimed to have landed on a Antarctic mainland where his men planted the Union Jack. He called the land New South

Shetland, which may have caused some confusion as to what Captain Smith actually discovered. He claimed to have seen Norway pine trees and to have traced a coastline for 250 miles.

When Smith reached Santiago, Chile, after his second southern voyage, his ship was chartered by Captain Shireff, commanding officer of the British Pacific fleet. He placed the vessel under the command of Edward Bransfield, who, on December 19, 1819, sailed south to discover a new continent and rich sealing grounds. The voyage lasted until March 1821. Because good sealing grounds were hard to find, the mission was confidential, and the results inconclusive. However, they did trace a shoreline "nine or ten degrees east and west" at 62°20′ south latitude, but they could not be sure that it was not some island or islands studded with high mountains. Bransfield, like Smith, did wax enthusiastic over the abundant seals and whales to be had for the taking. The secrecy of the expedition was broken when Dr. Adam Young, surgeon of the expedition, and one J. Miers, could not resist publication of the exploit in the *Edinburgh Philosophical Journal* for April 1821. They have sometimes been blamed for starting the "seal rush" that virtually exterminated the creatures from the South Shetlands.

Young and Miers were not entirely responsible, however. Earlier, after his first southern voyage, when he landed at Montevideo, Smith had told his tale to American sealers and whalers who attempted without success to persuade Smith to lead them to New South Shetland. As a patriotic Englishman he refused. However, for some years, Captain Edmund Fanning of Stonington had been fascinated with the prospect of land to the south of Cape Horn. He believed that should new islands or a mainland be discovered, vast new seal rookeries would also be revealed. By 1799, poring over ancient Spanish and Dutch charts, he believed that he had located at least one unexplored island group, called by the Spaniard Atrevida the Aurora Islands, and further lands discovered by the Dutch Captain Dirk Gherritz. On hearing of Smith's discovery of the South Shetlands, Fanning wrote in the *New England Palladium and Commercial Advertiser* for December 5, 1820:

> . . . the fact is, I do not consider this land as a new discovery. It was first seen by a Dutch Captain in the latter part of the 15th Century, and Frazier saw it in 1712, and called it South Iceland. This came to my knowledge in the year 1799, and I now have before me a manuscript chart of this *New South Iceland* as we call it to an extent between 11 and 12 degrees longitude and of between 5 and 6 degrees of latitude.

Several things are significant about Fanning's statement. It indicated that news traveled fast even out in the far South Atlantic, for Fanning knew of Smith's find even before Surgeon Young had published it in the *Edinburgh Review*. It further indicated that the sealers were not simple illiterate exploiters but men of considerable geographic and scientific knowledge. And finally it indicated that Fanning and other Americans intended to dispute to the fullest Britain's possible control of the South Shetlands.

Accordingly, on July 20, 1819, Fanning sent the big *Herselia* south on a voyage of discovery under the command of his nephew James Sheffield and carrying his son William Fanning as supercargo. Fanning's instructions to Sheffield are important in the history of exploration:

> The master and supercargo of the *Herselia*, both possessing nautical talents, and both able lunarians, were therefore directed in their instructions, to touch first at the Falkland Islands, there to fill up their water and refresh the crew, thence to proceed in search of the Aurora Islands, and should seals be found, to procure their cargo, if not to return to Staten Island (near Tierra del Fuego), and after wooding and watering, to stand to the southward keeping in the latitude of about 63° south, then to bear up and steer east, when it was confidently expected they would meet with land. . . .

Accordingly Sheffield sailed south, rediscovered the Aurora Islands, now called Shag Rocks, and proceeded on to the South

Shetlands, the westernmost of which he explored between January 18 and February 8. A reconstruction of his voyage from his recently discovered logbook indicates that he sighted South Island, traversed Boyd Strait, and made a landing at what is now called Herselia Harbor on Rugged Island. He may also have sighted Antarctica fifty miles away from a peak in the South Shetlands. It seems clear that though Fanning's instructions were explicit, he would have learned about the South Shetlands anyway. Somewhere on the voyage south, undoubtedly at Montevideo, Sheffield learned of Smith's prior voyage and something of the precise location of the Shetlands. This seems clear from the fact that while at the South Shetlands he was joined by Captain Thomas Davidson, who, hearing of Smith's discovery, had fitted out a brig in Buenos Aires and quickly sailed south.

At any rate, the voyages of Smith, Sheffield, and Davidson created a flurry of attention directed at the Antarctic. Fanning wrote in the *New England Palladium and Commercial Advertiser* on November 20, 1820, "From the knowledge I possess respecting New South Iceland, I have no doubt that Cook's Southern Thule and this land belong to one and the same continent. . . ." Even earlier in the year, the shipping magnate James Byars of New York, a former employee of Sheffield's, wrote three letters to Brigadier General Daniel Parker of the United States Army to be forwarded to Secretary of State John Quincy Adams. In a letter of August 25, 1820, Byars asserted that Sheffield saw "the great new Island or Continent in Lat. 61:10 So— Long 57-15 Wt. Coasted about 50 miles. Saw no end South Wt. Returned to what he thought the St. Wt. end and came to anchor between a number of islands a short distance from the Mainland. . . ." And from Valparaiso, Consul Jeremy Robinson had written on January 22, 1820, to Secretary of State Adams giving news of Smith's voyage and calling for an official U.S. exploring expedition to the region as a "means of throwing new light upon navigation, geography and the theory of the earth." Fearing that things had gotten out of hand and that a Nootka Sound incident might be precipitated, Adams on August 26,

1820, informed President Monroe that more than twenty U.S. vessels were sailing for the South Shetlands. He called for the dispatch of a warship to protect them and to take possession of the South Shetlands and other lands in the frozen but seal-rich region. In an immediate reply of September 1, 1820, President Monroe promised to look into the practicability of such a project. Meanwhile Consul Robinson had already sent a copy of his letter to Adams to Dr. John Latham Mitchell of the New York Lyceum of Natural History. This letter found its way into the *New York Evening Post* for September 16, 1820. Rumors were spreading that all these rich southern islands had long since been discovered by American sealers, who had kept the discoveries secret, but now they were about to be snatched away by Britain. Maritime interests from New York to New Bedford were putting maximum pressure on Monroe's administration to do something to protect American "rights" to the bottom of the world.

On an international level, the problem was not resolved until much later. Instead greed and free enterprise lessened the stakes of conflict by almost entirely wiping out the seal population of the coveted frozen isles to the south. In the summer of 1820, among the many ships (more than thirty from the United States) that hurried to the South Shetlands was a fleet put together by Edmund Fanning and Benjamin Pendleton. This fleet's activities were crucial to Antarctic exploration. It consisted of five ships: the *Frederick*, Capt. Benjamin Pendleton; the *Free Gift*, Capt. Thomas Dunbar; the *Herselia*, Capt. James Sheffield; the *Express*, Capt. Ephraim Williams, and the *Hero*, Capt. Nathaniel Palmer. The Fanning-Pendleton Fleet reached the South Shetlands on November 10, 1820, when it sighted Smith's Island capped by a mountain which they named Mount Pisgah. Searching for seals, the fleet split up and headed in different directions, eventually establishing a main base at Yankee Harbor on Greenwich Island in the McFarlane Strait.

The most significant voyages of discovery were undertaken by Captain Nathaniel Palmer aboard the *Hero* in November of

1820 and in January of 1821. Between November 14 and 18, Palmer sailed the *Hero* south through a heavy snowstorm from Livingston Island to Deception Island, a half-submerged volcanic cone which he discovered and explored. In the interior of the island into which he penetrated through a narrow channel dubbed "Neptune's Bellows" he found a spacious lagoon and a series of protected harbors. On November 16 he left the island and on the seventeenth headed south, passing amid immense icebergs until he reached a strait "Tending SSW and NNE. . . . Literally filled with Ice," which could only have been Orleans Strait between Trinity Island and the Antarctic mainland. He wrote in his logbook, ". . . the shore unaccessible we thought it not Prudent to venture in we Bore away to the Northward and saw a small Island and the shore everywhere Perpendicular. . . ." Palmer had sighted the Antarctic continent.

Later, in January of 1821, it appears that Palmer, probably accompanied by Pendleton, made another exploratory voyage south along the west coast of the Antarctic Peninsula as far as 68°, but the data on this are vague. Some time later, in February of 1821, perhaps returning from his second exploratory voyage, Palmer, emerging from a smothering fog, encountered two foreign vessels in the strait between Deception and Livingston islands. There were the *Vostok* and the *Mirny*, commanded by Captain Fabian Gottlieb Benjamin von Bellinghausen of the Imperial Russian Navy. Bellinghausen was a great admirer of Cook, and under the auspices of the Russian czar was making a scientific voyage around the world. At the end of the earth, so to speak, much to his surprise he encountered the youthful Palmer. Accounts vary as to this meeting. Fanning gives a rather complete account, asserting that Palmer led the Russian to safe harbor at Deception Island and described Antarctica to him. Palmer remembered drawing maps of the region for Bellinghausen, who in turn named Palmer's Land for him in gratitude. Bellinghausen's journals, on the other hand, make no mention of these details beyond noting the February meeting. Bellinghausen himself is commemorated by the great icebound Bellinghausen Sea on the west of Antarctica. Like Cook, he had circumnavigated the frozen continent, but unless Fanning's account of his meeting with Palmer is true, he never sighted the mainland.

Meanwhile news of the discoveries to the south, especially detailed information about the South Shetlands, quickly reached the geographical media. As early as the tenth edition of *The American Coast Pilot*, published in 1822, an extremely detailed and remarkably accurate set of sailing instructions for the South Shetlands appeared, including the location of dangerous reefs, channel depths, and the location of a safe harbor on "Ragged [Rugged] Island."

Though Palmer had sighted the Antarctic continent, he had not set foot on it. This honor belongs to Captain John Davis of New Haven, Connecticut. When he set sail aboard the *Huron* in March of 1820, he was not even aware that the South Shetlands had been discovered and seemed to be headed toward the Cape of Good Hope. However, he met Captain Christopher Burdick of the *Huntress* in the Falkland Islands; Burdick knew of Smith's discovery, and together they headed south accompanied by Davis's small shallop, the *Cecelia*. On December 7, 1820, the three ships reached Yankee Harbor, where they joined the ships of the Fanning-Pendleton fleet.

By this time the Shetlands were crowded with seal hunters, including some twenty-four British vessels in addition to the thirty American craft; at least three fights had broken out between the British and American sealers, and the seals themselves were hard to find because of overkilling. Davis, employing the shallow-draft *Cecelia*, made repeated reconnaissances of the islands, to little avail. But in early February 1821, he headed south from Smith Island, past Low Island and Hoseason Island, through very heavy weather to Cape Sterneck on the Antarctic mainland. On Wednesday, February 7, 1821, he recorded in his log

Standing for a Large Body of Land in that Direction SE at 10 a.m. close in with it out Boat and Sent her on Shore to looke for seal at 11 a.m. the Boat returned but found no signs of Seal at noon our Lati-

tude was 64°... 01' South stood up a Large Bay the Land high and
covered entirely with snow. . . .

The latter was Hughes Bay, but Davis did not have time to examine it closely because by 4:00 p.m. a heavy gale arose, thick
with snow, and the ice-dotted sea began to roll and swell, so
with reefed mainsail he edged northward off the coast and eventually into the Bransfield Strait between the South Shetlands
and the Antarctic. Davis's first landing had been a historic one,
but it was lost to history until his logbook was discovered in
1956 by Alexander O. Vietor, curator of maps at Yale University.

Shortly after Davis had landed at Cape Sterneck, Captain
Christopher Burdick sighted Antarctica himself. On February
15, while heading for Low Island, he noted in his log the sighting of "Land from South to ESE which I suppose to be a continent." The cruise of the *Huron*, the *Huntress*, and the *Cecelia*
had been a memorable one.

During the great "seal rush" of 1820-21, at least seven other
American fleets arrived in the South Shetlands. The most prominent of these was one sponsored by James Byars of New York,
but others arrived from Stonington, Boston, Salem, Nantucket,
New Bedford, and Fairhaven. If any new geographical discoveries were made by these fleets, history does not record them. In
fact, even the Fanning-Pendleton fleet, which returned to the
Shetlands in 1821-22, managed only one important "find."
Nathaniel Palmer and the British sealer George Powell, cruising
eastward together, discovered the South Orkney Islands on December 6, 1821. Other than that there were only three significant developments. By 1822 most of the seals had been
slaughtered, thus making the South Shetlands no longer a mag-
net for hunters. This lessened considerably the national rivalry
between the United States and other nations in that quarter of
the globe, as is suggested by the joint Palmer-Powell exploring
venture. And finally, the sealers began to look about for more
things than seals. This resulted in the first crude attempts at sci-

entific analysis of the Antarctic. The *New York Gazette and General Advertiser* for May 16, 1821, reported on returns from the Byars fleet which included a "manuscript chart" of the South Shetlands made by Hampton Stewart, and a collection of minerals forwarded to Dr. Samuel Latham Mitchell of the New York Lyceum by Mr. B. Astor. The *Gazette* reporter commented:

> Geologists will learn with surprise that the high grounds and summit of the rocks in several of the spots that have been visited, are strewn with skeletons of whales, and relics of other marine animals, leading to the belief that the whole of the materials have been hove up by the operation of volcanic fire, from the depths of the ocean.

In some ways this was not news, because the southern tip of South America had for nearly a century been called Tierra del Fuego, "Land of Fire." But in Europe and certainly in America the controversy between the Wernerians, who believed the world's landmasses were solely the result of precipitation from the world's oceans, and the Huttonians, who believed that much of the land was created by volcanic eruptions from the center of the earth, was still a significant issue with biblical overtones. Donald Mackay of the Byars fleet added fuel to this controversy with another letter to the *New York Gazette and General Advertiser* on May 22, 1821, in which he, like the previous correspondent, clearly recognized a continental landmass fifty to seventy miles south of the Shetlands, which like the islands seemed obviously volcanic in origin. He reported smoke seen issuing from a volcanic cone, an island so hot that, despite the freezing Antarctic temperatures, men could hardly walk on it, and what looked to him like an extinct volcanic crater that formed an island. Indeed it should have been obvious to him and to others that Deception Island fit just this description. By the 1820s, observations such as these made in the Antarctic and among the various islands of the South Pacific and East Indies should have made it clear that the Wernerian thesis was hopelessly inadequate.

While the desire for riches to be gained from the hunting of seals and whales remained uppermost in the minds of most Eastern Seaboard mariners, a fascination with scientific knowledge also had not died since the days of Captain Cook. Despite the exploits of the great navigator in the far southern latitudes, the mystery of Terra Australis Incognita remained a challenge to Americans and western Europeans alike. For Americans, national pride was at stake as well. From 1799 onward, Captain Fanning, touting his research in the ancient and more modern charts of the eighteenth century, lobbied for an official United States government exploring expedition in search of a southern continent. Such an expedition had been authorized by President Madison, and Fanning had been placed in command of two ships, the *Volunteer* and the *Hope*, designated for the mission. But just as they were about to sail, the War of 1812 broke out and the expedition was canceled.

vi

HOLES AT THE POLES?

FANNING and others never ceased their clamor for scientific information, however, and in 1825 President John Quincy Adams recommended such an expedition in his message to Congress. Meanwhile, Fanning and his cohorts were joined by a public relations genius, Jeremiah N. Reynolds of Wilmington, Ohio. Reynolds, like many of his time, was caught up in enthusiasm for global exploration. As such he was a representative figure of the grass-roots interest that sustained the Second Great Age of Discovery.

Reynolds's initial interest was aroused by the theories of Dr. John Cleves Symmes of Cincinnati, Ohio, who believed that the earth was hollow, and that at the poles, once one passed beyond the ice barrier, there existed a warmer climate and an entrance into the center of the earth. On April 10, 1818, he began proclaiming these doctrines, but he was a shy man and Reynolds

John Cleves Symmes's wooden model of the globe with holes at the poles. *(Academy of Natural Sciences of Philadelphia)*

took over his cause. They made an eastern tour, with Reynolds
doing most of the lecturing, using beautifully made wooden
models of the globe to illustrate Symmes's point. Many times
they were laughed out of the hall, and Symmes, fatigued by the
tour, went back home to Cincinnati to die. Reynolds persisted,
however, and gradually learning more, partially abandoned or
soft-pedaled the Symmes theory. As he did so he gained more
credibility and more allies among knowledgeable seafaring men,
until at last he became their acknowledged spokesman. Reynolds's assertions of the existence of warmer climates within the
Antarctic ice pack received some support from the reports of
volcanic activity observed by the sealers mentioned above, and
by the writings of the British explorer James Weddell. In February of 1822, Captain Weddell sailed south to 73°15'S, farther
than any man before the twentieth century. Though he cruised
what is now the ice-packed Weddell Sea, he wrote of a warm
climate. According to him, the weather was "summery," and
"Not a Particle of ice of any Description was to be seen." The
Symmes-Weddell-Reynolds theories took firm hold on the popular imagination. In fact, Reynolds's Baltimore friend Edgar
Allan Poe scored his first success when he won a literary contest
sponsored by the *Baltimore Emerald* with the story "Ms. Found
in a Bottle," based on a fictionalized elaboration of Symmes's
theories. The whole concept fascinated Poe; he wrote other
stories on the same theme, such as "The Descent into the Mael-
strom" and especially the long tale "The Narrative of A. Gordon Pym." As late as the end of the century, writers like Arthur
Conan Doyle and H. G. Wells, not to mention Jules Verne
slightly earlier, were still using the theme in their very popular
writings.

But Reynolds gained credibility himself as he abandoned
Symmes's theory in favor of hardheaded conversations with sea
captains and experienced naval officers. In 1827 the Secretary of
the Navy sent Reynolds to New England to do research among
the whaling and sealing logs and to interview veteran sea captains. Reynolds made this a labor of love and delivered his fa-

mous report to Congress in 1828, together with petitions from interest groups all up and down the Eastern Seaboard. As a result, Congress authorized an official exploring expedition to the southern latitudes and to the Pacific. Upon assuming the presidency in 1829, however, Andrew Jackson vetoed the expedition on the grounds of economy.

Reynolds persisted. In 1829 he persuaded Captains Benjamin Pendleton and Nathaniel Palmer to undertake a private exploring expedition. Though the expedition had as its main mission scientific exploration, it was also to engage in sealing activities to pay for the costs and especially to attract sailors, who volunteered to work for shares or "lays." Accordingly, three ships, the *Seraph* under Captain Pendleton, the *Annawan* under Nathaniel Palmer, and the smaller *Penguin* under Alexander S. Palmer (Nathaniel's younger brother), set out for a great world cruise, first to the Antarctic in search of the lost continent, then to the vast Pacific as far north as Bering Strait.

From the beginning things went awry. The ships failed to rendezvous off Montauk Point as planned. In fact, they never effected a rendezvous among all three vessels. The *Annawan* with Reynolds aboard caught up with the *Penguin* at Port Hatches in the Staten Islands, and together they sailed through the Shetlands from Elephant Island to Yankee Harbor. The *Penguin* also apparently reexplored Elephant Island while the men looked for seals. On Elephant Island, Reynolds and a shore party were stranded for four days because of fog, sleet, and snow. It is possible that Reynolds's account of this experience formed the basis for James Fenimore Cooper's novel *The Sea Lions*, just as his stories influenced Melville and Poe, and the launching of the first real government-sponsored oceanic expedition.

At any rate, once having arrived at the antipodes, Palmer, who had already seen the Antarctic continent, seemed less than fascinated with exploring its possibilities. Instead he devoted his efforts toward taking seal and cruising far to the west, into the empty Pacific, fruitlessly looking for seal islands reported by

Captains James C. Swain and Richard Macy. Meanwhile, far behind, Captain Pendleton pursued the same strategy with the same effect. Ultimately he caught up with Palmer at Valparaiso, Chile, where the men, disappointed at having taken so few seals, threatened desertion or mutiny. The expedition was called off. The *Penguin* cruised the coast of Chile hoping to make up the losses, while Captains Palmer and Pendleton closed out their otherwise brilliant careers by taking the *Seraph* and the *Annawan* ignominiously home.

The promoter, Jeremiah N. Reynolds, along with a scientific colleague, John Frampton Watson, was put ashore on a suicidal diplomatic mission to make peace with the warlike Araucanian Indians. Reynolds not only survived, he prevailed—over the Indians and over the captain of the U.S.S. *Potomac*, John Downes, who made him his private secretary and brought him home to continue the fight for a U.S. exploring expedition.

By far the most significant result of the Palmer-Pendleton expedition of 1829–31 was the scientific activity of James Eights of the Albany Academy, the training ground for Joseph Henry, who became the first Secretary of the Smithsonian Institution. Eights was the first trained naturalist to visit the Antarctic, and he published seven papers as a result of the expedition. These appeared in the *Boston Journal of Natural History*, the *Transactions of the Albany Institute*, and the *American Journal of Agriculture and Science*. Eights was primarily a mineralogist, and he described the South Shetlands as having a conglomerate base overlain with basalt (lava), thus adding proof to the Hutton thesis of igneous eruptions as part of the earth's landbuilding process. Eights also discovered a fossilized warmweather tree—the first fossil found on the Antarctic and one which suggested a previous warm-weather cycle or warmer lands to the south. Several years before Agassiz articulated his descriptions of the Ice Age and Darwin noted their significance, Eights pointed out the importance of boulders embedded in icebergs as an indication of the basic composition of Antarctic landmasses. He never got close enough to make any definitive statement about the Antarctic continent and was inclined to believe that Terra Australis Incognita was a chain of islands. He made no comment about Symmes Hole, but he did note, "During our cruise to the southwest above the 60° of south latitude we found the current setting continually at a considerable rate towards the northeast, bearing the plants and ice along in its course, some of the latter embracing fragments of rock, the existence of which we could discover no where on the islands we visited."

When the various components of the Palmer-Pendleton expedition reached home, thirteen chests of natural history specimens were presented to the New York Lyceum and two chests were given to the Philadelphia Academy of Natural Sciences. Reynolds gave his collection to the Boston Society of Natural History, while Eights contributed his to the Albany Institute. There is no evidence that anyone worked further with them. Nor, surprisingly, does it appear that the expedition produced any maps—possibly because no one had the ability to draw one accurately, and Navy lieutenant Charles Wilkes, scheduled to go on the expedition as astronomer and navigator, was left behind with a collection of instruments paid for out of his own pocket.

Because the sealers and the whalers produced so little in the way of overt contributions to organized science does not mean, however, that their contributions to science were negligible. They did make crude maps, not unlike those of the mountain men. They did keep hundreds of logbooks, storing them in marine society repositories, and these contained a wealth of information about the positions of islands and reefs, natives and natural history, great whales and little fishes, winds, currents, climate, and perhaps most subtle of all, the earth as a changing, almost circulatory system. As they followed the whales and the seasons and the currents, and as they described the phenomena, they created a composite picture, perhaps most vividly revealed to oceanic men, of a world in circulation and in effect recycling. Theirs was a dynamic instead of a static worldview that would come to have an importance that in many ways transcended or at least outlasted the equally powerful worldview of Charles Darwin. But their real significance lay hidden—obscured by the formal, organized, official scientific activities of the day upon which so much credence was placed, upon which national and international progress and prestige depended, and out of which the mighty thesis of Darwin emerged to change space into linear time.

CHAPTER VII

Exploration and Empires for Science

i

ADAMS'S CHALLENGE

THE FIERCE COMPETITION between American and British sealers in the ice-packed seas of the Antarctic merely symbolized what was happening on a larger scale across the oceans of the world. "No sea but what is vexed by their fisheries," declared Edmund Burke before Parliament, "no climate that is not witness of their toils." He was voicing alarm at the rapid emergence of the United States as a global force in oceanic commerce. Unhampered by traditional monopolistic controls over trade such as that exercised by the British East India Company and the Russian American Company, Americans made free to apply their seaborne enterprise whenever and wherever they chose—but largely at their own risk. They soon realized the disadvantages that went with the risk-taking inherent in such rugged individualism. And so, in the 1820s, just as the pioneers on the western frontier were calling for public roads and military protection from the Indians, the maritime interests of the Eastern Seaboard also clamored for the help of the United States government. In 1825, their spokesman, President John Quincy

Adams, strongly asserted that "a flourishing commerce and fishery extending to the islands of the Pacific and to China . . . require that the protecting power of the Union should be
deployed under its flag as well upon the ocean as upon the land."
By the 1819 Transcontinental Boundary Treaty that he had
concluded with Spain, Adams had given the United States a
window on the Pacific. Now he called upon Congress to involve
the federal government in commercial and imperial rivalries that
reached far beyond the shores of the continental United States
with the creation of Asiatic and Pacific squadrons of the United
States Navy. For Americans an era of global Manifest Destiny
had begun.

But Adams went even further. He saw the all-important link
between sophisticated knowledge and the growth of commerce.
Thus he called for global scientific exploring expeditions comparable to those of France, England, and Russia. He said, "The
voyages of discovery prosecuted . . . at the expense of those nations have not only redounded to their glory, but to the improvement of human knowledge. We have been partakers of that
improvement and owe for it a sacred debt, not only of gratitude,
but of equal or proportional exertion in the same common
cause." And in a statement that has a familiar ring today in the
age of space exploration, he concluded, "One hundred expeditions of circumnavigation like those of Cook and La Pérouse
would not burden the exchequer of the nation . . . so much as the
ways and means of defraying a single campaign in war." Adams
knew that knowledge was power, that knowledge commanded
world respect, that knowledge could win a far-flung American
empire. He was the first to call for permanently established federal scientific institutions. Such advanced notions cost him the
presidency in 1828, as strict-constructionist Republicans still
ruled American politics. But such institutions did come into
being, and even before the Civil War the United States government launched fifteen exploring expeditions over the high seas
to different parts of the world.

The next three chapters chronicle that story. Often it consists of tales of high adventure and danger as sailor explorers confronted the exotic ocean frontiers of the world. But the story must also include startling adventures of the mind that took place during this era as some very great men brought forth ideas and concepts of the first order, despite jealousies, bureaucratic bickerings, the inhibitions of narrow nationalism, provincialism, sectional disputes, national depressions, and the emergence of strong organized party politics. The great men who first brought forth respectable science in America were not always good men. In fact, the striking contrasts of their personalities, while they often got in the way of progress, also enhanced the human quality of the age. And because they were wrong as often as they were right, to follow the course of the progress they generated is sometimes a difficult task. But the story of these fiercely dedicated men illustrates the fact that if science had to include exploration within its purview, exploration also had to include science of a high and difficult order. It was a lesson hard won in the years before the Civil War and one not yet fully understood by politicians, the public, or even the historians of science of today. The result of this merger of physical and mental high adventure, however, had far-ranging results for western civilization. During this period a whole new worldview in which and by which we now live emerged to pit itself against the visionary certainties of previous centuries. This story marks the turning point in America's participation in the Second Great Age of Discovery. From 1830 to 1860, during the height of the Romantic Age, America dramatically emerged as a scientific civilization.

In the early nineteenth century the Pacific Ocean and the polar antipodes had become the focus of very extensive European scientific attention. Beginning in 1818, serious efforts at finding a way through the Arctic ice floes to a Northwest Passage had been undertaken by Great Britain. Between 1819 and 1822, Sir John Franklin had journeyed overland to what he viewed as the north polar sea. He continued to lead subsequent expeditions, and in 1845 his efforts to sail his way around north of Baffin Island and westward through the ice-locked islands north of the continent resulted in a loss of Franklin and all his men of the vessels *Erebus* and *Terror*. His countryman Lieutenant Edward Parry, had almost made the fabled passage between 1819 and 1825, and then had abandoned the attempt at the edge of the Beaufort Sea. Afterward he sailed his ship *Hecla* out of Spitzbergen farther north than any man had ever sailed, reaching 82° 45′ N, a record that was to stand for forty years. From 1819 onward there had been, in fact, continuous and heroic efforts by British explorers, later joined by Americans and Russians, to locate the all-water passage north of the continent finally discovered by the Norwegian Roald Amundsen in 1903–06. Much of the north polar sea activity was generated by the gallant efforts of men of all nations to rescue or find the remains of the lost Sir John Franklin. His widow, Lady Jane Franklin, made a career out of sending men to their death in vain sentimental searches among the Arctic seas. It was an age of romantic chivalry.

Perhaps more significant, the European nations also turned to the Pacific in efforts to chart its potential. Exclusive of three cruises of Captain Cook, since 1767 Britain had sent twenty-seven exploring expeditions to the Pacific, France seventeen, Spain five, Russia seven, and Holland one. This resulted in an immense backlog of information in addition to the great work of Captain Cook. La Pérouse of France had coursed the Pacific from Australia to the Bering Straits. Matthew Flinders had circumnavigated and mapped Australia, and the Russian von Bellinghausen had sailed all around the Antarctic continent, though he never knew it as such. A host of British and French explorers had discovered, mapped, and landed on virtually every island in the South Pacific, staking out territorial claims and raising flags over paradises owned by fierce cannibals and soft Polynesians alike. It was a rare expedition that did not come equipped with a full cargo of its nation's flags and territorial emblems. They also carried cartographers, astronomers, naturalists, ethnologists, and artists who pictured the exotic natives in far-away lands for the people back home. So many collections of exotic plants and animals had flowed back into Europe that they necessitated the creation of national museums and royal or public gardens and zoos. Ethnological collections abounded with vivid feathered helmets from Hawaii, bird-of-paradise cloaks donated by Polynesian royalty, sacred stone and wood effigy gods bartered for nails and brandy, splendidly decorated shields and Maori war clubs from New Zealand, as well as carved war canoes from that land and outriggers from the equatorial paradises. Decorated tapa cloth from the islands became so common that British shipbuilders began using it as undercoating for men-of-war.

By the 1830s specialists were able to devote their lives to studying specimens of all sorts from the Pacific Basin. In Europe, specialization quickly led to professionalization, and there was plenty of employment. If one puts the bombardment of specimens, charts, and astronomical data flowing in from the Pacific together with that coming back from Africa, South America, India, China, Arabia, and Egypt, it is easy to see why all the sciences took a quantum leap in the nineteenth century. It is also easy to see why exoticism and romanticism became the stylistic vogue in Europe.

In 1831, inundated by a surfeit of "discoveries," the British Admiralty concluded that no new discoveries beyond those at the antipodes were left to be achieved. Instead it turned its attention to exceedingly careful mapping of the coasts and harbors of the major continents, straits, and islands. It was on this sort of mundane mission that Captain Robert FitzRoy, R. N., set out in command of the *Beagle* with the earnest but amiable young Charles Darwin along as volunteer naturalist. The preceding synopsis of six decades of oceanic exploration by the advanced scientific nations of Europe suggests the already crowded field of endeavor into which the United States officially launched its own ventures into oceanic exploration. That America discovered anything novel at all is truly surprising. That it achieved the great magnitude of scientific discovery that it did finally is nothing short of astonishing.

ii
PLANNING A GREAT EXPEDITION

IF AMERICA was to compete successfully with the great European exploring expeditions, it was clear that her first venture would have to be something grand and spectacular. From the beginning, the enthusiastic Jeremiah N. Reynolds had envisioned a large-scale operation, and he was clearly disappointed by the Fanning-Pendleton venture. He pictured a whole squadron circumnavigating the world's oceans, complete with a full complement of the nation's best scientists and himself as the official historian of the epic event. In a speech before Congress that lasted three hours, he urged "a great United States exploring expedition" that would catch the attention of the world. If he did not arouse the instant enthusiasm of Congress, Reynolds at least managed to captivate Andrew Jackson.

One of the ironies in the history of American exploration is the fact that our most memorable expeditions—those by Lewis and Clark, Zebulon Pike, Stephen H. Long, and John C. Frémont, and even the great Pacific Railroad Surveys of 1853— were all launched by strict-constructionist Democrats. Jackson was no exception. He responded very positively to the stream of petitions from the maritime interests, which reached a crescendo just as he was taking office in 1828. He had little enthusiasm for science, but the idea of a grand global maritime expedition appealed to him on several levels. It was a significant outlet for his nationalistic feelings. It would also result in a careful inspection of the Pacific Coast, whose ports he had already determined to acquire. And since he had always hated the British, such an expedition provided the perfect opportunity not only to challenge Britain's assumed superiority over the seas, but also to thwart any ambitions she might have for acquiring Oregon and California and thus bringing to a halt American expansion.

Jackson's first attempt to push "The Great United States Exploring Expedition" through Congress was thwarted by the Southern bloc, whose spokesman was the eloquent Senator Robert Y. Hayne. The project languished for nearly eight years, during which time Jackson had already attempted to purchase from Mexico the ports of San Diego and San Francisco. But finally in May of 1836, very near the end of his presidency, Jackson's forces pushed the exploring expedition bill through Congress.

The planning for the great expedition was largely left in the hands of three men: Van Buren's Secretary of the Navy, Mahlon Dickerson, and two of Jackson's friends, Jeremiah N. Reynolds and the old sea dog Commodore Ap Catesby Jones. Almost immediately, political jealousies and crosscurrents of intrigue and blatant opportunism arose to plague all connected with the expedition. It was to be clear from the outset that this was an exclusively American venture. No foreign scientists need apply for positions on the cruise. It was also clear that the Navy was extremely suspicious of civilian scientists and considered its own officers superior in the skills necessary to achieve the main objectives of the expedition, namely mapping and hydrography. Few officers of rank wanted anything to do with shepherding a boatload of effete "scientifics" around the world. On the other hand, with Reynolds's encouragement, dozens of would-be "scientifics" applied for positions on the expedition. All of this caused Secretary Dickerson no end of irritation. He became especially annoyed at Reynolds's constant barrages of advice and soon wearied of all the political and technical complexities of the expedition itself. Claiming ill health, he largely ignored the expedition and spent most of his time at his favorite hobby, horticulture, hoping that the whole expedition project would simply die of neglect.

Reynolds soon lost his influence, while Commodore Jones, who knew nothing about scientific exploration, was forced to take charge. A befuddled man, he at least knew that his mentor, ex-President Jackson, wanted the expedition to be on a grand scale, so he had the *Macedonian*, the largest ship in the Navy, designated as flagship to the squadron. In addition, influenced by the politically powerful Renwick family of New York, he sent their relative, Lieutenant Charles Wilkes, to England to purchase instruments, books, and charts for the expedition. Young Wilkes was well qualified for the task. Almost unique among naval officers, he had studied with the great Bowditch himself, and with the erudite director of the Coast Survey, Ferdinand Hassler. When Wilkes returned from a year's stay in England, he brought with him the largest collection of scientific instruments and foreign charts ever assembled in the United States. He also brought with him the firm conviction that only he was qualified by training and intellect to command the exploring expedition. For more than a year, he schemed and plotted while Commodore Jones only became more confused with this task—especially when confronted with the inadequacy of the ships he had chosen for the expedition. For example, the *Macedonian* was too large to sail close inshore to take hydrographic or sea-depth soundings. Commodore Jones also could not deal with the question of the scientific personnel necessary for the expedition. Like his fellow flag officers, he saw no need for civilian scientists at all. Because of peer pressure as much as disgust with its political complexities, Jones resigned as commander designate of the expedition. Wilkes, because of his knowledge, his connections, and the fact that he seemed to be able to handle "the scientific question," was selected over a number of senior officers to command the expedition. Wilkes, in turn, blithely passed over a number of worthy officers in the process of staffing the naval positions in the squadrons. The fact that this did not endear him to his peers in the service bothered him not a whit. In many ways, Wilkes, who proved to be superior even to the notorious Captain William Bligh as a paranoid martinet, was an unfortunate choice to command America's greatest naval venture up to that time. But in 1837, with the whole enterprise facing disastrous collapse and consequent national embarrassment, he was a last desperate choice.

The arrogant Wilkes wasted no time with what had become a

scientist's lobby. He declared that the main mission of the expedition was that of charting the seas. Anything else was secondary. That was clear from his instructions, which he wrote himself over Secretary Dickerson's signature. With this focus to the mission, it was clear that naval officers were the best-qualified scientific men, since they were professional navigators. However, he condescended to carry along a minimal complement of civilian supernumeraries. Some of them proved to be qualified. The best men were Professor James Dwight Dana of Yale, who shipped on as a mineralogist; Dr. Charles Pickering, ethnologist; and Horatio Hale, the son of Sarah Josepha Hale, celebrated publisher of *Godey's Lady's Book*. Young Hale, a graduate of Harvard, was assigned the duties of "philologist," or collector of native languages. The other members of the scientific contingent included Titian Peale, a veteran of Major Stephen H. Long's expedition to the West in 1819–20; William Rich and William D. Brackenridge, two amateurs, as botanist and horticulturist respectively; and John Pitti Couthouy, conchologist. Asa Gray, America's foremost botanist, resigned from the scientific corps in disgust at Wilkes's cavalier view of the importance of natural science to the expedition. And since Wilkes himself intended to write his own history of the expedition, not wishing to share the "glory" with anyone, he dropped Jeremiah N. Reynolds from the expedition's company, coldly and without ceremony, barely one month before the squadron was to sail. Thus Reynolds, sadly enough, was never to participate in the great endeavor that he, almost single-handedly, had generated.

iii

A PASS AT THE SOUTHERN CONTINENT

ON AUGUST 18, 1838, Lieutenant Wilkes aboard the *Vincennes* led The Great United States Exploring Expedition out of Hampton Roads, Virginia, bound for a cruise around the world and a race against a French expedition under Captain Dumont d'Urville to discover the contours of the Antarctic. Wilkes's squadron consisted of the sloops-of-war *Vincennes* and the *Peacock*, the brig *Porpoise*, the storeship *Relief*, and two schooners, the *Sea Gull* and the *Flying Fish*. This represented the largest and most elaborate exploring squadron that any nation had yet sent to sea at one time.

The first part of their mission took them via the Madeira Islands to Rio de Janeiro, thence to Rio Negro, and finally to Orange Harbor off Tierra del Fuego at the tip of South America. They rendezvoused there on January 30, 1839. So far they had sailed through familiar waters, but in February, Wilkes, aboard the *Porpoise* accompanied by the *Sea Gull*, set out through blustery weather for Palmer's Land, Antarctica. His second-in-command, Captain Hudson, Wilkes sent with the *Peacock* and *Flying Fish* southwest in an effort to beat Captain Cook's record to the farthest southern latitude.

The first week of March, Wilkes and his men sailed steadily south through blustery winds, gales, and snowfalls to the South Shetlands and beyond, heading with determination for Palmer's Land, which they sighted on March 3 surrounded by barrier ice. Still Wilkes pushed on through stinging sleet and dangerous drift ice that could crush his ships or close behind them, locking them into the frozen antipodes forever. The men stared in awe at opalescent icebergs as large as cathedrals, dazzled by their fantastic shapes and unaware that what they could not see beneath the surface could rip out the copper-sheathed hulls of their fragile ships. The storms and the sleet concerned them most, however, as the decks were sheets of ice and the sails were freezing so fast that they would soon be useless. All around them mist, fog, and sleet together with high rolling waves began to cut off visibility. Wilkes finally turned back for Orange Harbor. At least for a brief moment, they had sighted the southern continent.

The *Peacock* and the *Flying Fish* managed to reach even farther south than had Wilkes's party. Despite the loss of a man from the maintop and the freezing of both deck and rigging, Captain Hudson on the *Peacock* reached 68°08′ before, as his artist-naturalist Titian Peale put it, "the dictates of common prudence" forced them to turn back.

The *Flying Fish*, a lighter vessel sailing farther west, had better weather and avoided the main ice barrier for a time. On March 21, 1839, Lieutenant Walker's vessel reached 68°41′ S and the crew confidently expected to break Cook's record the next day. But fog and drift ice closed in, the latter so tightly that they were forced to ram their way through it, straining the hull as they glided past icebergs against which giant hundred-foot waves crashed. To one gloomy but poetic diarist they were "a mere skiff in the moat of a giant's castle." On March 27, despite all the terrifying difficulties, they reached "about" 70° S and saw stained ice and "appearance of land," but then, about a hundred miles north of Thurston Peninsula, they turned back, almost in a panic, and rammed their way through the ice northward to the open sea of the Pacific. Today their feat is commemorated by the Walker Mountains and Cape Flying Fish, named after their commander and their vessel respectively.

The squadron's next task was to head for the Chilean coast at Valparaiso and then make a final rendezvous at Callao, Peru, before heading out to survey the Pacific. As they left Orange Harbor at Tierra del Fuego, the *Sea Gull* went down in a fierce storm, unbeknownst to the other vessels of the squadron. No trace of her was ever found. Wilkes, on the other hand, at the time had to be less worried about the *Sea Gull* than about negotiating Valparaiso and Callao harbors, where he managed to run afoul of ships from his own squadron and other foreign vessels, thus embarrassing all hands on the Great United States Exploring Expedition. Beyond this, Wilkes was a troubled man for other reasons. He suspected virtually every officer of conspiring against him, and he positively hated the "scientifics" and surgeons aboard. At each of their landings since Rio, he shuffled the crews and promoted and demoted officers capriciously. At Callao, paranoia got the better of him, and he shipped a whole boatload of the crew home, including Herman Melville's nephew. A possible reason for his paranoia became apparent when out in the mid-Pacific, headed for the Tuamotu Islands, he suddenly appeared in a captain's uniform and ran up the appropriate blue officer's pennant. He had, as he had intended all along, promoted himself to captain on the high seas, well beyond the sight of any brother officers save those under his stern, even vindictive command.

iv
SURVEYING THE SOUTH SEAS

WHEN the squadron reached the large Tuamotu Archipelago, Wilkes introduced a new method of surveying the vast South Seas. He divided his sizable flotilla, designating each a survey area, instead of pursuing a single track as previous smaller expeditions had been forced to do. Throughout his cruise in the South Seas, Wilkes pursued this method, sometimes endangering his men by using the small ship's launches to cover even wider areas and more islands and atolls. By this means, however, he was able to survey in one operation a great deal more of the South Pacific than had ever been possible before. In the course of the expedition, his flotilla managed to chart accurately the Tuamotus, Tahiti, the Society Islands, the Samoans, Tonga, the Union Group, the Gilbert and Ellice islands, the Phoenix Islands, the Hawaiian Islands, the Marquesas, the Marshalls, the Fijis, parts of the Philippines, especially the Mindoro Strait, the piratical Sulu Sea, and the Balabac Strait before he finally reached Singapore on the homeward journey. Wilkes had anticipated the era of "the Great Surveys" that characterized the exploration of the American West in the latter half of the nineteenth century.

This method did not endear Wilkes to his men. The scientifics complained that too much time was spent surveying and mapping and not enough time ashore collecting natural history

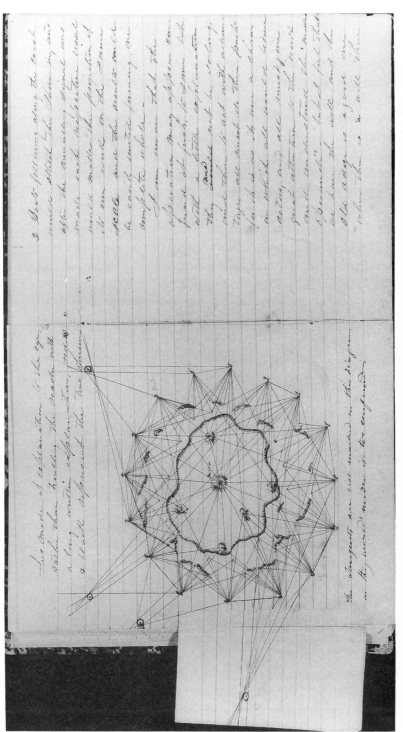

Captain Charles Wilkes, diagram showing how to conduct a "running survey," through triangulation, of a Pacific island. Manuscript. (*Smithsonian Institution, Washington, D.C.*)

specimens or studying the natives. The naval officers resented the long, hot, dangerous, boring hours spent charting reefs when they could see lush islands and native dancing girls only a few hundred yards away. However, Wilkes spent ample time ashore, especially in the Fijis, Tahiti, and Hawaii, points at which he needed to set up astronomical observation stations or check his instruments against previously determined positions. And when Wilkes did land and make contact with the natives, disaster invariably resulted. On his very first contact with the Polynesians of the Tuamotus he peppered them with birdshot. At Malolo in the Fijis, after enjoying over a month of hospitality, he wore out his welcome, and two of his men were killed. This called forth a full-scale attack by his ships in which two villages were burned, crops destroyed, and fifty-six natives were killed—two of them in fantastic rifle shots of 215 yards by Titian Peale.

Wilkes, however, was not alone in feeling the need to chastise the natives. Even his amiable second-in-command, Captain Hudson, while sailing on his own, launched an attack on islanders who had killed one of his crew. Behind this bellicosity was the feeling that since American traders, whalers, and more recently missionaries had increasing "business" in this land of "savages," the natives had better be taught to respect and even fear them. Wilkes unabashedly put his scientific expedition to the service of white, Anglo-Saxon Protestant imperialism.

Clearly not everyone in the squadron agreed with Wilkes. The scientific men became fascinated with ethnology, particularly Horatio Hale and the artists Agate, Drayton, and Peale, while the naturalists welcomed the help and cooperation of the native peoples. Couthouy wrote in his journal an essay on the unfair struggle between "natural man" and the "Spirit of the Age." Even members of the crew were scornful of Wilkes's policies with respect to the natives. Midshipman William Reynolds confided to his secret diary, "I could not help thinking, how much better it would be to let them [the natives] go their own old way, but No, No! We must have all the world like us, if we can." The nonmissionary literature of the Pacific indicates that a

great many others, including Melville, agreed with these sentiments. They also would have agreed with Midshipman William
Reynolds that missionaries like the Rev. John Williams delivered nothing but "a gross, absurd tissue of nonsense, ignorance
and fanaticism." Some may even have rejoiced when they heard
the news that the Rev. Mr. Williams had been killed and eaten
by the outraged cannibals of the New Hebrides. Because the islands seemed like a paradise, because the natives, especially the
women, seemed friendly and generous of their gifts, and because
tough sea captains and unyielding missionaries attempted to re-
strict or alter natural relations in "paradise," cultural relativism
came more naturally as a concept to South Seas adventurers
than to any other group long before anthropologists formalized
the term.

Wilkes's itinerary was a busy one. From Tahiti the squadron
sailed west, surveying the Samoan Islands and then making
speed for Port Jackson, Australia. Spurred on by competition
from France's d'Urville and Britain's James Clark Ross, Wilkes
meant to be the first to reach the Antarctic continent in the limited winter sailing season. On November 29, 1839, they reached
Australia, and the day after Christmas, December 26, leaving
the "scientifics" behind, Wilkes with the *Vincennes*, *Peacock*,
Porpoise, and *Flying Fish* headed south into the ice toward what
would be his greatest discovery.

v

ANTARCTICA FOUND!

WHEN Wilkes's squadron left Port Jackson, experienced captains looked with skepticism at sending such a fragile fleet into
the vast, frozen dangers of the Antarctic. In no way were
Wilkes's ships properly equipped for their dangerous mission.
But having already experienced its perils, the crews were confi-
dent. Aboard the *Peacock*, William Reynolds confided that he
had high hopes that they would find "a Continent, the Existence

of which has been so much disputed; if we do . . . the Nation May reap the fame of at last Contributing Something to the general Knowledge of the World!" Later, amid the sporting whales and pack ice of the glistening Antarctic waters, he recalled some lines from *The Rime of the Ancient Mariner:*

> We were the first that ever burst
> Into that silent sea.

This was not quite true. Palmer, Davis, and most recently, in 1831, John Biscoe of the Royal Navy had sighted land to the south. And most immediately, in his haste to be "the first that ever burst into that silent sea," Captain Wilkes had sailed ahead of his squadron, bypassing their appointed rendezvous point at Macquarie Island.

Nonetheless the *Peacock*, rather than Wilkes's *Vincennes*, was the first of the squadron to sight land. On January 16, 1840, Henry Eld and William Reynolds, aloft in the rigging, saw mountains towering in the distance. They rushed down for a spyglass and saw "conical forms" distinctly, in the especially clear weather that critical day. Reynolds exclaimed that "it burst upon [us] with the utmost Vividness and we unhesitatingly pronounced it the Southern Continent." The peaks of the George V Coast were later named Eld's and Reynolds' peaks. But on that day, unfortunately, Captain Hudson was distinctly unimpressed and failed even to go aloft to see for himself, thus abetting an international controversy that persists to the present day as to priority of discovery of the southern continent. Even more significant, deck officer Thomas A. Budd did not record the sighting in the logbook.

Unfortunately, too, Reynolds's letter to his mother, sent from Sydney, Australia, on March 4, 1840, after their return from the Antarctic, asserts that it was on January 17, not the sixteenth, that he and Midshipman Eld first sighted the southern continent. He does add that on the nineteenth he was "again at the mast head, spectacles on, and was the first to descry it." By January 19, all hands had a clear view of that part of Antarctica now known as Mawson's Peninsula. Five days later the crew of the *Peacock* gathered rock fragments from 360 fathoms down. But then, as they sailed ever closer into an inlet, disaster struck. Drift ice shattered the *Peacock*'s rudder, and the ship was tossed by the waves toward a towering ice cliff. The ship's boats could not tow her off, and ice anchors laboriously planted by the crew on nearby pack ice failed to hold. With death apparently imminent, a strange calm came over the crew, and the mesmerized Eld even paused to write in his journal about the "grandeur and beauty of this stupendous Mountain of Ice." Captain Hudson, however, with great skill as well as luck, got the ship around so that it was sent crashing sternwise into the ice mountain. The recoil from the collision propelled the ship through the floes and out toward the open sea. With the bottom planking being ground ever thinner by the ice floes, the carpenters worked against time to rebuild the rudder and remount it in the icy sea. They succeeded, and by January 26, with the ship in bad condition, Captain Hudson prudently made for Sydney.

Meanwhile on the *Vincennes*, Midshipman James Alden sighted land on January 21 and 22. Captain Wilkes ignored him. Not until the twenty-eighth did Wilkes declare, "There is no mistake about it." They had reached Piner Bay on the Adelie Coast, where mountains rise to thirty-six hundred feet. Wilkes named his "discovery" "the Antarctic Continent" as the crew took on rocks and a stone weighing seventy pounds that had drifted out in ice from the newfound continent. Later in Sydney they would sell even pebbles from the craws of penguins as souvenirs comparable to today's moon rocks.

By February 21, Wilkes had sailed along and charted fifteen hundred miles of the Antarctic coast, definitely establishing it for the first time as a new continent. Cook's search for Terra Australis Incognita was over. However, on the evening of January 20, 1840, d'Urville in the *Astrolabe* also sighted land and later landed on the continent, thus precipitating a priority-of-discovery dispute. This dispute was exacerbated by British

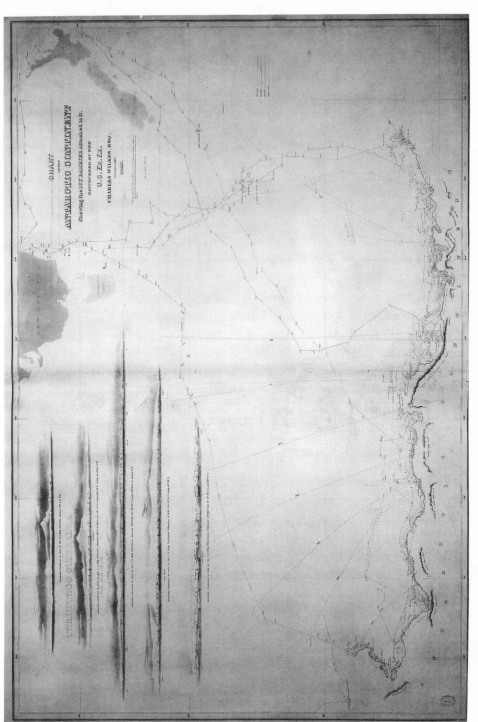

Captain Charles Wilkes, detail of "Chart of the Antarctic Continent Showing the Icy Barrier Attached to it." 1840. *(Library of*

Captain James Clark Ross's claim to priority of discovery later that same year and by his clearly fraudulent assertion that Wilkes never saw the Antarctic at all, despite the fact that Wilkes had even given him a copy of his map of the coastline. D'Urville, who also claimed to have cited land on the nineteenth but had forgotten the international dateline, which made his first sighting on January 20, retained an open mind, asserting that there was glory enough for all, but Ross never gave in to either the French or the Americans. There is indeed clear evidence that Wilkes, realizing his and Hudson's bungling with their logbooks, at a later time added to and doctored his entries, thus casting doubt, even in his own day in America, upon the validity of his discovery. And because he wished to capitalize financially on the publication of his narratives of the expedition, Wilkes withheld the evidence in the daily diaries of Eld, Reynolds, Alden, Emmons, et al. that would have immediately confirmed the sightings. Moreover, in his avarice he witheld publication of his charts until his *Narrative* was finished in 1845, while d'Urville and Ross published their charts in 1840 and 1841 respectively. If not Wilkes, then his men and his country deserved a better fate.

vi

FROM THE SOUTH PACIFIC TO THE NORTHWEST COAST

AFTER the travails in the Antarctic, Wilkes's next mission was to survey as many island groups in the South Pacific as possible. His method of dividing his flotilla has already been described. The first stop of the squadron was Tonga, then the Fiji Islands, where they spent three months in the first careful survey of that geologically complex and dangerous group. The difficulty of surveying in the Fijis was illustrated by Wilkes's meeting with Captain Edward Belcher. That veteran British officer, commanding the frigate *Sulphur* and the schooner *Starling*, had ignominiously run aground at Rewa. But it was nothing unusual for him. In the course of his survey he had run aground on reefs fifty-two times. Under the circumstances, Wilkes's exchange with Belcher was not particularly cordial.

For the most part, Wilkes's stay in the cannibal Fijis was productive and relations with the natives were pleasant, thanks to the help of David Whippey, who had swum ashore from a wrecked whaleship and had resided with the Fijis for nearly ten years. Wilkes established an astronomical observatory at Levuka to match Cook's station at Point Venus in Tahiti. When he was through, Wilkes had thoroughly mapped the Fiji Group, despite having had his unfortunate skirmish at remote Malolo. At Fiji, too, Wilkes took aboard a hostage, Chief Vendovi, who had murdered a seaman. Vendovi, a likable native, made the rest of the voyage with the squadron to America, which he soon became anxious to see. In fact, rumors began to circulate among the islands that one way to see the great land of America was to kill an American and become a hostage.

Wilkes found Honolulu much more to his liking. Almost completely acculturated, it resembled to him "a New England village." The captain spent nearly three months in Hawaii, the highlight of which was his ascent of the volcano Kilauea, where he and his men looked down into the crater at a cherry-red lake of molten fire a thousand feet below. They also stayed a month atop Mauna Loa performing pendulum experiments to determine the shape of the earth, similar to those performed by La Condamine in Peru as long ago as 1735.

On Monday, April 5, Wilkes with the *Vincennes* and *Porpoise* left Hawaii for his final task—a United States survey of the Northwest Coast of America. Captain Hudson, with the other vessels, sailed southwest to make the long and tedious surveys of the archipelagoes on either side of the equator. Their activities too were accompanied by violent skirmishes at Saluafata and Drummond's Island, where they killed twenty natives and burned the extensive village of Utiroa. Reynolds confided to his diary, "Our path through the Pacific is to be marked in blood."

When their survey of the equatorial island groups was finished, Captain Hudson and his ships headed east across the Pacific for a rendezvous with Captain Wilkes off the mouth of the Columbia. When they reached dangerous Cape Disappointment on July 17, 1841, they did not find Wilkes, who was farther north near the Strait of Juan de Fuca. Hudson determined to test the Columbia's possibilities as a harbor, and sailed his ship into the huge tidal flow from that mighty river. The *Peacock* ran aground, and despite efforts to save her, she was finally totally wrecked. The men, however, did manage to get the supplies and collections ashore on the beach not far from where Lewis and Clark had built Fort Clatsop.

The squadron's exploration of the Northwest Coast was among the most important accomplishments of the whole expedition. Wilkes, using Vancouver's excellent charts, determined that Puget Sound was the ideal harbor in the whole region, and the wreck of Captain Hudson's ship made it clear that the Columbia estuary would not do as a major port. Wilkes's report, though largely scorned by Congress, did stiffen the resolve of President Polk to acquire the territory north of the Columbia at least so as to include Puget Sound just below the 49th parallel. Polk's campaign slogan, "Fifty-four forty or fight," aimed to drive the British off the rich sea otter coasts and hence out of the North Pacific trade altogether. Polk also had an inkling of the importance of securing Puget Sound as a major port on the Pacific.

From the Northwest Coast, Wilkes's squadron sailed back across the Pacific to Hawaii, thence on through the Philippines, the Mindoro Straits (so critical in the World War II battle of the Philippine Sea), and the Sulu Sea, and finally to Singapore. At Singapore the *Flying Fish* was sold to a local yachtsman as a pleasure craft that would on occasion run opium into China. This seemed not to concern Wilkes. At this point he was eager to return home in triumph. On February 22, 1842, the squadron sailed from Singapore south between Java and Sumatra bound for the Cape of Good Hope. From there they rendezvoused at St. Helena in the South Atlantic, where Wilkes paid homage at

Napoleon's grave. Then the ambitious commander sent Captain Hudson and some ships to Rio to pick up scientific specimens while he raced for home and glory. The *Vincennes* and its crew arrived off Sandy Hook, New Jersey, on June 10, 1842. They had been at sea cruising the world nearly four years, though more than half the original crews had been dismissed and replaced before the end of the voyage. So strong was the feeling against Wilkes that the officers waited in anticipation to see him reprimanded for assuming a captain's rank. But Wilkes surprised them. He slipped ashore inconspicuously on the pilot boat, leaving the rest of the squadron to land almost unnoticed—and uncared for. It was a bitter return from an incredible voyage. And, in a final irony, just as he was carried ashore to a hospital in New York, Vendovi, the Fiji captive, died. His view of America was very brief.

vii
THE MANY LEGACIES OF THE GRAND ADVENTURE

THE AFFAIR of the Wilkes Expedition dragged on in recriminations for years. First there was a barrage of charges and countercharges between Wilkes and his men, then an endless series of courts-martial. Midshipman Reynolds, who began the cruise greatly admiring Wilkes, summed up the crew's opinion of the captain near the end of the voyage. Wilkes, he wrote his father from the mouth of the Columbia River, was "more . . . a monster than a man." Notwithstanding abundant testimony against him of a similar nature, Wilkes was finally let off with a mild reprimand in the end. Despite his paranoia and cruelties, Wilkes had done an extraordinary job, and he felt slighted by his country. The haughty Briton James Clark Ross had received a knighthood; Wilkes got only a reprimand from his country. He had expected national glory and a promotion in rank at the very least. For the rest of his life, Wilkes worked on a mammoth, self-justifying autobiography that remained unpublished until

1978 and when published only made him look worse. Like the case of the infamous Captain Bligh, it was a situation where a man's overbearing personality obscured his own truly astounding achievements, tenacity, and courage.

Even in the matter of publishing the results of the voyage, Wilkes remained a dastard to his own detriment. He impounded all diaries, journals, logbooks, and charts, and then, between 1843 and 1845, pieced them together in a badly written five-volume account of the voyage. Congress thought so little of it that it authorized the printing of only one hundred copies, though Wilkes presumably made considerable money by securing copyright and contracting with private printers for its re-publication in several editions. And it did have an impact on American literature. As William Stanton points out, James Fenimore Cooper drew on it for his novels *The Crater* (1847) and *The Sea Lions* (1849). Even Melville purchased a set of the *Narrative*, and he was said to have modeled Queenqueg in *Moby Dick* on a New Zealand Maori chief, Kotowatowa, described in Wilkes's *Narrative*.

The artistic aspects of the expedition, however, have been almost completely ignored by those who have concerned themselves with Wilkes's *Narrative*. It was graced by a large number of extraordinary illustrations by Alfred T. Agate and Joseph Drayton. The best of these appeared as steel engravings of the finest quality. In an age of high romantic excitement they depicted the exotic peoples of the South Seas in their ceremonies and villages as well as in a series of finely wrought portraits by Agate. Working from sketches by Wilkes himself and some of the other officers, Agate also caught the awful dangers, the perils and high adventure amid the towering waves and menacing ice mountains of the Antarctic seas. So far as is known, these represent the first views of the Antarctic, though Agate derived them from the sketches of those such as Henry Eld and Charles Wilkes who actually confronted its stormy shores. He deserves to be ranked among the most important of early American artists. Years later in the 1870s, Titian Peale also executed a series of oil paintings derived from on-the-spot sketches and his own memory. These, too, have been largely overlooked as have been oil paintings of considerable merit rendered by Wilkes himself. With the rising interest in scientific and ethonographic art, Agate, Drayton, and Peale will have their day. They will take their place alongside those other intrepid artists, like George Catlin, who captured the landscapes and the villages, ceremonies, and portraits of the Indians of the American West.

The scientific results of the Great United States Exploring Expedition have always been ambiguous. The "scientifics" returned with over 160,000 specimens and so overwhelmed national facilities that many were lost or destroyed as they were carelessly stored and displayed under the auspices of the National Institute in the newly built Patent Office Building. Ultimately, concern over what to do with these and other quantities of specimens arriving daily from federal expeditions caused the bequest left by James Smithson to be used for the construction of a national museum—the Smithsonian Institution—contrary to the wishes of its distinguished first secretary, Joseph Henry. In 1856 the specimens from the expedition were transferred to and displayed in the Great Hall of James Renwick's Smithsonian "Castle on the Mall."

Despite the protestations of Henry, the Wilkes Expedition played a critical role in the organization and structure of science in America. Solely in provoking the creation of a national museum the expedition provided a national focus for science. The Smithsonian became a highly visible clearinghouse for American scientific endeavor, and eventually it provided a political locus for the organization of American science—especially since employment for scientific specialists was very largely dependent on the federal government. This gave Henry and his successor, Spencer F. Baird, greatly enhanced control over science in America as it became institutionalized and its aims and standards better defined, first by the American Association for the Advancement of Science, and then by the National Academy of Science. Both of these were an outgrowth of the concentration of power in the Coast Survey and a national museum in the nation's capital.

Further, the Wilkes Expedition forced the creation of a national herbarium in Washington that almost instantly matched similar institutions in Europe. Its quality was quickly acknowledged by visiting European scientists. The United States Exploring Expedition's astronomical and geodetic returns forced Congress to construct the first permanent astronomical observatory of the first rank in the United States. Much of the scientific equipment purchased in Europe by Wilkes could not be taken along on the voyage and hence was deposited in a Depot of Charts and Instruments under the supervision of Lieutenant Melville Gilliss. The return of the expedition was one influence that persuaded Congress to turn the depot into an astronomical observatory—a "lighthouse of the skies," which John Quincy Adams had called for over two decades earlier. The only thing that Washington lacked by the 1850s was a major scientific research library, which Joseph Henry stoutly opposed. This caused the "scientifics" who wrote up the expedition's reports no end of vexation.

The full scientific results of the United States Exploring Expedition were never finally placed before the scientific world. As late as the 1920s, new genera and species of fishes, collected on the expedition and described by Louis Agassiz in a massive unpublished work, were still being discovered among the museum's collections. The results of the expedition were larger and more complex than anyone could have imagined, and they far outran the intellectual resources of the country. John James Audubon almost immediately recognized their significance. "I have some very strong doubts," he wrote to his young protégé Spencer F. Baird on July 30, 1842, shortly after the *Vincennes* had docked in New York, "whether the results of the Antarctic Expedition will be published for some time yet; for, alas, our Government has not the means, at present . . . to produce publications . . . connected with the vast stores of Information, collected by so many Scientific men in no less than Four years of

Constant Toil and privation, and which ought to come to the World of Science at least as brightly as the brightest rays of the Orb of Day during the Mid-summer Solstice."

Wilkes's original plan was to publish fifteen volumes of text including his five-volume narrative, plus nine volumes of atlases containing maps and illustrations. In the end, some twenty-three volumes, including atlases, were published, and the project was left unfinished in 1874. By that time most of the original scientific explorers were dead, though Wilkes himself remained very much alive and very much disappointed at the termination of his long labors.

Wilkes's own contributions were straightforward, and, despite the poor quality of his *Narrative*, impressive. He produced two massive atlases of charts—in all, some 241 in number—that remained virtually definitive until World War II, far outstripping the efforts of other nations. He also produced a volume containing eight hundred pages of meteorological tables, and a detailed volume on hydrography. Only his final work, "Physics," which he intended to be a pioneer work on the ocean floor, failed to appear because of the cessation of Congressional appropriations. Wilkes's charts, which he considered the main business of the expedition anyway, constituted the most lasting scientific contribution, especially since they incorporated surveys of 280 islands, eight hundred miles of the Oregon coast, one hundred miles of the Columbia River, the inland route via Oregon to San Francisco Bay, and fifteen hundred miles of the Antarctic coastline.

The other areas of science bewildered him and Congress as well. A staunch advocate of democracy and American nationalism, Wilkes was averse to drawing upon European scientists and scientific institutions for help in his mighty project. He believed that the American "scientifics" of the expedition were more than able to write up descriptions of what they had found. He wanted no "speculations," just factual descriptions, and these written in English rather than the Latin of scientific specialization, so that all the people of America could understand them. With no sense that a rapidly developing worldwide "culture of science" had emerged with its own methods, special literature, and judgmental institutions and even its own nontranslatable language, Wilkes felt that virtually anybody who was a close observer and a conscientious worker could do the job. He was soon surprised. Titian Peale, one of the old-school all-purpose, commonsense naturalists, provided the test case. His efforts at analysis and description for the volume on zoology proved totally inadequate to an age that had grown into scientific specialization. Peale's general volume *Zoology* had to be withdrawn and today is an exceedingly rare book. The volume, significantly retitled *Mammalogy and Ornithology*, was entirely rewritten by a Philadelphia "closet naturalist," John Cassin, one of an increasing number of Americans who had kept up with the latest specialized world literature on the subject.

Wilkes continually ran into the objections of the specialists with new training in the complexities of modern science. James Dwight Dana refused even to work in Washington away from his New Haven research library. And when his manuscript on corals was presented, Wilkes objected to it as being too speculative. Dana's friend Asa Gray, now an international figure and the doyen of botany in America, had to go over Wilkes's head to get Dana's work published. It was a work that contained "important principles," he argued. The volume became a classic that conclusively defined for the first time the nature and function of corals, which up to that time had been considered rocks rather than living organisms. Dana also helped to prove Charles Darwin's tenuous theory that Pacific atolls were indeed zoological constructions that had once surrounded mountains and volcanoes that had sunk into the sea. Even more important, in his *Geology* volume, Dana first determined the relative ages of the volcanoes that formed Pacific island chains, like the Hawaiian Islands, through the relative amount of erosion that had taken place on the great basaltic shield volcanoes. In this study, he was able to trace the sequence of volcanic eruptions and hence island-making in the Pacific island chains. He saw not only Hawaii but also other island chains emerging in the same northwest direction, but in sequence, volcano after volcano, as if the ocean

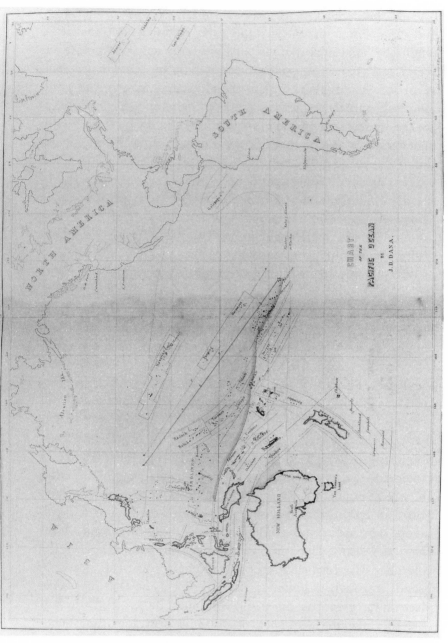

James Dwight Dana, "Chart of the Pacific Ocean." (*Smithsonian Library*) Derived from his work on the Wilkes Expedition,
his study of volcanic island chains and hence foreshadows the current theory of plate tectonics.

floor had passed over a hot spot or vent that channeled hot molten lava up from the earth's core to its surface beneath the sea. In order for this to happen in sequence the earth's surface had to be moving—like a floating raft atop a fiery sea. Dana's work in *Geology* anticipated the modern theory of plate tectonics and continental drift by over half a century. In all, working feverishly, Dana produced four masterful volumes for the report series, one of which contained 1,008 species drawings which he had personally executed. These volumes included *Zoophytes*, *Crustacea*, and *Geology*, plus the atlas of illustrations, and a fifth volume which he privately printed himself, *On Coral Reefs and Islands*. In the meantime, like the conchologist John Couthouy, he bombarded the scientific journals on both sides of the Atlantic with articles and notices. Unlike Captain Wilkes, they were well aware that date of publication, not date of discovery, gave priority in identifying new species.

The volume *Molluscs and Shells* was ultimately completed not by Couthouy but by B. A. Gould, though the most intriguing aspect of the work was a statement in a paper in the volume written by Samuel S. Haldeman. The young naturalist had suggested that "some individuals of a species were better adapted to the environment and so reproduced their kind, while those less well adapted tended to succumb." Modest though it was, and generally overlooked, Haldeman's brief conclusion clearly anticipated Darwin's theory of survival of the fittest through natural selection.

Volume VI, *Ethnography and Philology*, was completed almost effortlessly by young Horatio Hale in 1846, who then left the proofreading to his mother, the editor Sarah Josepha Hale, while he went off to Europe and the Middle East to study more languages. Hale's work was deceptively important. In addition to producing careful grammars of the Polynesians and other South Sea Island cultures, plus a careful study of the Indian languages of northwestern North America, he had also studied the "jargon" or acculturated trading languages of Oregon, Patagonia, and South Africa.

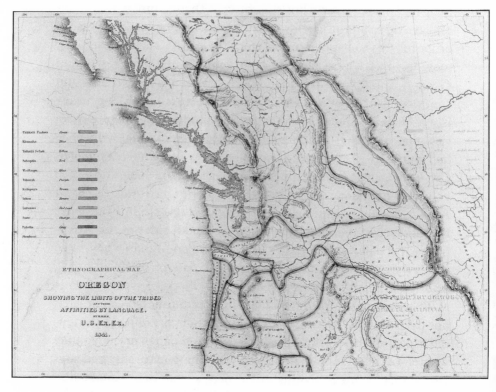

Horatio Hale, "Ethnographical Map of Oregon Showing the Limits of the Tribes and Their Affinities by Language." U.S. Exploring Expedition. 1844. *(Library of Congress)*

His three maps also had great implications. The first was a chart of native oceanic migration. The second was an ingenious chart representing the South Sea Islands according to the notions of the centrally located Tahitians. Clearly he was seeking by linguistic means to trace the *origins* of the South Seas cultures. His third map began to untangle the complex histories and culture areas of the natives of the Northwest Coast through linguistic boundaries and language crossovers. He made this particular study the hobby of his life despite spending twenty-six years as a workaday lawyer in Canada.

In the late 1870s, Hale resumed his linguistic interests. He felt compelled to refute the great Lewis Henry Morgan, who had just written what would become an anthropological classic, *Ancient Society* (1877). In that work Morgan had seen mankind as one worldwide species in different stages of cultural evolution from savagery to barbarism to civilization. Hale pointed out that Morgan was indeed right—mankind was one species—but that in ranking cultures Morgan touted the vlues of his own culture as those against which all others should be measured. Moreover Morgan, because of lack of fieldwork, which was absolutely essential if anthropology was to become a science, had misread the Polynesians completely. He saw them as promiscuous savages because he did not know their language, which would have shown him that in extended families incest taboos still held. The Polynesians simply had no word for brother or sister.

And finally in the early 1890s, an aged Horatio Hale provided basic instructions to the young Franz Boas as he set out to study the Indians of the Northwest Coast. It was Hale who insisted, somewhat to Boas's irritation, that all his studies should first be grounded in linguistics. In 1896, Boas wrote Hale's obituary thus: "Ethnology has lost a man who contributed more to our knowledge of the human race than perhaps any other single student." Today insistence on fieldwork and training in linguistics is standard practice in anthropology, as, according to Clifford Geertz, the social scientist seeks cultural meaning through being able simply to converse in an ordinary manner with the natives of the culture—and understand what they mean.

Charles Pickering, whose *Races of Man* was published as Volume IX in 1848, took a different approach. Challenging the mighty German J. J. Blumenbach, founder of anthropology, Pickering declared that he had delineated not five races as postulated by Blumenbach but no less than eleven. Moreover, each was perfectly adapted to its climate and natural environment. Though he saw man in terms of races specially created for adaptation to his environment, Pickering also saw no basis for hierarchical distinctions among races such as Lewis Henry Morgan would propose. He was an early cultural relativist despite his espousal of separate creationism. The latter Hale refuted during his two-year sabbatical to study the languages of the Middle East, in which he proved that mankind was one and simply had evolved into separate adaptive cultures. Thus the work of the two expedition ethnologists, Pickering and Hale, together provided a vision of the outlines of modern anthropology.

In a sense the common ground of these two men had to do with the questions of distribution and history or origins. Pickering himself had written a volume for the expedition reports, *Geographical Distribution of Animals and Plants*, to follow up his studies of man. It was never printed by the government, but Pickering himself published part I in 1854 and II in 1876.

Distribution had been the question that set Darwin on his quest, and it fascinated the American botanist Asa Gray, who not only worked with the plants coming in from the American West but ultimately took charge of the botanical publications of the Wilkes Expedition. Alas, however, the Wilkes collections buried him in data as he published one volume on *Phanergamia*, saw another stillborn because of federal parsimony, and supervised the volume on *Cryptogamia* by the expedition's original collector, who was by then the official Smithsonian gardener, William D. Brackenridge. Gray also supervised, with much labor, a second multiauthored volume on *Cryptogamia*, which was finally printed in 1874 but never officially distributed. It is tempting to say that Gray, inundated with collections, had no time for more profound speculations, but, as William Stanton has pointed out, thanks to these labors he made himself master of the botanical facts of the northern hemisphere, and this enabled him to make a solid major contribution to the Darwinian-special creationist debate.

What in the end had Wilkes and the United States Exploring Expedition accomplished? They had sailed 87,780 nautical miles around the globe making vast collections, charting innumerable islands, reefs, and continental shores. They had made a monumental set of charts of the Pacific and the Antarctic, which they had proved for the first time, though not without controversy, to be a continent. They had met and dealt with some of the world's strangest people, though perhaps none stranger than their own kind in the scientific, military, and political worlds in America. They had, in effect, created the outlines of modern anthropology and helped to professionalize science in America. But perhaps Wilkes's greatest contribution was to force the institutionalizing of science in the nation's capital despite the traditional know-nothingism of the people's representatives in Congress. As William Stanton has so elegantly put it, "The Exploring Expedition helped to bear the equalitarian society through its cruelest test, the survival of intellect, and in so doing placed liberty in debt to science."

Wilkes and his men scarcely knew the magnitude of their accomplishment, of course, since most of them were either frustrated in their scientific ambitions or caught up in the Great Civil War which obscured the Great United States Exploring Expedition. A good many of them faded from history altogether, and those who were remembered, as was Wilkes, were remembered for such front-page blunders as the *Trent* Affair in the Civil War, which nearly brought Britain into the war on the side of the Confederacy. His and his men's exploits at the ends of the earth were almost completely forgotten by the people of the United States until the early twentieth century, when a new age of discovery would revive old controversies over the discovery of the Antarctic and, more important, the nature of man.

CHAPTER VIII

Two Roads to Discovery: An Intellectual Drama

GIVEN the debacle of the Great United States Exploring Expedition, one might have expected that Congress had soured on all federally sponsored exploration, especially if it involved science. Quite the reverse was true. During the Era of Manifest Destiny, the spirit of nationalism and commerce ran ever higher, as did the public demand for practical information, not only about the continental United States, but of the seas and all the territories of the globe as well. More than anything, Wilkes's expedition symbolized these ambitions and desires even if it did not fulfill them. During the 1840s, such scientific establishments as the Smithsonian, the National Herbarium, the National Observatory and Depot of Charts and Instruments as well as the Coast Survey became important, entrenched national institutions.

i

ALEXANDER THE GREAT AND THE COAST SURVEY

THE UNITED STATES COAST SURVEY, begun under Ferdinand Hassler in 1818, had long languished for lack of Congressional interest. From 1843, under the energetic new leadership of

Alexander Dallas Bache, it began to grow rapidly until its annual appropriation of $500,000 made it the largest and most powerful of government bureaus. The logic of the Coast Survey's rapid growth was simple. In systematically and simultaneously conducting efficient surveys of the harbors of America's rapidly expanding coastline, including the Gulf of Mexico and, after 1848, California and Oregon, it performed a very practical service for the growing maritime interests of the country. It was also backed by a very subtle but powerful lobby composed of a new class of college-educated scientific men who, by virtue of their education among the elite at places like Harvard and Princeton, had access to rich merchants and well-placed politicians who had been their classmates or were their relatives. As the largest employer of scientifically trained men in the country, the Coast Survey commanded the fierce loyalties of the educated while at the same time proving to Congress and the public that education was not useless "humbuggery." Bache himself, with his experimental work at the Franklin Institute in Phildelphia in improving the safety of steamboat boilers, had earned the admiration of the merchant-industrialists of the Eastern Seaboard and the riverine heartland of the country.

Bache, a professor of natural philosophy and chemistry at the University of Pennsylvania, as well as an astronomer-physicist and later president of Girard College, stood for more than practical or applied science, however. From the time of his appointment as director of the Coast Survey, which had been urged by the eminent Princeton physicist Joseph Henry, whom he in turn sponsored as the first Secretary of the Smithsonian Institution, Alexander Dallas Bache, great-grandson of Benjamin Franklin, became the most powerful force for professional pure science in America. In concert with Henry, as well as Louis Agassiz and Benjamin Peirce at Harvard, in 1851 he took over the leadership of the American Association for the Advancement of Science—a national lobby which he controlled through a small group of Harvard-based scientists who styled themselves "the Scientific Lazzaroni." Their overt objective was to upgrade pure or disinterested science in America—to professionalize it, and to deprovincialize it through extensive contacts with the leading savants of Europe. They also wished to break the military monopoly on the control of science in America of the kind that the tyrannical Wilkes represented. This was relatively easy to do with the Army; Colonel John James Abert of the Corps of Topographical Engineers readily hired civilian scientists for the many western expeditions sponsored by the corps. It was more difficult to do with respect to the Navy, whose officer corps regarded even Wilkes as a suspect "intellectual." Nonetheless, Bache, who had graduated from West Point himself and employed numbers of naval officers on Coast Survey duty, was determined to wrest the nation's scientific activities away from the Navy. The naval establishment threatened the independence and power of his Coast Survey, which served under the Treasury Department. But more important, the Navy's flag officers' contempt for "scientifics" stood in the way of national progress as Bache and Henry saw it. Bache's crusade brought him and his following of "scientifics" into conflict with perhaps America's most famous scientific man of the nineteenth century—Lieutenant Matthew Fontaine Maury, U.S.N.

ii

ALEXANDER'S NEMESIS

IN THE 1840s, just as Bache was beginning to make startling progress in his movement on behalf of an elite-led science in America, Lieutenant Maury, a Virginian who was raised near Nashville in Tennessee, emerged as a kind of American Humboldt. Like his idol, Humboldt, Maury created a whole new science appropriate to the age—a "physical geography of the sea," Humboldt called it in a letter to Maury. Later it would be termed "oceanography." Others, including Wilkes, several European savants, and especially Humboldt himself, who collected information on ocean currents, temperature, specific gravity, and the relationship of the sea to the atmosphere, had preceded Maury in studying the geography of the sea. But Maury's ability to bring together all of the complex elements that related to the study of the sea resulted in a new science that eventually took him beyond geography. Maury perhaps expressed the Humboldtian aspect of his work best. He was certain "that all human phenomena were inextricably correlated with environmental conditions and that each discrete element could be understood or comprehended only as an integral segment of the whole." He thought it was possible to know everything about everything in the physical universe because all things were interrelated.

Such a vast, sweeping, comprehensive approach to science is a difficult concept to understand today. It seemed obvious to thinkers of the Romantic Age, for whom large, heroic, Faustian figures like Napoleon in Ralph Waldo Emerson's *Representative Men* or Captain Ahab of Herman Melville's *Moby Dick* constituted the roles to which men of the time aspired and the worldviews which they often assumed. In such a climate of opinion, Maury emerged as an American scientific hero fit to take his place with the giants of European science.

Latter-day scientists find fault with virtually all of his theories (some of which proved to be keys to later, more solid works). Many of the "scientifics" of his own day found him deficient because he "speculated." In a pre-Darwinian age in which pure science was pure induction, a person like Joseph Henry, who allowed no generalizations or speculations to appear in the Smithsonian monographs, found Maury's work anathema. Henry preferred the *Annual Reports of the Coast Survey* delivered by his friend Bache. But when Maury's work *The Sailing Directions* and *The Winds and Currents Charts* of the world's oceans went out to the public from the government printers, together with his highly influential book *The Physical Geography of the Sea*, he became a world figure and a kind of nemesis to the elitist Lazzaroni or Washington-Harvard axis.

It is important at the outset to understand Maury's point of view with regard to science because, like Prince Henry the Navigator in the days before Columbus, he was a key figure in what was rapidly becoming an "American Age of Discovery." For Maury, science grew out of practical tasks that were directly related to the needs of commerce. He did not scorn the information and support provided by whalers and merchantmen, by captains of men-of-war and newly minted passed midshipmen. By the same token he did not reject the information provided by scientific specialists like the microscopist Jacob Whitman Bailey at West Point. All information about the world, however mundane, was somehow interrelated and could be linked together at higher levels, as Humboldt had shown. Out of vast amounts of data—and quantity was important—concepts could be formed and hypotheses could be generated. These could then be subject to constant testing in the course of which new concepts would be formed that explained the data more completely and usefully. Many of Maury's concepts, such as that of the existence of an open polar sea, proved to be wrong, but in attempting to prove his hypotheses, Maury not only prompted important new discoveries and techniques; he also created, out of his questions, the science of oceanography. Thus the *process* of his endeavors was more important than the product in many cases. *The Physical Geography of the Sea*, for example, was a worldwide symbol of the emergence of the new science, but one writer has more correctly identified it as a dramatic "progress report" rather than the definitive work because of the changes in the numerous editions of Maury's best-selling book. Like Prince Henry and Hakluyt, he was really reporting the discoveries and adventures of other men whom he had sent on missions across the world's oceans. It was Maury's concepts and experiments, as well as the practical results that he and his men achieved, that were really important, not the highflown speculations of the *Physical Geography of the Sea*. Moreover, the emergence of oceanography as an interdisciplinary science demonstrates, better than anything else, the critical role of exploration, carried out by men who were often rather ordinary thinkers and technicians, to the development of a whole paradigm in science.

Maury came into his own literally by accident. On the night of October 17, 1839, as he was heading east from a Tennessee visit to his parents, the stagecoach upon which he was riding overturned and Maury's right leg was crushed. He lay for months an invalid in the ramshackle Hotel Phoenix in backwoods Somerset, Ohio, tended by quacks and sometimes by respectable doctors, all of whom despaired of his recovery. His leg had to be rebroken and reset without anesthesia. Only through force of will and an extreme tolerance for pain did Maury save his leg. And then, his kneecap shattered, he limped for the rest of his life. This would have been a tragedy for anyone, but Maury was a lieutenant in the United States Navy. His injury made him unfit for sea duty, and hence his promising career seemed to have come to an abrupt end.

Prior to the accident, Maury was a very active and able young officer. In 1829–30, he had sailed aboard the *Vincennes* in the United States Navy's first around-the-world cruise. Then in 1831 he had served as sailing master aboard the *Falmouth* as it rounded the Horn and took up patrol duties along the west coast of South America for two years. On this cruise, Maury first began to note the almost complete absence of accurate charts of the critical Cape Horn region, and for that matter of the whole southern Pacific. About the same time the British Admiralty also recognized the deficiency and sent Captain Robert FitzRoy to sea in command of the *Beagle* to remedy the situation.

After his return from South American duty, Maury married and began to establish a family. Promotions were slow in the Navy, but Maury was attached to the service. He did not, as so many other military officers did, turn his talents to a career in civilian life during a period of frontier boom. Instead he served aboard ship on coastal and harbor surveys, and at one point he even managed the United States Gold Mine in Virginia. His great love, however, was the science of navigation. In 1834, he published an article in the *American Journal of Science*, the first scientific article published by a United States naval officer. And in 1836, he wrote a textbook entitled *A New Theoretical*

and Practical Treatise on Navigation, based on all the latest authorities since Bowditch. It was immediately adopted by the
Navy for instructing its midshipmen. Ever so solidly, he was
building a reputation and demonstrating that naval officers were
capable of competent scientific work. At the same time, in letters
to various journals and newspapers, he strongly advocated the
reform of the Navy promotion system and the launching of the
Great United States Exploring Expedition. At one point, when
Commodore Ap Catesby Jones was assembling the expedition,
Maury was slated to be the chief scientific officer. But when
Jones resigned, Maury's appointment went with him.

After the stagecoach accident and his partial recovery, Maury
tried desperately to get sea duty. His friend Commodore Jones
offered to make him flag lieutenant aboard his vessel, but the
Navy's doctors turned Maury down. Then in 1842, Maury was
urged to apply for the position as superintendent of the Navy's
Depot of Charts and Instruments in Washington. The depot,
though housed in a small building at the time (actually Lieutenant Wilkes's house), had suddenly become a large institution
because of the return of so many charts and instruments from
the Wilkes expedition. At first Maury refused to put himself
forward as a candidate, but when he heard that George Blunt, a
civilian chartmaker from New York, might get the position, he
declared himself interested. Upon receiving the appointment,
Maury made his loyalty to the Navy very clear: he was, he
wrote in a letter, "determined to ask no advice or instruction
from the savants, but to let it be out and out a navy work." He
soon learned that this was impossible, but his role as superintendent of the depot enabled him to form a scientific corps
within the Navy composed of young officers, Navy professors of
science and mathematics, and civilian specialists dedicated to research in four areas: hydrography, astronomy, meteorology, and
magnetism. The teams that he assembled helped create oceanography. But this wide range of interests and this process of interdisciplinary creativity aroused the enmity of some practitioners,
spurred on by Bache, who preferred narrower definitions in the

science of astronomy and who believed that they had a monopoly on professionalism in the discipline.

The Depot of Charts and Instruments had been headed by Lieutenants Louis M. Goldsborough, Charles Wilkes, and Melville Gilliss previously, and Gilliss, backed by Bache, was in the process of pushing through a bill to have it made the first U.S. astronomical observatory as well. The able Gilliss had already compiled the first American star catalogue, and he expected to superintend the new observatory. But in 1844, two years after Maury's original appointment, and in the wake of Maury's equally genuine achievements in astronomy, he was selected over Gilliss and moved into a sumptuous new building which now housed the Observatory and the Depot. Lieutenant Gilliss, bitter over what he mistakenly believed to be Maury's political maneuverings, went to join Bache on the Coast Survey.

Meanwhile Maury, enthusiastic about astronomy since his first treatise on navigation, had turned his attention to the stars. Among the first things he did was to invite John Quincy Adams, the Observatory's earliest advocate, over to look through the telescope of one of the federal government's first "lighthouses of the skies," then still housed in an old building on Capitol Hill. He also compiled another star catalogue, brought in a staff of four astronomers, and, on the night of January 13, 1843, made the world's first observation of the splitting of Biela's Comet. This observation was a spectacular achievement in an era of omens and portents that produced Mormonism and in which many citizens anxiously awaited the millennium.

Because of his interest in navigation at sea, Maury clearly recognized the value of an observatory. It enabled the fixing of longitudes and, through continuous astronomical observations, the establishment of time itself with precision. He read widely in the works of European authorities and acquired a thorough knowledge of the subject. Thus in 1846, when the French scientist Urbain J. J. Leverrier and the Cambridge, Massachusetts, astronomer Couch Adams jointly discovered the new planet Neptune, Maury was shrewd enough to commission a civilian

scientist, Sears Walker, to search back through the history of recorded star sightings to note if it had ever been seen before.
Walker discovered that it had been sighted and noted as a fixed
star in 1795. In compiling subsequent sightings, he found a correct orbit for Neptune, precipitating an international feud with
Leverrier. By that time, however, Maury had dismissed Walker
because he had turned his observatory work over to Joseph
Henry, who published it without acknowledgment to Maury
and the National Observatory. Walker then went to work for
Maury's rival, Bache.

iii
A NEW SCIENCE OF THE SEA

LIEUTENANT MAURY'S major work was not to be in astronomy,
however. Instead, intrigued by the huge collection of long-
neglected naval logbooks deposited at the Observatory, he introduced an innovation so simple that it revolutionized the
study of the sea. He introduced statistical analysis to the study
of the oceans. Setting a team of midshipmen and civilian em-
ployees to work correlating data concerning winds, weather,
water temperature, and currents derived from the logbooks, he
began to build up a statistical picture of the world's oceans.
Maury's team of assistants scrutinized the logbooks for "every
scrap of information that might assist the navigator." As Maury
put it, "the compiler wades through log-book after log-book, and
scores down in column after column, and upon line after line,
mark after mark" until he had completed the study of logbooks
for a particular 5 ° square segment of the ocean. This laboriously
acquired information was then laid down on specially designed
charts or represented in ingenious circle graphs. Using this
method, Maury's men and navigators at sea could tell at a
glance, for example, the percentage of prevailing winds in 5°
squares in the Atlantic for any given month or even week of the
year—provided the logbook data was available. This team effort

and broad data base took Maury far beyond the individual efforts of even the mighty Humboldt.

As early as 1831, the British scientists Sir John W. Lubbock
and William Whewell had published a series of articles and
maps concerning the causes and directions of the ocean's tidal
currents. Their speculations were expanded on the basis of
writings by Humboldt and put in systematic form by the Scotsman Alexander Keith Johnston in a popular Humboldtian work
entitled *The Physical Atlas of Natural Phenomena*, published
in 1848. One quarter of Johnston's *Atlas* was devoted to hydrography, in which he now included generalized wind and current
charts of the world's oceans, as well as tidal charts juxtaposed
with an analysis of the river systems of the world. In addition,
Johnston's hydrography section was immediately followed by a
section on the meteorology of the world, which he saw as being
directly related to the oceans' currents. Many of Johnston's generalizations were based on data from individual voyages. Even
though the Scotsman's comprehensive work linked the world's
oceans, river systems, and meteorology together, it did not serve
as the basis for Maury's much broader statistical approach to the
subject in his *Winds and Current Charts* and *Sailing Directions*. Neither did the relatively sophisticated *Physical Geography* published by an Englishwoman, Mary Fairfax Somerville,
in 1848. Like Johnston, Mrs. Somerville was inspired by and
encouraged to write her book, the first of its kind by a woman,
by Humboldt and Sir John Herschel. In her work she included a
long chapter on the oceans, based, like Johnston's *Atlas*, on the
reports of the great voyagers, and, in addition, J. Scott Russell's
Theory of Waves. In a strikingly succinct passage she summed
up the multiple causes of ocean currents—a question with
which Maury struggled in some confusion:

> Constant currents are produced by the combined action of the rota-
> tion of the earth, the heat of the sun, and the trade-winds; periodical
> currents are occasioned by tides, monsoons, and other long-contin-
> ued winds; temporary currents arise from the tides, melting ice, and

from every gale of some duration. A perpetual circulation is kept up in the waters of the main by these vast marine streams; they are sometimes superficial and sometimes submarine, according as their density is greater or less than that of the surrounding sea.

Works such as these by Johnston and Mrs. Somerville, along with Humboldt's writings, undoubtedly provided a conceptual basis for Maury's later classic *The Physical Geography of the Sea*, but in the publication of his *Winds and Current Charts* and *Sailing Directions*, Lieutenant Maury preceded both the Scotsman and the Englishwoman. His work in this vein was produced between 1843 and 1847, culminating at least a year before their publications appeared. And, if not conceptually, then methodologically Maury's works were far in advance because of his statistical approach through the correlation of logbook data.

A statistical analysis based on logbooks had previously been employed with striking success by William C. Redfield, a former harnessmaker in Middletown, Connecticut. In 1831, Redfield, who soon became an important figure in American scientific circles, had published "Remarks on the Prevailing Storms of the Atlantic Coast of the North American States" in *The American Journal of Science*. Later, in 1833, he had published "Observations on the Hurricanes and Storms of the West Indies and the Coast of the United States" in the same journal. His work was based on some seventy logbooks that he studied through the auspices of E. and G. W. Blunt, publishers of *The American Coast Pilot*. In these articles, Redfield went far beyond narrow study and generalized about the winds and currents of the Atlantic and Pacific basins as well as their relationship to the winds sweeping over the continents. Redfield's work and Humboldt's comprehensive studies of isothermal or climatic zones formed the methodological and theoretical basis for Maury's larger enterprise at the U.S. Naval Observatory.

Statistical analysis was perhaps the most critical of these concepts. It is now so commonplace, especially with computers, that Redfield's and Maury's innovation can easily be over-looked. But only in astronomy, especially the worldwide observations of the transits of Venus, in calculations of terrestrial magnetism and plant distribution by Humboldt, and in Jeremiah N. Reynolds's crude compilations from New England whaling logs had anything like it been tried before in the world of science. The use of a broad data base, however uneven in quality the observations were, had something that seemed characteristically American and democratic about it. In one sense, Wilkes had set the style when he deployed a larger exploring squadron over the Pacific rather than, as was the European custom, using one or two ships following a single track. But Wilkes, unlike Maury, demanded precision in hydrography and astronomy. Maury, at first using logs of naval vessels, then those of civilian commercial ships—whalers, traders, etc.—which he supplied with standard forms and instructions, was basically forced to rely upon cruder observations and what today would be called a "calculus of probability." For this he was roundly criticized by the scientific elite in America. In 1865, after Maury had joined the Confederate Navy, Bache threw out his data as "worthless." But Maury's *Winds and Current Charts* and his *Sailing Directions* proved to be a spectacular practical success.

As early as 1842, Maury had persuaded his chief, Commodore Crane of the Bureau of Ordnance and Hydrography, to require Navy captains to send in hydrological, navigational, and meterological data to the Observatory upon returning from a voyage. The old salts did this grudgingly, but Maury, pushing forward, devised a standard form or *Abstract Log* which was distributed to the officers and made reporting easier. He also employed James P. Espy, a distinguished meteorologist, known as "the Storm King," to help analyze the data. By 1843, Maury had enough data to make a crude winds-and-currents chart of the Atlantic, but he focused principally on the route south to Rio de Janeiro.

When Maury's first chart was published in 1847, Captain Jackson, commanding the brig *W. H. D. C. Wright*, used it, and made the round trip to Rio in thirty-five days less than had ever been done before. Maury's charts soon were in great demand among merchant ship captains, and Maury employed agents in New York and Boston to encourage their distribution. The charts were issued routinely to Navy captains, but civilians had to agree to return a filled-in *Abstract Log* in order to obtain them. For civilian captains, Maury devised a simplified *Abstract Log* which called for daily data on latitude, longitude, currents, temperature, barometer readings, forms and directions of clouds, probability of clear skies, hours of fog, rain, snow, and hail, magnetic variations of the compass, and the rate, direction, and velocity of the winds.

Maury made the raw data meaningful by turning it into enormous amounts of information ingeniously expressed by symbols and graphs. The maps and graphs showed many times more "bytes" of information than large books. They could also be utilized virtually at a glance. Like the curved-handle ax, they were a characteristically simple and efficient American tool. As he explained to John Quincy Adams, the symbols were all-important. Winds were shown by small brushlike images, "the head of the brush showing the direction from whence the winds blow, the length of the brush showing the comparative force." He also delineated currents by arrows of varying length according to the strength of the current. Roman numerals indicated the degree of magnetic variation; numbers with lines drawn under them showed the temperature of the water, while the name of the ship, its route, and the year the voyage was undertaken were printed right on the chart. Maury also devised the previously mentioned circular charts that indicated "the relative times in every 5° square of the South Atlantic that the wind had been reported by mariners as blowing from each direction during a particular month."

Between 1847 and 1860, Maury issued six series of maps which included, in all, over sixty charts and diagrams. Series A were *Track Charts* that indicated routes taken by previous voyagers. They included wind and current data and were perhaps

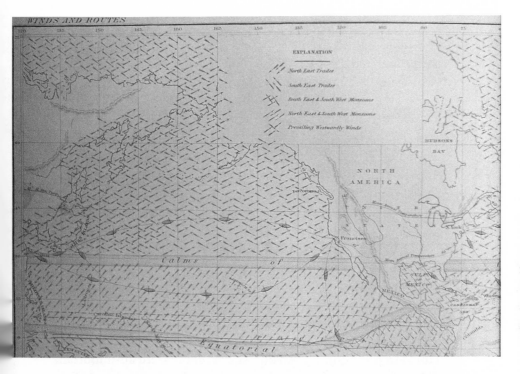

Section of one of Matthew Fontaine Maury's wind and current charts. Winds are indicated by brushlike symbols in which the head of the brush points towards the direction from which the wind is blowing. The width of the brush indicates the variations of the winds during a given day and the length of the tail gives some idea of the winds' strengths. The currents are indicated by lines, arrows, and numbers that represent their relative strength. As time passed, Maury and his men charted the tracks of actual ships on these detailed maps, which became extremely popular. From Matthew Fontaine Maury, *Sailing Directions*. 1858. *(William H. Goetzmann Collection)*

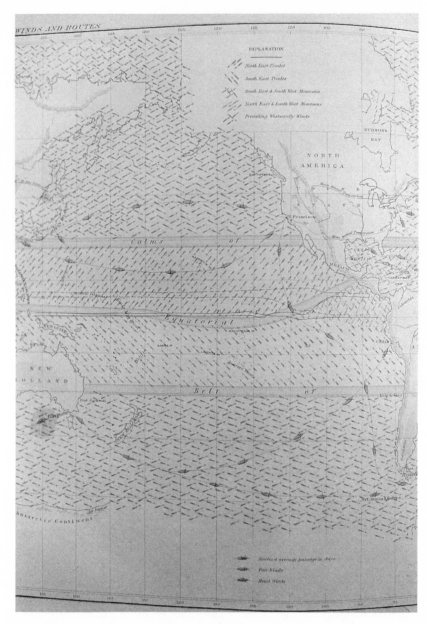

Matthew Fontaine Maury, "World Winds and Current Chart." From Maury, *Sailing Directions*. (*William H. Goetzmann Collection*)

Maury's unique wind rose that accompanied his pilot charts. This chart shows the relative number of times in every five-degree square of a portion of the ocean that mariners had reported the winds blowing from a certain direction during a particular month. From Maury, *Sailing Directions*. *(William H. Goetzmann Collection)*

the easiest to use. Series B were *Trade-wind Charts;* Series C were more complex *Pilot Charts* which contained much greater detail; Series D were *Thermal Charts;* Series E were *Storm and Rain Charts;* and Series F were *Whale Charts,* which recorded sightings and migrations of various kinds of right whales and sperm whales. These charts were constantly updated as new *Abstract Logs* came into the Observatory.

With the Gold Rush to California, Maury's charts assumed enormous importance. They immediately shortened the passage from New York to California by forty to forty-four days, and they enabled the great clipper ships like the *Flying Cloud* to establish records as they raced one another around the Horn and north through the Pacific Ocean. In one day, for example, the *Flying Cloud* sailed 374 nautical miles. Maury's maps, as much as the vessels' beautiful design, helped make the clipper ships famous. By the end of 1851, Maury could report that a thousand American ships were sending data to him and using his charts. In that year too, by means of Maury's *Charts and Sailing Directions,* the floundering U.S.S. *San Francisco* was located just in time, out in the storm-tossed Atlantic, and its surviving crewmen rescued. Dramatic feats such as these made Maury and his work famous, as year after year he produced his *Charts and Sailing Directions.*

In 1853, at Maury's instigation, an International Maritime Meteorological Conference met in Brussels. Representatives from ten nations, including the United States, attended, although Britain, already assuming technological superiority on the seas, did so reluctantly. It was only after Maury made a speech on the utility of his charts and *Abstract Logs* before the marine insurers Lloyd's of London that his friend Lord Wrottesley of the Royal Society was able to persuade his government to send Captain Frederick William Beechey of South Seas fame to the conference. Other nations represented were Belgium, Denmark, France, the Netherlands, Norway, Sweden, Portugal, and Russia. Out of the conference came an international agreement whereby the mariners of all these nations would employ a specially devised *Abstract Log* and share information used to compile international marine charts. Maury and all men of the sea now had access to information from tens of thousands of vessels every year, thus greatly increasing the probable accuracy of the charts. For Maury personally and for the United States, the Brussels conference was a great triumph. For the first time, the United States had indisputably led the way in a branch of world science. The many decorations and honors that Maury received from foreign countries as a result of his work paled in significance before this fact.

iv

MAURY AND OCEANOGRAPHY

IN THE MEANTIME, Maury was pushing on into other aspects of the science he had helped to create. In March of 1849, Maury persuaded the Secretary of the Navy to assign him three small vessels to carry out advanced research in the Atlantic Ocean. He was already collecting all the data he needed about the winds and surface currents, but now Maury hoped to investigate the depths of the sea. He knew from the French cartographer Philippe Buache's formulations that the oceans could be thought of as distinct basins, but how deep were these basins, what was the nature of their floors, and what caused the ocean waters to circulate from one basin to the other? These and dozens of other questions, such as the relative temperatures at different ocean depths and the chemical composition of the waters, fascinated him. Maury was gradually moving from a two-dimensional surface study of the world's oceans to the complex multidimensional studies that characterize modern oceanography.

On October 25, 1849, Maury's first experimental exploring vessel, the U.S.S. *Taney*, sailed from New York with orders to trace a zigzag course across the Atlantic, sounding its depths and underwater currents as well as surface phenomena. Maury ordered the commander of the vessel, Lieutenant Joseph Walsh, to make frequent observations of the temperature of the ocean at various depths and test the specific gravity and saltiness of the ocean in addition to his sounding activities and meteorological observations. The voyage of the *Taney* was the world's first true oceanographic undertaking. Unfortunately both the vessel and its equipment proved unequal to the task. The ship was a "floating coffin" of rotting timbers that somehow survived a stormy crossing of the Atlantic. It was condemned by a naval board in the Cape Verde Islands. Nonetheless they ordered Walsh to sail it back across the Atlantic to the Virgin Islands, a feat which he accomplished only through pluck and luck. Though Walsh collected a significant amount of oceanographic data, he was hampered by his inability to make true soundings of the ocean floor. With existing equipment and techniques, sounding lines invariably snapped. Moreover, frequently it was impossible to tell when a sounding lead landed on the bed of the ocean because the heavy line coiled on the bottom beside it.

After some experimentation with new sounding techniques and a lighter line, Maury launched a second voyage in October of 1851, using the *Dolphin*, commanded by Lieutenant Samuel P. Lee. This had better results, though they were still inconclusive in many respects. Lee and his crew did perfect sounding methods with respect to line and lead and the use of small boats. In the meantime, working under Maury at the Observatory, an ingenious young graduate of the Naval Academy's first class, Passed Midshipman John M. Brooke, had devised a novel sounding lead that enabled one to tell when it hit bottom. In Brooke's device a thirty-two-pound lead ball fell off the line when it hit bottom, signaling the event. It also released a small sample capsule that could be brought to the surface. Because of the weight of the ball, the capsule stuck into the ocean floor at first stroke and took a bottom sample before it was released. Thus, for the first time, man could sound the deepest parts of the ocean. It was now theoretically possible to map the ocean floor accurately.

In September 1852, Maury sent the *Dolphin*, commanded by

Lieutenant Otway Berryman, into the Atlantic to begin this task with the proper equipment. Brooke's Patented Sounding Device was a rousing success, and Maury was able to send the world's first specimens from the deep ocean floor to Professors Jacob Whitman Bailey at West Point, Benjamin Silliman at Yale, and Charles Lyell in Britain. The whole cruise of the *Dolphin* in 1852–53 was so successful that Maury was able to compile two important maps of the Atlantic. One, which he called an "Orographic Map," gave a profile of the bottom on the 39th parallel. A second, pretentiously titled *Bathymetrical Map of the North Atlantic Basin with Contour Lines Drawn in at 1,000, 2,000, 3,000 and 4,000 Fathoms*, was the world's first map of an ocean floor. These were published in Maury's *Winds and Currents* volume for 1854.

Maury's ocean floor research and Samuel F. B. Morse's success in sending telegraphic signals over a two-thousand-mile distance made an underwater Atlantic telegraph connection feasible. By 1855, the project was under way, under the auspices of an international consortium headed by Cyrus W. Field of New York. It became the great work of the age. And because it was the great project of the age, Alexander Dallas Bache deemed it too important to be left to the likes of "amateurs" like Maury. Accordingly, he persuaded Secretary of the Navy Dobbin to give him the new steam-powered sounding vessel *Arctic* that had been assigned to Maury. He also persuaded Lieutenant Berryman to command the vessel. But instead of using Maury's tested methods for sounding and mapping, the Coast Survey introduced new devices such as Massey's Depth Indicator and a plumb-bob variant of Brooke's sounding device. Neither of these worked, as the *Arctic* steamed back and forth across the Atlantic between Newfoundland and Ireland in 1856, improbably extending the U.S. "Coast" Survey all the way to Europe.

Upon Berryman's return, Maury, furious at the perfidy of Bache, Berryman, and Secretary Dobbin, checked the results of the expedition and found them full of gross errors. He turned the information over to a naval examination board, which deter-

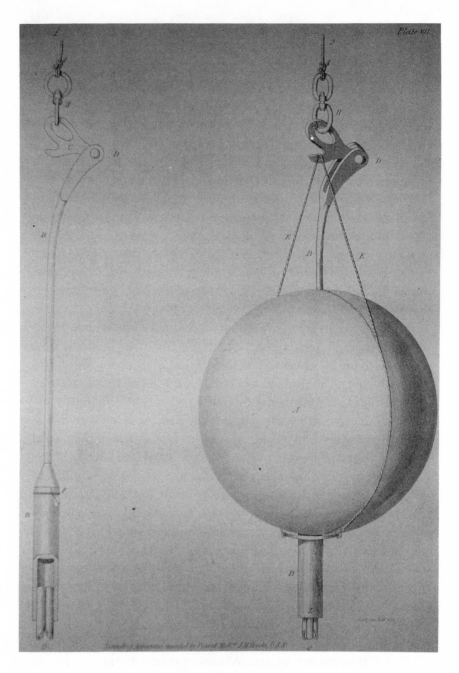

Diagram of Lieutenant John Mercer Brooke's Deep Sea Sounding Apparatus. From Maury, *Sailing Directions*. *(William H. Goetzmann Collection)*

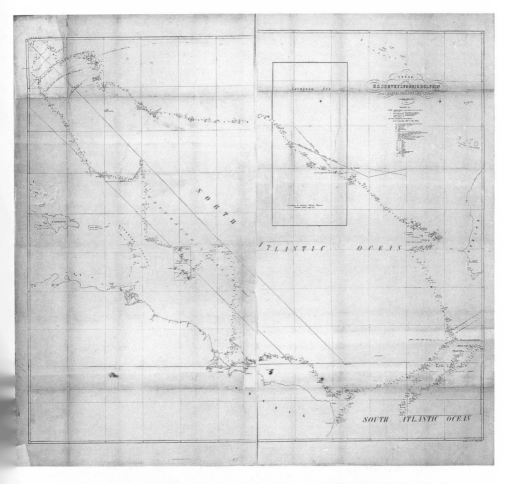

Matthew Fontaine Maury, "Track of the U.S. Surveying Brig *Dolphin*." 1851–52. Track chart of voyage in the Atlantic. *(The National Archives)* The world's first oceanographic chart.

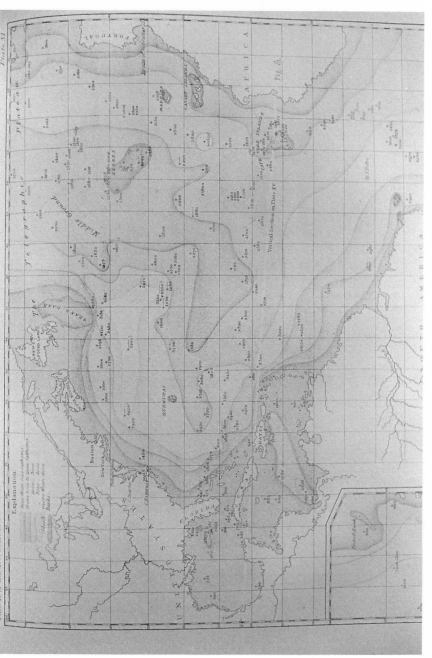

Lieutenants Berryman and Lee, "Deep-Sea Soundings of the North Atlantic." 1852. From Maury, *Sailing Directions*. (*William H. Goetzmann Collection*) This map is the first major map of an ocean floor with soundings indicated. Note Maury's depiction of what he called the "Telegraphic Plateau." Maury also shows, however, the deep trench off Newfoundland.

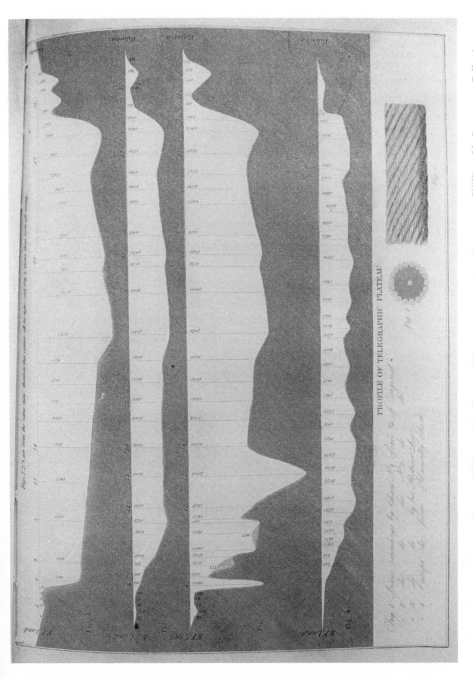

Matthew Fontaine Maury, "Profile of 'Telegraphic Plateau.'" From Maury, *Sailing Directions*. (*William H. Goetzmann Collection*)

mined that Berryman's eastward and westward logs for approximately the same position did not agree with each other. This was difficult to discern because Berryman did not even bother to note the positions where he had made soundings. His ocean floor maps, which he had illegally released prematurely to the Transatlantic Telegraph Company, were deemed completely fraudulent. Maury did not hesitate to bring these facts to the attention of the Secretary of the Navy, the Transatlantic Telegraph Company, and the public press on both sides of the Atlantic. He called for another expedition. The British volunteered at this time, however, and Lieutenant Dayman on the H.M.S. *Cyclops* did the job—using Brooke's Patented Sounding Device. The Prussian government awarded Brooke its highest scientific honor.

On the basis of his own *Dolphin* expedition and the additional data collected by Dayman, Maury announced that in the very place where it was proposed to lay the cable, there was a vast underwater "marine plateau," which, Maury opined, "seems to have been placed there especially for the purpose of holding the wires and of keeping them out of harm's way." Thereafter, Maury habitually referred to it as "the Telegraphic Plateau." He also claimed to have discovered no strong current on the floor of this portion of the Atlantic. He described this evidence thusly, in a dramatic passage characteristic of Maury's often poetic prose:

> The specimens of deep-sea soundings, for which we are indebted to Lt. Brooke, are as pure and as free from the sand of the sea as the snow flake that falls when it is calm upon the lea. . . .The sea . . . is always letting fall upon its bed showers of . . . microscopic shells. . . . This process, continued for ages, has covered the depths of the ocean as with a mantle, of organisms as delicate as the mailed frost and as light as the undrifted snow flake of the mountain.

If there were strong currents there would be rough sand and pebbles and no delicate undisturbed organisms. Professor Jacob

Whitman Bailey, West Point's microscopist, had analyzed the evidence which had been brought up with Brooke's sounding device on the cruise of the *Dolphin*. But the *Dolphin's* researches and those of Lieutenant Dayman on the *Cyclops* also disclosed the existence of deep underwater trenches off the coasts of Newfoundland and Ireland respectively. Maury, in what appeared to be a contradiction of his "Telegraphic Plateau" thesis, also believed that the Newfoundland trench was the deepest part of the Atlantic.

Maury's advice concerning the cable was that, except close to shore where the pull was heaviest, it ought to be light in weight—"no more than a strand of copper wire encased in gutta percha." In this he was partially correct, as in 1857, on the first attempt, the great heavy cable parted because of its weight. A second attempt was made in 1858, using lighter cable and starting the cable ships from mid-Atlantic, then proceeding east and west respectively. This method worked, and for a time the great wire spoke across the ocean. But then it broke again. In fact, there was no gentle submarine plateau, but there were deep canyons, particularly off Newfoundland, as Maury's map actually showed. There were also many smaller canyons and ridges as well, and it was not until 1866 that the cable was successfully laid. However, with regard to the Great Atlantic Telegraph Cable, Maury managed to share the limelight on both sides of the Atlantic with Cyrus W. Field in the 1850s.

A different aspect of the telegraph cable problem led directly to a hypothesis Maury was developing about the Arctic Ocean currents. Dayman's maps indicated that the "Telegraphic Plateau" was really an extension of Greenland over which three ocean currents collided and deposited the debris of centuries, which in turn built up the plateau. As Maury put it, "The polar current, which comes down between Iceland and Greenland, meets on this middle ground the ice-bearing current from Davis' Straits; and these two are met again and crossed by the Gulf Stream." He concluded dramatically, "Many a load of earth, rock, and gravel has, we may suppose, in the process of ages, been dropped from icebergs down upon the middle ground." One wonders how Maury squared this image with that picture of the ocean depths covered with an undisturbed mantle "as delicate as the mailed frost" which he conveyed to Cyrus W. Field. But for Maury hypothesis sometimes worked backward. The "Telegraphic Plateau" was really proof that these polar currents and the Gulf Stream all came together in a circular motion and eventually created an "open polar sea."

The "open polar sea" concept had long preoccupied Maury. He had read with interest Sir John Barrow's article "Behring's Strait and the Polar Sea," published in 1818, which raised anew the age-old question of a direct polar great circle route to China that had launched Davis and Baffin and Frobisher in the sixteenth century. Maury had also been convinced by the whaler Captain William Scoresby in *The Arctic Regions and the Northern Whale Fishery* (1820, reprinted 1848) that there was something to Barrow's thesis. Accordingly, he assigned his brother-in-law, Lieutenant William Lewis Herndon, to begin compiling data on the habits of whales as early as 1847, with the objective of "showing where the whalemen have hunted and where they have found their game; consequently," Maury wrote, "this chart enables us to designate those parts of the ocean where [sic] the whales 'use,' and those parts where they never go, and to tell where in each month the animal is likely to be found." Maury deemed this to be important information on a practical level because the value of the whaling industry "far exceeds that of the gold mines of California."

A number of facts and speculations emerged from the study of whales and their peregrinations. Maury first found that "tropical regions of the ocean are to the right whale as a sea of fire, through which he cannot pass, and into which he never enters." Thus the right whale was solely confined to the cold waters of the northern hemisphere. The sperm whale, on the other hand, cruised in warm waters near the equator and in the tropics. Maury noted two further curiosities. Sperm whales were frequently seen in northern seas or at very high latitudes to the south near the Antarctic. Maury concluded that Antarctic waters near Cape Horn were warmer and that the sperm whale followed the warm currents of the Gulf Stream and Humboldt Current northward in the Atlantic and Pacific respectively. A second conclusion he reached fascinated explorers of his day. Drawing on the work of Scoresby and others, he noted that right whales harpooned near Baffin Island (on the Atlantic side) had been taken in Bering Strait (on the Pacific side), suggesting that there was indeed an unobstructed, ice-free Northwest Passage. Whales could not stay down long enough to cross under a sea of ice. According to Maury, who used whales as tracers to study the flow of currents, this connoted the distinct possibility that in the far north there existed an open polar sea.

V

THE PHYSICAL GEOGRAPHY OF THE SEA: AN ASSESSMENT

IN THE FALL of 1853, when Maury delivered the copy for the sixth edition of his *Explanations and Sailing Directions to Accompany the Winds and Currents Charts* to his publishers, E. C. and J. Biddle of Philadelphia, they pointed out to him that he owned no copyright to the material. According to Maury, they asserted that he would soon see "some Yankee bookmaker steal his thunder and reap a fortune from it." They advised him to compile and copyright his own book and to call it by the Baron von Humboldt's felicitous phrase "The Physical Geography of the Sea." An alarmed Maury set to work in haste and by June of 1854 had produced his classic book—the first comprehensive text on oceanography and a work that should have defined the field. It was first published by Harper and Brothers in 1855, and went through countless subsequent editions, five in the first year alone. Several British editions were also published in short order, and within a decade there were numerous foreign-language editions. The book was repeatedly published in many languages down through the 1870s, when the results of the British *Challenger* expedition began to replace it.

Maury was able to write *The Physical Geography of the Sea*

so rapidly because it was essentially a compilation of papers which he had delivered earlier before such bodies as the American Association for the Advancement of Science and a digest of materials from his official *Winds and Currents* books. In the introduction to the first edition of his book Maury admitted this. But just as the *Winds and Currents* volumes often varied as to subjects, so too did *The Physical Geography of the Sea.* In the sixth edition of 1856, Maury covered a vast range of topics— "the Gulf Stream and its Influence on Climates, the atmosphere, land and sea breezes, red fogs and dust from the Sahara and South America, the probable relationship of magnetism to the circulation of the atmosphere, currents of the sea, salts of the sea, the equatorial cloud rings, the open arctic sea, the geological agency of the winds, the depth of the ocean, the basin of the Atlantic, the climates of the ocean, winds, storms, the drift of the sea"—and included two chapters concerning the effectiveness of his charts and the Brussels International Maritime Meteorological Conference.

It was a strangely fascinating yet wildly disorganized book whose details critics in his own day and in the present have argued about and largely dismissed. Popular British and American journals gave it high praise, though the comment in the French periodical *Revue des Deux Mondes* must surely have been made with tongue in cheek. The reviewer declared, "Often indeed his powerful imagination makes of Maury a veritable poet and his descriptions recall those stories of the *Thousand and One Nights....*" Bache's friend Benjamin Apthorp Gould, in *The American Journal of Science*, was more direct: "While the work contains much instruction, we cannot adopt some of its theories, believing them unsustained by facts."

Despite the previous existence of at least one German work by Heinrich Berghaus, which could have been based on nothing like the systematic data collected by the U.S. Naval Observatory, Maury's book must be considered the pioneer comprehensive work on the science of oceanography. With the exception of the relationship of the rotation of the earth to the circulation of the atmosphere and oceans, a question dealt with and resolved by William Ferrel of Tennessee in 1856, Maury had confronted most of the basic questions that defined the new science. He did so, as he admitted, on two levels. The first rested on the empirical data collected through the logbooks and expeditions such as that of the *Dolphin*. The second arose as multiple hypotheses which Maury saw logically arising from these data and subject to change with new data. In his day it was not fashionable to hypothesize in science, and Maury was criticized for it. Yet not all of his hypotheses were wrong. He was in general correct when, in debating the great Sir William Herschel, he argued that density and temperature had more to do with the circulation of the oceans than did the winds. And the cruise of the H.M.S. *Lightning* in 1868 confirmed his belief in deep currents in the oceans. The British research vessel H.M.S. *Challenger*, which exhaustively studied all aspects of the oceans in the 1870s, issued reports that tended to support Maury's theory of cold undercurrents and warm uppercurrents simultaneously stemming from the Antarctic. Later expeditions confirmed his assertions about red land dust blowing out to sea combining with a "rainfall" of organisms to make up the surface of the ocean floor. In the late nineteenth century, German scientists observed in accordance with Maury that "cold water at the poles was continually sinking and flowing towards the equator," and "to replace the sinking polar waters, masses of warm surface water from the tropics floated towards the poles." This, of course, was what Maury was trying to prove with his polar sea model. He saw polar circulation as the key to the whole nature of the flow of the oceans, whose currents were primarily generated by changes in temperature and density.

It is thus not true, as one modern commentator, John Leighly, has asserted, that "the application of physical theory to the sea and the atmosphere would have been little different if the book had never been written," except insofar as later oceanographers continually rediscovered and considered questions that Maury had raised. In fact, it was not until the 1890s, when the Norwegians undertook the task off their coast, that anyone else recognized the value of conducting ocean research by means of a statistical method based on thousands of standard logbooks. Even the celebrated *Challenger* expedition was not based on a matrix of information, but on a linear cruise that covered far less of the oceans than did the larger Wilkes Expedition.

The grandiosity of Maury's method and the grandiosity of his vision dramatized and reified the emergent science of the sea. And yet this grand vision seemed to be something old rather than something new. Like his idol Alexander von Humboldt, Maury was an exemplar of the closed Newtonian world view of the seventeenth and eighteenth centuries. He saw the earth and its atmosphere as a gigantic machine functioning in harmony, "like the music of the spheres," a phrase he used often. For Maury there was no sense of clash or conflict as there would be for Darwin or Wallace. Instead, there was before him the perfect world machine which if examined carefully would yield its secrets to mankind. It was also paradoxically a static machine that at the same time moved within limits. In short, the earth, with its oceans and atmosphere, was a replica of Newton's closed system of planetary motion. It was also a mechanism controlled by God through design—a concept that nearly every scientist in the America of Maury's time held to be true, including Joseph Henry, James Dwight Dana, Asa Gray, Benjamin Silliman, Louis Agassiz, and Alexander Dallas Bache.

What Maury introduced that was new to this standard model of the Creator's world was the view from the sea. More than any other place on the globe the sea seemed to afford a vision of endless cycles—the circulation of whales and plankton, clouds, storms, winds, ocean currents, and the starry firmament. The sailor, whether rude whaleman or educated officer, had more reason to be aware of a cyclical world than anyone else save perhaps the astronomer. In his grand work Maury had at base simply provided a unique vantage point for observing a world that would temporarily disappear with the linear progression theories of Charles Darwin.

But, as Voltaire observed, history has a way of playing tricks on the dead. As of 1859, Darwin's evolutionary theory with its linear, open-ended implications replaced the cyclical world-views of men such as Maury and Humboldt. But in the twen-tieth century, plate tectonics, generated out of studies of the ocean floor, took science right back to systems, systems analysis, and "feedback mechanisms" that bear more than casual resem-blance to the worldview held by Maury. The cyclical worldview today appears to exist respectably side by side with the linear view introduced by Darwin in 1859.

The work of Bache and Maury, following on the experience of the Wilkes Expedition, represented contrasting viewpoints as to the purpose, nature, and proper method of discovery at a time when the United States was taking a prominent place among the world's nations in that activity. Though Alexander von Hum-boldt was Maury's hero, Bache and his constituency of profes-sional scientists more closely represented the great German's scientific ideal. Humboldt, a Prussian who insisted on working in Paris during the Napoleonic Wars, transcended nationalism in favor of a world culture of science and scientific men. He also believed in precision of observation, in pure science, no matter how abstract and impractical, and in the highest possible pro-fessional training. He became a dominant world figure of his time because his colleagues were professional scientific men everywhere on the globe. This was precisely the kind of disin-terested, pure-science-oriented, transnational professionalism that Bache, Henry, and their followers were trying to bring about in an America that was reaching the heights of nationalis-tic fervor.

Maury, on the other hand, was an exemplar of mainstream American values. Though he conducted precise experiments and delved deeply and profoundly into pure science, Maury did so with no elitist limitations. His style of scientific investigation was an American style—Jacksonian in that he relied not only on the elite but on the work of midshipmen who were sometimes impressive innovators like John Mercer Brooke, amateurs like the Connecticut harness maker William C. Redfield, and the *Abstract Logs* returned by thousands of common seamen whose observations were often less than precise. Maury saw as his primary duty the mobilization or mass production of practical information that could be put to the immediate service of the country. He was not insulated by a college professorship or a secure administrative position in a learned institution. He was under the direction of the Navy, whose ranking officers were always skeptical of his scientific activities just as they had disapproved of the Great United States Exploring Expedition. He also had to serve a Congress that was not easily persuaded of the value of science and certainly not science shared with "foreigners." Thus in spectacular fashion, as "The Pathfinder of the Seas," Maury went with the democratic and nationalistic flow of his times. This made him famous. It led to the creation of a whole new science. It also thrust him into the forefront as an avatar of the Era of Manifest Destiny.

CHAPTER IX

From Manifest Destiny to Survival of the Fittest

THOUGH the rapid rise of a world "culture of science," with its own high priests, priorities in pure research, judges, tests for truth, and methodologies, was the hidden agenda of the nineteenth century, science in America, was largely seen by businessmen and their representatives in Congress as the instrument or occasion for commercial and territorial expansion. It was also seen by many religious idealists as part of the fulfillment of a romantic dream involving the spread of Anglo-Saxon Christianity, republican government, and new technologies around the world—especially into the nether regions where dwelt the heathen savage and the victims of Spanish superstition. European authorities such as Humboldt, Karl Ritter, and the Swiss geographer Arnold Guyot, then teaching at Princeton, believed that the races of man were determined by climate. Humboldt, for example, believed that the most vigorous peoples of the world had migrated westward around the globe along an "isothermic zodiacal belt," by which he meant the temperate zones. It was generally agreed that the peoples of the tropics needed awakening and invigorating by means of formidable doses of Anglo-Saxon energies. Most Americans in the Era of Manifest Destiny, and indeed down to the end of the century when the phrase "white man's burden" became popular, eagerly espoused the European theories, if only as rationales for crasser commercial and geopolitical aims.

This complex of baser motives along with the loftier aims of science stimulated mid-nineteenth-century American exploration. The Jacksonian Democrats, and the commercially minded Whig Party as well, viewed the United States as being locked in intense competition with the world's greatest power, Great Britain, over control of world markets and hence the future growth of American commerce. The period from 1840 to 1860 saw a whole series of confrontations with Britain at strategic borders around the world, whether in the continents of South America and Asia or on the remote islands of Hawaii in the vastness of the Central Pacific. It is in this context, as well as a scientific one, that American exploring expeditions of the period must be seen. The most important objective of the Wilkes Expedition was its mission to examine the western and northwestern coasts of America for fear that Britain might seize California and Oregon. American geopoliticians, Whig and Democrat alike, began to concern themselves with the commercial route to China, especially as it linked up with a contemplated railroad across the western United States. This, in turn, led them to a vital concern for the opening up of Japan to commerce, and expansion northward to a new frontier in Alaska. Men of both parties hoped that the North Pacific might become a vast American lake which held the key to the fabled riches of the East.

i

RELIGION AS SCIENCE

AMERICAN expeditions were not solely confined to those objectives, however, nor were they often so well thought out. The first of the fourteen expeditions sent out after the Wilkes Expedition was a wildly impractical junket to the Holy Land and the Dead Sea commanded by Maury's friend Lieutenant William Francis Lynch, a pious but ambitious Virginian who had been fifteen years without promotion in the Navy. Scientific research was ostensibly the objective of Lynch's venture, but he took no real scientist with him, only his nephew as botanical collector.

In 1847, Lynch sailed first for Constantinople, capital of the Ottoman Empire, and thence to Acre in what is now Israel. From there he marched overland across deserts and among fierce Bedouin tribes with a small contingent of men who carried prefabricated metal boats for cruising the Dead Sea. When they reached the Jordan River, accompanied by an armed escort of one thousand of the Sultan of Turkey's best soldiers, they put their boats into the holy river and coursed downstream to what was claimed to be the very spot where John baptized Christ. Lynch promptly duplicated the ceremony with himself in the Savior's role. It was an ecstatic moment for him. But his real objective was to locate as many biblical sites as possible to prove the truth of Divine Revelation. He did manage to find what he believed were the doomed cities of Sodom and Gomorrah under the Dead Sea, and he was very disappointed when orders from the Navy Department recalled him before he could march to the Euphrates River and locate the Garden of Eden.

Along the way, however, he did make a thorough survey of the saline waters of the Dead Sea. He also hired a vacationing professor of chemistry from Columbia College to analyze the rocks in the region. Lynch saw the Dead Sea as the remnant of a previous creation, and he believed the rocks in the area, being of two distinct kinds and running along a massive fault line, confirmed the existence of two ages of creation and the destruction of Sodom and Gomorrah, which had sunk into the Dead Sea. The Columbia College professor refused to reach any such conclusion, much to the consternation of Lynch and possibly Maury, who also believed in a literal interpretation of the Bible.

Maury, however, unlike Lynch, Louis Agassiz, and many geologists of his day, was not much concerned with the theory of catastrophism or the idea that the Creator had built and destroyed and rebuilt the world on several occasions which were labeled "catastrophes." He was certain of the biblical account of creation, however, though he espoused the "long day" theory of Edward Hitchcock of Amherst College in which God's "day" was not twenty-four hours but "a day that had its 'evening and morning' before the sun was made." The controversy over Genesis versus geology concerned Maury far less than biblical evidence for his studies of the winds and currents which he found in Job, who, Maury believed, had long since discovered gravitation and the empty spaces in the universe where, as Maury put it, "comets most delight to roam and hide," which were just now being located by men like Sir John Herschel with powerful new telescopes. Maury was also delighted with Solomon's words "Into the place from whence the rivers come, thither they return again," because he believed that Solomon "in a single verse, describes the circulation of the atmosphere as actual observation is now showing it to be." Like Lieutenant Lynch and the majority of scientific men of his age, Maury believed, as Agassiz put it, that studying nature was studying "the thoughts of the Creator." Perhaps not fully realizing the implications of the slogan "Manifest Destiny," the Secretary of the Navy believed that Revelation was none of the Navy's business, and so prevented poor Lynch from being the first man since Adam to enter the lost Garden of Eden.

ii

"SOUTH AMERICA CALLED THEM"

THE WAR WITH MEXICO had turned American attention to Central and South America. The discovery of gold in California only enhanced this interest as gold seekers raced around Cape Horn or struggled across the Isthmus of Panama. Along the way, they, like the Spaniards of long ago, perceived the possibilities of further riches in the lands and continents to the south. Such opportunities beckoned, especially to shipping entrepreneurs in New York and New Orleans. Together they began to dream of a Caribbean empire, and in the 1850s, American filibustering bands with grandiose plans invaded Cuba, Nicaragua, and parts of Mexico. William Walker, "the gray-eyed man of destiny," became for a time the infamous dictator of Nicaragua with its natural canal route to the Pacific. He was largely supported by Commodore Vanderbilt's steamship company out of New York.

But when Americans looked to the south with dreams of a commercial empire they always found Britain in their way. Britain controlled the trade of the Río de la Plata, which ran through Argentina to Paraguay. Britain was the only foreign nation given the right by Brazil to navigate the Amazon. Britain even occupied the Mosquito Coast and the islands off Nicaragua in an effort to thwart any United States attempts to build or control an isthmian canal; war with the United States over this issue was only averted when the Whig Secretary of State William Clayton capitulated to Britain and signed the Clayton-Bulwer Treaty of 1850. The treaty guaranteed all nations right of passage across the isthmus by a canal or any other means. Given the fact of British competition, it comes as no surprise that in the years after the Mexican War the United States Navy sent seven expeditions to South and Central America.

The first of these was undertaken by Lieutenant Melville Gilliss, partially out of disappointment at not being selected as superintendent of the Naval Observatory, but primarily in the true disinterested spirit of the Humboldtian culture of science. He wished to go to Chile to make observations of Venus in relation to the sun to determine more precisely the solar parallax and thus make it possible to compute more accurately the distance of the sun from the earth, which had become a standard of measurement for the solar system. The idea had been suggested to him by the German astronomer C. L. Gerling in 1847. Quickly Gilliss secured letters of support from Gerling and most of the prominent German astronomers. He secured the support of Maury's rivals Bache and Joseph Henry and, along with this, the endorsement of the American Philosophical Society, the Boston-based American Academy of Arts and Sciences, Professor Benjamin Peirce of Harvard, and the Smithsonian. Gilliss's expedition would show what a real scientist could do and clearly reveal Maury's shortcomings at the Naval Observatory. With such powerful backing Gilliss was able to get an appropriation of $5,000 from Congress.

Thus in 1849, Lieutenant Gilliss sailed for Chile to make the same kind of observations of Venus that La Condamine had done as long ago as 1735. Gilliss had many of the same frustrating experiences endured by the French astronomer. He labored in Chile for four years, conscientiously making his astronomical sightings and also studying terrestrial magnetism and the nature of earthquakes. The latter, he concluded, were the result of vertical upthrusting from the center of the earth, a theory now discredited by modern plate tectonics. In addition, at Congress's insistence, Gilliss made a thorough study of Chilean geography, society, and its economy with an eye to trading possibilities. He also went further in the spirit of Humboldt. He helped to establish scientific institutions in Chile and presented some of his instruments to the government. Thus he tried to return full measure for the support he received from the Chileans and was one of the few American explorers to leave a reservoir of goodwill behind when he left in 1852.

When he returned to Washington, Gilliss discovered that Maury, so engrossed in his oceanic studies, had not even attempted to make the corresponding solar observations from the northern hemisphere upon which the success of the whole venture depended. Thus, in terms of pure science Gilliss's venture was a failure, though it is curious that, knowing of Maury's recalcitrance long before 1852, neither Bache nor Benjamin Peirce attempted to make the necessary observations from their respective observatories at Girard College and Harvard. Despite his disappointment, Gilliss published a four-volume report on his expedition, a charming geographical account of Chile. One writer called Gilliss's expedition "the first technical assistance mission to Latin America." The lieutenant was not unmindful of United States commercial interests, however. Upon his return, he became a lobbyist for William Wheelwright, who was attempting to secure a federal subsidy for a line of steamships that would cruise from Valparaiso to Panama along the west coast of South and Central America.

Gilliss was a true scientist at heart, however, and persisted in his astronomical work. In 1858, under the auspices of the Smithsonian and private companies, he observed from Peru the great eclipse of September 1858. In 1860 and in 1862 he conducted expeditions under private sponsorship to Argentina to observe the transits of Mars across the sun. His dedication to pure science was in strong contrast to the attitudes of the other expedition leaders sent to South America during this period.

The most notorious of these expeditions was undertaken by Maury's brother-in-law, Lieutenant William Lewis Herndon, in 1851. This venture was entirely Maury's conception. On March 29, 1850, Maury proposed to Secretary of the Navy William Preston Ballard an expedition to explore Peru, Bolivia, and the immense basin of the Amazon. The plan was approved by both Ballard and his successor, William A. Graham. Passed Midshipman Lardner A. Gibbon was assigned to assist Herndon on the expedition. Clearly they were not exploring new territory; Peru, Bolivia, and the Amazon River were well known since the days of Humboldt at least. There were other motives for the expedition.

Ostensibly it was a venture for science, but Maury made it clear to the U.S. authorities that Herndon and Gibbon were reconnoitering the commercial possibilities of the resources of the three countries. The expedition was also designed to force Brazil into opening the Amazon River to the commercial traffic of all nations. Peru and Bolivia had already agreed to this, and Maury hoped to break the British monopoly of the Amazon trade. But he also had more sinister motives. He saw all three countries as being not unlike Texas—potential lands for Anglo-Saxon, especially American, colonization. He said as much in a long, secret letter of instructions to Herndon.

There was more. Maury was worried that Britain might turn from the American South to the Amazon Basin for the source of its cotton, whereas he envisioned the South creating a Caribbean empire that reached to the Amazon, whose valley he saw as "the safety valve for our Southern States." Seized with anxiety over the compromise crisis of 1850, which effectively blocked southern expansion into the West, Maury was a staunch racist who confirmed his prejudices by reference to the researches of Arnold Guyot, who had firm ideas as to racial hierarchies. Maury looked toward the South's expansion to the Caribbean and

South America for "philosophical" as well as commercial reasons. He saw the Amazon's "imbecile" and "indolent" people being swept aside to make way for "American citizens from the free as well as from the Slave States" to settle there "with their goods and chattels" [meaning slaves] and to "revolutionize and republicanize and Anglo-Saxonize that valley." Herndon's expedition was to be "the first link in a chain which is to end in the establishment of the Amazonian Republic." Because cotton could only be cultivated by "compulsory labor," the Amazonian Republic would be a slave republic. At the time of the crisis of 1850, Maury envisioned nothing less than a massive exodus of southern slaveholders into Brazil's Amazon Basin. Herndon was to use his scientific exploring expedition to spy out the land in preparation for this southern exodus.

Meanwhile, at Maury's urging, and undoubtedly that of more powerful persons than he, the State Department was putting maximum pressure on Brazil to open up the Amazon to American vessels. The remonstrances with Brazil had been undertaken by Secretary of the Navy William B. Preston and Secretary of State John M. Clayton, two moderate Southern Whigs who favored union. When Daniel Webster of Massachusetts took over as Secretary of State in 1851, he put even more pressure on Brazil. He demanded passports for Herndon's expedition, which he declared had as its object "to gratify a liberal curiosity and extend the limits of geographical knowledge in which Brazil and all other civilized states have a common interest." He also pressed hard for a treaty of commerce and navigation. Had Webster and other members of the Whig Party, as a result of the bitter struggle over the Compromise of 1850, determined that it was best for the Union to "let the erring [Southern] sisters depart in peace"—to South America?

It is also of more than passing significance that in the same year Herndon and Gibbon departed for the Amazon, Lieutenant Lynch sailed to scout out the west coast of Africa, ostensibly on a scientific mission to collect plants and animals and to look into legitimate trading possibilities. In the same year, Captain Martin R. Delaney, the first black officer in the U.S. Army, led an expedition to the Valley of the Niger, where he purchased land from native chiefs upon which he intended to resettle American slaves. In 1852, he also published a book calling for black migration to New Grenada (Colombia) and Nicaragua. While Maury envisioned a new republic of southern slaveholders in Brazil, where slavery was common and legal, others, like Lynch and Delaney, followed the lead of the American Colonization Society and looked toward returning blacks to freedom in Africa.

Herndon and Gibbon carried out their expedition with remarkable aplomb. At Herndon's suggestion they divided forces. Gibbon scouted out the Bolivian river routes to the Amazon while Herndon descended the swift-flowing rivers from the towering mountains and high plateaus of Peru. Both men showed an intense interest in gold and silver mining, while Gibbon also made a detailed study of ancient Inca monuments. He concluded that there had been transpacific contact with Asia at least two thousand years ago.

On the way over the mountains, Herndon was seemingly delighted with everything he saw. He became used to eating monkey soup, and he got on well with the natives, the ubiquitous priests, and the local traders and merchants. He became somewhat calloused about the hardships and the dangers of travel by canoe on the mighty Amazon. Once, in a series of rapids, a companion canoe, piloted by a friendly priest, went over a falls, almost certainly dooming the priest to a watery death unless help came quickly. Herndon, despite pleas by the survivors, did not think he had the time to stop and look for the missing priest. He also shrugged his shoulders at laments of a man whose wife had recently provided a ghastly feast for the crocodiles that swarmed in the river.

Instead, he paid careful attention to agricultural possibilities, exploitable resources, the town life along the river, the prices and kinds of goods, and the transportation facilities. He kept extensive tables of commodities and prices, and came to the conclusion that the valleys of the Amazon and the Mississippi would inevitably be linked by trade, commerce, and compatible cultures as well as by Maury's winds and currents. The latter made this linkage a geographic certainty.

Herndon also found the river crowded with British and
French naturalists as well as German miners and traders. The
dash of his exploit in descending the Amazon was somewhat
dimmed when he learned that only the year before, an American
circus company had preceded him by the very same route from
Lima. Apparently grand plans for Anglo-Saxon migration to
Brazil were not really necessary, since people of all nations were
constantly going up and down the river despite the government's decrees. In any case, Brazil declined to yield to U.S.
pressure and the river remained officially closed. Largely as a
result of Herndon and Gibbon's best-selling published reports,
however, after the Civil War a sizable contingent of unrecon-
structed Confederates resettled forever in Satarem, Brazil, 650
miles up the Amazon. Maury and Herndon were not among
them.

Lieutenant Thomas Jefferson Page's exploring expedition up
the Río de la Plata through Argentina, Paraguay, and southern
Brazil revealed another dimension of U.S. interest in South
America. This venture appears to have had its genesis in the
promotional efforts of Edward A. Hopkins, U.S. Special Agent
to Paraguay. Hopkins viewed Paraguay as comparable to China
and Japan in its potential yield of exploitable resources. An en-
thusiast, perhaps second only to Jeremiah N. Reynolds, he made
himself *persona non grata* with Secretary of State Daniel Webster and ultimately the U.S. Congress. But he did catch
the attention of the American Geographical and Statistical
Society of New York, an organization of merchants and capitalists who were always interested in expanding America's overseas interests. With their influence and the strong support
of Maury, Hopkins persuaded Whig Secretary of the Navy
John Pendleton Kennedy, himself an advocate of aggressive
commercial expansion, to authorize an expedition up the Río de
la Plata.

In 1853, Lieutenant Page sailed the paddlewheel steamer
Water Witch up the La Plata, ostensibly on a scientific reconnaissance, but actually on a mission aimed at ousting British in-

terests from Argentina and Paraguay. He was hardly able to provide the desired show of force, but he did work hard at making vast miscellaneous scientific collections. He also managed to call forth an official protest from the British Foreign Minister; to involve himself and his men in an Argentine revolution; and to illegally supply the dictator of Paraguay with arms, which the dictator eventually used to blow away the wheelhouse of the *Water Witch* as Page defied his decree and headed upstream for Brazil.

It was clear that Page did relatively little for either commerce or diplomacy that was not disastrous. He did, however, privately publish perhaps the most complete geographical report yet written by an American on any Latin American country. He was also conscientious in his collection of live animal specimens for science. In 1855, as he sailed proudly up the Potomac with cages of jaguars and other captured beasts aboard his vessel, he confidently believed he was laying the groundwork for a national zoo. This sorely vexed the Navy Department and Congress, which had not contemplated creating such an institution. The problem was solved, however, with the suggestion that the animals be transferred to the National Insane Asylum "for the amusement of the inmates."

In the 1850s, too, the Navy sent three expeditions to Central America to search for an isthmian canal route. Maury had earlier convinced Congress that the longer route across Tehuantepec in southern Mexico was too big an undertaking and too disease-ridden to be feasible. Besides, the Mexican government had already leased the Tehuantepec route to a European consortium. In 1853, as Secretary of War Jefferson Davis was sending out the Pacific Railroad Surveys across the West, Lieutenant William M. Jeffers, accompanied by Dr. Samuel Woodhouse of the Philadelphia Academy of Natural Sciences, reconnoitered Nicaragua, reporting so favorably on its potential for an interoceanic canal that William Walker and his backer, Commodore Vanderbilt, were inspired to take over the country.

A second expedition to the isthmus was less successful. In 1854, Lieutenant Isaac I. Strain led a party across Panama that became lost in the jungles. Before they could find their way out and secure help, three expeditioners died of starvation.

Finally, possibly despairing of naval officers, the government sent Army lieutenant Nathaniel Michler of the U.S. Topographical Engineers, who was seasoned on the plains of Texas with the Mexican Boundary Survey, to explore the Atrato River route in southern Panama. He took along with him an old friend from the Mexican Boundary Survey, the German artist-naturalist Arthur Schott. Michler's expedition was very thorough and lasted a year, from the fall of 1857 to the fall of 1858. He returned to New York with significant scientific collections, which were parceled out to an eager array of closet scientists.

With the exception of Lieutenant Gilliss's expedition to Chile, it must be concluded that all of the Navy's expeditions to South and Central America of the 1850s had economic and geopolitical aims rather than serious scientific objectives. Though only Herndon's expedition was Maury's exclusive conception, Maury has somehow been made the mastermind behind most of them. Clearly more people than Maury, especially the merchants and steamship line owners operating out of New York, were far more interested in the southern continent than he. The merchant capitalists were, in turn, backed by a host of jingoistic journalists, including Charles A. Dana of the *New York Sun*, Henry Raymond, founder of the *New York Times*, and Freeman Hunt, proprietor of *Hunt's Merchant's Magazine*. Also among the staunch supporters of New York expansionism were the bellicose historian George Bancroft and G. P. Putnam, who published the literary works of the politically aggressive Young America Movement. New York's boosters were, at this time, strongly competing with Boston, Baltimore, Philadelphia, and other Eastern Seaboard ports for dominance over the nation's commerce. In this, because of their aggressive policies, they succeeded. Congress, invariably skeptical of scientific missions since the Wilkes Expedition, which was still calling for appropriations, was receptive only to expeditions that promised practical commercial results or else, for Whigs as well as Jacksonians, thwarted British ambitions of the same sort.

iii
"ON JAPAN"

IN 1852, at the same time that it was concerned with countering British influence in South America, the jingoistic American Geographical and Statistical Society of New York also looked to the far Pacific, the China trade, and the long-protected potential of the Japanese Empire. Their concern was to open forever the fabled trade of the East to American merchant ships and to provide support for hundreds of whaling vessels now swarming over the North Pacific from Alaska to Japan. Thus, strongly supported by New England whaling interests, they lobbied for a significant show of American naval force in the western Pacific. Congress and the Navy listened; the immediate consequence was Commodore Matthew Calbraith Perry's famous expedition to Japan.

From the American point of view, Japan represented a problem as much as an opportunity. Because of the vastly increased whaling in the North Pacific and the booming China trade, both Britain and Russia were stepping up attempts to gain most-favored-nation trading status with Japan. The Dutch, who clung precariously to Deshima, a small sealed-off island trading compound in the harbor of Nagasaki, seemed destined to be replaced or ejected altogether. They had served a purpose since 1609 as Japan's limited window on the western world, but in the mid-nineteenth century the Dutch had lost their vigor and were virtual prisoners on the tiny island. American policymakers seemed convinced that Japan would soon be opened to commerce by the British or the Russians, thus forever thwarting American aims in the Far East, and perhaps the American Northwest Coast.

Recent American attempts to establish good relations with Japan had received humiliating rebuffs. In the spirit of the modern Soviet Union, the "Celestial Empire" would let no foreign vessels (except Dutch ships) enter its harbors or coastal waterways without the threat of attack and destruction. In 1837 an American merchant vessel had attempted to return some Japa-

nese fishermen washed ashore at the mouth of the Columbia
River. The American merchantman, on its goodwill mission,
was fired on and sent scurrying away from Edo (Tokyo Bay).
In 1846, Commodore Biddle with the *Columbia* and the *Vincennes* was surrounded by nearly one hundred Japanese war
vessels in Tokyo Bay, treated contemptuously by Japanese officials, and sent packing. A few years later, in 1849, it was learned
that sixteen shipwrecked American sailors were being held
under intolerable conditions in Japan. They were ill-fed, continually humiliated, and on occasion forced to trample upon a
Christian cross. Commander Glynn, with the *Preble*, was dispatched to Japan's only open port, Nagasaki, to secure their release. He was threatened by an armada of Japanese ships backed
up by shore batteries. Glynn stood fast in the face of Japanese
insults and threats. The American sailors were finally delivered
up, but this was only a temporary solution to the international
problem of the treatment of mariners shipwrecked in Japan.
Factors and incidents such as these figured as importantly to
American naval and maritime interests as did the possibilities
for trade with Japan. Glynn's show of force seemed the most
promising way of getting Japan to relate in some humane way to
the rest of the world's nations.

Perry himself favored strong activity in the western Pacific, as
well as a strong show of force. He saw the onset of an age of
steam-powered ocean vessels, and he called for the establishment of coaling stations and United States bases in the Pacific to
fuel our warships, which he thought should be greatly increased
in strength and number. In 1852, he sailed for the Far East on
this and a far more ambitious mission—the opening up of the
empire of Japan to American enterprise, by force if necessary.
Initially he commanded a squadron of four black-hulled warships, two of them new steam-powered vessels, the *Mississippi*
and the *Susquehanna*. But when he reached Hong Kong he also
took command of the whole Asiatic Squadron in preparation for
his mission. From the island of Madeira on his way to the Far
East, Perry issued this dispatch, which clearly outlined his primary motives:

When we look at the possessions in the east of our great maritime rival England and at the constant and rapid increase of their fortified ports, we should be admonished of the necessity of prompt measures on our part. . . . Fortunately the Japanese and many other islands in the Pacific are still left untouched by this unconscionable government; and as some of them lay in a route of commerce which is destined to become of great importance to the United States, no time should be lost in adopting active measures to secure a sufficient number of ports of refuge.

Perry took no "scientifics" with him on his voyage of open confrontation, except James Morrow, an agricultural expert attached to the State Department. The commodore was not opposed to science. Indeed, he had even founded the Brooklyn Lyceum of Science. But the Navy Department remained firm against civilian "scientifics." This was a military and diplomatic mission. So Perry shipped aboard two artists, Eliphalet Brown, Jr., and William Heine, and a telegrapher, John P. Williams, and instructed his officers to do what they could in the cause of science. He then headed east for Hong Kong on the other side of the world. There he reorganized the Asiatic Squadron, took aboard at Shanghai Bayard Taylor, the greatest American travel writer of his day, and steamed full ahead to Tokyo Bay, where he arrived with his four warships on July 8, 1853. Through firmness and the intimidation of his heavily armed smoke-belching black ships, Perry forced the Japanese emperor to consider a treaty that opened three ports to American commerce and promised aid to shipwrecked whalers and merchantmen. Confronted by nearly twenty thousand aroused Japanese warriors clad in medieval armor and manning batteries of antique cannons, Perry's bluejackets nonchalantly went about sounding and mapping Tokyo Bay while the diplomatic negotiations were in progress. They rowed their longboats daily under the guns of Japanese forts, and ignored the threats from archers who might have stepped out of the Battle of Hastings in 1066. Perry was a firm but remote negotiator who concealed himself aboard ship like some celestial deity until serious representatives of the em-

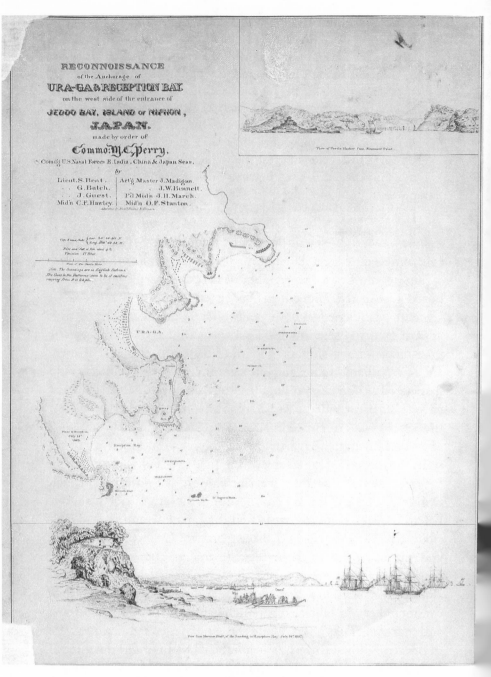

"Reconnoissance of the Anchorage of Ura-Ga & Reception Bay, on the west side of the entrance of Jeddo Bay, Island of Niphon, Japan." 1853. Perry map with views and insets. *(The National Archives)*

peror appeared to accept his ultimatum. As a representative of a new empire, the commodore was intent upon opening up the old Empire of Japan to American commerce and international standards of behavior. Nothing could deter him.

But he was also a patient and sagacious man. Well briefed on the history and culture of Japan, Perry was aware that decisions were not easily made in that complex country. So, having delivered his proposed treaty, he departed, promising to return for an answer the following year. He also promised to return with a larger force and refused joint rights with the humiliated Dutch in Nagasaki.

In addition to his confrontation with Japan, Perry also secured a coaling station at Chichi Jima (Peel Island) in the Bonins, and forced a coaling concession at Noka, near the southern end of Okinawa. The Bonin Island station proved to be unnecessary, but the Noka base was important to subsequent U.S. naval expeditions.

In early February of 1854, fearing that he would be anticipated by the British or the French, Perry left for Japan. By February 13 he had returned to Tokyo Bay with a full squadron of ten warships—three of them formidable steam-powered frigates. Negotiations began. On March 31, 1854, Perry had his treaty. In addition to a show of military power, Perry's diplomatic strategy also involved winning over the Japanese by a display of American technology. Consequently, when he returned to Japan in August of 1854, he brought with him a quarter-sized steam locomotive and the necessary rails to enable him to run it as an entertainment for Japanese officials. He also demonstrated the uses of the telegraph, the telescope, ingenious American clocks, and farm implements.

An indication of the impact of technology on the people of both China and Japan is perhaps best demonstrated by the introduction of the daguerreotype. One member of Perry's squadron, Eliphalet Brown, a daguerreotypist as well as an artist, set up his equipment in Hong Kong and later Japan. At almost the same time, Edward Kern of the United States North Pacific Exploring Expedition was also making daguerreotypes in Hong

Kong and Japan. The populace in both places was fascinated, and Hong Kong became by 1860 an important world center of early photography. It was there that the famous California photographer C. L. Weed first learned his trade. And in Japan, photography caught on so strongly that by the mid-1860s there were forty Japanese commercial photographers operating in Osaka alone. In 1872, when the Emperor Meiji allowed himself to be photographed, it was the world's first picture of "a living deity." Though the emperor suppressed the pictures, the fact that he had allowed himself to be photographed at all made photography fashionable among the elite of Japan. So popular had photography become that in 1889 a Japanese Photographic Society came into being, and by 1893 it hosted a world photographic exhibition. Technology as much as gunboat diplomacy helped open Japan to Americans and Europeans. The treaty was not as full and complete as Perry and the United States government wished. The Japanese rulers agreed to open two ports to American commerce: Shimoda, in the south of Japan, and Hakodate, at the northern tip of Honshu Island. They also promised aid to any foreign sailors shipwrecked or stranded on Japanese shores, as well as assistance in the mapping of their dangerous storm-ravaged coastlines.

When he returned to the United States, the results of Perry's mission were received with less enthusiasm from the public press than he expected. Nonetheless, with the acknowledged aid of his officers' journals and those of Bayard Taylor, Perry soon produced a popular yet complete volume on his expedition written by his friend the Rev. Francis Hawks, a New York minister. In reading this volume, it is difficult not to regard Perry as a second Columbus who had finally fulfilled that great mariner's mission to the Indies. This fit right in with the inflated ambitions of the day, and Perry ultimately became a national hero. Eventually, after the Meiji restoration of 1868, he became an admired hero in Japan as well. Surprisingly enough, his squadron also had collected enough scientific data and specimens to delight the professionals at the Smithsonian, and to provide two further volumes of scientific reportage. In addition, Lieutenant

Silas Bent, a Maury protégé on the expedition, managed to publish the first scientific analysis of the Japan current in the *Bulletin of the American Geographical and Statistical Society* for 1856.

Belligerency on the part of the United States in the Pacific was running high in the early 1850s. As recently as 1842, both Britain and France had guaranteed the integrity of the Hawaiian Islands, but first Britain, in 1843, then France, in 1849, had taken over the islands out of fear of an American occupation. By 1853, with Hawaii clearly overrun by Americans and standing directly in the track of the long-awaited "passage to India" from newly acquired California, Secretary of State William L. Marcy informed the British minister Crampton that the United States stood ready to accept an invitation from the islands for annexation, and "would surely resist any British or French attempts to annex them." The moment for annexation passed, however, with the ascendancy of Prince Alexander to the Hawaiian throne. The prince stopped all attempts at annexation and called upon Britain, France, and the United States to uphold the territorial integrity agreements of 1842. The United States checked its desire to acquire the strategic islands, for the time being, and concentrated on the great circle route to Japan and newly acquired treaty ports on the Chinese coast.

iv

THE NORTH PACIFIC EXPEDITION

WHILE PERRY was penetrating Japan by military and technological means, the Whig administration of President Fillmore was persuaded by the scientific establishment in America to launch a second purely scientific and hydrographic expedition to Japan, the China Sea, and the North Pacific. Most of these coasts were uncharted and thus not safe for whalers or merchantmen intent upon commercially invading the western Pacific. For American science, this was a virtually unknown part of the world. For once, the Smithsonian, the Coast Survey, and Maury's Naval

Observatory cooperated enthusiastically in planning what they regarded as a second Great United States Exploring Expedition. This expedition was to have a full complement of scientific men aboard.

The command of the North Pacific Expedition was given to Lieutenant Cadwallader Ringgold, who had commanded one of the ships in Wilkes's fleet. Second–in–command was Lieutenant John Rogers, member of a powerful Navy family. Rogers did most of the liaison work with the various scientific communities. Among the scientific men recruited for the expedition were Louis Agassiz's able assistant, William Stimpson, and Asa Gray's assistant, Charles Wright, a Harvard-educated Texan who had seen long service in the field on the U.S.-Mexican Boundary Survey.

In addition, an artist was added to the company. He was Edward "Ned" Kern, who had served in the West with John C. Frémont and had once briefly commanded Fort Sutter in California during the Bear Flag Revolution that directly preceded the Mexican War. Kern, as mentioned, took along a daguerreotype apparatus. Before sailing he went to New York for special instruction in the use of the apparatus by the firm of Edward and Henry Anthony, the most prominent photographers in the United States. He also took along Henry Hunt Snelling's *The Art of Photography*. Perhaps even more than Brown of Perry's expedition, Kern introduced photography into the Far East. He took many photographs—of Chinese temples, of Japanese shrines and fishing villages, of the Chukchis on the coast of Siberia, and of dozens of other exotic subjects, which he also sketched in elegant fashion. None of his valuable daguerreotypes—along with Brown's, the first ever taken in the Far East—have ever come to light, though it is highly probable that Kern returned to the United States with them.

Ringgold's squadron, which sailed from Chesapeake Bay on June 11, 1853, consisted of the *Vincennes* and *Porpoise*, veteran ships of Wilkes's expedition, the tender *John Kennedy*, the rickety New York harbor steamer *John Hancock*, and the small sloop *Fenimore Cooper*. One of the officers was Maury's protégé Lieutenant John Mercer Brooke, whose deep-sea sounding apparatus had been responsible for the success of Maury's Atlantic Ocean floor-mapping operation. Brooke, a southerner like Maury who would one day join the Confederate Navy and design the famous *Merrimack* ironclad, was clearly the ablest officer on the expedition. Both Bache and Maury respected his abilities, and he had already been decorated by the Prussian government for his contributions to science.

The route of Ringgold's squadron took it via the Madeiras to the Cape of Good Hope, where it languished for two months. Then the *Vincennes* and *Porpoise* sailed for Sydney, Australia. The other ships sailed more directly past Java, into the China Sea, and to port at Hong Kong. On the route north from Sydney, Lieutenant Brooke successfully took soundings from two and one half miles down in the Coral Sea which yielded specimens of foraminifera, tiny shell-covered marine animals. This was an important scientific find. It refuted current European theories that at great depths, in an "azoic zone," the pressure was so great that nothing could penetrate it. Some scientists had believed that drowned sailors and ships lost at sea floated forever suspended at an intermediate depth of the ocean.

Seeking a fast commercial route from Australia to the China Coast, Ringgold did not bother to reexplore the many island groups charted by Wilkes a decade previously, though he corrected a few of Wilkes's charts. Consequently, the *Vincennes* and the *Porpoise* were reunited with the rest of the fleet in Hong Kong in March. There they sat until September. Ringgold's behavior suddenly turned downright strange. He violated his orders and allowed the *Porpoise* to cooperate with the British H.M.S. *Rattler* in attacking a fleet of pirate junks, and he took his flagship, the *Vincennes*, to Canton to aid the Manchu government in beating off attacks by rebel forces, thereby officially entering a Chinese civil war. He felt that he was protecting the interests of American traders, but to botanist Charles Wright he had cheapened the scientific expedition by defending the local "dime-grasping Anglo-Saxons" who were already helping to smuggle opium into China.

While engaging in these rash actions, Ringgold also turned uncharacteristically cautious with respect to the condition of his ships. He had them overhauled repeatedly, conducting himself in a manner strangely reminiscent of the hated Captain Wilkes. Finally, he came down with delirium—some said because of alcohol, others malaria, and still others declared it was due to overdoses of opium and morphine. Meantime, Perry had returned from Japan. He held an immediate court of medical inquiry, which declared Ringgold insane. He was removed from command and sent home, where he recovered sufficiently to prefer charges against his fellow officers and Commodore Perry. Lieutenant Rogers assumed command of the North Pacific Expedition.

In September the steamer *John Hancock* and the *Fenimore Cooper* sailed north to survey the long stretch of the China Coast as far as Korea. They also surveyed the island of Formosa and some of the Pescadores, narrowly avoiding conflict with cannibals on Formosa's southern shore and shipwreck in typhoons and fog in the dangerous Formosa Straits. Before returning to Hong Kong in January of 1855, they had surveyed the huge area of the Yellow Sea.

The *Vincennes* and the *Porpoise* headed due east toward Okinawa and the Bonin Islands. Somewhere between the Formosa Straits and the East China Sea, the *Porpoise* was lost in a typhoon with all hands aboard. Nothing was ever again heard of that sturdy veteran of the Wilkes Expedition. In the meantime, Lieutenant Rogers had the first of his many confrontations with Japanese authorities on Okinawa. He returned to Hong Kong in January, disgruntled and determined to enforce Perry's treaty the following year. Despite the loss of the *Porpoise*, the squadron had done well for science. It had carefully charted dangerous and relatively unknown seas, and it had collected over three thousand scientific specimens.

In the spring and summer of 1855, the North Pacific Expedition completed its work in spectacular fashion. Its ships surveyed the main Japanese island of Honshu, both east and west coasts from Kagoshima in the south to Hokodate in the north. Lieutenant Brooke, along with the artist Ned Kern and eleven sailors, coasted 450 miles of the typhoon-exposed eastern shores of Honshu in the launch of the *Vincennes*, making landings in forbidden territory where they encountered both hostile and friendly representatives of the Empire of Japan. Only Lieutenant Brooke's incredible courage, perseverance, and tact pulled them through.

Meanwhile, in Tokyo Bay, Lieutenant Rogers remonstrated with the Japanese government for failing to uphold the treaty forced upon it by Perry. With the arrival of consul Townsend Harris in 1856, the situation improved through the great patience and tact of Harris, one of the ablest diplomats in American history. Lieutenant Rogers and his men, with the exception of Brooke's small company, were no diplomats. They drew pistols and fired at local officials. And when they weren't doing that, they frequently went out of their way to kick haughty Japanese officials in the seat of their balloonlike trousers, laughing wholeheartedly as the officials "lost face." Diplomacy was principally Rogers's concern, though clearly not his forte.

Meanwhile, the rattletrap steamer *John Hancock* chugged through fogs and furious storms up past the Sakhalin Islands, through the Tatorskiy Straits (between Japan and the Russian mainland), and all around the giant Sea of Okhotsk. Its crew surveyed the mouth of the Amur River in Siberia, and spent weeks ashore with Russian emissaries of the czar, who welcomed their penetration of the British blockade (stemming from the current Crimean War). While the *Hancock* was sounding the Sea of Okhotsk, the *Fenimore Cooper* was mapping the long, fogbound Aleutian Islands chain and searching for the lost whaleship *Monongahela* without success.

From Tokyo, Rogers took the *Vincennes* north to Kamchatka Peninsula, where Brooke made the deepest sounding of the ocean floor yet completed. His samples of marine infusoria were taken from a depth of three and one half miles. This kind of work undertaken on the North Pacific Expedition, coupled with

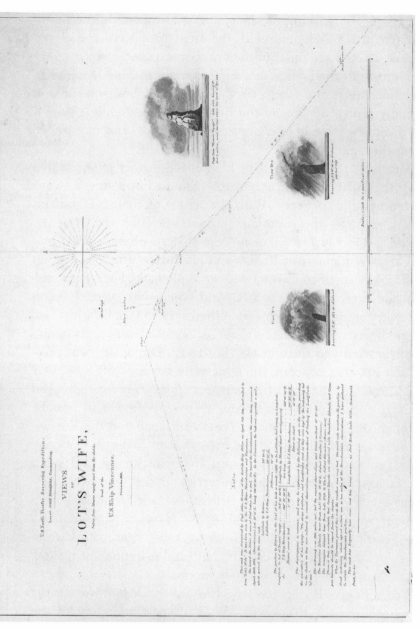

"U.S. North Pacific Surveying Expedition. . . . Views of Lot's Wife, taken from Meares voyage and from the sketchbook of the U.S. ship *Vincennes*, November 1854." Three views by artist Edward M. Kern and chart showing the ship's track. (*The National Archives*)

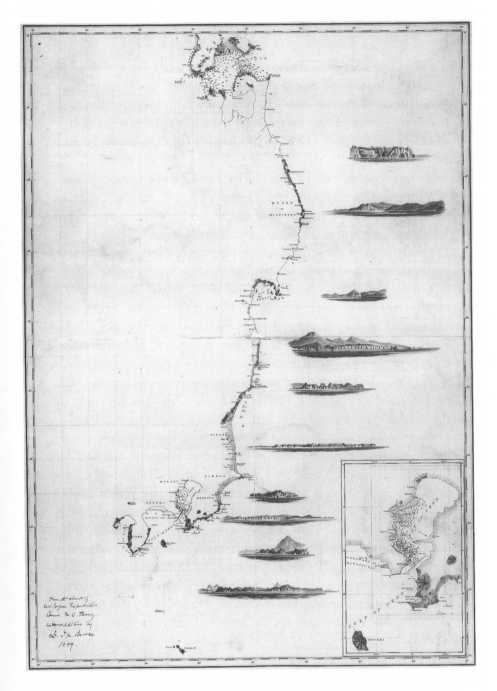

"East Coast of Honshu from Tsugaru Strait to Izu Peninsula (Tokyo Bay)." 1859. From M. C. Perry Expedition. Additions by Lieutenant J. M. Brooke. Views by Edward M. Kern. Tokyo Bay. 1859. *(The National Archives)*

his Atlantic Ocean work for Maury and his later transpacific sounding cruise on the *Fenimore Cooper*, made Lieutenant Brooke one of the premier oceanographers of the age. Much of his work preceded and anticipated the more celebrated, because more complete, discoveries of the British *Challenger* expedition of 1872–75.

Brooke further served the North Pacific Expedition by commanding a shore station at Glazenop Harbor on the Siberian mainland at the western shore of the Bering Strait. In a camp fortified against the Chukchi, or Siberian natives, Brooke and the naturalists made critical natural history collections and accurately determined the land's end of Siberia.

Lieutenant Rogers, at Maury's request, sailed the *Vincennes* far north through Bering Strait to the vicinity of 70° north latitude heading for Wrangel Island far above the Arctic Circle. Rogers hoped to penetrate the "open polar sea" from the west, or at least find evidence of warm currents circulating in the arctic regions. To this end, he took water temperature samples that Maury used to support his polar sea theory. But the ice packs of the Beaufort Sea finally turned him back south to the Pacific.

After collecting Lieutenant Brooke and the scientific crew, the *Vincennes* headed for San Francisco, which it reached on October 16, 1855. The North Pacific Expedition was officially over. Though its returns to science were exceedingly rich, and its mapping and hydrography bordered on the spectacular, the expedition received little notice outside scientific circles. The Civil War prevented publication of any official reports in the style of those of the Wilkes Expedition, and even today the story of its important operations in the northern seas must be pieced together from records in the National Archives. Only one book in English was published on the cruise. That came out in 1857, written by Lieutenant A. W. Habersham, appropriately titled *The North Pacific Surveying and Exploring Expedition, or My Last Cruise*. One important person, however, who remembered the North Pacific Expedition was one of its enthusiastic sponsors, Senator William F. Seward of New York, who engineered the purchase of Alaska in 1867.

v

REINFORCING A NEW WORLD VIEW

THOUGH distinguished scientists from Harvard to the Smithsonian worked on the vast collections brought back by the North Pacific Expedition, certainly the most important result of the whole undertaking was provided by Charles Wright, the botanist. In looking through Wright's field notebooks, Asa Gray noted a number of similarities between the flowering shrubs of Japan and those of eastern North America. This confirmed other similar observations that he had noticed in the work of Linnaeus's collector Thurnberg, and in Zaccarini's *Flora Japonica* (1840, 1844). William Stirling Sullivant found similar correlations among the mosses and liverworts. These finds could only mean one thing: related species on almost opposite sides of the globe had evolved from a common ancestor. Somehow, Japan, Siberia, and eastern North America had been biologically connected, eons ago, then separated long enough for varieties of the same species to evolve. The operative word was *evolve*. Gray had discovered strong evidence for the proof of a theory of evolution such as that soon to be proposed by Charles Darwin.

Darwin regularly corresponded with Gray, who was one of the world's authorities on global distribution. In 1858, he sent Gray advance proofs of his great work *On the Origin of Species*. Based on the strong evidence from the North Pacific Expedition, Gray saw validity in Darwin's theory. In the spring of 1859, at the American Academy of Arts and Sciences in Cambridge, Massachusetts, Gray used his data to confront his rival Louis Agassiz, the foremost apostle in America (along with Maury) of special creationism. This was the theory that the earth and everything on it had been created just as they were by God in the six days of creation. There were no extinct species and no evidence of change or evolution within each species. Agassiz scoffed at the thought of a connection between Japan and eastern North America. Gray, at the suggestion of his friend James Dwight Dana of the Wilkes Expedition, used Agassiz's own descriptions of the polar ice age to show how the great cap had pushed seeds and plants southward and then receded, leaving warm germination periods in a process that happened several times. In each recession the species were widely separated and left on their own—to evolve according to natural selection. After Gray's confrontation of Agassiz in the spring of 1859 in Boston, and with the publication of Darwin's work, special creationism was on its way to an extinction in the eyes of the scientific world as complete as that of the fossil fishes Agassiz so loved.

Darwin, aided by Gray's (and Wright's) data, had ushered in a new way of looking at nature. By 1860, two world views generated out of the culture of science stood opposed. The old view, espoused by Agassiz, Maury, and even Humboldt (who mercifully had died in 1859 before seeing his life's work replaced), was a closed world—a mighty cycling and recycling machine that wasted nothing, not even a species, and was presumably kept in motion by the Divine Creator. The new view, presented by Darwin, was anything but closed, cyclical, and without waste. It was open to chance mutations, linear in the relentless survival of the fittest, wasteful in that the unfit species perished, and in espousing chance, it cast doubt on the immanent causal presence of the Almighty. Strangely enough, Darwin's vision of a chance universe, like Maury's belief in the Creator's special creation, came from observations on a sea voyage where endless cycles of winds, curents, and clouds were prevalent. But it also came as a result of cooperation between explorers in the field and scientists in institutions poring over learned articles and distribution maps of plants and animals produced by their colleagues in the culture of science all over the world.

It is testimony to Darwin's imagination that he triumphed over the conventional wisdom of the culture of science and even the complexities of taxonomy to focus on the global distribution of biological specimens, which enabled him to hypothesize a whole new view of nature that turned the focus from space to time. Darwin's *On the Origin of Species* was a product of the Second Great Age of Discovery as important as Galileo's *Dialogue on Two World Systems* was to an earlier age. In the natural world, geography had given way to history as Darwin turned space into infinite time. American explorer-scientists, such as Wright and Dana, had played a significant role in the process of the development of this new world view.

vi
THE SEARCH FOR THE OPEN POLAR SEA

AS THE 1850s came to a close, American explorer-scientists did not cease activities in the name of commerce and sheer romanticism. In 1858–59, just as Gray was preparing to confront Agassiz, Lieutenant Brooke, on the *Fenimore Cooper*, was sailing across the Pacific tracing out the fastest route from San Francisco to Japan. On this voyage he made deep sea soundings and water temperature and density experiments all across the Pacific. The chance to publish this important pioneering oceanographic data was unfortunately lost when Brooke defected to the Confederacy in 1861. His ship, too, was wrecked in Tokyo Bay, and he returned on a hair-raising storm-lashed voyage to the United States aboard the *Kanrin Maru*, ineptly manned by its Japanese crew. It was the first warship from the "Celestial Empire" to visit America.

The 1850s also saw Americans turn to the Arctic, first in a romantic attempt to rescue the lost British captain Sir John Franklin, who was searching for a Northwest Passage, then in an attempt to sight, and therefore prove, the existence of Maury's "open polar sea." Sponsored by Henry Grinnell and his New York associates, Lieutenant Edwin J. De Haven in the *Advance* and the *Rescue* spent 1850 and 1851 frozen among the ice floes of the Davis Straits.

Then his lieutenant, the intrepid Philadelphia physician Elisha Kent Kane, spent an even more harrowing two and one-half years frozen in far above the Arctic Circle at 78°41', beyond where anyone save Admiral William Edward Parry of the Royal Navy had ever gone before. Kane, like De Haven, was searching for Maury's open polar sea. His search caused him and all his men to be locked into the far northern ice pack. For two long, dark winters, they huddled aboard the *Advance*, ill from starva-

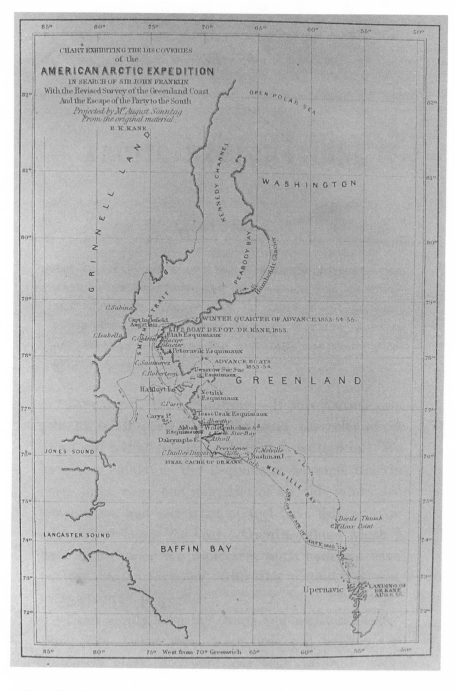

Elisha Kent Kane map. From *Arctic Explorations in the Years 1853, '54, '55. 1856*, vol. 1. Map is frontispiece of vol. 1. *(William H. Goetzmann Collection)*

tion, scurvy, frostbite, typhoid fever, and gangrene. Three men of the party died. A number of others suffered amputation of toes, feet, and even legs. Two men tried to desert in despair. Only Kane's incredible spirit and ability to learn from the Greenland Eskimos pulled them through. In the summer of 1855, truly more dead than alive, they struggled over four hundred miles across the ice pack which blocked their way to the south, pulling improvised sleds loaded with the ship's boats and a dwindling supply of unmentionable foodstuffs. Finally, they reached relatively open water among the floating ice and emerged at the Danish settlement at Upernavic on August 6, 1855. Kane, fraught with emotion, wrote, "We hugged the land by the big harbor...." A short while later, they were taken aboard the rescue vessel U.S.S. *Release*, commanded by Lieutenant H. J. Hartstene, and they arrived in New York on October 11, 1855.

Despite the hardships, Kane had returned with a complete set of scientific notes taken over the two-and-one-half-year stay in the Arctic wastes. But perhaps the most important aspect of his whole experience was the knowledge of the Greenland Eskimo culture that he acquired. From the Eskimos, he and his men learned to survive in and adapt to the Arctic. Before the end of the century, as they learned more from the Eskimos, men like the Canadian explorer Vilhjálmur Stefánsson would come to view the whole northland as "the friendly Arctic," difficult as it seems even today to believe.

But in 1855, the intrepid Kane wrote one of the great bestselling travel adventure books of the age, *Arctic Explorations in the Years 1853, 54, 55*. Soon after, he died as a result of his strenuous Arctic experiences, which had taxed an already weakened heart. In the climax of his stirring account, Kane described how William Morton, a member of his party, standing on Cape Constitution at 81°22′ north latitude, had seen open water stretching away for forty miles and had heard "the novel music of dashing waves ... and a surf, breaking in among the rocks at his feet."

Kane and all the members of his party dared to hope that this was the long-sought polar sea. Armchair scientists thought not; so in 1860, Dr. Isaac Hayes, a surviving member of Kane's party who had lost a foot to amputation, sailed north once again in the schooner *United States*, in quest of that fatal chimera. He returned to report with strong emotion that he had penetrated to 81 °35′, where he had seen, far in the distance, that elusive polar sea of circulating waters that so many explorers from Scoresby onward through Maury and Kane knew in their imaginations was there. Few believed him. A later generation would reach even higher latitudes, and, looking out toward the pole, they would see nothing but an endless frozen icecap at the top of the world. Nature lacked the perfection to match man's imagination.

Histories of oceanography, ironically in view of Matthew Fontaine Maury's extensive work, date a new age of oceanic exploration with the voyage of the British *Challenger* expedition in 1872. The round-the-world deep-sea sounding and oceanic collecting expedition of the *Challenger* was followed by relatively sophisticated new-style voyages by the American vessels *Tuscarora* (1873–74), *Blake* (1877–88), and *Albatross* (1900). Both the *Blake* and the *Albatross* were research vessels for Alexander Agassiz, Louis Agassiz's son, who had made both a fortune in copper mines and a prominent reputation in the world of science—a world far different from that of his distinguished father, who believed the hand of the Creator was ever-present in nature. The new focus in the late nineteenth century was not on God's marvels, though there was some concern with discovering "missing links" or living fossils from archaic ages in the depth of the ocean. Such hope still persists, as from time to time in the twentieth century million-year-old species like the coelacanth are brought up from the "azoic" depth of the ocean. But a newer age of systems analysis applied to ocean floor mapping, advanced geophysics, sophisticated chemistry, and the study of marine biological processes definitely replaced the old romantic age, leaving only Edward Harriman's summer cruise to Alaska in 1899, aboard the *George W. Elder*, to remind us of the good old days of the explorer-adventurer among the winds and currents of storm-tossed seas at the very ends of the earth.

BOOK THREE

THE BOOK OF TIME

PORTFOLIO II

New Men

IN ADDITION to discovering exotic new lands around the globe, the explorers of the Second Great Age of Discovery also came upon strange new peoples and cultures. They found, as well, mysterious remnants of buildings and monuments of entire civilizations that seemed to have vanished. These new men and lost civilizations brought the biblical story of man's descent into question. How, for example, did man spread over the globe down as far as Patagonia, or off as far as the archipelagoes of the Pacific in just the 4004 years indicated by the genealogical sequence in the Bible? Then there was the question of the *origin* of these creatures and cultures. Did they really spread out from a Mesopotamian Garden of Eden? And were they really human—like Adam and Eve and Thee and Me? Some thought not. Others thought that the strange peoples encountered were Ur men and women—humans at a very early stage of development—true primitives reflecting life at the dawn of time. Still others saw them, particularly North American Indians, as bestial, humans who had degenerated from an earlier time, when higher civilizations existed, as evidenced by the ancient prehistoric mounds of the Ohio and Mississippi valleys. Under the auspices of the Smithsonian, Ephraim George Squier and E. H. Davis produced an exhaustive survey of them in 1847, entitled *Ancient Monuments of the Mississippi Valley*. Pseudoscholars like Josiah Priest, whose *American Antiquities* was a best-seller of its day, declared the mounds and other sites remnants of the lost tribes of Israel, as well as Egyptians, Phoenicians, Greeks, Romans, Mongols, and Hindus. Joseph

Smith founded the Mormon religion on just such data as these. For him, the mounds were the forts and former cities of the vanished tribe of the Angel Moroni—the Mormons. All of this tended to refute eighteenth-century assertions by Voltaire and the Abbé DePauw that American Indians were the as yet unformed prepubescent children of the globe. Thus, the discovery of ancient ruins in the Americas became a national cause, and few men were more celebrated than Alexander von Humboldt, Ephraim George Squier, and John Lloyd Stephens, who produced scholarly, yet readable and exciting illustrated works on the ancient civilizations of America. The historian William Hickling Prescott chipped into the discussion with two monumental histories that described the prehistoric cultures of America vividly. Prescott's *History of the Conquest of Mexico* (1843) and *History of the Conquest of Peru* (1847) were also best-sellers in their days because people were fascinated by the mystery of the antiquity of America. Discoveries of the ruins of ancient civilizations in America's far Southwest continued after the Civil War. In 1875 William H. Holmes and the photographer William H. Jackson discovered Anasazi ruins high up on the walls of Mancos Canyon, and when they visited Chaco Canyon, Jackson drew a highly accurate reconstruction of the giant Pueblo Bonito. In the winter of 1881, while rounding up stray cattle atop Mesa Verde, Richard Wetherill happened upon the ghostly Anasazi Cliff Palace, looking like some magical village lost in time.

And time was the central focus of the study of man in the Second Great Age of Discovery. Darwin's theory of evolution merely accented the question. Not until Franz Boas and the new theory of cultural relativism, developed in *The Mind of Primitive Man* in 1911, did time cease to be the central concern of students of man. Time was integrally related to questions of diffusion, as well as apparent stages of cultural development envisioned by men like Lewis Henry Morgan, who, in *Ancient Society*, published in 1877, saw mankind progressing, at different paces in various parts of the globe, from "savagery" to "barbarism" to "civilization." By the latter he meant the technological urbanized society of his own day.

For certain students of the American Indian, like George Catlin and the German Prince Maximilian of Wied, who went up the Missouri River in the 1830s, time was important in another sense. They, and others like them, felt that the Indian and other primitive men would soon vanish, and they wished to record them in their wild and pristine state for posterity. The result of this was the extensive writings of Catlin and the prince, as well as the hundreds of stunning paintings of the Native Americans by

Catlin, and the prince's exquisite painter, Karl Bodmer. On the other hand, out in the far Pacific, where similar primitive people were encountered, missionaries took steps to usher the natives out of the primitive stage as fast as possible—much to the dismay of serious students of ethnology, and astute observers like Melville, who in his South Sea novels, *Moby Dick* and *Typee*, provided the first glimmerings of cultural relativism.

All over the globe, however, whether on Pacific islands, in the mountain fastnesses of North America, or in the jungles of Central and South America, observers of new men and ancient ruins, like the geologists analyzing strata, tried to fit what they saw into a historical framework. It was an age where geographical and ethnographical discoveries, like the wondrous archaeological finds at Troy and Mycenae, Herculaneum and Pompeii, Easter Island and Palenque, were all seen from the vantage point of evolution and history. One could truly say that for the Second Great Age of Discovery, "time was of the essence."

i

WHAT ARE THESE NEW MEN?

THIS CLUSTER of pictures offers a glimpse of the range of ideas concerning man that were visually represented. Josiah Priest's Garden of Eden–diffusionist view is engagingly represented by his biblical portrayal of "The Deluge and Confusion of Tongues," an allusion to the story of Noah's Ark and the Tower of Babel.

On the other hand, when the African explorer Paul Du Chaillu discovered the gorilla in Gabon in 1847, some thought that the troglodyte was the ancestor of man. Professor Jeffries Wyman of Harvard and Thomas Savage of Yale considered the question carefully in the first scientific article on the gorilla, published in the *Boston Journal of Natural History* in December 1847. Du Chaillu had already furnished dramatic illustrations of the great ape in his *Explorations and Adventures in Equatorial Africa* (1861).

Still other observers of primitive man, in this case American Indians, saw them either as cruel savages, as did La Page du Pratz in his *Histoire de la Louisiane*, published in 1758, or as the dumb, lascivious brutes pictured by Heinrich Balduin Möllhausen on an expedition to the American Southwest.

Josiah Priest, "The Deluge and Confusion of Tongues." From *American Antiquities and Discovery of the West*, 1833. *(William H. Goetzmann Collection)*

Paul Du Chaillu, "The Gorilla." From Du Chaillu, *Explorations and Adventures in Equatorial Africa*, 1861. *(William H. Goetzmann Collection)*

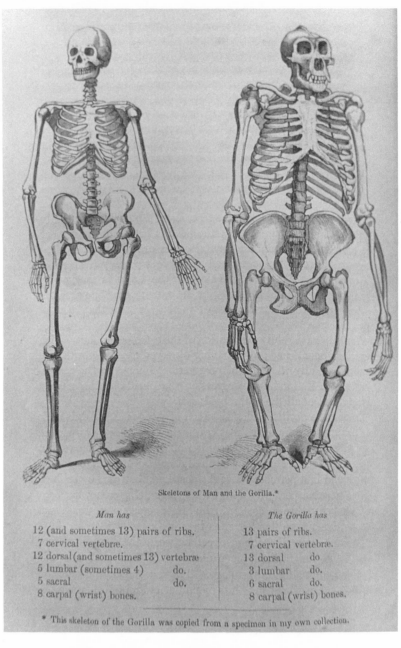

Skeletons of Man and the Gorilla.*

Man has	The Gorilla has
12 (and sometimes 13) pairs of ribs.	13 pairs of ribs.
7 cervical vertebræ.	7 cervical vertebræ.
12 dorsal (and sometimes 13) vertebræ	13 dorsal do.
5 lumbar (sometimes 4) do.	3 lumbar do.
5 sacral do.	6 sacral do.
8 carpal (wrist) bones.	8 carpal (wrist) bones.

* This skeleton of the Gorilla was copied from a specimen in my own collection.

Paul Du Chaillu, "Comparison of Skeletons of Man and Gorilla." From Du Chaillu, *Explorations and Adventures in Equatorial Africa*, 1861. *(William H. Goetzmann Collection)*

La Page du Pratz, "Plan of the Fort; Prisoner on the Fire-Frame; Scalping Scene."
(Apaches) From *Histoire de la Louisiane*, Paris, 1758. *(Barker Texas History Center,
The University of Texas, Austin)*

Paul Du Chaillu, "Ouganza Exorcising a Sorcerer." From Du Chaillu, *Explorations
and Adventures in Equatorial Africa*, 1861. *(William H. Goetzmann Collection)*

H. B. Möllhausen, "Ceremonial Visit of Chemhuevies."
(Oklahoma Historical Society)

ii

VESTIGES OF SOME PREVIOUS CREATIONS

ROMANTICISM AND SCIENCE were never better wedded than in the melancholy contemplation of ruined temples and abandoned or fallen idols. Such monuments to the futility of man's vanity were celebrated by Shelley in his poem *Ozymandias* (1817):

> I met a traveller from an antique land
> Who said: Two vast and trunkless legs of stone
> Stand in the desert . . . Near them, on the sand,
> Half sunk, a shattered visage lies, whose frown,
> And wrinkled lip, and sneer of cold command,
> Tell that its sculptor well those passions read
> Which yet survive, stamped on these lifeless things,
> The hand that mocked them, and the heart that fed:
> And on the pedestal these words appear:
> "My name is Ozymandias, king of kings:
> Look on my works, ye Mighty, and despair!"
> Nothing beside remains. Round the decay
> Of that colossal wreck, boundless and bare
> The lone and level sands stretch far away.

Artists from the days of Captain Cook to the mid-nineteenth century typically portrayed archaeological discoveries in emotion-filled scenes— even when they were making accurate renditions.

William Hodges, "A View of the Monuments of Easter Island." 1775.
Oil on panel. *(National Maritime Museum, London)*

One of the most moving and beautiful paintings rendered by Captain
Cook's artist, William Hodges, was this view of Easter Island. It should
lay to rest all speculation concerning the artist's supposed objectivity as a
scientific painter.

Thomas Jefferson was the first known American to investigate the contents of the mysterious mounds scattered across the eastern United States.
Here a St. Louis artist provides a cross-sectional view of a mound that is
part of the massive Cahokia complex across the Mississippi from St.
Louis. Note how he contrasts the ancient mound and its contents with a
nearby Indian tipi.

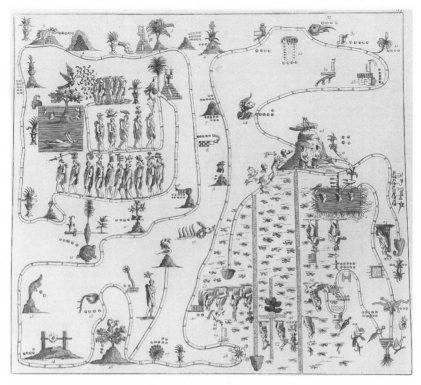

Alexander Humboldt, "Meso American Ruins." Lithograph. From *Researches Concerning the Institutions and Monuments of the Ancient Inhabitants of America*, 1814. *(The University of Texas, Humanities Research Center)*

John J. Egan, "Cross Section of a Mound Near St. Louis." Oil on canvas. From his *Panorama of the Monumental Grandeur of the Mississippi Valley*, 1850. *(The Saint Louis Art Museum, Purchase Eliza McMillan Fund)*

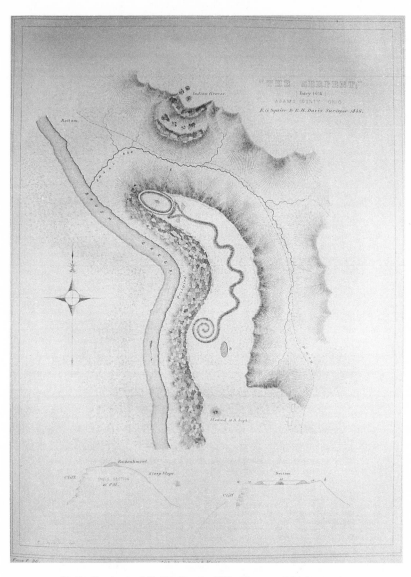

E. G. Squier and E. H. Davis, "The Serpent." Lithograph.
From *Ancient Monuments of the Mississippi Valley*, 1847.

Remarkably, Squier and Davis were able to trace out the serpentlike configurations of this mound near Marietta, Ohio. The serpent shape suggested some giant sculptor.

376

William H. Jackson, "Reconstruction of Pueblo Bonito, Chaco Canyon."
Lithograph. From F. V. Hayden, *Report of the U.S. Geographical and
Geological Survey of the Territories*, 1876.

Frederick Catherwood, "First View of Palenque." Lithograph.
From *Incidents of Travel in Central America, Chiapos, and Yucatán*, vol. 2, 1841.

In 1839, the American John Lloyd Stephens together with a British artist,
Frederick Catherwood, left on a diplomatic mission to Central America,
Mexico, and Yucatán. In addition to his diplomatic duties, Stephens
intended to explore and visually record the vanished jungle civilization of
the Mayans. In all, Stephens made two trips, the first from 1839–41, the
second in 1841–42. Stephens's writing about the long-hidden ruins con-
veys a romantic sense of wonder, as do Catherwood's amazingly accurate
and sensitive drawings.

377

Frederick Catherwood, "Fallen Idol, Copan." From *Incidents of Travel in Central America, Chiapas, and Yucatán*, vol. 2, 1841.

Frederick Catherwood, "Bas Relief on Inside of Door of Altar at Palenque." From *Incidents of Travel in Central America, Chiapas, and Yucatán*, vol. 2, 1841.

This evil-looking character seems to be having curious dreams as he smokes something exotic in his open-ended pipe.

MYSTERIOUS PEOPLES OF THE PACIFIC

So MANY expeditions crisscrossed the Pacific from 1768 to 1855 that its island peoples were arguably the most studied natives in the world. From Alexander Buchan's early painting of miserable Tierra del Fuegans to the work of Alfred T. Agate, Titian Peale, Joseph Drayton, and other artists on the Wilkes Expedition of 1838–42, representations of these peoples were invariably romanticized in one way or another.

Artist unknown, "Patagonian Giants." This picture is very probably from the Malespina Expedition sent out by Spain. *(William H. Goetzmann Collection)*

In contrast to Buchan's picture of wretched people painted on Cook's first expedition, these Patagonians at Tierra del Fuego are a race of classical giants who dwarf the European.

William Hodges, "Portrait of a Maori Chieftain." 1773. Lithograph.
(William H. Goetzmann Collection)

William Hodges, "Review of the War Galleys at Tahiti." 1775–76. Oil on canvas.
(National Maritime Museum, London)

John Webber, "Cook observing a ceremony involving human sacrifice on Tahiti, 1 September 1777." *(British Museum)*

William Hodges, "The Landing at Erramanga." Oil on canvas.
(National Maritime Museum, London)

Alfred T. Agate, "Vendovi." Engraving. From Charles Wilkes,
Narrative of the United States Exploring Expedition.

Agate's portrait commands respect for this cannibal prince from Fiji.

Artist unknown, "Fiji Major Drummer." Pictured in Charles Erskine,
Twenty Years Before the Mast, 1890; reprinted in 1985.

Midshipman S. F. Emmons, "The Burning of Sualib on Malolo" in the Fiji Islands. Pencil or pen sketch. *(Western Americana Collection, Beinecke Rare Book and Manuscript Library, Yale University)*

Alfred T. Agate, "Drummond's Island Warriors." Woodcut. From Charles Wilkes, *Narrative of the United States Exploring Expedition*.

CULTURAL CONFRONTATIONS

William Heine, "Commodore Matthew Calbraith Perry Meeting Japanese Officials." From Francis L. Hawks, *Narrative of the Expedition of an American Squadron to the China Seas and Japan*, 1856.

384

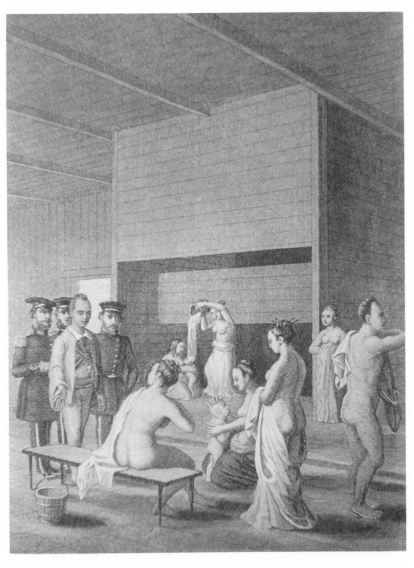

Anonymous, "Bathing Scene in Japan." Engraving. From A. W. Habersham,
The North Pacific Surveying and Exploring Expedition, or My Last Cruise.
(William H. Goetzmann Collection)

Habersham and his Victorian mates were taken aback at the Japanese custom of mixed bathing. They soon got used to it.

Van Ingen Snyder, "An American officer and his friends accord the Japanese officials little respect." From A. W. Habersham, *The North Pacific Surveying and Exploring Expedition, or My Last Cruise*.

BELOW: Chinese justice revealed to western eyes. The artist does not seem particularly shocked by the scene which is, however, considerably cleaned up.

Anonymous, "Execution Yard, Canton." From A. W. Habersham, *The North Pacific Surveying and Exploring Expedition, or My Last Cruise*.

"Good Cheer." From Isaac Hayes, *Arctic Boat Journey*, 1860.
(University of Texas Library)

Christmas in the Arctic brings "good cheer" for natives and explorers alike.

The picture below is meant to show Stanley's heroic punishment of the local "terrorists" in Central Africa. Technology in the form of rifles made the difference.

"The Attack of the Sixty-three Canoes of the Piratical Bangala."
Illustration from Henry Morton Stanley, *Through the Dark Continent*.
(William H. Goetzmann Collection)

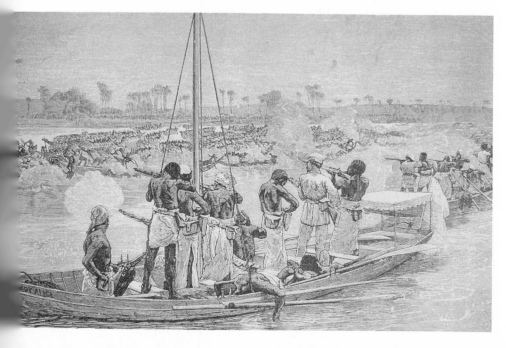

GEORGE CATLIN dedicated his life to painting the American Indian. To him they were nature's noble people, and he was a pioneer champion of Indian rights, even incurring the wrath of President Andrew Jackson. Catlin sensed the mystery, as well as the grand simplicity of Indian life.

In the 1850s, after he lost his Indian Gallery to an American locomotive manufacturer, Catlin traveled through the entire western hemisphere, from Patagonia to Alaska, painting all the indigenous tribes. These form what is today called "The Catlin Cartoon Collection." Most of Catlin's paintings also manage to convey his real zest for adventure.

George Catlin, "Catlin Painting a Portrait of Mah-to-toh-pa." Lithograph. From *Letters and Notes on the Manners, Customs, and Conditions of North American Indians*. 1841. *(American Museum of Natural History)*

George Catlin, "Medicine Man." *(National Museum of American Art,*
Smithsonian Institution. Gift of Mrs. Joseph Harrison, Jr.)

George Catlin, "Rainmaker," a Mandan Shaman. *(National Museum of American Art, Smithsonian Institution. Gift of Mrs. Joseph Harrison, Jr.).*

George Catlin, "Mandan Torture Ceremony." *(National Museum of American Art, Smithsonian Institution. Gift of Mrs. Joseph Harrison, Jr.).*

George Catlin, "Dance to the Berdash." Oil on canvas. *(National Museum of American Art, Smithsonian Institution. Gift of Mrs. Joseph Harrison, Jr.)*

Here some Pawnee warriors are entertaining a homosexual tribesman who looks serene and pleased with his/her new status in the tribe.

Catlin was the only artist to witness the Mandan Okipa ceremony, an annual event that tested the young men of the tribe and called forth buffalo for the year ahead. Few believed his description of the ceremony in *Letters and Notes* . . . because he also believed that the Mandans were Welsh people, descendants of Price Madoc, who sailed for America in 1170, according to *Hakluyt's Voyages*. In 1867 Catlin published *Okipa*, a further discussion of the Mandan ceremony complete with testimonials from virtually everyone familiar with the Mandans.

George Catlin, "A Mayoruna Village, north shore of the upper Amazon."
(National Gallery of Art, Washington, D.C., Paul Mellon Collection)

Catlin is sketching from a canoe while his friend Smythe dazzles the natives with a revolver-rifle.

Of course Catlin tricked the chief and painted his portrait too, together with his amused friends.

George Catlin, "Tapuya Encampment. The author ashore, and the Indians
giving the war dance, north shore of the Amazon, above Obidos."
(National Gallery of Art, Washington, D.C., Paul Mellon Collection)

George Catlin, "A man of Herculean strength, said to be the chief, holding his
young wife for her portrait to be made, *not willing to have his own painted . . .*"
(National Gallery of Art, Washington, D.C., Paul Mellon Collection)

KARL BODMER'S INDIANS

WHEN PRINCE MAXIMILIAN of Wied Neu Wied traveled up the Missouri River in 1837, he took along a twenty-three-year-old Swiss view painter named Karl Bodmer. So far as scholars know, Bodmer had never painted the human figure. On this voyage he produced masterpieces in this genre that revealed both the savage and the gentler nature of the mysterious redmen, who called themselves "people of the first man."

Karl Bodmer, "Mehkskéhme-Sukáhs (Iron Shirt),
a Piegan Blackfoot Chief." Watercolor, ink and pencil on paper.
(The InterNorth Art Foundation, Joslyn Art Museum, Omaha, Nebraska)

Karl Bodmer, "Péhriska-Rúhpa (Two Ravens) Hidatsa Man."
Watercolor on paper. *(The InterNorth Art Foundation,
Joslyn Art Museum, Omaha, Nebraska)*

This warrior is doing the Dog Dance, signifying that he is a Dog Soldier,
or defender of the tribe. Though this is a static painting, one can almost
hear the chants and feel the motion of the Dog Dance. To Bodmer, despite
his passion for accuracy, the Indian was also a highly exotic creature.

Karl Bodmer, "Interior of a Mandan Hut." Watercolor and ink on paper.
(Northern Natural Gas Company Collection, Joslyn Art Museum, Omaha, Nebraska)

This view of the interior of a Mandan hut is replete with a wealth of ethnographic detail. It is also composed in such a way as to suggest the importance, if not majesty, of the hut's occupants.

BELOW: Here Bodmer calls up all the mystery and exoticism of the plains Indian buffalo ceremony.

Karl Bodmer, "Bison Dance of the Mandan Indians." Hand-colored aquatint.
(Northern Natural Gas Company Collection, Joslyn Art Museum, Omaha, Nebraska)

THE BANDITTI OF THE ROCKY MOUNTAINS

IN 1837 Captain William Drummond Steward, a Scottish nobleman, took Alfred Jacob Miller, a young Baltimore painter, with him into the Rocky Mountains. Miller painted Stewart's exploits with the mountain men, as well as capturing, with misty romantic strokes, the Indian untainted by the white man. Miller was the only artist to paint the mountain men in their heyday, and one of the first to paint the intermontane Indians of the Rockies.

The final picture in the portfolio is an engraving after a watercolor by Frank Mayer, Miller's only student. Mayer's work is a rare picture of the Dakota Sun Dance.

Alfred Jacob Miller, "Attack by the Crow Indians." Oil on canvas.
(Walters Art Gallery, Baltimore, Maryland)

Here Miller is painting a story told to him by Stewart. The Scottish captain and Antoine, his mountain man friend, are being taunted by the normally friendly Crow Indians. To move a muscle was to start a massacre. Stewart and Antoine remained rigid, much to the amusement of the squaws in the foreground.

Alfred Jacob Miller, "The Yell of Triumph." Watercolor. *(Walters Art Gallery, Baltimore, Maryland)*

Frank Mayer, "Dakota Sun Dance, 1851." Engraving. *(Collection of William H. Goetzmann)*

CHAPTER X

Time and the Heroic Age of Geological Exploration

i

GEOLOGY BECOMES "BIG SCIENCE"

DURING the second half of the nineteenth century, expeditions were increasingly sponsored and supervised by large national organizations and federal bureaus. And though these bureaus grew in size and sophistication as the decades passed, they did not entirely obscure the role of the individual explorer. In America the age of the "Great Surveys" emerged, as opposed to individual expeditions, but the leaders of these surveys were themselves towering, adventuresome figures who lent drama to even the most elaborate of organizations.

It was also during this Gilded Age that the last phase of exploring the American West was completed. Major John Wesley Powell discovered the last unknown river and the last unknown mountain range in the West. Dr. Ferdinand V. Hayden revealed the wonders of Yellowstone, while other men, including photographers, painters, and the inimitable "old man of the mountains," John Muir, dramatized the rediscovery of Yosemite. Railroads and stagecoach lines began to push across the West, and mineral prospectors searched out the remotest of places—often in advance of the "official" explorers. Important discoveries, often made by accident by amateurs, sometimes led to the rapid organization of whole fields of exploration and scientific investigation. No more dramatic instance of this took place than the discovery, one winter day in 1888, of Mesa Verde's Cliff Palace by the rancher Richard Wetherill, who thereafter devoted his life to archaeology. His work at Mesa Verde and Chaco Canyon helped to launch the whole field of southwestern archaeology.

The late nineteenth century saw an intense preoccupation with the discovery of time. Fields like anthropology and archaeology took root and flourished, especially after the creation of the Bureau of American Ethnology in 1879. But the primary investigation of time was the exploration of the planet's remote past. The geologic explorer became perhaps the most important explorer of the period. He combined two approaches to the discovery of the past—paleontology, or the dating of the remote past through the fossil remains of long-extinct creatures, and geomorphology, or the measurement of crustal uplift, mountain-making and massive erosion that had to have taken place over eons of time. The vast empty spaces of the American West provided the best natural laboratory in the world for the study of such phenomena. Thanks to the work of its geological explorers, the United States took the lead in the earth sciences.

On March 3, 1879, President Rutherford B. Hayes signed the legislation creating the United States Geological Survey. His action marked the end of more than ten years of intense competition within the federal government that more than matched the rugged individualism of American business in the Gilded Age. Though it came to be dominated for the next fifteen years by one-armed Major John Wesley Powell, a rugged individualist if there ever was one, the U.S. Geological Survey became one of the largest and most effective federal agencies in the history of the nation. Until well into the twentieth century, when the rise of great science-oriented universities assumed some of the task, the Geological Survey virtually defined the scope of the earth sciences in America. The progress in geology in nineteenth-century America, stemming largely from explorations, surveys, and dramatic discoveries in the Far West, commanded respect from geologists all over the world and represented the nation's "coming of age" scientifically.

ii

THE BEST AND THE BRIGHTEST

TO A WHOLE GENERATION of young men keen with ambition—with what the historian Henry Adams was to call "knives in their brains"—the trans-Mississippi West beckoned as a great theater of opportunity. "What untold treasures must there be in the whole Rocky Mountain region," wrote the soon-to-be-famous paleontologist Othniel Charles Marsh of Yale in the summer of 1868. Other men of talent were having similar thoughts at about the same time, and their paths often crossed, even in the immense spaces of the Far West. As early as 1864, young Clarence King, also of Yale, wrote on the cover of his California Geological Survey notebook: "The U.S. Interior Survey, C. R. King, Supt." He was twenty-two years old and fresh with the high adventure that he was to write about so lucidly in *Mountaineering in the Sierra Nevada*. By 1867, thanks to his friend Secretary of War William Stanton, he was chief of his own western survey, charged with the responsibility of making a detailed map and resource survey one hundred miles wide along the proposed route of the transcontinental Union and Central Pacific Railroads, from the slopes of the Sierras to the front range of the Rockies. King's Ivy League manner, his elegant derby and lemon-yellow gloves worn in the field, and even his employment of a black manservant to wait table for him in the most godforsaken regions of the West belied the keen mind, gusto for real adventure, courage, and capacity for organizing large projects that made him a forerunner of Teddy Roosevelt. Year after year, as Director of the United States Geographical Survey of the Fortieth Parallel, he led parties of explorers, surveyors, geologists, artists, and photographers across the barren wastes of the Great Basin, over the Wasatch Range, and straight through the Rockies. Struck by lightning atop a bald mountain, King laughed it off. And he loved combat, whether in a struggle with pistols with a hard-bitten Army deserter, or in a confrontation with an enraged grizzly bear in a dark cave. Neither mountaintops nor alkali deserts, nor the War Department, which sponsored his expedition, intimidated him. In fact, he emerged as one of the country's great heroes as a result of exposing a great "diamond hoax" in the fall of 1872. Through astute deduction, King and his men located a secret mesa in the West which two unscrupulous men had salted with diamonds, then sold to San Francisco entrepreneurs, who in turn floated a $12 million public stock company. King's exposure of the hoax, beyond saving thousands of small investors and the San Francisco Stock Exchange from disaster, also proved the practical importance of modern science to an admiring public and a grateful government.

Before the work of his survey was terminated in 1878, King would be responsible for some remarkable work in both theoretical and practical science. He commissioned a series of extensive studies of large questions by the principal men of his survey. The survey's first publication, James D. Hague and Clarence King's *The Mining Industry*, was largely the work of Hague, a European-trained geologist from the Freiburg School of Mines. It was the definitive work on the subject. King had also sent the great Civil War photographer Timothy O'Sullivan deep into the Gould and Curry Mine (part of the Comstock Lode), where, using magnesium flares, he photographed the dark and terrifying world of the miner. Except for one shot of Mammoth Cave, Kentucky, these were the first photographs ever taken underground in America. King's survey also produced other important publications that were either innovative or exhaustive in their completeness. These include Ferdinand Zirkel's *Microscopic Petrography*, O. C. Marsh's *Odontorniths, or the Extinct Toothed Birds of North America* (warm-blooded dinosaurs?), Arnold Hague and S. F. Emmon's *Descriptive Geology*, James Terry Gardner's masterful *Atlas*, and King's own masterpiece, a

James Terry Gardner, "Topographical Map of the Wasatch Mountains." Fortieth Parallel Survey, C. King, Superintendent. *(The National Archives)*

James Terry Gardner, "Geological Map of Wasatch Mountains." Fortieth Parallel Survey, C. King, Superintendent. *(The National Archives)* These two maps are typical of the kinds of thematic maps that began to be developed by the "Great Surveys" after the Civil War in the age of "Big Science."

catastrophist reconstruction of the entire earth history of the West, modestly entitled *Systematic Geology*. King never lost sight of the practical needs of a growing nation. He saw mining as the key to western development, and to this end he located and mapped the now all-important coal deposits of Wyoming. His studies increased the yield of silver from the Comstock Lode from 66 percent to 93.7 percent. It is no wonder that his sedentary friend, the historian Henry Adams, called him "the best and brightest man of his generation."

iii

THE POWELL PHENOMENON

THIS title could as well have belonged to John Wesley Powell. In 1869, Major Powell, undaunted by the loss of his arm at Shiloh, took nine companions down the mighty Colorado River of the West where no man, not even an Indian, had ever gone before. His feat of daring electrified the nation and made Powell an instant authority on the West, as well as chief of his own federally sponsored survey—the Geographical and Geological Survey of the Rocky Mountain Region. Powell, fond as he was of adventure, was, like King, also a serious man. His two chief interests were structural geology, a branch of the science virtually created by him and the men of his survey, and the overall relation of people to the arid lands of the West. So serious about these questions was Powell that, like Lindbergh repeating his flight to Paris, he risked his life coursing down the Colorado a second time in 1871–72. Then he wrote about the trips as if they were one in an exciting book, *The Exploration of the Colorado River of the West* (1875). Read by most people as an adventure story, Powell's book actually revolved about the very large question of the earth-shaping processes that had created the rugged Colorado Plateau country, which included everything from the North Rim of the Grand Canyon to present-day Zion and

Bryce Canyon national parks and the Capitol Reef National
Monument, and extended east and south to the Uinta Mountains
and the Canyonlands National Park area. Powell believed that
the key to the whole region was river drainage and erosion,
especially that of the Colorado. The river he saw as antecedent
to the uplifting of the massive plateaus. As the plateaus were
uplifted, the sometimes meandering river cut faster and faster
into them. As he put it in the account of his canyon voyage:
"The river preserved its level, but mountains were lifted up; as
the saw revolves on a fixed pivot, while the log through which it
cuts is moved along. The river was the saw which cut the
mountain in two." The result of this process was far more than
the carving out of the deep recesses of the Grand Canyon.
Powell and his subordinate Captain Clarence Dutton proved
that a "great denudation" had taken place over the entire Colorado Plateau from the Zion Cliffs to the north to the San Francisco Mountains to the south. The erosion process was
staggering in terms of the tons of earth moved and the millions
of years it took to move it. Powell's exploration of the Grand
Canyon dramatized the discovery of time as had nothing else in
the world. In 1876 he amplified upon this thesis in *The Geology
of the Uinta Mountains,* but it took many years and the help of
such colleagues as Clarence Dutton, Grove Karl Gilbert, and
William H. Holmes before Powell was able to present a clarified
picture of the plateau province as the product of a grand system
of erosion. When the final reports written by Dutton, *Report
upon the Geology of the High Plateaus of Utah* (1880) and *The
Tertiary History of the Grand Canyon District* (1882), finally
came out, it was clear that Powell's persistent questioning had
led to a model for erosion applicable the world over. He and his
colleagues had defined all the basic terms and processes.

Powell's other interest, the relation of people to the arid lands,
grew out of his fascination and close association with the Mormons and the Indians of the plateau province. He eventually
carried these interests so far that he established and became
chief of the Bureau of American Ethnology, which he headed

until his death in 1902. It was the world's first government bureau exclusively dedicated to the science of man. In 1878,
Powell, with the very important help of Grove Karl Gilbert,
published the American classic *Report upon the Lands of the
Arid Regions of the United States.* In this powerful work,
Powell argued that because of lack of rainfall, the traditional
160-acre Land Office farm was inappropriate in the West.
Rather, he called for classification of lands according to soil coverage and water availability. Farms could be as small as eighty
acres, but ranching and grazing lands should be parceled out in
units as large as twenty-five hundred acres. All water rights
should inhere in the land. That is, no water company or greedy
citizen should be able to monopolize water upstream. In later
years he called for water basin communities in which, through
meetings of citizens, the resources of the region, especially
water, could be shared. Powell's ideas directly influenced the
Newlands Reclamation Act of 1902 and the formation of the
Tennessee Valley Authority in the Great Depression. At heart,
perhaps because he grew up on farms in Illinois, Powell was a
Jeffersonian, and agriculture, rather than mining, loomed largest
in his vision of the West. Great man though he was, his vision of
mining, ranching, and farming was frequently not shared by
westerners, nor was his love for the Indian.

iv

LT. WHEELER'S DOOMED SURVEY

KING and Powell were by no means the only federal entrepreneurs in the West after the Civil War. Two others commanded
great attention, and in the end sparked the crisis that led to the
creation of a single U.S. Geological Survey. One, Lieutenant
George M. Wheeler, who graduated from West Point in 1866,
longed for the prewar glories and fame of Captain John C.
Frémont. From 1871 to 1878 he commanded the Army's United
States Geographical Surveys West of the 100th Meridian. This

was largely a topographical mapping project in which Wheeler first intended to cover the entire Southwest below the limits of King's 40th-parallel survey as far east as the Great Plains. Eventually he planned to map the entire West in ninety-eight enormous quadrants in a system similar to that in use by the Geological Survey today. But Powell, King, and even pre–Civil War explorers like Lieutenant Joseph Christmas Ives, who had steamed up the Grand Canyon in 1857, had already preceded him in many of his activities. His projects and expeditions only duplicated theirs. He restudied the Comstock, reexplored furnace-hot Death Valley, and captained a small fleet of boats rowed and poled up the Colorado River—nearly perishing in the process—to Diamond Creek in the Grand Canyon, a point reached by Lieutenant Ives before the war in 1857. Wheeler also took along on his surveys two photographers, William Bell and Timothy O'Sullivan, as well as the Boston journalist Frederick Loring, for public relations purposes. Unfortunately, before Loring could get to the telegraph office at Wickenburg, Arizona, to announce the news of Wheeler's "conquest" of the Colorado in 1871, he was massacred by Apaches.

Lieutenant George M. Wheeler turned out maps—some seventy-one in all—annual reports, and large scientific monographs produced by his survey scientists. But his work was little appreciated. The scale on his maps was too large to be of much help to General Crook, then in desperate conflict with the Apaches, and they were seldom satisfactory to civilian scientists. His best men, Grove Karl Gilbert and Archibald Marvine, deserted the survey for work with his rivals. He was not, in Adams's terms, "the Alcibiades or Alexander" of his age. In fact, he was viewed as a poacher and a menace to the leaders of the other great surveys. He had duplicated the work and invaded the domains of both King and Powell, and his sharp confrontation with Ferdinand V. Hayden of the Interior Department's United States Geological Survey of the Territories at Twin Lakes, Colorado, in 1872 so provoked Congress that all four western surveys were in jeopardy in the winter of 1874. At that time, the Townsend Committee of Congress became the focus for what was becoming a last desperate battle between military and civilian science. On May 13, 1874, James Terry Gardner, Hayden's chief assistant, wrote to Josiah Dwight Whitney of Yale, "It is a great crisis for the science of the country. There must now be decided whether civilians who have devoted years to science are to direct the scientific work of the country." Later he informed the faculties of both Yale and Harvard that "we shall remember the friends that stand by in this awful struggle. The weak-backed men will be marked by the stand they take." The men of Yale were not quite pleased with this more or less direct threat, but in usual fashion they produced a protest against the military anyhow. Perhaps they were more impressed by King's urgings and Powell's misstatements that "there is not a single square mile of the Rocky Mountain region sufficiently accurate and in detail on the engineer maps that we could use for geological purposes." At any rate, when Yale saw that the Townsend Committee was not going to penalize the Wheeler survey, nor any other survey for that matter, it discreetly withdrew the protest letter. Embarrassed, certain powerful members of its science faculty began to resent Gardner's blackmail and Hayden's survey.

V

EXPLORER IN WONDERLAND

FERDINAND V. HAYDEN was the ultimate federal entrepreneur in the West. Hayden was one of the Gilded Age's most brilliant and most promotion-conscious scientists. He and Fielding B. Meek, a strange, eccentric man who lived in a Washington bawdy house without knowing it, had made geologic history before the Civil War. On dangerous expeditions to the Indian country in the Nebraska and Dakota Badlands and excursions far up the Missouri, they had uncovered and carefully described an entire cretaceous horizon in the West. They also found so many fossil bones of larger animals that they provided their friend Professor Joseph Leidy of the University of Pennsylvania with the opportunity of writing two classics, *The Ancient Fauna of Nebraska* and a treatise on the evolution of the fossil horse. The latter was published the same year as Darwin's *On the Origin of Species* (1859) but was ignored because of the onset of the Civil War.

When Hayden emerged from four years of service as a doctor in the war, he once again turned to the West. In 1867 and 1868 he surveyed the economic resources of Nebraska, and his reports were so glowing the entire first printings were snatched up immediately. From that time on, Hayden knew he would be the businessman's explorer. In 1869, as head of the United States Geological Survey of the Territories, he surveyed the high plains and the foothills of the Rockies as far south as Raton Pass, then returned north to Denver via the great interior parks of Colorado. The season of 1870 found him even deeper in the Rockies beyond Denver, with the extraordinary western photographer William H. Jackson as part of his entourage. Another member of his party was Professor Cyrus Thomas, who, out on the Great Plains, saw the definite applicability of the current European theory that rain followed the plow—that the tilling and planting of arid regions would actually draw more rain from the sky. The Dust Bowl of the 1930s was the fruit of such speculations.

When Hayden heard of the Washburn-Doane expedition to the Yellowstone region in 1870, he resolved to turn his attention in that glamorous direction. In 1871, at the head of a federally sponsored scientific cavalcade that also included the photographer Jackson and the famous painter Thomas Moran, Hayden explored Yellowstone. He found a military party under Captains J. W. Barlow and D. P. Heap also exploring the region, but Hayden's report, accompanied by hundreds of stunning photographs by Jackson and paintings by Moran, so overwhelmed the public and Congress that Barlow and Heap's expedition report remained forever buried in the government document series.

Hayden touted and exploited the wonders of Yellowstone with its spectacular hot springs, roaring geysers, color-spattered mud fountains, deep cerulean pools, and burning rivers and its own sublime Grand Canyon. While N. P. (National Park) Langford, an earlier explorer of the region, worked assiduously and effectively with the Northern Pacific Railroad behind the scenes, Hayden, with his generous distribution of Jackson's photographs, seemed to gain the major share of credit for the creation of the world's first national wilderness park by President Grant in 1872. More than any other explorer or survey leader, Hayden dramatized the West as a wonderland—a paradise for tourists. He created "the Tourist's West."

In 1873, Hayden turned south to survey Colorado. He intended to carry his survey all the way to the Mexican border, despite Lieutenant Wheeler's known presence in the area. From 1873 to 1877, Hayden conducted a masterful survey of Colorado, the highlights of which were the confrontation with Wheeler's survey at Twin Lakes and the discoveries of the Mount of the Holy Cross and the lost Anasazi Pueblos of Mancos Canyon on the edge of Mesa Verde. The Mount of the Holy Cross, a towering peak in western Colorado with a white snowy cross emblazoned across its face, became a symbol of the sublime wilderness to millions of Americans. Jackson, its discoverer, photographed it, and Moran painted it.

In southern Colorado, Hayden's parties were chased and besieged by hostile Ute Indians, but the photographer William H. Jackson and the artist William H. Holmes, guided by an old prospector, Captain John Moss, discovered, explored, mapped, illustrated, and photographed the high exotic cliff dwellings of Mancos Canyon. In 1876, they covered the whole Southwest, examining cliff dwellings. Holmes was so moved that he switched his energies to ethnology; he eventually became the foremost anthropologist in the country, and Powell's successor as chief of the Bureau of American Ethnology. The Colorado survey produced spectacular results, but Hayden was running afoul of too many rival explorers. He had blatantly resurveyed the country covered by King's 40th-parallel survey, and then there was the dispute with Wheeler over who would survey Colorado, a dispute that had caused the Congressional Crisis of 1874. Finally, upon feinting toward a reexploration of the Colorado Plateau and Colorado River, he trespassed on Powell's territory. Government service was beginning to be as cutthroat and wasteful as the railroad, mining, and cattle industries. Major Powell complained. Secretary of the Interior Carl Schurz gave him his choice—ethnology or geology. Powell chose ethnology. Hayden was left with geology and sent north to survey Wyoming, Montana, and Idaho in 1877. But the confrontation generated another congressional crisis in 1878, which led to the creation of the unified national Geological Survey.

vi

CRISIS AND CONSOLIDATION

IN THE SPRING of 1878, concerned about waste and duplication in the western surveys, the House Appropriations Committee ordered Powell, Hayden, and Wheeler to submit reports on their activities. Powell was ready for the showdown. As early as the spring of 1877 he had been using John Strong Newberry as a conduit to influential congressmen such as Abraham Hewitt of New York and James Garfield of Ohio. Moreover, Newberry was a personal friend of President Hayes. In a letter to Garfield and Hewitt, who chaired the Appropriations Committee, Newberry described Hayden as "a fraud" who had "lost the sympathy and respect of the scientific men of the country." On the other hand, he described Powell and his team as "men of first-rate ability." Powell's and Hayden's reports to the Appropriations Committee soon proved Newberry correct. Hewitt suggested that the matter of the possible unification of the western surveys be turned over to a special committee of the National Academy of Sciences. The acceptance of this proposal meant doom for the Wheeler Survey and the Army, and it did not bode well for Hayden. In May of 1878, because of the death of Joseph Henry, Othniel Charles Marsh of Yale, a friend of both King and Powell, became president of the National Academy. In addition to his friendship, especially with King, of whose survey he was a member, Marsh particularly disliked Hayden because of Gardner's threatening letter to Yale in 1874, and because the Hayden Survey sponsored the work of his hated paleontological rival Edward Drinker Cope. Even then, Marsh and Cope were raiding each other's dinosaur fossil finds in Wyoming and competing for priority in naming and describing new species. Their differences eventually hit the public print when Marsh hijacked a trainload of fossil bones and took them to Yale. He proved as well that Cope had described a dinosaur upside down. The Academy committee that Marsh appointed reflected these friendships and animosities. Only one military man was represented, and no one known to be friendly with Hayden. One member of the committee, Alexander Agassiz, was a silent partner with King in a large ranch venture near Cheyenne, Wyoming. And for good measure, Congressman Hewitt, who had called for the advice of the Academy in the first place, was a partner with King in at least three large western ranch ventures. Given the agribusiness outlook on both the Appropriations Committee and the National Academy Committee, Powell's *Report on the Arid Lands* calling for large ranching grants takes on something more than the character of a straightforward scientific report, great document that it was. Clearly, with tremendous Washington support marshaled against them, including the members of Powell's newly formed scientific social circle, the Cosmos Club, Wheeler and Hayden had no chance at all.

Powell seized the initiative at every hand. In November of 1878 he sent the Academy a sweeping series of recommendations that in effect called for the abolition of the Wheeler and Hayden surveys and the Public Land Office as well. These were to be replaced by a United States Coast and Interior Survey, for geodetic work, and a United States Geological Survey, both of which would be under the Department of the Interior. He also called for a special commission to reorganize the surveying and distribution of the public domain. Powell's recommendation reached the floor of Congress on February 10, 1879, with the endorsement of President Hayes. It was defeated by the western bloc in Congress, who strongly objected to interference by the Washington scientific lobby in the parceling out of lands in their local districts and states. Hewitt, however, managed to salvage most of the bill by having it transferred to a joint committee of the House and Senate, from which it emerged as part of the Sundry Civil Expense Bill and easily passed both houses. Thus the United States Geological Survey came into being, thanks to Powell, King, Newberry, Marsh, and the National Academy of Sciences, and no little legerdemain on the part of King's silent partner, Abraham Hewitt.

In retrospect, too, the selection of the first director of the new Geological Survey was easier than it looked at the time. Hayden made a run at it, depending upon western congressmen, the business community, and the large public following who admired Jackson's photos and Moran's paintings to support him. Powell and King worked furiously behind the scenes marshaling support from the leading colleges and learned societies. But really all it took was a visit to President Hayes by Marsh and Brewer of Yale, and Hayes's old friend John Strong Newberry of Ohio. Hayes appointed King the first Director of the United States Geological Survey.

vii

BIG SCIENCE PROVES ITSELF

KING almost immediately turned the Survey toward mining. He organized four districts: one under Emmons in Leadville, and later Denver, one under Dutton on the Colorado Plateau, one in the Great Basin, where Gilbert worked on a study of Lake Bonneville and Arnold Hague examined the Eureka Mining

District, and one under G. F. Becker, who restudied the Comstock Lode. King did not bother about the sensitive question of surveying, mapping, and classifying the western domain, but he did establish a laboratory in the East, the basic structure for carrying the Survey across the Mississippi, and an annual statistical census, the *Mineral Resources of the United States*. His was definitely a business-oriented Survey, though the able men under his command, Emmons, Hague, Gilbert, Becker, and Dutton, produced some of the most important theoretical studies of the entire century. Gilbert's *Lake Bonneville*, Dutton's *Tertiary History of the Grand Canyon District*, and Emmons's *Leadville, Colorado*, sometimes known as "the miner's bible," in particular have held up as classics. But then, with the Survey well underway, King abruptly resigned in 1880. Unknown to most, he had a conflict of interest and a genuine lust for wealth. By the terms of his appointment he could have no "pecuniary interest" in any lands under his jurisdiction. What was he to do? He owned parts of three large ranches and many mining interests, so he gave up the Survey after his long and brilliant struggle. The rest of his life he spent in the tragic pursuit of wealth as a mining speculator and consultant, acting out the alternate charades of a clandestine marriage to a black woman in Brooklyn and playing the *bon vivant* at the elite clubs of New York and San Francisco. He died in poverty of tuberculosis in Arizona in 1901.

Powell was appointed Director of the Survey. He was mainly concerned with reform of the land system and settlement patterns, but he proceeded on many fronts at once. He merged the Bureau of American Ethnology, of which he was Chief, with the Geological Survey; he greatly expanded the staff, placed Othniel Charles Marsh in charge of paleontology, set Gilbert to work on irrigation and water flow studies, established a chemistry laboratory in Washington under Becker, and commenced to map the entire West and then the nation. In addition, he attempted to work closely or in tandem with the numerous state geological surveys that were springing to new life all over the nation. By

1882 a national topographic map of the United States was under way, with parties already at work in the South as well as the West. On top of all this, his best men continued theoretical studies—Dutton on volcanoes, Gilbert on the physics of geology and the geology of the moon, W J McGee and T. C. Chamberlin on glaciation, etc.

All of these were fundamental works that virtually recreated and markedly changed the science of geology. Dutton's *Tertiary History of the Grand Canyon District*, accompanied by William H. Holmes's wondrous drawings—some of the greatest art works of the century—provided a spectacular vision of massive erosion that documented the incredible age of the earth. The work provided a new scale and hence a new meaning for the concept of time. It also focused on a geological process as did the works of T. C. Chamberlin and Grove Karl Gilbert. The concept of process in geology led directly to the necessity for measurement and mathematics as well as history. It also called for the formulation of models demonstrating physical principles. Here Gilbert, with his work on loccolith or domed mountains and his study of the ancient bed of long-vanished Lake Bonneville as well as his basic insights into the physical workings of glaciers turned geology in a whole new direction—toward applied physics and engineering principles. Thanks to the vast natural laboratory that the West provided and thanks to the genius of men recruited by Powell and King, geology took a giant step forward in sophistication. But such work required the training, support system, and resources of an ever-expanding scientific community that had been principally supported by the federal government through the 1880s, despite the rapid growth of the nation's colleges and universities.

Such empire-building, such expensive, widely varied, and often esoteric work, worried Congress, and in 1883 Powell was ordered to explain his direction of the Survey to the Allison Commission, which was studying efficiency in government. With his tremendous command of the facts and his great presence before Congressional committees, Powell managed to convince the Allison Commission that what he was doing was in the national interest. He had created a vast cooperative scientific research bureau—a far cry from the days of the rugged individual explorer at the head of a survey, of which species Powell seemed to be the only surviving member. Perhaps Powell's persistent ruggedness was what ensured the permanence of the Survey as it emerged from the Allison Commission hearings.

By 1888, Powell was soaring higher than ever. The summer of 1887 saw an extreme drought in the West, and Powell seized this opportunity to secure the backing of powerful Senator William Stewart of Nevada for a comprehensive irrigation and water resource survey of the West. The bill was passed in 1888 and authorized the Geological Survey to map all possible reservoirs, catch basins, and dam sites in the West. Stewart and the western representatives expected quick results. They wished to use the Survey to prospect for water in an effort to gain immediate relief for their constituents. Instead, Powell planned a long-range project that would span a generation. Moreover, a provision in the bill prevented the Public Land Office from issuing land grants to settlers until Powell finished his work. Powell himself was unaware of the provision, but nonetheless, in 1889, with President Harrison's approval, the Land Office began canceling grants from the previous year and holding up all future movement into the West. Stewart and virtually all western congressmen were furious, and in 1890 they retaliated. The Survey budget was cut drastically, and cut further each year after that as long as Powell remained the Director. Some of his loyal men continued their duties at no pay or "con amore," as Powell put it, but it was obvious that the Major had to resign for the good of the Survey, which he did in 1894. The end of Powell's career marked the end of the Survey's direct role in national land reform policy, as well as the "Heroic Age" of American geological explorations and surveys, except in far-off Alaska Territory.

Under Charles D. Walcott, Powell's friend and successor, the Survey grew dramatically. In 1901 its budget reached $1 million, ten times the original budget of the Survey and nearly three times Powell's final budget. Congress was obviously pleased with Walcott and with the Survey's expanding service to the nation. Under his directorship the Survey concentrated on the search for mineral resources. The Alaskan gold rush of 1898–99 dramatized the need, and by 1900, Walcott, at the behest of Congress, had established a Division of Mining and Mineral Resources. He also, however, accelerated the irrigation surveys to such an extent that in 1902, a special Hydrographic Branch was added to the Survey, along with the newly created Reclamation Service, the brainchild of Senator Francis Newlands. The Survey also began to map the forest reserves of the nation, and in 1897 sent a geologist to Nicaragua to study a proposed isthmian canal route. Walcott was clearly the benefactor of Theodore Roosevelt's Progressive Era enthusiasms.

When Walcott resigned to become Secretary of the Smithsonian Institution in 1907, his successor, George Otis Smith, who was Director from 1907 to 1930, continued Walcott's policy of stressing "practical geology." It was an age of pragmatism in the public philosophy and applied science in the service of the nation. Some, however, believed that theoretical studies had just as much practical value as applied science. In 1912 the geologist C. R. Van Hise, a Wisconsin Progressive, complained that the Survey was not "contributing in any large way to the advancement of science." In the days of King and Powell, he declared, the Survey had been "the center of the world" for the advancement of science. And Professor Thomas Manning has more recently confirmed this assessment of the Survey's "Heroic Age." He declared, "The Geological Survey was the leading scientific bureau of the post–Civil War period, and was the government's most productive research agency during the nineteenth century." He added that the Survey "had the advantage of a dual organization, wielding the power of the government bureau, yet enjoying the freedom of the scientific society. It used this advantage to make geology and paleontology the primary research sciences in the United States after 1865."

CHAPTER XI

"On, Beyond Greenland's Icy Mountains"

i

SCIENCE AND POPULAR CULTURE

SHORTLY AFTER New Year's Day in January of 1888 the following letter was circulated in Washington and in scientific circles elsewhere:

Dear Sir:
    You are invited to be present at a meeting to be held in the Assembly Hall of the Cosmos Club, Friday evening, January 13, at 8 o'clock, for the purpose of considering the advisability of organizing a society for the increase and diffusion of geographic knowledge.

The letter was signed by some of the most distinguished scientists and explorers in America, such as Henry Gannett, chief topographer of the U.S. Geological Survey, the astronomer Henry Mitchell, and the doyen of Arctic exploration, Lieutenant Adolphus W. Greely. The first signature on the letter, however, was that of Gardiner Greene Hubbard, a Boston lawyer who served as the first president of the Bell Telephone Company.

Hubbard also became the first president of the National Geographic Society, which was incorporated at the Cosmos Club on January 27, 1888. The articles of incorporation were signed by fifteen distinguished men, including the redoubtable Major John Wesley Powell. Initially there were 165 members of the society. The objectives of the new society were clearly set forth by President Hubbard in his keynote address. The society hoped to bring together "the scattered workers [in geography, science, and exploration] of our country" with "the persons who desire to promote their researches." Hubbard went on to explain: "By my election you notify the public that our society will not be confined to professional geographers, but will include laymen, like myself, who desire to promote geographic research and to diffuse that knowledge so that we may all know more of the world upon which we live."

Thus, the National Geographic Society, heavily supported by government scientists, set up shop in the nation's capital as a public lobby for the geographical sciences and for exploration as an ongoing cultural process. The new society was in direct competition with New York's venerable agent of expansion, the American Geographical Society.

What did all of this new organizational activity and the shift to Washington signify? It was symbolic of a shift from private funding of exploring activity on an *ad hoc* basis of the sort that was characteristic of the years just after the Civil War to a dependence on large federal bureaus like the U. S. Geological Survey. The scientific establishment was clearly reaching out to the public for support of its expeditions and geographic activities. The development of a public lobby seemed to be an objective as important as the massive bureaucratization of science itself.

When Hubbard was succeeded as president of the society in 1898 by Alexander Graham Bell, inventor of the telephone and founder of the Bell telephone system nationwide, the relationship of the scientific establishment to the mass media, of course, became evident. This became all the more so when Bell hired twenty-three-year-old Gilbert Grosvenor to be full-time editor of the society's magazine. Grosvenor's avowed objective was to transform the sedate journal into a popular magazine, profusely illustrated and devoted to the wonders of geographical discovery. Photo offset printing made this possible, and clearly Grosvenor succeeded in popularizing geography beyond what even he could have imagined. In the National Geographic Society and in its magazine both organized science and individual heroism were celebrated and dramatized. The kind of armchair adventuring that had so captivated Henry David Thoreau in Concord in the mid-nineteenth century had, by the end of the century, become available to a vast American public. It represented a wonderful paradox: as the activities of science became ever larger, more organized, and more complex, by the same token the demand for individual explorer media heroes increased tenfold.

All along, however, popular papers like *Harper's Weekly* and the *Illustrated London News* had celebrated explorers and new discoveries. The most noted impresario in this respect was young James Gordon Bennett of the *New York Herald.* In 1869 he commissioned a reporter, Henry Morton Stanley, to go to Africa and find the "lost" missionary David Livingstone. Ten years later Bennett sponsored the disastrous Arctic voyage of the *Jeannette*, which sank in the frozen seas off the Lena River delta in Arctic Russian seas while trying to locate a Northwest Passage from Alaska across the north pole to Greenland. Deep in the heart of northern Siberia, Bennett's reporters were on hand to take down the accounts of the survivors of the *Jeanette* expedition. Bennett created the occasion for heroic exploration from Siberia's icy waters to Africa's "sunny clime." Throughout the late nineteenth and early twentieth centuries the image of the explorer as an exotic hero of science and progress continued to engross the public. The explorer was a symbol of indomitable courage, endurance beyond belief, a kind of superhuman Odyssean vision, and ultimately mankind's biblical urge to "dominate the earth."

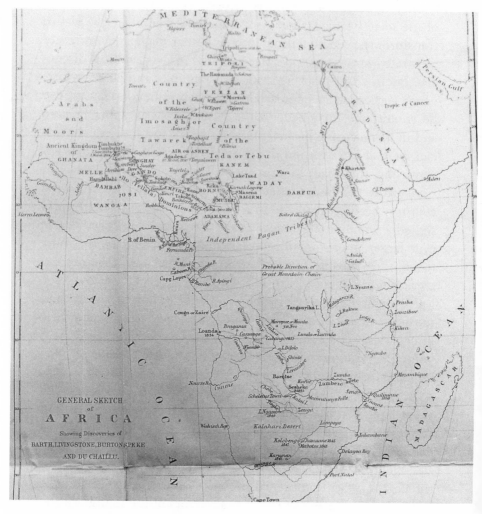

Paul Du Chaillu, "General Sketch of Africa Showing Discoveries of Barth, Livingstone, Burton, Speke and Du Chaillu." From *Explorations and Adventures in Equatorial Africa*. 1861. *(William H. Goetzmann Collection)*

ii

ALASKA: THE EXPLORATION OF THE WEST REPEATED

IN 1867, Secretary of State William H. Seward succeeded in persuading the United States government to purchase the immense territory of Alaska. His detractors deemed Seward's purchase either another instance of American quixoticism or a further example of the new nation's overweening ambition. "Seward's icebox" became a familiar phrase, and critics like the English Alaskan artist-explorer Frederick Whymper reported that Seward was also ready to purchase Iceland and Greenland for America. Whymper asserted, "Mr. Seward's mania for icebergs and snowfields seems insatiable." But clearly Seward had something else in mind. The friend of whalers and China traders, supporter of both the Perry and the Rogers expeditions to Japan, prime mover in the mercantile group behind the expansionist New York–based American Geographical Society, Seward was simply pursuing his plan to turn the North Pacific into an "American lake." All of the American jingoists did not look away from Dixie to the Caribbean and South America. Seward of New York also looked north to the eventual annexation of Canada and the domination of East Asia. In addition to his geopolitical interests, however, Seward may well have been tipped off to reports of the discovery of large coal deposits in Alaska, which would fuel the steam-powered navy of the future, and to news of the discovery of gold in Alaska coming out of Sitka and Victoria, British Columbia. One party of prospectors asserted that they had picked up gold in lumps off the ground. Seward may well have seen Alaska with its strategic location, its wonderful harbors, and its potentially rich resources as another California. At any rate, when approached by the Baron de Stoeckl of the Imperial Russian Government offering to sell Russia's remote Alaskan lands, Seward leaped at the chance.

The United States purchase did not set off the American exploration of Alaska. Cyrus W. Field's Atlantic telegraph cable provided the initial stimulus. Noting Field's grand venture, in 1856 one Perry McDonough Collins, supported by then Senator William Seward of New York, ventured across Russia and down the Amur River to the Pacific even as elements of the North Pacific Exploring Expedition were being entertained by Russian traders at the mouth of that remote river. Collins saw the transoceanic telegraph line heading west fifty miles across the Bering Strait, not east across the vast Atlantic. To this end, even in the climate of the Crimean War hostilities, Collins obtained charters from both Russia and Britain to cross their territories with a telegraph line. Collins merged his company with Western Union, and with the initial failures of Field's Atlantic cable, it looked as if Western Union might be the first to connect the Old World with the New.

In 1865, under the leadership of Colonel Charles Bulkley, Western Union began to explore Canada, Alaska, and Siberia for the United States. An elaborate team of explorers with special blue uniforms and silver insignia was sent into the field on both continents in that year. The Alaskan contingent was commanded by Robert Kennicott, curator of Northwestern University's Museum of Natural History and one of the few Americans who had spent time in the interior of Alaska. In 1860–61, he had wintered at the Hudson's Bay post at Fort Yukon, where he collected nearly forty boxes of specimens for the Smithsonian Institution.

Kennicott was an excitable man of large ambition, but he disliked the responsibility of supervising a large corps of explorers—one comparable to that of the pre–Civil War Pacific Railroad Surveys. According to William Healey Dall, Kennicott was in a "fiery furnace" of anxiety over his responsibilities and he felt betrayed by the Telegraph Company in underequipping his expedition. In May of 1866, having reached Nulato, the old Russian post far up the Yukon, Kennicott had a sudden heart attack and died. His men, especially Dall, Frank Ketchum, Ivan Lukeen, Mike Lebarge, and Ferdinand Bischoff, carried on the work of exploration. All except Bischoff, who worked out of Sitka, journeyed up the Yukon with Ketchum and Lebarge, reaching the British post at Fort Selkirk. They also explored the vast Seward Peninsula and collected thousands of specimens for science. Bischoff, in addition, provided critical testimony before the U.S. Senate that helped push the Alaska treaty through that deliberating body with remarkable dispatch. The work of the Telegraph Company explorers, commanded by Dall, was remarkable considering the task, the absolute lack of knowledge concerning Alaska, and the resources committed to the venture. It was a work of frustration, however. On June 25, 1867, Ketchum and Lebarge reached Fort Selkirk, the first men ever to traverse the Yukon River that far inland from the Alaskan side. Less than a month later they learned that because of the success of the Atlantic cable, the Russian-American Telegraph Expedition had been abruptly terminated. Dall determined to remain in Alaska, exploring its wilderness and studying its numerous tribes of Indians. He produced the first American classic on the vast unknown territory, *Alaska and Its Resources* (1870), and he became the chief authority on Alaska, which, he learned on February 3, 1868, at Nulato, had become officially American territory.

The telegraph expeditions had laid out a feasible route for a telegraph line through Alaska's wilderness. The explorers had also tested the navigability of the Yukon, which flowed two thousand miles through the heart of Alaska; they had collected thousands of natural history specimens for science, some of which helped to make a beginning for the study of Alaskan geology, others of which tended to prove Asa Gray's theory of the migration of plant species from eastern Asia; and above all, they had pointed up Alaska's rich resources. This led almost immediately to the formation of the Alaska Commercial Company, a U.S. rival to the Hudson's Bay Company, and the beginning of ruthless American exploitation of Alaska's resources and its native peoples.

The American exploration of Alaska continued in the 1870s,

under the auspices first of the U.S. Army, and then after 1877 of the Coast Survey of the Treasury Department. Both of these agencies explored and mapped huge stretches of territory in a rugged land nearly as large as "the lower" American West, and, most significantly, acted as advance scouts for the Alaska Commercial Company—even to the point of forcing the British to move out of Fort Yukon and cease trading with "our" noble savages on the American side of the international boundary. This was the real significance of U.S. Army Captain Charles Raymond's expedition up the Yukon River to Fort Yukon in 1868–69 aboard the first steamboat ever to ply that remote river.

Captain Raymond's expedition left St. Michael's Island, opposite the mouth of the Yukon, on June 29. He and his men chugged 1,040 miles upriver to Fort Yukon, towing two whaleboats. The little paddlewheel steamer *Yukon* was the first ever seen on the river; it appeared to be a "huge monster" to the natives in the villages along the river. The vessel, belching smoke and fiery cinders, seemed to the Indians like some "chariot of the gods." They were soon to get used to such craft, however, as rival American trading companies following in the wake of the explorers each felt obliged to have its own river steamer.

Captain Raymond's expedition was hardly a heroic feat, though the daily jousts with the swarms of gnats and mosquitoes that are characteristic of Alaska in the summer season put the Captain and his men to the test. Still, his experience was a far cry from some of the early mountain man excursions up the Missouri River. Perhaps the closest Captain Raymond and his men came to "adventure" was their near starvation on the return trip downriver in native skin boats. Ironically, they were rescued by an Indian, "Brother of New Years," a veteran Telegraph Expedition guide. Primarily Captain Raymond's mission was in the interests of San Francisco capitalists who hoped to intimidate the British and force them out of the Indian trade in Alaska.

Beyond the pioneering work of Captain Raymond, two other military expeditions to Alaska stand out as important. The first of these was the result of an international Polar Congress held in Hamburg, Germany, in 1879. There the United States and the European nations with an interest in the Arctic agreed to establish stations all around the polar region. On the Alaskan side, this duty was assigned to Lieutenant P. Henry Ray, who left San Francisco with an elaborate party which included a photographer—perhaps the first to photograph the extreme Arctic landscape—aboard the schooner *Golden Fleece* on July 18, 1881. Lieutenant Ray and his men were bound for Point Barrow on the northern coast of Alaska, far above the Arctic Circle. Technically, this was not unexplored territory, because daring whaleship captains frequently searched for the leviathans off Alaska's northern coasts. However, these ships came in the summer, while Lieutenant Ray and his men intended to spend nearly two years in a landlocked icy station collecting meteorological, magnetic, tidal, and natural history data that would link up with comparable polar ventures around the Arctic Circle. Lieutenant Ray's mission was far different from that of Captain Raymond. It was not made in the interests of narrow nationalism, or even especially those of commerce. He was part of the world culture of science.

Lieutenant Ray's expedition was well planned—in contrast to its counterpart led by Lieutenant Adolphus Greely on the eastern margin of North America at Ellesmere Island. Ray reached his destination, and with his men erected efficient winter quarters, which included a wooden blockhouse "pierced for musketry below and for the Gatling gun above." What enemies they expected to repel with a frozen Gatling gun will forever remain a matter for conjecture. Nonetheless, Ray's expedition was enormously successful. In two seasons he and his men collected all the necessary data. They made frequent contact with whalers, who supplied them with more data, and Ray himself tested the frozen winter tundra on an inland expedition to the Meade River. On June 29, 1883, Lieutenant Ray and all his men—in excellent health and spirits—having completed their mission, departed on the schooner *Leo* for San Francisco. Ray's venture, because it was so efficient, is easily overlooked, but it was he and his men who made survival in the Arctic wastes at 70° below zero look routine to Americans for the first time. And Lieutenant Ray had been the first inland explorer of Alaska's northern regions.

On the way home, the *Leo* stopped at St. Michael's and there took on board the complement of another, more flamboyant expedition, that of Lieutenant Frederick Schwatka. Lieutenant Schwatka was already a famous Arctic explorer by 1883. A lawyer, a doctor, a graduate of West Point, and a member of the 3rd U.S. Cavalry, Lieutenant Schwatka might well be seen as the John C. Frémont of Arctic and Alaskan exploration. He had a well-developed sense of publicity to go along with his considerable skills as a thorough and accomplished scientific explorer.

As early as 1878, in company with William Henry Gilder of the *New York Herald*, Schwatka had sailed from New York in search of relics and possibly long-lost survivors of Sir John Franklin's disastrous expedition of 1845 in search of a Northwest Passage. In his mission, Schwatka was extremely successful. "Schwatka's search," as the newspapers called the expedition, succeeded in finding the frozen graves of many of Franklin's party, various relics collected from the natives, scattered remains of Franklin's men who had almost reached northern Canada's Back River estuary, and the wreckage of one of Franklin's ships. Schwatka also accomplished the longest Arctic sledge journey on record, vividly described in Gilder's book *Schwatka's Search*. The lieutenant's journey of 3,251 miles across the northern coast of Canada, among Eskimo tribes who had never seen a white man, was indeed truly remarkable.

In 1883, Schwatka was on a different mission. In that year, starting at Chilkoot Pass—soon to be the route to the fabulous Yukon gold fields—along with a party of explorers aboard a homemade raft, he traced the entire course of the Yukon River from its sources in the glacial lakes of the mountains of British Columbia all the way to its outlet on the western shores of Alaska. Schwatka's was the first complete exploration of the

Yukon River. However, he failed to note significant traces of the golden bonanza that would soon transform Alaska. Ignoring the mysterious activities of Mr. Ed Schlieffelin, "a mining capitalist" whom he met making his way far up the Yukon, Schwatka concentrated on mapping the course of the river accurately for the first time and applying names to the land—names of important friends like Professor O. C. Marsh, the Yale paleontologist, and Mr. James Gordon Bennett, owner of the *New York Herald*, who was already responsible for the Stanley and Livingstone incident and the tragic dispatching of the *Jeannette* to the Arctic seas. But though he missed Alaska's gold deposits, and seemed somewhat too eager for publicity, Lieutenant Schwatka had completed another remarkable mission. His official report was complete with detailed maps and woodcuts made from photographs taken by his topographer, Charles A. Homan, as well as a thorough survey of the countless Alaskan Indian tribes and bands he had encountered. Schwatka's ethnological report is a landmark in the study of Alaska's native peoples.

As a result of this expedition, Schwatka became a popular lecturer and author. He resigned from the Army and published two Arctic books, *Along Alaska's Great River* (1885) and *Nimrod in the North* (1885). The year after their publication, he persuaded the *New York Times* to sponsor an expedition that climbed Mount St. Elias, then thought to be the highest mountain among the many that dominate Alaska. Schwatka clearly combined the talents of the serious scientist, the courage and drive of the adventurer, and the desire to be a public media hero that so captured mass enthusiasm at the end of the nineteenth century.

The last of the important Army Alaskan expeditions of the period was accompanied by far less publicity and fanfare. In 1885, Lieutenant Henry T. Allen of the 2nd U.S. Cavalry explored Alaska from south to north. He followed the Copper River north out of the Gulf of Alaska near Nuchek, then crossed over to the totally unexplored Tanana River, which runs northwest into the Yukon, and then traced the course of the Kayukuk

River as it runs down from the Arctic Circle into the Yukon just above Nulato. Much of the territory traversed by Lieutenant Allen was inhabited by fierce Indians, many of whom had never seen a white man. Allen's published report, like Schwatka's, was a model example of the old-style all-purpose reconnaisance. He included accurate maps, natural history data, a sense of the mountainous geography complete with topographical profiles, meteorological data, and descriptions of native tribes never before seen by their neighbors, let alone white men. Lieutenant Allen's report has been termed a classic in the literature of Alaskan exploration. But like the reports of many of the Army Topographical Engineers in the lower American West in the days before the Civil War, such important contributions to American literature as Allen's were largely ignored in favor of more spectacular events and personages.

In later times Captain P. H. Ray and Lieutenant W. P. Richardson captured headlines as a result of their expeditions "for the Relief of the Destitute in the Gold Fields," and the railroad magnate Edward H. Harriman garnered world publicity for his summer cruise with a boatload of scientists aboard the *George W. Elder* to Alaska in a possible search for a railroad route around the world—a sequel to the quixotic telegraph mission.

In the 1890s, before, during, and after the great gold rushes that began in the Yukon in 1896, much of Alaska's interior was explored and mapped in detail by teams of unsung heroic explorers from the U.S. Geological Survey. The Brooks Range in northern Alaska stands as a monument to perhaps the best-known of the Geological Survey explorers. But more typical and no less heroic was Josiah Spurr, who in 1896 had crossed Chilkoot Pass and followed the Yukon to its source while mapping the geology of the vast Yukon River country.

In 1898, at the height of the Alaskan gold rush, he led another, more spectacular expedition of mapmakers and geologists. Spurr and his men landed from the U.S. gunboat *Wheeling* on the north shore of Cook Inlet in a snowstorm. Even as they were preparing to make their way into the interior via native canoes up the Susitna River, they were startled to see two hundred men and two women suddenly land on that remote shore of Cook Inlet, where they set up tents and began to look for gold gravel. Spurr observed ironically, "They had been lured by the general excitement and by the steamship companies to come up to Cook Inlet." But finding no gold to be picked up in nuggets, "the majority rushed back to the off-lying ships as whole-heartedly as they had come ashore."

Spurr's party, consisting of six men, made their way with great difficulty up the south fork of the Kuskokwim River past Mount McKinley, the highest mountain in North America. Spurr surmised that this was the case. As they moved up the Kuskokwim, past towering Mount McKinley, which another Geological Survey party named the following year, they were traveling deep into the heart of Alaska, in territory and among peoples no white man had ever seen. They eventually ascended the mighty Kuskokwim River to its source, and from high atop a peak they gazed upon a splended panorama of rivers and lowlands stretching for miles, divided from the Yukon by the Kuskokwim Mountains, which were "grey, awe-inspiring, like vast Gothic cathedrals." Spurr added that "no white man, I thought in this moment of exhilaration, has ever gazed on this vast and beautiful country." It was no accident that a mountain in Alaska is named after him.

Eventually the Spurr expedition descended the Kuskokwim River to the Bering Sea. Then in Eskimo boats they made their way along the shore and across stormy Bristol Bay to present-day Egegik on the north shore of the Aleutian Peninsula. There they went inland through a country full of geysers and smoking steam pots, dominated by the very active Katmai volcano. This mysterious country would soon be visited by amateur explorers and dubbed the Valley of the Ten Thousand Smokes. Today it is a national park, but when Spurr and his by now thoroughly exhausted party traversed it, few, if any, Americans knew of its existence. It was like discovering another Yellowstone.

The last leg of their long, circuitous journey required them to

cross the treacherous, oceanic Shelikof Strait in a small dory.
This they proceeded to do. Fortunately they were rescued by a
fishing schooner from Kodiak and put on a ship that would take
them home with their maps, their botanical specimens, their
rock samples, and their memories of having gone deep into the
unexplored beauties of America's last frontier. They had not
preceded the amateur adventurers, the gold seekers, and the
tourists by much, but the maps they made as a result of the expedition made entry into the far northern country all the easier
for those who came after them.

But the most famous person associated with Alaska was the
old man of the Sierras, John Muir. In the summer of 1879, in
company with his missionary friend Hall Young, Muir had explored Glacier Bay, affixed his name to Muir Glacier, below
which he built a Thoreauvian hut, and immortalized the little
dog, Stikeen, that accompanied him on his dangerous travels
across the remarkable Alaskan glaciers. All this adventure Muir
recounted in his best-selling books *Stikeen* (1909) and *Travels
in Alaska* (1915).

In the summer of 1881, Muir accompanied Edward W. Nelson on an expedition aboard the revenue cutter *Corwin*, in a
vain search for the lost *Jeannette*. The result of this cruise was to
cast Muir even larger as the nation's expert on glaciers, the most
obvious element of Alaskan scenery—despite the fact that
Muir's theories on glaciation were almost all wrong. And though
his companion on the *Corwin* cruise, Edward Nelson, was to
become Chief of the U.S. Biological Survey, it was Muir who
became identified in the popular mind as the national spokesman, not only on glaciers, but on all things biological. He became the patron saint of preservationists in Alaska, as well as
California.

And this perhaps explains as well as anything why the monumental task of exploring Alaska—first by the Army, then by the
Revenue Service of the Treasury Department, and finally by
teams of men from the U.S. Geological Survey and Biological
Survey—has remained for the most part obscure. In Professor

Daniel Boorstin's apt phrase applied in another context, Alaska was "settled before it was explored." Nature lovers like Muir helped bring boatloads of summer tourists, who invaded the coasts admiring the mile-long glaciers he made famous. On these boats were photographers like Eadweard Muybridge, who began a whole industry depicting scenic Alaska. At the same time, a massive monopoly, the Alaska Commercial Company, invaded the streams for salmon and the Indian fur trade, and before long ACC canneries polluted Alaska's coasts in the name of progress. And finally, of course, all this was topped off by the dramatic gold rush of 1897–98. Even today there are parts of Alaska that have never been explored or accurately mapped. In the late nineteenth and early twentieth centuries, the American public wanted sensation and adventure that seemed to stand for science, progress, and a morality so sublime that it was always beyond the grasp of ordinary men, who were nonetheless devoted to it. This linkage of adventure and morality is nowhere better exemplified than in America's last grand adventure—the conquest of the mysterious frozen Arctic and the attainment of the North Pole.

iii

THE EXPLORER AS ECCENTRIC BUT TRAGIC HERO

THE LURE of the mysterious frozen North—the end of the earth, so to speak—was symbolized for millions on both sides of the Atlantic by the loss of the British explorer Sir John Franklin. It was one of the nineteenth century's most publicized tragedies; it was kept playing on the world's stage by Franklin's widow, Jane, Lady Franklin. Between 1847 and 1879 some forty-two expeditions were launched into the frozen north, ostensibly to search for survivors of Franklin's failed search for a Northwest Passage.

One of those caught up in the romance of the Franklin tragedy was Charles Francis Hall, a plain bourgeois printer and newspaper publisher in Cincinnati, Ohio. Like Cervantes's immortal Knight of La Mancha, Hall heated his brain to a fever pitch reading accounts of the Franklin expedition and of those adventurous voyagers to Ultima Thule who sailed in search of Sir John. Lacking any nautical skills whatsoever, Hall volunteered for several rescue expeditions, but was, of course, rejected. The vision of himself as rescuer of Franklin and his men took over his life. And even after Sir Francis Leopold McClintock returned to England with definite news of Franklin's demise, Hall refused to part with his vision. Influenced primarily by Kane's account of his symbiotic relationship with the Eskimos, Hall reasoned that survivors of the Franklin Expedition must certainly have made their way to Eskimo villages and were even now, in 1859, over ten years after the tragedy, living somewhere in the Arctic, waiting to be rescued. The thing to do, then, was to go to some strategic jumping-off point in the Arctic, learn to live and converse with the Eskimos or "Inuits," and have them lead him to the fabled survivors of the expedition. Accordingly, in his own eccentric way, Hall began practicing for his Arctic rescue mission. He drew up plans to secure transportation to Frobisher Strait, Foxe Basin, and King William Island (where Franklin was last seen), and then to the vast amusement of the citizens of Cincinnati, he began camping out each chilly autumn night in a tent on a hill behind the old astronomical observatory. He also began the serious study of navigation and triangulation via the stars in the night sky. Most important, he began corresponding with Ohio politicians, who soon put him in touch with potential expedition sponsors in New York. The chief of these was Henry Grinnell, president of the American Geographical and Statistical Society.

In 1859, virtually abandoning his family in his obsession with Arctic exploration and the Franklin quest, Hall journeyed to New York to meet Grinnell and read further on Arctic subjects in the American Geographical Society library and the sizable Astor Library. Despite Grinnell's strong support and that of influential New York citizens like Henry Brevoort, the best Hall could do was to assemble a minimum of equipment and take passage in May of 1860 aboard the whaleship *George Henry*, bound for the Frobisher Strait area. By late autumn, the small whaling fleet was berthed for the winter at Cyrus Field Bay on the extreme southeastern tip of Baffin Island.

As soon as he could, Hall moved off the whaler and in with the Eskimos of the region—adapting as much as he could to their sometimes revolting and shocking customs. He made friends with two Eskimos who had been to England and had even met Queen Victoria. Their names were Ebierbing and Tookaalito, otherwise known as Joe and Hannah. They were to stand by Hall in all his Arctic travels, and even to return with him to the States, where they earned their keep appearing with Hall on the lecture platform, and as features in P. T. Barnum's extravaganza shows.

Hall, more than any other Arctic explorer, learned the ways of the Eskimos. In many ways he became the very model of the modern anthropologist, who in Clifford Geertz's terms could converse in ordinary terms with the natives and comprehend their levels of meaning. For over two years Hall served a rugged apprenticeship in the vicinity of Frobisher Strait, where his exploring efforts produced spectacular results. He proved that Hall Island was indeed the sixteenth-century British explorer's first American landfall. He also located coal and red brick deposits laid down by Frobisher's expeditions, a cairn raised atop Warwick Peak by the British adventurer some three hundred years before, and the actual site of Frobisher's headquarters in the New World. The Frobisher relics that Hall brought back from his lonely expeditions of 1860–62 made him famous in both Britain and America. He also proved that Frobisher Strait did not lead to Foxe Basin and a Northwest Passage, but was actually an enormous bay or inlet.

Hall spent the year 1863 back on the East Coast of the United States raising funds for a revised plan to locate Franklin's missing men. In this venture he resorted to showmanship, using Joe and Hannah whenever he could and lecturing in stuffy overheated halls clad in full Arctic fur regalia. Hannah contracted pneumonia, and her child, Butterfly, died. But still Hall persisted. So persistent was he that in June of 1864 he and his two Eskimo friends boarded the whaler *Monticello* and headed north for Repulse Bay on the far western shore of Foxe Basin, hundreds of miles west beyond Baffin Island, and much closer to the last known whereabouts of Franklin's party, as it was known to have come ashore from the wreckage of the *Erebus* and the *Terror*. Unfortunately for Hall, the skipper of the *Monticello*, having no soul or sympathy for expeditions in search of dead men, disembarked Hall and his Eskimo friends at Noowook on Roe's Welcome Sound, hundreds of miles from Hall's intended destination. As a result of this, Hall spent five years making his way from Foxe Basin to King William Island, where Franklin was known to have perished. He did, however, find relics and physical remains of the Franklin expedition. Some of these, such as a monogrammed spoon and scientific instruments, made their way to the Smithsonian Institution. Others were bones and bodies—at least one of which, that of Lieutenant Le Vesconte, was identified and sent back to England for burial. Other bodies, Hall found, showed signs of saw and knife marks, indicating that the flower of the Royal Navy had taken to cannibalism *in extremis*. Perhaps the saddest thing he learned was that Lieutenant F. R. M. Crozier and a sizable contingent of the Franklin party had survived, crossing via the Todd Islands to the estuary of the Great Fish or Back River. There they were refused aid by the local Eskimos and hence starved to death in a region not far from the grazing ground of the tasty musk oxen. At this point Hall's faith in the Eskimo faltered. He wrote bitterly in his diary, "Civilize, Enlighten and Christianize them and their race." He did not mean through gentle persuasion.

By the time Hall returned to the United States in the summer of 1869, he had spent ten years mastering the ways of the Arctic. He had gotten to know the ways of the Eskimo and the tricks of living off the land in the Arctic beyond any other man, including most Eskimos. He had been forced to shoot a mutineer, one

Patrick Coleman, in cold blood, and he had published books about his adventures, carefully leaving out such lurid misadventures. But by 1869 Hall had come quits with the Sir John Franklin conundrum. Instead, he set his sights on being the first man to reach the North Pole.

In November of 1869, he wrote to his friend Grinnell: "Having now completed my Arctic collegiate education, I feel [inclined] to spend my life extending our knowledge of the earth up to that spot which is directly under Polaris—the crowning jewel of the Arctic dome."

iv

THE MURDERED AND THE MAROONED

CHARLES FRANCIS HALL, engraver, printer, backwoods newspaper editor from Cincinnati, the haunt of the eccentric John Cleves Symmes, had begun the race for the Pole.

By March of 1870 Hall's Ohio political friends had introduced a bill before both Houses of Congress authorizing a polar expedition to be led by Hall. Hall lectured ceaselessly and lobbied assiduously for the passage of the bill—even to the point of cultivating President Grant. The latter came in handy because Dr. Isaac Hayes at the last moment succeeded in having Hall's name removed from the Polar Expedition Bill, with the leader left to the discretion of the President. When the bill passed, naturally Grant chose Hall—a rough, self-made man like himself, who even bore a striking resemblance to the President.

Hall was given a steam tug of 287 tons renamed the *Polaris* and specially reinforced for Arctic travel. First choice for captain of the vessel was George E. Tyson, but he was committed to a whaling voyage, so Hall persuaded his old friend Captain Sydney Buddington to take command, which Buddington did with some reluctance. It proved difficult to find an American-born crew for the northern venture as well, so the crew members were Germans and Scandinavians, with a few exceptions, including William Morton, the veteran of Elisha Kent Kane's expedition of 1855, who had last laid eyes on the "open polar sea." Eventually Tyson joined the expedition as navigation officer, as did the Eskimos Joe and Hannah, and Hans and his family from the Kane expedition, making nine Eskimos in all as part of the exploring crew.

But before the *Polaris* even sailed, an old problem arose that quite possibly spelled the doom of the expedition. In the summer of 1869, Lady Franklin, then nearly eighty, journeyed to Cincinnati to persuade Hall to continue his search for her husband's remains. Failing this, she recommended Dr. David Walker of the U.S. Army, an experienced Arctic hand, as chief scientific officer for the expedition. But Joseph Henry and Spencer F. Baird had a different idea. They hoped to lift the professional scientific tone of the expedition by securing the appointment of Heidelberg-trained Dr. Emil Bessels as chief scientist. They felt that this civilized man would compensate for the boorish Yankee amateur Charles Francis Hall. Bessels did more than compensate for Hall. Throughout the duration of the expedition, he assumed the superior airs of the European-trained savant. He was contemptuous of Hall, Captain Buddington, and most of the scientific aspects of the voyage. To most of the men, he was a sinister figure whom they did not trust.

After a rousing send-off banquet thrown by the American Geographical Society, in which Grinnell presented Hall with a flag from Wilkes's Antarctic expedition, the *Polaris* sailed from New London, Connecticut, on July 3, 1871. It was an unusual season in Arctic waters, and the expedition vessel steamed north through Smith Sound, through Kane Basin, and even the narrow ice-filled Kennedy Channel, between Ellesmere Island and Greenland, with relative ease. It was only when they reached the Robeson Strait near 82°11' that they at last confronted the vast impenetrable ice pack of the polar sea. They had sailed farther north via this route than any other vessel, and though they didn't know it, no land lay between them and the Pole, five hundred miles away.

But then the ship was cast back by the pack ice and went into winter quarters just below Cape Lupton at shallow Thank God Harbor on the Greenland shore of Kennedy Channel.

From Thank God Harbor, Hall began to lead sled expeditions northward, testing the feasibility of a dash for the Pole. Then, on October 24, just after he returned from one of these land expeditions, in which from atop Cape Brevoort he had at last seen the Lincoln Sea—the polar sea—Hall downed a cup of coffee and suddenly fell ill. He soon became delirious and believed himself poisoned by the mysterious Dr. Bessels, with whom he had been feuding. The intrepid explorer lingered in agony until November 8, when, with William Morton in attendance, he died. The expedition was left without its dauntless leader. Both Bessels, head of the scientific corps, and Buddington, captain of the *Polaris*, were relieved. But most of the rest of the party were grief-stricken and slightly panicked as they buried Hall in the far northern wasteland in the Arctic semidarkness at 11:00 a.m., the service lit only by lanterns and stars shining through an eerie boreal glow.

The men of the *Polaris* continued to make overland exploring expeditions to the shores of the polar sea throughout the winter, with Chester, Tyson, and Meyer leading the parties while Bessels set up an astronomical station near the ship. Captain Buddington took no interest in science, and only waited for the day he could free his ship from the ice and return to his beloved New London. On August 12 that day arrived, and the ship sailed south out of Thank God Harbor. This departure was not to be their deliverance.

At 6 p.m. on October 15, far up in Smith Sound, disaster overtook them. The *Polaris* was nipped by ice, the stern rose, and she began taking on water in the engine room. Captain Buddington ordered everybody and all longboats and supplies tossed overboard onto the ice floe in preparation for abandoning ship. Tyson supervised this operation, managing to rescue three Eskimo children and most of the supplies. All that was lost, perhaps deliberately, was the box containing many of Hall's personal journals and papers.

At about 10:00 P.M. the floe seemed to explode. The ship tore loose, its hawsers and ice anchors ripped apart. And while the moon shone through the clouds, the ship, with fourteen men, including Captain Buddington, aboard, drifted away into the darkness. Tyson and nineteen people were marooned on an ice floe far up in the frozen Arctic waters. The ship did not sink after all, however, and twice they hailed her, receiving no response. To those marooned on the ice floe, the *Polaris* had become a ghost ship.

When the panic died down, the marooned survivors looked to their own problems. The ice floe on which they found themselves was about four square miles in area, so they constructed an igloo village and hoped to drift south with the Greenland current. On one occasion they missed an opportunity to use their boats and make for the Eskimo settlements on Greenland because of the reluctance of the German sailors to take to the icy waters in small boats. Eventually, however, the floe began to break up in warmer waters, and the party found themselves shuttling by boat from one floe or ice cake to another. They had just about run out of ice platforms when on the last day of April, off Newfoundland, they were rescued by the steamship *Tigress*. They had drifted nearly two thousand miles through icy Arctic seas in perhaps one of the greatest epic voyages of all time. Later they learned that Captain Buddington and his men, forced to take to small boats, had been rescued by Scottish whalers after a far easier time. Thus ended the impossible moonlight dream of Cincinnati's Charles Francis Hall—one of the strangest men in the annals of world exploration.

The demise of the expedition did not end the story. An inquest was held back in the States concerning the circumstances of Hall's death and the desertion by Buddington of Tyson and his marooned companions. Both men, Bessels and Buddington, were cleared. Hall was declared to have died of apoplexy. However, in 1968, Hall's biographer, Chauncey Loomis, led a party to his lonely grave near Thank God Harbor, disinterred the body, and performed an autopsy. They discovered that Hall had imbibed massive concentrated doses of arsenic over the last two weeks of his life. Dr. Bessels, who attended to him in those two weeks, indeed proved to be Hall's implacable enemy to the end. In a sense he represented a kind of ruthless elitism that was becoming part of the culture of science. Such a culture had no place for a crude mountain man type like Charles Francis Hall. As his biographer asserts, Hall's explorations were "a quest for the kind of independence that was gone from American life."

V

GREELY'S FOLLY

WHILE LIEUTENANT RAY, with his log fort and his frozen Gatling gun, was conducting his International Circumpolar Year experiments in comparatively routine fashion at Point Barrow, Alaska, in 1881, something quite different was happening to the other American expedition under Lieutenant Adolphus Greely, stationed far up on Ellesmere Island. In the summer of 1881, Lieutenant Greely of the 5th Cavalry and twenty men of the U.S. Army, plus two Eskimos and one civilian meteorologist, took ship aboard the sealing vessel *Proteus* for Lady Franklin Bay on Ellesmere Island. Their destination was far up the island at 81°44′ north latitude, at a spot called Discovery Bay where a British expedition had wintered the year before.

Lieutenant Greely's mission was roughly the same as that of Lieutenant Ray in Alaska. He was to conduct pendulum experiments and record such things as the daily weather and the earth's magnetic variations in the far northern region. Actually, he was closer to the true north magnetic pole of the earth than the astronomically determined one. Following orders, Greely and his men constructed Fort Conger, a well-supplied base, and prepared to wait out the winter doing their duty. Operating from a safe, secure base, Greely's mission seemed almost routine. In the summer of 1882, a relief ship would bring further supplies and cache others up and down the coasts of Ellesmere Island and Greenland. If necessary, due to freakish Arctic weather, still other relief ships would be sent out in 1883. Meanwhile, Fort Conger was admirably situated for an Arctic base. It was in an area covered with grass and flowers, close to the grazing lands of the caribou and the musk ox, and with plenty of seals and fish to be had. It was an oasis in the Arctic— one comparable to that at a similar latitude across the Kennedy Channel in Greenland. All Greely really had to do was to wait it out in this Arctic paradise doing his meteorological duty. Instead he was ambitious. He sent the expedition's doctor, Oliver Pavy, and Lieutenant J. B. Lockwood north, headed for the Pole. They did not reach the Pole, but Lockwood did reach latitude 83°24', four miles farther north than a British expedition led by Sir Clements Markham the previous year. The Americans set up a rock cairn on what they named Lockwood Island and displayed from it a flag made by Mrs. Greely. And beyond this they named a promontory that they could just barely see, Cape Washington. Meanwhile, Greely conducted expeditions inland up and down Ellesmere Island, covering some five thousand square miles. Thus far Greely's expedition was a rousing success—except in one respect. The corps was wrought with dissension. The doctor resigned, but stayed to do his medical duties only. Greely's second-in-command, Lieutenant Kislingburg, also resigned and plotted mutiny. In some ways this dissension was perhaps due to the fact that the party was large and there was not enough to do. When things turned grim in succeeding times, the morale improved.

After reaching a high point of advancement that first season, Greely and his men waited in vain for the relief ship of 1882 to arrive. It did not; the *Proteus* had been nipped in the ice off Cape Sabine and had sunk. In addition, Lieutenant E. A. Garlington of the ill-starred 7th Cavalry disobeyed his orders and did not cache supplies at designated places in Kennedy Channel as had been agreed, should an emergency arise. As the historian Jeanette Mirsky has calculated, "from July 1882 to August 1883, fifty thousand rations were taken northward through Smith Sound and . . . of these only a bare one thousand were cached in various places." And some of these were on the Greenland side and hence inaccesssible to Greely and his men.

After the third summer had passed with no relief, Greely and his officers decided to make their way southward where they might expect to make contact with relief vessels. On August 9, 1883, they left the relative comforts of Fort Conger and made their way down Ellesmere Island to Cape Sabine, where they hoped to reach a major cache of supplies. They were bitterly disappointed. Thus they faced the prospect of a long Arctic winter with twenty-eight men and forty days' food rations.

Greely and his men, supplementing these rations with an occasional seal, Arctic shrimp which they caught in nets, and seaweed, managed to keep alive until May 1, 1884. Then, beginning with the engineer William Cross, they began to weaken and die. One by one they were buried on a gravel ridge above the camp, which consisted of a four-foot rock wall enclosure, a whaleboat roof, and a tent. Among the first to die was the intrepid Lieutenant Lockwood, but others, including the Eskimos, soon followed. Yet through it all, Greely maintained his spirit, while Sergeant D. L. Brainard, with incredible energy and heroism, kept the dwindling company together. One man, Private C. B. Henry, had to be shot for stealing food—a sentence which was officially carried out on June 6, 1884.

Gradually the exploring party dwindled to seven men huddled in a tent, slowly freezing and starving to death. Only F. J. Long and Sergeant Brainard were really functional, and they were all so weak that they could not even push the corpse of Private Schneider out of their tent, so he lay half in and half out, rotting before their eyes. By the time a relief party did arrive under Commander Winfield S. Schley, there was evidence that some of Greely's party had taken to cannibalism. But at last the seven were rescued at the end of June 1884, thanks to the daring of Commander Schley, who set out north so early in the spring as to put his own ship in some jeopardy.

When he arrived at Cape Sabine, the first sight Schley and his men saw was Long pitifully trying to raise a signal pole. Then he led them to the tent where Greely sat clad in a red skullcap, trying to read his Bible. One more day and they would all have perished.

Greely has not gone down in the annals of exploration as a great discoverer, but rather as a symbol of Arctic disaster and, to some extent, for his poor judgment in leaving Fort Conger. Yet he carried out his mission with great thoroughness, and all his scientific records survived. Moreover, Greely went on to become the recognized U.S. authority on the Arctic. No explorer departed for those perilous regions without seeking his advice. And just as he was a pillar of the American Geographical Society, he became a founding father of the new National Geographic Society. He was, to use a time-worn phrase, "a hero in spite of himself."

vi

THE HERO

TWENTY-FIVE years later, on April 6, 1909, Commander Robert Edwin Peary of the United States Navy at last reached the goal that men like Greely and Hall had struggled so hard to attain. Peary stood at the North Pole, atop the world. He had taken exploration full cycle from those days in the early eighteenth century when Sir Isaac Newton alerted mankind to the fact that the earth was an "oblate spheroid," flattened at the poles. Peary now stood at a point that Newton could see only in his mind's eye, and then only in terms of mathematics, not icy wastes. The commander wrote in his diary for that April day: "The Pole at last. The prize of three centuries. My dream and goal for twenty years. Mine at last! I cannot bring myself to realize it. It seems all so simple and so commonplace."

After making sure of his astronomical sightings and taking a photograph, Peary almost matter-of-factly planted the American flag and four other flags, including the colors of Delta Kappa Epsilon, left a record of his arrival there in a bottle, and departed at 4:00 p.m. the next day, April 7, 1909. How had Peary succeeded when all others failed? What were the results of this achievement? And, most important of all, what was its meaning—in its own time and for all times?

Robert Peary (pronounced like "cheery") was born in Cresson, Pennsylvania, May 6, 1856. Three years later his father died, and he was raised by his mother, who devoted her life to him—even to the extent of attending Bowdoin College with her son. Peary's early post-college years were devoted to civil engineering. In 1881, he became a draftsman for the Coast and Geodetic Survey, with the rank of first lieutenant in the United States Navy. In 1884, he went with the famous Colonel Goethals to Central America, where he assisted in making a survey for an isthmian canal across Nicaragua. This duty recalled to his mind his recurring dreams of becoming an explorer—the characteristic hero of his age. Even while on monotonous duty in Washington, D. C., Peary wrote: "I never come under those glorious influences of nature . . . but my thoughts turn to those first few views which have turned themselves into the eye of Columbus, Cortez, Livingstone . . . Balboa, De Soto, and all the host of travelers and explorers."

As a child, Peary had read of the exploits of Elisha Kent Kane in the Arctic, but what focused his dreams of being an Arctic explorer most directly was his purchase one day at a Washington bookshop of Baron Nordenskiöld's *Exploration of Interior Greenland*. Greely's harrowing Arctic experiences were also fresh in his mind from the daily newspapers. Peary began to read all existing Arctic exploration accounts and, in a notebook which he kept, to lay out his own plan for what was to be his life's goal—the attainment of the North Pole. The question as to why an otherwise perfectly normal man, who on August 11, 1889, married his sweetheart, Jo Diebitsch, should wish to attain the North Pole above all else, can only be left to the psychohistorian. But it is clear that from Greely's return in 1885 onward, Peary single-mindedly planned a rendezvous with the top of the world.

Within a year, in 1886, on leave from the Navy, Peary

mounted an expedition that took him 120 miles into the interior of Greenland. He hoped that his first noteworthy feat would be the first expedition to cross that frozen waste, but he was anticipated in this by the Norwegian Fridtjof Nansen in 1887. As a result of this, Peary turned to northern Greenland. His plan was to set up a base on the Greenland coast and trek farther north than Lieutenant Lockwood of Greely's expedition. In 1891 he secured financial backing and leave from the Navy to carry out this plan.

As the Canadian historian Neatby has pointed out, Peary's campaign falls into three phases. In the first, from 1891 to 1895, Peary experimented with overland routes to northeast Greenland, looking for a jumping-off point to the Pole. Eventually he rejected this, but only after exploring the whole north coast of Greenland and proving it an island, for which he received a gold medal from the Royal Geographical Society.

In the second phase, from 1898 to 1902, he turned his attention to "the American route" up Kane Basin and the Kennedy Channel—the route followed by American explorers from Kane to Greely. Finally, by 1902, he realized that he did not have a ship that could carry him far enough north so that he could effectively launch a dash for the Pole. He needed a vessel like Nansen's famous *Fram* that rode above the crunching ice floes.

From 1891 onward, Peary kept his name and his Arctic feats before Congress and the public. In 1891, he took to Greenland his wife and a Dr. Frederick Cook, as well as a black servant who was to remain his most faithful Arctic companion, Matt Henson. Mrs. Peary, the first white woman to winter in the Arctic, of course made headlines. That summer, despite having broken his leg, Peary crossed northern Greenland in a thousand-mile trek to what he named Independence Fiord, which he saw erroneously as the termination of Greenland to the northeast. It was not until 1900 that he plunged on farther, corrected this error, and proved that Greenland was an island. In 1893, however, he was back in Greenland, this time with a pregnant wife and a nurse who would help deliver "snow baby," born at Bowdoin Bay on September 12, 1893, and christened Mary Annighito Peary. Headlines again. But on August 28, 1894, Jo Peary, the baby, and the nurse, Susan Cross, as well as all the rest of Peary's party except Matt Henson, sailed back to civilization, leaving Peary virtually alone in the Arctic. It was at this point that Peary began to realize the value of living with, and like, the Highland Eskimos around Etah. Like Henson, they became his faithful companions, and one of them even his mistress, as he relied less and less on Europeans or Americans on his expeditions. The 1890s were years of extreme hardship, peril, and desperation for Peary. But he persevered, always conscious of keeping his name in the newspaper. In 1896, for example, he supervised the collecting of three giant meteors from Greenland, including one called the Tent that weighed over a hundred tons.

In the spring of 1898 he sailed in great haste up the "American route" for the Pole aboard a totally inadequate vessel, the *Windward*, because he learned that the Norwegian Otto Sverdrup was taking the *Fram* up the same route in an effort to "steal his glory." Both expeditions failed that season because of heavy ice, and eventually Sverdrup gave up attempting to reach the Pole. The Danes and the Norwegians were far less interested in exploration stunts than they were in the systematic scientific survey of the Arctic, and Greenland in particular.

While Peary was snowbound in Kane Basin during the winter of 1898–99, back in New York his two friends Morris K. Jessup and Herbert L. Bridgeman launched the Peary Club to provide a financial base for Peary's further Arctic adventures. Peary, meanwhile, managed to insult Sverdrup, Scandinavia's most famous explorer after Nansen. But he also led a party of Highland Eskimos to Cape Hecla at the tip of Ellesmere Island, where he selected his jumping-off point for the North Pole expedition. That excursion, which took them to Greely's abandoned Fort Conger, cost Peary the amputation of eight frozen toes and Greely's undying enmity because the perfectionist Peary publicly criticized the old major's handling of his 1884 expedition.

After his brush with Sverdrup, Peary grew impatient. In 1900 he rounded off his survey of northern Greenland. Then, in 1901 and 1902, he made two futile attempts to head north from Ellesmere Island to the Pole. In the summer of 1901, Mrs. Peary and his by now seven-year-old "snow baby" had journeyed north to Fort Conger to provide encouragement. They were no help then or in the frustrating year of 1902 when he reached 84°06′ before "a hellish tangle of erupted ice blocks" forced him to turn back. At that point Peary almost gave up. He confided to his journal, "The game is off; my dream of sixteen years is ended!" All his previous achievements he counted for nothing, declaring that "no man would exchange a few facts of so-called scientific information for the gorgeous title of discoverer of the Pole." For Peary it had turned into a public relations world, but then fame had always been his spur.

After 1902, Peary knew he needed a proper ship that could edge him closer out onto the Lincoln Sea ice pack. Thanks to the widow of Morris K. Jessup and other friends, the *Roosevelt*, a vessel like the *Fram*, was built to his specifications in 1904–1905. In the summer of 1905, he sailed it farther north than any previous ship. On February 19, 1906, at fifty years of age, he launched what he thought was to be his final polar expedition. He was halted less than a hundred miles from land by a large lead (a river in the ice) that he could not cross. Again he faced disappointment, but at least he had worked out a plan for the dash for the Pole. He would create igloo relay stations constructed out on the floating ice pack by advance parties leap-frogging one another and caching supplies. Then he sailed back to the States, arriving at New York harbor on Christmas Eve, 1906. His almost forgotten daughter was by now thirteen years old.

But away out there on the ice floes of the Polar Sea lay Peary's soul. He confided to his diary: "And what I saw before me in all its splendid, sunlit savageness was *mine* by right of discovery, to be credited to me, and associated with my name, generations after I have ceased to be."

In the spring of 1909, Peary was again ready to make his move on the Pole. He sailed north in the *Roosevelt* with a large complement of Highland Eskimos, Matt Henson, his friend and navigator Bob Bartlett, 246 sled dogs, and a newly graduated Yale man, the athletic youth George Borup. This time, starting in March, Peary was to attain his goal. The weather, which was cold enough to keep the ice firm, cooperated, and his expedition team functioned to perfection. By April 1 he had reached 87°47′ and was 133 geographical miles from the Pole. This was his last jumping-off station. And it was here that Peary foolishly left behind Captain Bob Bartlett, the only man who could confirm his astronomical determination of the Pole. Instead, he took five Eskimos and Matt Henson with him, thus forever leaving open to question his actual attainment of the exact location of the Pole.

Peary said he did this because it was according to plan and for the safety of his men. Each Eskimo relay party had to have at least one man who could navigate it back to the previous station, and at the last outpost Captain Bob Bartlett was that man. Even the disappointed Bartlett, who had come so far and so long with Peary, agreed with that judgment, though he later declared, "But my mind had been set on it for so long that I had rather die than give it up then." And so Peary, his five Eskimos, and Henson departed over the ice horizon for the top of the world and the fulfillment of the dream of his life.

Peary, making incredibly fast time, returned from the Pole to the *Roosevelt*, anchored at the foot of Cape Columbia, in sixteen days, or by April 23. The return party had averaged over thirty miles a day while suffering no delays from leads or other mishaps. As Ootah, one of the returning Eskimos, remarked, "The devil is asleep or having trouble with his wife or we should never have come back so easily!"

The return trip aboard the *Roosevelt* to the Etah settlement on the coast of Greenland was a triumphant one. But once Peary reached Etah, he learned that one of his old expedition mates, Dr. Frederick Cook, was already on his way to Denmark claiming to have reached the Pole in the season of 1908. Peary had been scooped. Thus began a long and tedious battle between the amiable Dr. Cook, who offered to share the glory with Peary, and the commander, who felt that Cook was a fraud who was attempting to dupe him out of the meaning of his whole life.

vii

THE HERO'S NEMESIS

COOK claimed that he had departed from the the northernmost point of Axel Heiberg Island, five hundred miles from the Pole, on March 18 of 1908, with two Highland Eskimos, and had arrived at the top of the world on April 21. He also claimed that he had all the celestial observations and logbook records to prove it, most of which he had left at Etah under the care of a young American sportsman, Caspar Whitney. Taking his rudimentary documentation with him, Dr. Cook sailed aboard the Danish vessel *Hans Egede* for Copenhagen. From Lerwick in the Shetland Islands he telegraphed James Gordon Bennett of the *New York Herald* announcing his feat. By the time Cook reached Copenhagen, the whole world was astir. Danish authorities, no friends of Peary's, accepted Cook's claim without much question, and when Phillip Gibbs did question Cook's story in the *London Chronicle*, he was challenged to a duel by one of Cook's Danish partisans. Cook was decorated by Denmark's king and its Royal Scientific Society. Back in America, his story was also accepted by both Greely and Schley, who also had no reason to be sympathetic to Peary, who had insulted them over the 1884 expedition.

Peary himself did his cause no good when, from Indian Harbor, Labrador, he sent the following rather frivolous telegram: "Do not trouble about Cook's story or attempt to explain any discrepancies in his installments. The affair will settle itself. He has not been to the Pole on April 21st, 1908 or at any other date. He has simply handed the public a gold brick. These statements are made advisedly and I have proof of them. . . ."

The "gold brick" reference was courtesy of Borup, the Yale man, and offended the sensibilities of the American scientific establishment and the newspaper-reading public. Thus, initially, opinion overwhelmingly sided with the amiable Dr. Cook and against the surly, arrogant Peary. Cook was given a testimonial dinner at the Waldorf-Astoria and went on a profitable lecture tour across the country. Peary headed into seclusion at his retreat on Eagle Island, Maine. Public relations seemed certain to defeat him—especially when he turned the matter over to his own friends at the National Geographic Society, for judgment in the matter.

Cook's claims were relatively easy to dismiss, however. From the beginning, the Royal Geographical Society had been suspicious of his skimpy documenation and had awarded priority of discovery to Peary without much hesitation. The society also awarded him another gold medal for achievement. And, as could be predicted, the National Geographic Society also found in Peary's favor. The most damaging evidence against Cook was the testimony of his two Eskimo companions that they had never been out of sight of land during their entire march to the Pole, plus the thinness of Cook's records when they finally did arrive from Etah. Cook's honor was further besmirched when it was proved that he had lied when he claimed to have been the first to climb Mount McKinley in 1907. And finally, a Captain Loose swore in an affidavit that he and an insurance salesman named Dunkle had, for $4,000, sold Cook a series of fake astronomical observations, which he used to substantiate his reaching the Pole.

Cook ended his public career in 1923, when he was convicted of using the United States mail to defraud people in a Texas oil swindle. He was sentenced to Leavenworth Prison for fourteen years, during which time he was visited by his last friend, Roald Amundsen, discoverer of the Northwest Passage and the South Pole. Cook was paroled in 1930 and died ten years later in 1940, just on the eve of World War II. By that time Admiral Peary had been dead for twenty years.

viii
DID PEARY REALLY REACH THE POLE?

IT IS by no means certain that the dour Peary died secure in the knowledge that he had truly reached the North Pole. In a neglected article in the *Boston American*, Matt Henson himself cast doubt on Peary's achievement without actually meaning to do so. According to Henson, Peary seemed "disappointed" after taking his last astronomical observations. And then:

> "Well, Mr. Peary," I spoke up, cheerfully enough, We are now at the Pole, are we not?"
> "I do not suppose that we can swear that we are exactly at the Pole," was his evasive answer.

Was it possible that neither Cook nor Peary reached the Pole? That the first expedition truly to reach the Pole was the nuclear submarine U.S.S. *Nautilus*, which cruised over the Pole underneath the ice pack on August 5, 1958, and radioed to the world, "*Nautilus* 90° north"? Several modern authors seem to think so. In 1973, Dennis Rawlins, in *Peary at the North Pole: Fact or Fiction*, concluded that Peary could possibly have gotten to within a hundred miles of the Pole, but could not have reached it. His primary argument is that Peary, without careful latitude and transverse or deviation observations, could not have known which way to aim toward the Pole. Peary nowhere makes clear that he made these observations, declares Rawlins, thus making the alleged march to the Pole the "most superhuman aiming achievement in the entire history of Polar exploration ... the equivalent of expecting a rocket aimed from Cape Kennedy to hit the moon without any in-flight guidance system."

But Rawlins and his latter-day disciple David Roberts, in *Great Exploration Hoaxes*, perhaps overlooked Peary's careful sightings when they reached the Pole. After his first sighting of

89°51′, Peary advanced ten more miles and made further observations that he determined placed him beyond the Pole. In fact,
he traveled in each of the compass directions and made sightings
back toward the Pole spot to cross-check his own first calculations. Though this is not conclusive, it does indicate that Peary
was sincere in thinking that he had reached the Pole. He was
perpetrating no hoax of the kind Dr. Cook attempted. Moreover,
Roberts's criticism of the rate at which Peary returned from the
Pole, estimating that he would have had to travel some fifty-six
miles per day, seems farfetched. His rate of speed from his last
camp to the Pole and back again figures out to about thirty-three
miles per day, traveling with a light sled and load—definitely
within the realm of plausibility. And the total time of his return,
sixteen days from the last camp, was only two days faster than
Captain Bartlett's, though Bartlett's party had to stop to rescue
him from a fall through the ice and to thaw him out. Thus, the
Englishman J. Gordon Hayes, who first questioned the rate of
Peary's return in 1929, as well as the latter-day writer David
Roberts, seem either spiteful or confused.

But then, as is still possible, and even Peary knew it, suppose
he did not in fact reach the exact location of the North Pole?
What did this mean? Clearly it meant little to science. The
Danish explorers of Greenland had long since concluded that.
And since 1880, after the Hamburg Conference, most of the
world's scientific establishment was concentrating on such profound questions as long-range meteorological and oceanic currents and chemical changes resulting from the Greenland ice
mass, the shifting of the earth's magnetic field, and, toward 1920,
the whole question of continental drift that would change the
entire way in which we look at the earth and its history. A
Third Great Age of Discovery had come into being—highly organized, team-oriented, and ultimately the creature of imper-
sonal systems analysis.

ix

CIVILIZATION AND ITS SUBTEXTS

Peary—the indomitable Peary—stood for something else. Sigmund Freud would have said that he, like the hundreds of other explorers in the Second Great Age of Discovery, stood for "civilization and its discontents." Clearly there were explorers with different motives. Some, like Lewis and Clark, were on a mission to scout out the dimensions of the Louisiana Purchase. Others, like Lieutenants Gibbon and Herndon, were looking to exploit economically the Amazon Basin and to resettle the American slave population there. Clarence King was searching out the mineral resources of the western United States and hoping to reconstruct its geologic history. And way off in the jungles of Central Africa, that naturalized American Henry Morton Stanley, who traced out the course of the mighty Congo, was laying the foundation for a white man's empire. He, like a number of other explorers of his age, such as the revered David Livingstone, carried on the ancient concept of a pagan "third world" that first needed Christianizing, then civilizing through westernized education, and then exploiting through phase capitalism and its multinational trading infrastructure. Stanley, Livingstone, and their type of explorer were naive avatars of that naked, aggressive imperialism that so characterized the nineteenth century.

More subtle, however, was the imperialism of the culture of science. Once the powerful scientific method was devised, gentle bespectacled men like Charles Darwin or towering figures of erudition like Alexander von Humboldt could roam the earth, establishing this scientific method—the western mind-set—as the only way of comprehending the realities of Nature and Nature's Earth. If this chronicle of American global exploration following after the Scientific Revolution of the seventeenth century has revealed anything, it should certainly have made clear the broad outlines of a rapidly emerging culture of science that, in its amoral search for empirical truth and laws that will "work" pragmatically, is taking over the world and washing over countries and cultures more powerfully than the ice floes of the long-sought polar sea.

But through it all, through all the decades of both the First and the Second Great Age of Discovery, there have been very special men—men like Robert Edwin Peary—who, deeply discontent with civilization, the walled city, the overorganization of life, have seen themselves as special mythical figures—Promethean men who would "light a fire on the moon," or else, like the cunning Odysseus, forever go afloating and aquesting on the terrifying wine-dark seas of space, time, and eternal questions, into the heart of darkness and the deep unknown that transcends even death itself.

ACKNOWLEDGMENTS

As my preface indicates, this book has had a long gestation period, going back, really, to my first works on exploration. It has also been enriched by an intensive study of American intellectual history over a long period of time when I was heavily engaged as Director of the American Studies Program at the University of Texas. My thoughts on the present book, however, crystallized at a meeting of the American Association for the Advancement of Science in Boston in the winter of 1975, when I delivered the lecture "Paradigm Lost" that became the germ of the book. Here, however, I wish to acknowledge the more immediate sources of support, collegial aid, and friendly comforts.

First of all I am indebted to the John Simon Guggenheim Memorial Foundation for a fellowship that helped me get started on the project. I also wish to thank Dr. Gardner Linzey and his staff at the Center for Advanced Study in the Behavioral Sciences, Palo Alto, California, for a year that allowed me to develop not only this but several other books and films. For me the Center experience was matchless. In connection with that experience, I also wish to thank the National Endowment for the Humanities for providing a supplementary grant that made the year possible.

457

And I should also like to acknowledge the help of the University of Texas Research Institute, which provided a matching grant on at least one occasion. The University Research Institute is especially important to active scholars because the University does not provide the sabbatical leave traditional in most leading universities.

The following institutions aided me in my research in various ways. I am indebted to the National Archives, particularly the Cartographic Records Group and the Still Pictures Group; Mr. William J. Heynen was especially helpful in the former instance. Likewise, Mr. William Stanley of the National Ocean and Atmospheric Survey supplied me with the first *Whistler's Mother*. Mr. Herman Viola and his co-worker, Carolyn Margolis, of the Smithsonian Museum of Anthropology, were extremely helpful, as were various other branches of the Smithsonian, such as the National Collection of American Art, where I must thank Mr. William Treuttner, the authority on George Catlin, and Nancy Anderson, who helped me through the Catlin Cartoon Collection, which she is currently cataloging. I would also like to thank the Cartographic Branch of the Library of Congress, especially John Wolter and Ralph Ehrenberg. Likewise, I am indebted to the U.S. Naval Historical Foundation and the Smithsonian Press for permission to reproduce paintings and drawings by Alfred T. Agate, the Wilkes Expedition artist, who deserves a book all to himself.

Other institutions which have come to my aid in allowing me the use of material or helped in my searches or those by my assistants are: the Beineke Library, Yale University; the Bancroft Library at the University of California, Berkeley; the Academy of Natural Sciences and the American Philosophical Society, both in Philadelphia; the Peabody Museum of Salem; the Kendall Whaling Museum, Sharon, Massachusetts; Mystic Seaport, Mystic, Connecticut; the British Museum; the National Maritime Museum; the British Library; the Royal Geographical Society; the Bernice P. Bishop Museum in Hawaii; and the Musée de l'Histoire Naturelle and the Bibliothèque Nationale in Paris.

The University of Texas itself is one of the world's great research centers. I have benefited from the use of the Harry H. Ransome Center, the University of Texas Geological Library, the Art Library, the Latin American Institute Library, the Barker Center for Research in Texas History, and, most of all, from the Perry Castañeda Library, where Ms. Jo Anne Hawkins, the Circulation Director, should be presented with a special award for her common sense in aiding scholars, particularly me.

Special thanks should be accorded to the Cartographic Laboratory, Geography Department, The University of Texas, and particularly to Dr. R. K. Holz and his assistant, Elaine Bargsley, for the endpaper maps.

A number of students, colleagues, and family members have also come to my aid. Sarah Shelby may be the best manuscript typist in the world. Mahala Waltser also struggled with my handwriting. Dr. Stephen Pyne, a former student of incredible accomplishments, spurred me on, while Dr. Nathan Reingold, former editor of the Joseph Henry Papers, gave me a critical reading of those chapters relating to Matthew Fontaine Maury, Alexander Dallas Bache, and Joseph Henry, a critical reading indeed for which I especially thank him. Dr. Stephen Spurr, the distinguished former president of the University of Texas, loaned me his father's unpublished autobiography and journals concerning his exploration of Alaska. Dr. Michele Aldrich of the American Association for the Advancement of Science provided her usual help, and sometimes her important critical insights. I also, almost accidentally, gained important insights from Dr. Stephen Jay Gould, and as this work related to a previous project, *Looking Far North, the Harriman Expedition to Alaska, 1899,* I benefited from the work of my co-author, Kay Sloan. My current research assistants, Lawrence Walker and Ann Graham, have provided crucial help, Ms. Graham in particular in matters relating to maps, where she is fast becoming an expert.

Bright and willing family members also helped in crucial instances. My daughter and son-in-law, Anne and Brooks Kelley, brought the computer to my aid in the commissioning of maps. My son, William N. Goetzmann, my co-author on another book soon to be released, researched the New England museums and libraries. And finally, my wife, who had been patient through my long struggle with this book, gave me that push at a critical time when, like Ishmael, it was "a damp, drizzly November in my soul." After such "encouragement," what gratitude is adequate?

Parts of this book in altered form have appeared in *American West Magazine, Exploring the American West* (a National Park Service Booklet, now out of print), Nathan Reingold, ed., *The Sciences in the American Context* (Smithsonian Institution Press), and in my lecture "The Ages of Discovery," delivered at the opening of "The Magnificent Voyagers" exhibition at the Smithsonian Museum of Natural History and Anthropology, November 1985.

BIBLIOGRAPHICAL NOTES

It should be clear from the large scope of this volume that it is not a monograph, nor has it been possible to extend the research into literally thousands of manuscript collections in literally hundreds of countries that survive from the past and bear on my subject. In certain areas where such research seemed necessary and not merely academically pretentious, I have reached down to the manuscript level, but in general my account is a historical landscape based on printed sources from the distant past and up-to-date authorities from the not-so-distant past. My principal aim has been to tell a remarkable story and reveal a remarkable phenomenon in the best way I could manage. I am aware that this is the first book on a large subject, and by no means, I hope, the last.

I have not included many of the more esoteric sources that I have consulted, nor have I made any special effort to distinguish between sources and authorities in this bibliographical essay. Instead, the bibliography is intended to indicate to the general reader, who may wish to pursue the subject further, the nature and kinds of materials that were particularly useful to me. In addition, I have called special attention to those authorities to whom I have been most indebted. Whenever it seemed feasible I have also referred to them in my narrative. Anyone wishing further information as to sources of particular quotations or information should feel free to write to me, care of the American Stud-

ies Program, 303 Garrison Hall, the University of Texas, Austin, TX
78712.

Chapter I.   THE COSMIC VOYAGERS

Some historians would date a Second Great Age of Discovery with the
exploration of the Pacific Basin and the circumnavigations of the eighteenth century. The chief proponents of this theory are J. C. Beaglehole, whose *The Exploration of the Pacific* is the comprehensive work
on the subject, and J. H. Parry in *Trade and Dominion*. Both are formidable authorities. Beaglehole's edition of *The Journals of Captain
James Cook* and his *The Life of Captain James Cook* are monumental
works of scholarship and the place where all students of Pacific history
must begin. Other helpful general works on the history of Pacific
Ocean exploration in the period are William Napier, John Gilbert, and
Julian Holland, *Pacific Voyages*; Roselene Dousset and Etienne Taillemite, *The Great Book of the Pacific*; and Jacques Brosse, *Great Voyages of Discovery: Circumnavigators and Scientists, 1764–1843*.

The point of the present work, however, is to indicate that something more than just the exploration of the Pacific Basin was involved
in the Second Great Age of Discovery. Consequently I have included
some explorers of the continental landmasses in this first chapter, as
well as astronomical explorers who took the whole globe for their province. In this respect four modern works were particularly important to
me: Victor W. Von Hagan's account of La Condamine in *South
America Called Them*; Edward J. Goodman, *The Explorers of South
America*; Douglas Botting, *Humboldt and the Cosmos*; and Harry
Woolf, *The Transits of Venus*.

These and other sources and authorities upon which I have relied
are listed below:

Auger, Helen. *Passage to Glory: John Ledyard's America*. Garden
City, N. Y.: Doubleday, 1946.

Banks, Joseph. *The Endeavor Journal of Joseph Banks*. Edited by J. C.
Beaglehole, 2nd ed. 2 vols. Sydney: Trustees of the Public Library of
New South Wales in association with Angus Robertson, 1962.

Beaglehole, J. C. *The Exploration of the Pacific*. 3rd ed. Stanford,
Calif.: Stanford Univ. Press, 1966.

————. *The Life of Captain James Cook*. London: Hakluyt Society, 1974.

Bedini, Silvio A. *Thinkers and Tinkers: Early American Men of Science*. New York: Charles Scribner's Sons, 1975.

Botting, Douglas. *Humboldt and the Cosmos*. New York: Harper & Row, 1973.

Bougainville, Louis Antoine de. *A Voyage Round the World*. Translated by J. R. Forster. London: Printed for J. Norse, 1772.

Brosse, Jacques. *Great Voyages of Discovery: Circumnavigators and Scientists, 1764-1843*. Preface by Fernand Braudel. Translated by Stanley Hochman. N. Y., Oxford: Facts on File Publications, 1983.

Bruhns, Karl. *Life of Alexander von Humboldt*. Translated by June and Caroline Larsell. London: Longmans, Green, 1873.

Byron, John. *Byron's Journal of His Circumnavigation, 1764-1766*. Edited by Robert E. Gallagher. Cambridge: Hakluyt Society, 1964.

Cobbe, Hugh. *Cook's Voyages and Peoples of the Pacific*. London: British Museum Publications, 1974.

Cook, James. *The Journals of Captain James Cook*. Edited by J. C. Beaglehole. 3 vols. Cambridge: Hakluyt Society, 1955-67.

Crone, G. R., and Skelton, R. A. "English Collections of Voyages and Travels, 1625-1846." In *Richard Hakluyt and His Successors*. London: Hakluyt Society, 1946.

Dampier, William. *Dampier's Voyages*. Edited by John Masefield. New York: E. P. Dutton, 1906.

————. *A Voyage to New Holland, etc. in the Year 1699 . . .* London: Printed for James Knapton at the Crown in St. Paul's Church-Yard, 1703.

Dousset, Roselene, and Taillemite, Etienne. *The Great Book of the Pacific*. Translated by Andrew Mouravieff-Apostal and Edita Lausanne. Secaucus, N. J.: Chartwell Books, 1979.

Forster, Johann Reinhold. *The "Resolution" Journal of Johann Reinhold Forster, 1772-1775*. Edited by Michael G. Hoare. 4 vols. London: Hakluyt Society, 1982.

Gilbert, William Napier John, and Holland, Julian. *Pacific Voyages*. Garden City, N. Y.: Doubleday, 1971.

Goodman, Edward J. *The Explorers of South America.* New York: Macmillan, 1972.

Hindle, Brooke. *David Rittenhouse.* Princeton, N. J.: Princeton Univ. Press, 1964.

Humboldt, Alexander von. *Aspects of Nature.* Translated by Mrs. Sabine. Philadelphia: Lea & Blanchard, 1849.

———. *Cosmos: A Sketch of a Physical Description of the Universe.* Translated by E. C. Otte. 5 vols. and Atlas. London: H. G. Bohn, 1848–58.

———. *Personal Narrative of Travels to the Equinoctial Regions of the New Continent.* 7 vols. London: Longman, Hurst, Rees, Orme, and Brown, 1814–24.

———. *Political Essay on the Kingdom of New Spain.* 2 vols. London: Longman, Hurst, Rees, Orme, and Brown, et al., 1811.

———. *Researches Concerning the Institutions and Monuments of the Ancient Inhabitants of America.* 2 vols. London: Longman, Hurst, Rees, Orme, Brown, Murray and Colburn, 1814.

———. *Vues des Cordillères, et Monuments des Peuples indigènes de l'Amérique.* 2 folio vols. Paris: F. Schoell, 1810.

Kellner, Charlotte. *Alexander von Humboldt.* London: Oxford Univ. Press, 1963.

La Condamine, Charles-Marie de. *A Succinct Abridgement of a Voyage Made Within the Inland Parts of South America.* London: E. Withers, 1747.

Parkinson, Sydney. *A Journal of a Voyage to the South Seas, in His Majesty's Ship, the Endeavour.* Edited by Stansfield Parkinson. London: Printed for S. Parkinson, 1773.

Parry, J. H. *Trade and Dominion.* London: Weidenfeld & Nicolson, 1971.

Rickman, John. *Journal of Captain Cook's Last Voyage to the Pacific Ocean.* New York: Da Capo Press, 1967.

Robertson, George. *The Discovery of Tahiti: A Journal of the Second Voyage of H.M.S. Dolphin . . . Written by Her Master George Robertson.* Edited by Hugh Carrington. London: Hakluyt Society, 1948.

Roggeveen, Jacob. *The Journal of Jacob Roggeveen.* Edited and translated by Andrew Sharp. Oxford: Clarendon Press, 1970.

Surville, Jean de, and Labe, Guillaume. *The Expedition of the St. Jean-Baptiste to the Pacific, 1769–1770, from the Journals of Jean de Surville and Guillaume Labe.* Edited and translated by John Dunmore. London: Hakluyt Society, 1981.

Taylor, E. G. R. *The Haven-Finding Art: A History of Navigation from Odysseus to Captain Cook.* New York: Abelard-Schuman, 1957.

Terra, Helmut de. *Humboldt.* New York: Alfred A. Knopf, 1955.

Thiery, Maurice. *Bougainville, Soldier and Sailor.* London: Grayson, 1932.

Ulloa, Antonio de, and Santarcilia, Jorge Juan y. *A Voyage to South-America.* 2 vols. London: Printed for J. Stockdale, 1806.

Chapter II. THE NORTH AMERICAN ADVENTURES
Chapter III. A CONTINENTAL CONSCIOUSNESS

There is a veritable torrent of published material concerning the early exploration of the North American continent. A number of general works have proved particularly useful to me. These include Justin Winsor, *Narrative and Critical History of America;* Bernard DeVoto, *The Course of Empire;* W. P. Cumming, S. E. Hillier, D. B. Quinn, and G. Williams, *The Exploration of North America, 1630–1776;* Warren Cook, *Flood Tide of Empire;* John Bartlett Brebner, *The Explorers of North America;* and Hugh Honour, *The New Golden Land: European Images of America from the Discoveries to the Present Time.*

Especially useful for tracking the confusing debate over the nature and merits of the New World are Antonello Gerbi's exhaustive *The Dispute of the New World: The History of a Polemic, 1750–1900;* Henry Steele Commager's stimulating *The Empire of Reason: How Europe Imagined and America Realized the Enlightenment;* and Howard Mumford Jones's *O Strange New World: American Culture: The Formative Years.*

Three important reprint series, from which individual volumes will be listed below, are Reuben Gold Thwaites, ed., *Early Western Travels, 1748–1846,* 32 vols. (Cleveland: Arthur H. Clark, 1904–1907); Reuben Gold Thwaites, ed., *The Jesuit Relations and Allied Documents: Travels and Exploration of the Jesuit Missionaries in New*

France, 1610–1791, 73 vols. (Cleveland: Burrows Bros., 1896–1901); and *The March of America Facsimile Series*, 101 vols. (Ann Arbor: University Microfilms, 1966).

The individual works mentioned above and others that I found useful are listed below.

Adair, James. *James Adair, The History of the American Indians*. Edited by Robert Berkhofer. London: 1775. Reprint. New York and London: Johnson Reprint Co., 1968.

Allen, John Logan. *Passage Through the Garden: Lewis and Clark and the American Northwest*. Urbana, Ill.: Univ. of Illinois Press, 1975.

Allen, Paul, and Biddle, Nicholas, eds. *Expedition of Lewis and Clark*. (Orig. title: *History of the Expedition Under the Command of Captains Lewis and Clark to the Sources of the Missouri, Thence Across the Rocky Mountains and Down the River Columbia to the Pacific Ocean. Performed During the Years 1804–5–6. By Order of the Government of the United States.*) Reprint of 1814 ed. *March of America Facsimile Series*, No. 56. Ann Arbor, Mich.: University Microfilms, 1966.

Alvord, Clarence W., and Bidgood, Lee. *The First Explorations of the Trans-Allegheny Region by the Virginians, 1650–1674*. Cleveland: Arthur H. Clark, 1912.

Alvord, Clarence W., and Carter, Clarence, eds. *The Critical Period, 1763–1765. British Series*, Vol. I. *Collection of the Illinois State Historical Library*, Vol. X. 1915.

———. *The New Regime, 1765–1767. British Series*, Vol. II. *Collection of the Illinois State Historical Library*, Vol. XI. 1916.

Bailey, Kenneth P. *Christopher Gist, Colonial Frontiersman, Explorer, and Indian Agent*. Hamden, Conn.: Archon, 1976.

———. *The Ohio Company of Virginia and the Westward Movement, 1748–1792*. Glendale, Calif.: Arthur H. Clark, 1939. (Includes explorations of Christopher Gist.)

Bartram, John. *An Account of East-Florida with a Journal Kept by John Bartram of Philadelphia, Botanist to His Majesty for The Floridas upon a Journey from St. Augustine up the River St. Johns*. London: W. Nicoll, at No. 51, St. Paul's Church Yard, and G. Woodfall, Charing Cross, 1766.

————. *Observations on the Inhabitants, Climate, Soil, Rivers, Productions, Animals, and Other Matters Worthy of Notice, Made by Mr. John Bartram in His Travels from Pensilvania to Onondago, Oswego and the Lake Ontario in Canada. To Which Is Annex'd, a Curious Account of the Cataracts at Niagara by Mr. Peter Kalm a Swedish Gentleman Who Travelled There.* London: J. Whirton & B. White, 1751. Reprint. *March of America Facsimile Series*, No. 41. Ann Arbor, Mich.: University Microfilms, 1966.

Bartram, William. *William Bartram, Botanical and Zoological Drawings, 1756–1788.* Edited by Joseph Ewan. Philadelphia: American Philosophical Society, 1968.

————. *Travels Through North and South Carolina, Georgia, East and West Florida.* Edited by Francis Harper. New Haven: Yale Univ. Press, 1958.

Batts, Thomas, and Fallam, Robert. "A Journal from Virginia, 1671." See Alvord and Bidgood, 1912, 183–95.

Beaglehole, J. C. *The Life of Captain James Cook.* London: A. and C. Black, 1974.

Berkeley, Edmund, and Berkeley, Dorothy S. *John Clayton, Pioneer of American Botany.* Chapel Hill: Univ. of North Carolina Press, 1963.

————. *Dr. John Mitchell: The Man Who Made the Map of North America.* Chapel Hill: Univ. of North Carolina Press, 1974.

Berry, Robert Elton. *Yankee Stargazer: The Life of Nathaniel Bowditch.* New York and London: Whittlesey House, McGraw-Hill, 1941.

Birkbeck, Morris. *Notes on a Journey in America, from the Coast of Virginia to the Territory of Illinois.* Reprint of 1818 ed. *March of America Facsimile Series*, No. 62. Ann Arbor, Mich.: University Microfilms, 1966.

Boorstin, Daniel J. *The Lost World of Thomas Jefferson.* Boston: Beacon Press, 1948.

Bowditch, Nathaniel. *Early American-Philippine Trade: The Journal of Nathaniel Bowditch in Manila 1796.* New Haven: Yale Univ. Press, Southeast Asia Studies, 1962.

Bradford, William. *Journall of the English Plantation at Plimoth. March of America Facsimile Series*, No. 21. Ann Arbor, Mich.: University Microfilms, 1966.

Brebner, John Bartlett. *The Explorers of North America*. Reprint. Garden City, N. Y.: Doubleday, 1955.

Buttrick, Tilly, Jr. *Voyages, Travels and Discoveries*. Boston, 1831.

Byrd, William. *William Byrd's Histories of the Dividing Line Betwixt Virginia and North Carolina*. Edited by William K. Boyd. Reprint. New York: Dover, 1967.

Cabeza de Vaca, Alvar Núñez. *Relation of Núñez Cabeza de Vaca*. Translated by Buckingham Smith. Reprint of 1542 ed. *March of America Facsimile Series*, No. 9. Ann Arbor, Mich.: University Microfilms, 1966.

Champlain, Samuel de. *Les Voyages du Sieur de Champlain*. Reprint of 1613 ed. *March of America Facsimile Series*, No. 20. Ann Arbor, Mich.: University Microfilms, 1966.

————. *Works*. Edited by H. B. Biggar. Toronto: Champlain Society, 1922–26. Reprint. Toronto: University of Toronto Press, 1971.

Collections of the Illinois State Historical Library. Vol. I. Springfield, Ill.: *Illinois Historical Collections*, 1903. (Contains accounts of Marquette, La Salle, Hennepin, and de Tonti, pp. 8-164.)

Collinson, Peter. *Brothers of the Spade: Correspondence of Peter Collinson of London, and of John Curtis of Williamsburg, Virginia*. Barre, Mass.: Barre Gazette, 1957.

Collot, Victor. *A Journey in North America* ... 3 vols. and Atlas. Paris: Arthur Bertrand, 1826.

Commager, Henry Steele. *The Empire of Reason: How Europe Imagined and America Realized the Enlightenment*. Garden City, N. Y.: Doubleday, 1977.

Cook, James. *The Journals of Captain James Cook on His Voyages of Discovery: The Voyage of the Resolution and Discovery 1776–1780*. Edited by J. C. Beaglehole. Vol. 3. Cambridge: Hakluyt Society, 1967.

Cook, Warren. *Flood Tide of Empire*. New Haven and London: Yale Univ. Press, 1973.

Cose, William. *Russian Discoveries Between Asia and America*. *March of America Facsimile Series*, No. 40. Ann Arbor, Mich.: University Microfilms, 1966.

Crane, Verner W. *The Southern Frontier, 1760–1782*. Ann Arbor: Univ. of Michigan Press, 1956.

Crèvecoeur, Michel-Guillaume St. Jean de. *Journey into Northern Pennsylvania and the State of New York.* Paris, 1801. Reprint. Ann Arbor: Univ. of Michigan Press, 1964.

―――. *Crèvecoeur's Eighteenth Century Travels—Pennsylvania and New York.* Lexington: Univ. of Kentucky Press, 1961.

―――. *Sketches of Eighteenth Century America: More "Letters by St. John de Crèvecoeur from an American Farmer."* Edited by Henri Bourdin, Ralph Gabriel, and Stanley T. Williams. New Haven: Yale Press, 1925.

Croghan, George. *George Croghan's Journal of His Trip to Detroit in 1767.* Edited by Howard W. Peckham. Ann Arbor: Univ. of Michigan Press, 1939.

―――. "Journals of Conrad Weiser (1748), George Croghan (1750-1765), Christian Frederick Post (1758) and Thomas Morris (1764)." In R. G. Thwaites, ed., *Early Western Travels*, Vol I. Cleveland: Arthur H. Clark, 1904.

Cuming, Fortescue. *Sketches of a Tour to the Western Country, Through the States of Ohio and Kentucky; a Voyage down the Ohio and Mississippi Rivers, and a Trip through the Mississippi Territory and Part of West Florida. Commenced at Philadelphia in the Winter of 1807, and Concluded in 1809.* Pittsburgh, 1810. Reprinted in R. G. Thwaites, ed., *Early Western Travels*, Vol. IV. Cleveland: Arthur H. Clark, 1904.

Cumming, W. P.; Hillier, S. E.; Quinn, D. B.; and Williams, G. *The Exploration of North America, 1630-1776.* New York: G. P. Putnam's Sons, 1974.

Custis, John, and Freeman, Thomas. *Jefferson and Southwestern Expansion: The Freeman and Custis Accounts of the Red River Expedition of 1806.* Edited by Dan L. Flores. Norman: Univ. of Oklahoma Press, 1984.

Cutting, Rose Marie. *John and William Bartram, William Byrd II and St. John de Crèvecoeur: A Reference Guide.* Boston: G. K. Hall, 1976.

Dana, Richard Henry. *Two Years Before the Mast.* New York: Harper's, 1840.

Darlington, William. *Memorials of John Bartram and Humphrey*

Marshall with Notices of Their Botanical Contemporaries. Edited by William Darlington. Philadelphia: Lindsay and Blakeston, 1849.

David, Richard Beale. *Intellectual Life in the Colonial South 1585–1767.* 3 vols. Knoxville: Univ. of Tennessee Press, 1978.

DeVoto, Bernard. *The Course of Empire.* Boston: Houghton, Mifflin, 1952.

Earnest, Ernest. *John and William Bartram, Botanists and Explorers.* Philadelphia: Univ. of Pennsylvania Press, 1940.

Evans, Estwick. *Estwick Evans, A Pedestrious Tour of Four Thousand Miles, Through the Western States and Territories during the Winter and Spring of 1818* . . . In R. G. Thwaites, *Early Western Travels,* Vol. VIII. Cleveland: Arthur H. Clark, 1904.

Fallows, Arthur. *Journal.* Reprint from *American Anthropologist* IX (1907). *March of America Facsimile Series,* No. 33. Ann Arbor, Mich.: University Microfilms, 1966.

Filson, John. *Kentucky and the Adventures of Col. Daniel Boone.* Facsimile reprint with Filson's First Map of 1784. Introduction by Willard Rouse Jillson. Louisville: John P. Morton, 1934.

———. *The Discovery, Settlement and Present State of Kentucke.* Wilmington, Del.: Printed by J. Adams, 1784.

———. *The Discovery, Settlement and Present State of Kentucke.* *March of America Facsimile Series,* No. 50. Ann Arbor, Mich.: University Microfilms, 1966.

Fite, Emerson D., and Freeman, Archibald, comps. and eds. *A Book of Old Maps Delineating American History from the Earliest Days down to the Close of the Revolutionary War.* Cambridge, Mass.: Harvard Univ. Press, 1976.

Gass, Patrick. *Journal of the Voyages and Travels of a Corps of Discovery Under the Command of Capt. Lewis and Capt. Clarke of the Army of the United States . . . During the Years 1804, 1805, and 1806* . . . 3rd ed. Philadelphia: Matthew Carey, 1811.

Gerbi, Antonello. *The Dispute of the New World: The History of a Polemic, 1750–1900.* Rev. and enlarged ed. Translated by Jeremy Moyle. Pittsburgh: Univ. of Pittsburgh Press, 1955.

Goetzmann, William H. " 'Savage Enough to Prefer the Woods'; The Cosmopolite and the West." In Lally Weymouth, ed., *Thomas Jeffer-*

son, The Man, His World, His Influence. New York, G. P. Putnam's Sons, 1973.

Gipson, Lawrence Henry. *Lewis Evans.* Philadelphia: Historical Society of Pennsylvania, 1939.

Gist, Christopher. *Christopher Gist's Journals.* Edited by William M. Darlington. Pittsburgh, 1893.

Golder, F. A. *Russian Exploration in the Pacific, 1641–1850.* Cleveland: Arthur H. Clark, 1914.

Grausteen, Jeanette E. *Thomas Nuttall, Naturalist: Explorations in America 1808–1841.* Cambridge, Mass.: Harvard Univ. Press, 1967.

Hariot, Thomas. *Thomas Hariot's Virginia.* Edited by Theodore De Bry. (Orig. title: *Briefe & True Report of the New Found Land of Virginia.*) *March of America Facsimile Series,* No. 15. Ann Arbor, Mich.: University Microfilms, 1966.

Harrison, Fairfax. "The Virginians on the Ohio and the Mississippi in 1742." *Virginia Magazine of History and Biography,* XXX (1922), 203–22.

———. "Western Explorations in Virginia Between Lederer and Spotswood." *Virginia Magazine of History and Biography,* XXX (1922), 323–40.

Hassrick, Peter, and Trenton, Patricia. *The Rocky Mountains: A Vision for Artists in the Nineteenth Century.* Norman: Univ. of Oklahoma Press, 1983.

Hearne, Samuel. *A Journey from Prince of Wales's Fort in Hudson's Bay to the Northern Ocean . . .* London: A. Strahan & T. Cadell, 1795.

Heckewelder, Rev. John. *History, Manners, and Customs of the Indian Nations Who Once Inhabited Pennsylvania and the Neighboring States, New and Revised Edition with an Introduction and Notes by the Rev. William C. Reichel. Pennsylvania Historical Society Memoirs.* Vol. 12 (1891). Philadelphia: Historical Society of Pennsylvania, 1891.

———. *Thirty Thousand Miles with John Heckewelder.* Edited by Paul W. Wallace. Pittsburgh: Univ. of Pittsburgh Press, 1958.

Herbst, Josephine. *New Green World.* New York: Hastings House, 1954. (On John Bartram.)

Hennepin, Louis. *A Description of Louisiana* (1683). Translated by John Gilmary Shear. *March of America Facsimile Series,* No. 30. Ann Arbor, Mich.: University Microfilms, 1966.

————. "Account of the Discovery of the River Mississippi and the Adjacent Country by the Lakes"; "Account of La Salle's Undertaking to Discover the River Mississippi by Way of the Gulph of Mexico." Reprinted in *American Antiquarian Society Transactions and Collections*, Worcester, Mass., 1820, pp. 61–104.

————. *A New Discovery of a Vast Country in America*. London: Printed for M. Bentley, J. Tonson, H. Bonwick, T. Goodwin, and S. Manship, 1698.

Henry, Alexander. *Travels and Adventures in Canada and the Indian Territories Between the Years 1760 and 1776*. Edited by James Bain. New York: I. Riley, 1809. Reprint. Toronto: G. N. Morang, 1901.

Herbst, Josephine. *New Green World*. New York: Hastings House, 1954. (On John Bartram.)

Holloway, Mark. *Heavens on Earth: Utopian Communities in America, 1680–1880*. London: Turnstile Press, 1951.

Honour, Hugh. *The New Golden Land: European Images of America from the Discoveries to the Present Time*. New York: Pantheon, 1975.

Howard, Robert West. *The Downseekers*. New York and London: Harcourt Brace Jovanovich, 1975.

Hutchins, Thomas. *A Topographical Description of Virginia, Pennsylvania, Maryland, and North Carolina*. London: Printed for the author and sold by J. Almon, 1778.

Ingram, David. *Relation of David Ingram*. From Richard Hakluyt, *The Principall Navigations, Voyages & Discoveries of the English Nation*. Reprint of 1589 ed. *March of America Facsimile Series*, No. 14. Ann Arbor, Mich.: University Microfilms, 1966.

James, Edwin. *Account of an Expedition from Pittsburgh to the Rocky Mountains, Performed in the Years 1819 and '20, Under the Command of Major Stephen H. Long . . .* 2 vols. and Atlas. Philadelphia: H. C. Carey and I. Lea, Chestnut Street, 1823. (The geological appendix, usually neglected by historians because omitted from the Thwaites reprint, is particularly interesting.)

Johnson, Adrian. *America Explored: A Cartographical History of the Exploration of North America*. New York: Viking/Studio Books, 1974.

Jones, Howard Mumford. *O Strange New World: American Culture— The Formative Years*. New York: Viking/Compass, 1967.

Joutel, Henri. *Last Voyage Performed by de la Sale.* Reprint of 1714 ed. *March of America Facsimile Series,* No. 31. Ann Arbor, Mich.: University Microfilms, 1966.

Karamanski, Theodore J. *Fur Trade and Exploration: Opening the Far Northwest, 1821–1852.* Norman: University of Oklahoma Press, 1983.

Kastner, Joseph. *A Species of Eternity.* New York: Alfred A. Knopf, 1977.

Kellogg, Louise P., ed. *Early Narratives of the Northwest, 1634–1699.* New York: Charles Scribner's Sons, 1917.

Lahontan, Louis d'Arce de. *New Voyages to North-America.* London: Printed for H. Bonwicke, T. Goodwin, M. Wotton, B. Tooke, and S. Manship, 1703.

Lawson, John. *A New Voyage to Carolina.* Edited by Hugh Lefler. Chapel Hill: University of North Carolina Press, 1967.

Leach, Douglas E. *The Northern Colonial Frontier, 1607–1763.* New York: Holt, Rinehart & Winston, 1966.

Lederer, John. *Discoveries of John Lederer, in Three Small Marches from Virginia to the West of Carolina.* Reprint of 1672 ed. *March of America Facsimile Series,* No. 25. Ann Arbor, Mich.: University Microfilms, 1966.

Lewis, Meriwether, and Clark, William. *Atlas of the Lewis and Clark Expedition.* Edited by Gary Moulton. Lincoln and London: Univ. of Nebraska Press, 1983.

———. *The Journals of Lewis and Clark.* Edited and abridged by Bernard DeVoto. Boston: Houghton Mifflin, 1953.

———. *The Letters of the Lewis and Clark Expedition.* Edited by Donald Jackson. Urbana: Univ. of Illinois Press, 1962.

Loomis, Noel M., and Nasatir, Abraham P. *Pedro Vial and the Roads to Santa Fe.* Norman: Univ. of Oklahoma Press, 1967.

Mackenzie, Alexander. *Voyages from Montreal on the River St. Lawrence, Through the Continent of North America to the Frozen and Pacific Oceans: In the Years 1789 and 1793 . . .* London: T. Cadell Jun. and W. Davies Strand, 1801.

McDermott, John D. *The French in the Mississippi Valley.* Urbana: Univ. of Illinois Press, 1965.

Marquette, Jacques. *Voyages. March of America Facsimile Series*, No. 28. Ann Arbor, Mich.: University Microfilms, 1966.

Masterton, James R., and Brower, Helen. *Bering's Successors, 1745-1780: Contributions of Peter Simon Pallas to the History of Russian Exploration Toward Alaska.* Seattle: Univ. of Washington Press, 1948.

Michaux, André. "Journal of Travels into Kentucky; July 15, 1793-April 11, 1796; François André Michaux, Travels to the West of the Allegheny Mountains in the States of Ohio, Kentucky, and Tennessee, and Back to Charleston by the Upper Carolinas . . . Undertaken in the Year 1802." In R. G. Thwaites, *Early Western Travels*, Vol. III. Cleveland: Arthur H. Clark, 1904.

Mitchell, Julia Post. *St Jean de Crèvecoeur*. New York: Columbia University Press, 1916.

Morris, Thomas. "Journals of Conrad Weiser (1748), George Croghan (1750-1765), Christian Frederick Post (1758) and Thomas Morris (1764)." In R. G. Thwaites, *Early Western Travels*, Vol. I. Cleveland: Arthur H. Clark, 1904.

Nasatir, A. P., ed. *Before Lewis and Clark: Documents Illustrating the History of Missouri, 1785-1805.* 2 vols. St. Louis: St. Louis Historical Documents Foundation, 1952.

Nichols, Roger L., and Halley, Patrick L. *Stephen Long and American Frontier Exploration.* Newark, Del.: Univ. of Delaware Press, 1980.

Nute, Grace Lee. *Caesars of the Wilderness.* New York: D. Appleton-Century, 1943.

Parkman, Francis. *La Salle and the Discovery of the Great West.* 12th ed. Boston: Little, Brown, 1880.

Pike, Zebulon M. *Account of Expeditions to the Sources of the Mississippi.* Reprint of 1810 ed. *March of America Facsimile Series*, No. 57. Ann Arbor, Mich.: University Microfilms, 1966.

Poesch, Jessie. "Titian Ramsey Peale, 1799-1885, and His Journals of the Wilkes Expedition." *Memoirs of the American Philosophical Society.* Vol. 52. Philadelphia: American Philosophical Society, 1961.

Post, Christian Frederick. "Journals of Conrad Weiser (1748), George Croghan (1750-1765), Christian Frederick Post (1758) and Thomas Morris (1764)." In R. G. Thwaites, *Early Western Travels*. Vol. I. Cleveland: Arthur H. Clark, 1904.

Pownall, Thomas. *A Topographical Description of the United States of America. Being a Revised and Enlarged Edition of a Topographical Description of Such Parts of North America as Are Contained in the Map of the Middle British Colonies.* Edited by Louis Mulkearn. Pittsburgh: Univ. of Pittsburgh Press, 1949.

Pratz, Le Page du. *The History of Louisiana* . . . 2 vols. London: T. Becket and P. A. DeHonst, 1763.

Purchas, Samuel. *Henry Hudson's Voyages* from *Purchas His Pilgrimes,* Pt. 3. Reprint of 1625 ed. *March of America Facsimile Series,* No. 19. Ann Arbor, Mich.: University Microfilms, 1966.

Richardson, Edgar P., Hindle, Brooke, and Miller, Lillian B. *Charles Willson Peale and His World.* New York: Harry N. Abrams, 1982.

Rogers, Robert. *Journals of Major Robert Rogers.* Edited and with an introduction by Howard W. Peckham. Reprint from orig. ed. of 1765. New York: Corinth Books, 1961.

Salley, Alexander S., ed. *Narratives of Early Carolina, 1650–1708.* New York: Charles Scribner's Sons, 1911.

Saumerez, Philip. *Log of the Centurion, Based on the Original Papers of Captain Philip Saumerez on Board H.M.S. Centurion, Lord Anson's Flagship During His Circumnavigation 1740–44.* Edited by Leo Heaps. New York: Macmillan, 1973.

Schwartz, Seymour, and Ehrenberg, Ralph E. *The Mapping of America.* New York: Harry N. Abrams, 1980.

Schoolcraft, Henry R. *Travels Through the Northwestern Regions of the United States.* Reprint of 1821 ed. *March of America Facsimile Series,* No. 66. Ann Arbor, Mich.: University Microfilms, 1966.

Severin, Timothy. *Explorers of the Mississippi.* New York: Alfred A. Knopf, 1967.

Smith, John. *Generall Historie of Virginia, New England, & the Summer Isles.* Reprint of 1624 ed. *March of America Facsimile Series,* No. 18. Ann Arbor, Mich.; University Microfilms, 1966.

Smith, William. *Historical Account of the Expedition Against the Ohio Indians.* Reprint of 1765 ed. *March of America Facsimile Series,* No. 45. Ann Arbor, Mich.: University Microfilms, 1966.

Stafford, Barbara Maria. *Voyage into Substance, Art, Science, Nature, and the Illustrated Travel Account, 1760–1840.* Cambridge, Mass., and London: M.I.T. Press, 1984.

Stearns, Raymond P. *Science in the British Colonies of America.* Urbana: Univ. of Illinois Press, 1970.

Stork, William. *An Account of East-Florida, with a Journal Kept by John Bartram of Philadelphia* ... London: Sold by W. Nicoll and G. Woodfall, 1766.

Susquehanna Company, The. *The Susquehannah Company Papers, Vol. I, 1750-1755.* Edited by Julian P. Boyd. Published for Wyoming Historical and Geological Society, Wilkes-Barre, Pa. Ithaca, N.Y.: Cornell Univ. Press, 1930.

Vancouver, George. *The Voyage of George Vancouver, 1791-1795.* Edited by W. Kaye Lamb. 4 vols. London: Hakluyt Society, 1984.

Verendrye, Pierre Gauthier de Varennes de la. *Journals and Letters of Pierre Gauthier de Varennes de la Verendrye and His Sons* ... Edited by Lawrence J. Burpee. Vol. 16. Toronto: Champlain Society, 1927. Vol. 16.

Volwiler, Albert T. *George Croghan and the Westward Movement, 1741-1782.* Cleveland: Arthur H. Clark, 1926.

Wainwright, Nicholas B. *George Croghan, Wilderness Diplomat.* Chapel Hill: Univ. of North Carolina Press, 1959.

Wallace, Paul A. *Conrad Weiser, 1696-1760, Friend of Colonist and Mohawk.* Philadelphia: Univ. of Pennsylvania Press, 1945.

Weiser, Conrad. "Journals of Conrad Weiser (1748), George Croghan (1750-1765), Christian Frederick Post (1758) and Thomas Morris (1764)." In R. G. Thwaites, *Early Western Travels.* Vol. I. Cleveland: Arthur H. Clark, 1904.

Wheat, Carl I. *Mapping the American West, 1540-1857: A Preliminary Study.* Worcester, Mass.: American Antiquarian Society, *Proceedings,* April 1954.

———. *Mapping the Transmississippi West.* 6 vols. San Francisco: Institute of Historical Cartography, 1960.

Williams, Samuel C. *Dawn of Tennessee Valley and Tennessee History.* Johnson City, Tenn.: Watauga Press, 1937.

Winsor, Justin. *The Mississippi Basin: The Struggle in America Between England and France, 1697-1763.* Boston: Houghton Mifflin, 1898.

———. *Narrative and Critical History of America.* 8 vols. Boston and New York: Houghton, Mifflin, 1889.

————. *The Westward Movement: The Colonies and the Republic West of the Alleghenies 1763–1798*. Boston: Houghton Mifflin, 1899.

Wood, Richard G. *Stephen Harriman Long, 1784–1864*. Glendale, Calif.: Arthur H. Clark, 1966.

Chapter IV. THE FUR TRADER AS EXPLORER

This chapter is largely based on my previous works on western exploration, particularly *Exploration and Empire: The Explorer and the Scientist in the Winning of the American West*. The original sources and historical authorities upon which the book was based can be found in the more than 2,500 footnotes that support it, as well as in the note on the sources at the end of the book. It should be noted, too, that much of the material in this chapter and in Chapter V represents a rewritten digest of my larger work, which in an earlier and considerably altered version was published by the National Park Service under the title *Exploring the American West, 1803–1879*. This material is reprinted here in altered form with permission of the National Park Service.

Because so much of this and the next chapter has been based on my previous works, which are fully—indeed exhaustively—documented, I have included with them in the list below merely works published subsequently upon which I have drawn for this book. The most important new addition to scholarship in this field is the bibliography by Robert E. Becker, ed., Henry R. Wagner, and Charles L. Camp, *The Plains and the Rockies: A Critical Bibliography of Exploration, Adventure and Travel in the American West, 1800–1865*.

Becker, Robert E., ed., Wagner, Henry R., and Camp, Charles L. *The Plains and the Rockies: A Critical Bibliography of Exploration, Adventure and Travel in the American West, 1800–1865*. 4th ed., rev. and enlarged. San Francisco: John Howell Books, 1982.

Berry, Don. *A Majority of Scoundrels: An Informal History of the Rocky Mountain Fur Company*. New York: Harper and Brothers, 1961.

Cline, Gloria G. *Peter Skene Ogden*. Norman: University of Oklahoma Press, 1974.

Clokey, Richard M. *William H. Ashley: Enterprise and Politics in the Trans-Mississippi West.* Norman: Univ. of Oklahoma Press, 1980.

Conner, Daniel Ellis. *Joseph Reddeford Walker and the Arizona Adventure.* Edited by Donald J. Berthrong and Odessa Davenport. Norman: Univ. of Oklahoma Press, 1956.

Gilbert, Bil. *The Trailblazers.* New York: Time-Life Books, 1973.

———. *Westering Man: The Life of Joseph Walker.* New York: Atheneum, 1983.

Goetzmann, William H. *Exploration and Empire: The Explorer and the Scientist in the Winning of the American West.* New York: Alfred A. Knopf, 1966.

———. *Exploring the American West, 1803–1879.* Washington: Division of Publications, National Park Service, U.S. Department of the Interior, 1982.

Savage, Henry, Jr. *Discovering America, 1700–1875.* New York: Harper and Bros., 1979.

Smith, Jedediah S. *The Southwest Expedition of Jedediah S. Smith: His Personal Account of the Journey to California, 1826–1827.* Edited by George R. Brooks. Glendale, Calif.: Arthur H. Clark, 1977.

Weber, David. Introduction to David Coyner, *The Lost Trappers.* Albuquerque: University of New Mexico Press, 1970.

———. *The Taos Trappers.* Norman: Univ. of Oklahoma Press, 1968.

Wisehart, David. *The Fur Trade of the American West, 1807–1840.* Lincoln: Univ. of Nebraska Press, 1979.

Chapter V. HUMBOLDT'S CHILDREN

As explained in the source note to Chapter IV, this chapter is largely based on my previous works on western exploration, particularly *Exploration and Empire: The Explorer and the Scientist in the Winning of the American West* and a digested version of the story of western exploration published by the National Park Service and entitled *Exploring the American West, 1803–1879.* This material is reprinted in this chapter in altered form with permission of the National Park Service.

The following list includes works by others that have been published subsequent to my earlier work and also some older works that I have drawn upon here for new material. This is particularly the case with regard to works on artists of the American West—they were very definitely explorers who helped to define the Second Great Age of Discovery.

Aldrich, Michele A. L. "New York Natural History Survey, 1836–1845." Ph.D. dissertation, Univ. of Texas, Department of History, 1974.

Ballinger, James K. *Beyond the Endless River: Western American Drawings and Watercolors of the Nineteenth Century.* Phoenix: Phoenix Art Museum, 1979.

Barba, Preston. "Balduin Möllhausen, the German Cooper." *Americana-Germanica Monograph Series*, No. 17. Philadelphia: Univ. of Pennsylvania, 1914.

Beltrami, Giacomo Constantine. *A Pilgrimage in Europe and America, Leading to the Discovery of the Sources of the Mississippi and the Bloody River with a Description of the Whole Course of the Former, and of the Ohio.* London: Hunt and Clarke, 1828.

Billington, Ray Allen. *Land of Savagery, Land of Promise: The European Image of the American Frontier.* New York and London: W. W. Norton, 1981.

Carr, Gerald L. *Frederic Edwin Church: The Icebergs.* Dallas: Dallas Museum of Fine Arts, 1980.

Catlin, George. *The Letters of George Catlin and His Family.* Edited by Marjorie Roehm. Berkeley and Los Angeles: Univ. of California Press, 1966.

———. *Letters and Notes on the Manners, Customs and Conditions of North American Indians.* 2 vols. 1841. Reprint. New York: Dover, 1973.

———. *O-Kee-Pa, a Religious Ceremony and Other Customs of the Mandans.* Reprint. Edited by John Ewers. New Haven and London: Yale Univ. Press, 1967.

Letters and South American Itinerary, Mss., Thomas Gilcrease Institute, Tulsa, Okla.

Dana, Richard Henry. *Two Years Before the Mast.* New York: Harper's, 1840.

Egan, Ferol. *Frémont, Explorer for a Restless Nation.* Garden City, N. Y.: Doubleday, 1977.

Egan, John J. *The Panorama of the Monumental Grandeur of the Mississippi Valley.* Painting. St. Louis Art Museum. (This is the only surviving panorama painting of the Mississippi.)

Ewers, John C., et al. *Views of a Vanishing Frontier.* Omaha: Center for Western Studies, Joslyn Art Museum, 1984.

Goetzmann, William H. *Army Exploration in the American West, 1803–1863.* New Haven: Yale Univ. Press, 1959.

———. *Exploration and Empire: The Explorer and the Scientist in the Winning of the American West.* New York: Alfred A. Knopf, 1966.

———. *Exploring the American West, 1803–1879.* Washington: Division of Publications, National Park Service, U. S. Department of the Interior, 1982.

———, and Orr, William. *Karl Bodmer's America.* Omaha and Lincoln: Joslyn Art Museum and University of Nebraska Press, 1984.

Huntington, David. *The Landscapes of Frederic Edwin Church: Vision of an American Era.* New York: George Braziller, 1966.

Jackson, Donald, and Spence, Mary Lee, eds. *The Expeditions of John Charles Frémont.* 3 vols. and Atlas. Urbana: Univ. of Illinois Press, 1970, 1973.

Long, Stephen H. *The Northern Expeditions of Stephen H. Long, the Journals of 1817 and 1823 and Related Documents.* Edited by Lucille M. Kane, June D. Holmquist, and Carolyn Gilman. St. Paul: Minnesota Historical Society, 1978.

Lottinville, Savoie, ed. *Paul Wilhelm, Duke of Württemberg, Travels in North America, 1822–1824.* Translated by W. Robert Nitske. Norman: Univ. of Oklahoma Press, 1973.

McCracken, Harold. *George Catlin and the Old Frontier.* New York: Dial, 1959.

Merrill, George P. *The First One Hundred Years of American Geology.* New Haven: Yale Univ. Press, 1924.

Miller, David H. *Baldwin Möllhausen: A Prussian Image of the American West.* Ph.D. dissertation, Univ. of New Mexico, 1970. Ann Arbor, Mich.: University Microfilms, 1971.

————. "A Prussian on the Plains: Baldwin Möllhausen's Impressions." *Great Plains Journal* 12 (Spring 1973), 175–93.

Noble, Louis Legrande. *After Icebergs with a Painter.* New York: D. Appleton, 1861.

Nuttall, Thomas. *A Journal of Travels into the Arkansas Territory During the Year 1819.* Introduction by Savoie Lottinville. Norman: Univ. of Oklahoma Press, 1980.

Porter, Mae Reed, and Davenport, Odessa. *Scotsman in Buckskin: Sir William Drummond Stewart and the Rocky Mountain Fur Trade.* New York: Hastings House, 1963.

Severin, Timothy. *Explorers of the Mississippi.* New York: Alfred A. Knopf, 1968.

Statistical Appendix to Annual Report of the Sec. of the Treasury on the State of Finances for the Fiscal Year Ended June 30, 1970. Washington: Government Printing Office, 1971. pp. 8–16. (This obscure set of tables is of critical importance in determining the proportion of federal expenditures on science and art from 1840 to 1860. I have supplemented this with a study based on an analysis of the printed *Annual Reports* of the federal bureaus for the period, made for me by Ann Graham.)

Thomas, David, and Ronnefeldt, Karin. *People of the First Man . . . The Firsthand Account of Prince Maximilian's Expedition Up the Missouri River, 1833–34.* New York: E. P. Dutton, 1976.

Treuttner, William. *The Natural Man Observed: A Study of Catlin's Indian Gallery.* Forth Worth and Washington: Amon Carter Museum and National Collection of Fine Arts, Smithsonian, Smithsonian Institution Press, 1979.

Tyler, Ron, ed. *Alfred Jacob Miller: Artist on the Oregon Trail.* Fort Worth: Amon Carter Museum, 1982.

Wilhelm, Paul, Duke of Württemberg. *Early Sacramento.* Edited by J. A. Hussey. Translated by Louis C. Butscher. Sacramento: Sacramento Book Collectors Club, 1973.

————. *Travels in North America, 1822–1824.* Edited by Savoie Lottinville. Translated by W. Robert Nitske. Norman: Univ. of Okla. Press, 1973.

Chapter VI. THE MOUNTAIN MEN OF THE SEA

The foremost authority on whalers is Edouard A. Stackpole and
in particular his two major works, *The Sea Hunters: The New England Whalemen During Two Centuries, 1635–1835*, upon which I
have relied heavily, and *Whales and Destiny: The Rivalry Between
America, France and Britain for Control of the Southern Whale
Fishery, 1785–1825*. Stackpole's *The Voyage of the "Huron" and
the "Huntress": the American Sealers and the Discovery of the
Continent of Antarctica* is also important in indicating United
States priority of discovery with regard to the Antarctic continent—
no small question at the present time when a new international Antarctic treaty is in the process of negotiation. Other works by Stackpole
that I found interesting were *William Rotch (1734–1828) of
Nantucket, America's Pioneer in International Industry* and *Mutiny
at Midnight: The Adventures of Cyrus Hussey of Nantucket Aboard
the Whale Ship "Globe" in the South Pacific, from 1822 to
1826*.

Four other classic historical and statistical works concerning whaling are Alexander Starbuck, *History of the American Whale Fishery
from Its Earliest Inception to the Year 1876* (pp. 711–63 contain an
index to voyages by vessels' names); Obed Macy, *History of Nantucket;* Charles W. Townsend, "The Distribution of Certain Whales as
Shown in Logbook Records of American Whaleships," an incredible
piece of statistical research; and R. Gerard Ward, ed., *American Activities in the Central Pacific, 1790–1870*.

On the story of the American sealers, particularly in the Antarctic
region, the indispensable book is Kenneth J. Bertrand, *Americans in
Antarctica, 1755–1948*. This work is virtually definitive, and I have
depended heavily upon it.

All the works mentioned and others important to this chapter are
listed below.

Aldrich, John. *Thoreau as World Traveller*. New York: Columbia
Univ. Press, with the cooperation of the American Geographical Society, 1965. (Includes a list of Thoreau's very extensive reading in the
literature of world exploration.)

Berry, Robert Elton. *Yankee Stargazer: The Life of Nathaniel Bowditch.* New York and London: Whittlesey House, McGraw Hill, 1941.

Bertrand, Kenneth J. *Americans in Antarctica, 1755–1948.* New York: American Geographical Society, 1971.

Bingham, Hiram. *A Residence of Twenty-one Years in the Sandwich Islands* . . . 3rd ed. Canandaigua, N. Y.: H. D. Goodwin, Auctioneer, 1855.

Boggs, S. Whittemore. "American Contributions to Geographical Knowledge of the Central Pacific." *Geographical Review,* vol. XXVIII, no. 2 (April 1938), 177–92. (This article also includes a facsimile of the manuscript track chart of the American whaleship *Hope,* as well as C. H. Townsend's whale charts cited above, and his important map "Pacific Islands Discovered, Named, Mapped, and Occupied or Frequently Visited by Americans.")

Bowditch, Nathaniel. *New American Practical Navigator.* Washington: Government Printing Office, 1802.

Burstyn, Harold L. *At the Sign of the Quadrant: An Account of the Contribution to American Hydrography Made by Edmund March Blunt and His Sons.* Mystic, Conn.: Maritime Historical Association, 1957.

Christmas, Margaret C. S., *Adventurous Pursuits: Americans and the China Trade, 1784–1844. Washington, D.C.; National Portrait Gallery and the Smithsonian Institution Press, 1984.*

Delano, Amasa. *Narrative of Voyages and Travels, in the Northern and Southern Hemispheres: Comprising Three Voyages Round the World; Together with a Voyage of Survey and Discovery in the Pacific Ocean and Oriental Islands.* Boston: E. G. House, 1817.

Dodge, Ernest S. *Beyond the Capes: Pacific Exploration from Captain Cook to the "Challenger" 1776–1877.* Boston: Little, Brown, 1971.

Fanning, Edmund. *Voyages and Discoveries in the South Seas, 1792–1832.* Salem, Mass.: Marine Research Society, 1924. (A bowdlerized version of Fanning's book of 1833.)

————. *Voyages Round the World; with Selected Sketches of Voyages to the South Seas, North and South Pacific Oceans, China, etc. . . . Between the years 1792 and 1832.* New York: Collins & Hannay, 1833.

————. *Voyages to the South Seas, Indian and Pacific Oceans, China*

Sea, North-West Coast, Feejee Islands, South Shetlands, etc. . . . Between the Years 1830–1837. New York: W. H. Vermilye, 1838.

Gordon, James D. *The Last Martyrs of Eromanga, Being a Memoir of the Rev. George N. Gordon and Ellen Catherine Powell, His Wife.* Halifax, N. S.: Macnab and Shaffer, 1863.

Hefferman, Thomas Feral. *Stove by a Whale: Owen Chase and the "Essex."* Middletown, Conn.: Wesleyan University Press, 1981.

McHale, Thomas, and McHale, Mary C., eds. *Early American Philippine Trade: The Journal of Nathaniel Bowditch in Manila 1796.* New Haven: Yale Univ. Press, Southeast Asian Studies, 1962.

Macy, Obed. *History of Nantucket.* New York: Research Reprints, 1970.

Morison, Samuel Eliot. *The Maritime History of Massachusetts, 1783–1860.* 1921. Reprint. Sentry ed. Boston: Houghton Mifflin, 1961.

Morrell, Abby Jane. *Narrative of a Voyage to the Ethiopic and South Atlantic Ocean, Indian Ocean, Chinese Sea, North and South Pacific Ocean in the Years 1829, 1830, 1831.* New York: J. & J. Harper, 1833.

Morrell, Benjamin, Jr. *A Narrative of Four Voyages to the South Sea, North and South Pacific Ocean, Chinese Sea, Ethiopic and Southern Atlantic Ocean, Indian and Antarctic Ocean, from the Year 1822 to 1831 . . .* New York: J. & J. Harper, 1832.

Newcomb, Harvey. *A Cyclopedia of Missions, Containing a Comprehensive View of Missionary Operations Throughout the World . . .* New York: Charles Scribner, 1854.

Porter, David D. *Journal of a Cruise Made to the Pacific Ocean by Captain David Porter in the United States Frigate "Essex" in the Years 1812, 1813 and 1814.* 2 vols. New York: Wiley & Halsted, 1822.

Reynolds, Jeremiah N. "A Report of J. N. Reynolds, in relation to islands, reefs, and shoals in the Pacific Ocean, etc." 23 Cong. 2d Sess., *H. R. Doc. 105,* Serial 273 (January 27, 1835).

———. *Voyage of the United States Frigate "Potomac" Under the Command of Commodore John Downes During the Circumnavigation of the Globe in the Years 1831, 1832, 1833, and 1834.* 3rd ed. New York: Harper and Bros., 1835.

———, and Pearce, Rep. James A., of Maryland. "Report: The Committee on Commerce, to which were referred numerous memorials from citizens of various sections of the United States, praying that an exploring expedition to the Pacific Ocean and the South Seas may be authorized by Congress . . ." 23rd Cong. 2d Sess., *H. R. Doc. 94*, Serial 276 (1835).

Smith, Sarah Tappan. *History of the Establishment and Progress of the Christian Religion in the Islands of the South Sea; with Preliminary Notices of the Islands and of Their Inhabitants.* Boston: Tappan & Dennet, 1841.

Stackpole, Edouard A. *Mutiny at Midnight: The Adventures of Cyrus Hussey of Nantucket Aboard the Whale Ship "Globe" in the South Pacific, from 1822 to 1826.* London: F. Miller, 1944.

————. *The Sea Hunters: The New England Whalemen During Two Centuries, 1635–1835.* New York and Philadelphia: J. B. Lippincott, 1953.

————. *The Voyage of the "Huron" and the "Huntress": The American Sealers and the Discovery of the Continent of Antarctica.* Maritime History Association Publication No. 29. Mystic, Conn.: Maritime History Assoc., 1955.

————. *Whales and Destiny: The Rivalry Between America, France and Britain for Control of the Southern Whale Fishery, 1785–1828.* Amherst: Univ. of Massachusetts Press, 1972.

————. *William Rotch (1734–1828) of Nantucket, America's Pioneer in International Industry.* New York: Newcomen Society in North America, 1950.

Starbuck, Alexander. *History of the American Whale Fishery from Its Earliest Inception to the Year 1876.* In *Report of the U. S. Commissioner of Fish and Fisheries for 1875–76.* Washington: Government Printing Office, 1878, pp. 1–779.

Tamarin, Alfred, and Glubok, Shirley. *Voyaging to Cathay: Americans in the China Trade.* New York: Viking, 1976. (A delightfully illustrated book.)

Townsend, Charles W. "The Distribution of Certain Whales as Shown in Logbook Records of American Whaleships." *Zoologica, Scientific Contributions of the New York Zoological Society* 19:1 (1935), 1–50.

Ward, R. Gerard, ed. *American Activities in the Central Pacific, 1790–1870.* 8 vols. Ridgewood, N. J.: Gregg, 1966–69.

Chapter VII. EXPLORATION AND EMPIRES FOR SCIENCE

The writings concerning the Great United States Exploring Expedition of 1838–42, both in print and in manuscript, are exceedingly voluminous. This note on the sources used in writing this chapter will not attempt to list all of the relevant materials, though I have examined the critically important manuscript diaries of Midshipmen Emmons, Eld, Calvacoresses, and Reynolds, as well as Reynolds's letters home to his family.

Any scholar interested in the subject should start with the following four seminal works. Daniel C. Haskell, *The United States Exploring Expedition, 1838–1842 and Its Publications 1844–1874*, is a masterful bibliography that also includes guides to the location of manuscripts relating to the expedition. Charles Wilkes, *Autobiography of Rear Admiral Charles Wilkes, U.S. Navy 1798–1877*, is a bitter book in which Wilkes settles some old scores. Charles Wilkes, *Narrative of the United States Exploring Expedition During the Years 1838, 1839, 1840, 1841, 1842 . . .* is obviously of value. William Stanton, *The Great United States Exploring Expedition of 1838–1842*, is surely one of the outstanding histories in the literature of exploration, and I have depended on it heavily both for facts and for judgments. Other works have also been helpful to me, especially quite recently the Smithsonian Exhibition and attendant catalogue, Herman Viola and Carolyn Margolies, editors, *Magnificent Voyagers; the United States Exploring Expedition 1838–1842*.

Adams, John Quincy. "First Annual Message to Congress, Dec. 6, 1825," calling for an American exploring expedition. In James D. Richardson, *A Compilation of the Messages and Papers of the Presidents*. Vol. II. New York: Bureau of National Literature, 1897, pp. 865–83. See especially p. 878.

Anderson, Charles Roberts. *Melville in the South Seas*. New York: Columbia Univ. Press, 1939.

Belcher, Edward. *Narrative of a Voyage Around the World*. 2 vols. London: 1843.

Bertrand, Kenneth J. *Americans in Antarctica 1775–1948*. American Geographical Society Special Publication No. 39. New York: American Geographical Society, 1971.

Conklin, Edwin G., et al. "Centenary Celebration of the Wilkes Exploring Expedition of the United States Navy, 1838–1842, and Symposium on American Polar Exploration." *Proceedings of the American Philosophical Society* 82 (1940), 519–947.

Darwin, Charles. *Journal of Researches into the Natural History and Geology of the Various Countries Visited During the Voyage of H.M.S. Beagle Round the World.* 2nd ed. London: J. Murray, 1845.

Dumont d'Urville, Jacques S. C. *Voyages au Pole Sud et dans l'Océanie sur les corvettes l'Astrolabe et la Zelée Executis par l'ordre du Roi pendant 1837, 1838, 1839 et 1840.* 23 vols. Paris: 1841–45. See espec. vols. 8 and 9.

Erskine, Charles. *Twenty Years Before the Mast; with the More Thrilling Scenes and Incidences while Circumnavigating the Globe under the Command of the Late Admiral Charles Wilkes, 1838-1842.* 1890. Reprint. Washington, D. C., Smithsonian Press, 1985.

Friis, Herman, ed. *The Pacific Basin: A History of Its Geographical Exploration.* New York: American Geographical Society, 1967.

Gates, W. B. "Cooper's *The Sea Lions* and Wilkes' *Narrative*." *Publications of the Modern Language Association (PMLA)* 65 (1950), 1069–75.

Gilman, Daniel Coit. *The Life of James Dwight Dana.* New York and London: Harper & Brothers, 1899.

Goode, George B. "The Genesis of the National Museum." *U. S. National Museum Annual Report for 1891*, pp. 273–380.

———. *The Smithsonian Institution 1846–1896: The History of Its First Half Century.* Washington, 1897.

Gough, Barry. *The Royal Navy and the Northwest Coast of North America.* Vancouver: Univ. of British Columbia Press, 1971.

Gruber, Jacob. "Horatio Hale and the Development of American Anthropology." *Proceedings of the American Philosophical Society* III (1967), 5–37.

Haskell, Daniel C. *The United States Exploring Expedition, 1838-1842, and Its Publications, 1844-1874.* New York: Greenwood Press Reprint, 1968.

Hobbs, William H. "The Discoveries of Antarctica Within the American Sector as Revealed by Maps and Documents." *Transactions of the American Philosophical Society* (N.S.), 31, Part I (January 1939), 1–71.

———. *Explorers of the Antarctic.* New York: House of Field, 1941.

Ivashintsov, L. A. *Russian Round-the-World Voyages: 1802–1849, with a Summary of Later Voyages to 1867.* Edited by Richard A. Pierce. Kingston, Ont.: Limestone Press, 1980.

Kazar, John D. *The United States Navy and Scientific Exploration, 1837–1860.* Ph.D. dissertation, Univ. of Massachusetts, 1973. Ann Arbor, Mich.: University Microfilms.

Merk, Frederick. *The Oregon Question.* Cambridge, Mass.: Harvard Univ. Press, 1967.

Mitchell, Lee Clark. *Witnesses to a Vanishing America.* Princeton: Princeton Univ. Press, 1981. (This is the first work to notice Melville's cultural relativism.)

Philbrick, Thomas. *James Fenimore Cooper and the Development of American Sea Fiction.* Cambridge, Mass.: Harvard Univ. Press, 1961.

Poesch, Jessie. "Titian Ramsey Peale, 1799–1885, and His Journals of the Wilkes Expedition." *Memoirs of the American Philosophical Society*, Vol. 52. Philadelphia: American Philosophical Society, 1961.

Ross, James Clark. *A Voyage of Discovery and Research in the Southern and Antarctic Regions During the Years 1839–43.* 2 vols. London: 1847.

Sanford, William F. "Dana and Darwinism." *Journal of the History of Ideas* 26: 4 (October–December 1965).

Smith, Bernard. *European Vision and the South Pacific 1768–1850.* Oxford: Clarenden Press, 1960.

Stanton, William. *The Great United States Exploring Expedition of 1838–1842.* Berkeley and Los Angeles: Univ. of California Press, 1975.

Tyler, David B. *The Wilkes Expedition: The First United States Exploring Expedition 1838–1841* [sic]. Philadelphia: American Philosophical Society, 1968.

Viola, Herman, and Margolies, Carolyn, eds. *Magnificent Voyagers; the United States Exploring Expedition 1838–1842.* Washington, D. C.: Smithsonian Press, 1985.

Wilkes, Charles. *Autobiography of Rear Admiral Charles Wilkes, U.S. Navy 1798–1877.* Edited by William James Morgan, David B. Tyler, Joye L. Leonhart, and Mary F. Loughlin. Washington: Naval History Division, Dept. of the Navy, 1978.

—————. *Narrative of the United States Exploring Expedition During the Years 1838, 1839, 1840, 1841, 1842 . . . In Five Volumes and an Atlas.* Philadelphia: C. Sherman, 1844.

Wolter, John. *Surveyors of the Pacific: Charting the Pacific Basin, 1768–1842.* Catalogue to an exhibition at the Library of Congress, November 1985.

Chapter VIII.   Two Roads to Discovery

The historical literature on the subject matter of this chapter is not as voluminous as it should be. There is no definitive work on Alexander Dallas Bache, certainly one of the most important men of science in nineteenth-century America, nor is there a detailed study of the United States Coast and Geodetic Survey, a study that is badly needed. In addition, historians, for various reasons, have tended to dismiss the work of Matthew Fontaine Maury out of hand, possibly because he joined the Confederate rebellion. Moreover, oceanographers for the most part have scarcely been interested in the history of their discipline, and the principal modern judgment of Maury's work rests on oceanographer John Leighly's introduction to a Harvard University Press reprint of Maury's *The Physical Geography of the Sea.* Harold Burstyn's article on Maury in the *Dictionary of Scientific Biography,* for example, takes its cue almost entirely from the Leighly introduction. Unfortunately, Leighly directed his attention, as was his assignment, almost entirely to *The Physical Geography of the Sea* and hence ignored Maury's more coherent scientific work. Most other writers, with the exception of Edward Leon Towle, Francis Leigh Williams, and George M. Brooke, have concerned themselves only with Maury's rather confusing *The Physical Geography of the Sea.* My analysis of Maury's work in this chapter stems largely from the other works in the following list and from helpful criticism afforded me by Dr. Nathan Reingold of the Smithsonian Institution, the distinguished former editor of the Joseph Henry Papers.

Brooke, George M. *John M. Brooke, Naval Scientist and Educator.* Charlottesville: Univ. Press of Virginia, 1980.

Bryant, Samuel. *The Sea and the States: A Maritime History of the American People.* New York: Thomas Y. Crowell, 1947.

Burstyn, Harold. Entry on Maury in *The Dictionary of Scientific Biography.* New York: Charles Scribner's Sons, 1974.

Caskie, Jacqueline Ambler. *The Life and Letters of Matthew Fontaine Maury.* Richmond: Richmond Press, 1928.

Cowen, Robert C. *Frontiers of the Sea: The Story of Oceanographic Exploration.* New York: Doubleday, 1960.

Deacon, Margaret. *Scientists and the Sea, 1650–1900: A Study of Marine Science.* New York: Academic Press, 1971.

Espy, James P. *Philosophy of Storms.* Boston: C. C. Little & J. Brown, 1841.

Graham, Ann M. "Oceanographic Methodologies in the Nineteenth Century: The Work of Matthew Fontaine Maury and Alexander von Humboldt." Seminar paper, Univ. of Texas American Studies Program, 1983.

Grosser, Morton. *The Discovery of Neptune.* Cambridge, Mass.: Harvard University Press, 1962.

Henry, Joseph. "Eulogy on Prof. Alexander Dallas Bache, Late Superintendent of the United States Coast Survey." *Annual Report of the Smithsonian Institution, 1870.* Washington, D.C., 1870.

Johns, Patricia. *Matthew Fontaine Maury and Joseph Henry: Scientists and the Civil War.* New York: Hastings House, 1960.

Johnston, Alexander Keith. *The Physical Atlas of Natural Phenomena.* American ed. Philadelphia: Lea and Blanchard, 1849, pp. 31–62.

Kohlstadt, Sally Gregory. *The Formation of the American Scientific Community: The American Association for the Advancement of Science, 1848–1860.* Urbana: University of Illinois Press, 1976.

Leighly, John. "Introduction to Matthew Fontaine Maury," *The Physical Geography of the Sea.* Cambridge: Harvard Univ. Press, 1963.

Lewis, Charles Lee. *Matthew Fontaine Maury, Pathfinder of the Seas.* Annapolis: U. S. Naval Institute, 1927.

Maury, Matthew Fontaine. *Explanations and Sailing Directions to Accompany the Wind and Current Charts.* Washington, D.C., 1858.

————. *The Physical Geography of the Sea*. New York: Harper & Brothers, 1855.

Odgers, Merle. *Alexander Dallas Bache: Scientist and Educator, 1806–1867*. Philadelphia: Univ. of Pennsylvania Press, 1947.

Pyne, Stephen. "From the Grand Canyon to the Marianas Trench." In Nathan Reingold, ed., *The Sciences in the American Context*. Washington, D.C.: Smithsonian Institution Press, 1980.

Redfield, William C. "Observations on the Hurricanes and Storms of the West Indies and the Coast of the U. States." *The American Journal of Science and the Arts*, 1833.

————. "Remarks on the Prevailing Storms of the Atlantic Coast of the North American States." *The American Journal of Science and the Arts*, 1831.

Schlee, Susan. *A History of Oceanography: The Edge of an Unfamiliar World*. London: Robb Hale & Co., 1973.

Scoresby, William. *The Arctic Regions and the Northern Whale Fishery*. London: Religious Tract Society, 1820, 1848. Modern edition. 2 vols. New York: Augustus M. Kelley Publishers, 1969.

Somerville, Mary Fairfax. *Physical Geography*. 2nd American ed. Philadelphia: Lea and Blanchard, 1850.

Thomson, C. Wyville. *The Depths of the Sea: An Account of the General Result of the Dredging Cruises of H.M.S.S. "Porcupine" and "Lightning" during the Summers of 1868, 1869 and 1870*. 2nd ed. London: Macmillan & Co., 1874.

Towle, Edward Leon. *Science, Commerce and the Navy on the Seafaring Frontier (1842–1861)*. Ph.D. dissertation, Univ. of Rochester, 1965. Ann Arbor, Mich.: University Microfilms, 1981.

Weber, Gustavus Adolphus. *The Coast and Geodetic Survey: Its History, Activities, and Organizations*. Service Monograph of the U.S. Govt. No. 16. Baltimore: Institute for Government Research, 1923.

————. *The Naval Observatory: Its History, Activities and Organization*. Service Monograph of the U.S. Govt. No. 39. Baltimore: Institute for Government Research, 1926.

Williams, Francis Leigh. *Matthew Fontaine Maury, Scientist of the Sea*. New Brunswick, N. J.: Rutgers Univ. Press, 1963.

Chapter IX.   FROM MANIFEST DESTINY TO SURVIVAL
OF THE FITTEST

The most comprehensive survey of the subject matter of this chapter is John Dryden Kazar, *The United States Navy and Scientific Exploration, 1837–1860.* Though I have studied the published official government reports of the various expeditions discussed in this chapter, I have also frequently relied on Kazar's authoritative work. Unfortunately, the complete results of the Ringgold-Rogers North Pacific Exploring Expedition were never published, and one must be grateful for Allan B. Cole's *Yankee Surveyors in the Shogun's Seas,* in which selections from the voluminous manuscript archives that remain from the expedition are printed, and which archive I have also examined. The only work by a member of the expedition published in English is Alexander W. Habersham's book, cited below, a rare copy of which I luckily found in a Palo Alto, California, bookstore. The complete story of the North Pacific Exploring Expedition still awaits its historian. The following works are those that I found most helpful in writing this chapter.

Basalla, George. "The Spread of Western Science." *Science* 156 (May 1967), 611–22.

Basso, Hamilton, ed. *Exploration of the Valley of the Amazon by William Lewis Herndon.* New York: McGraw-Hill, 1952.

Bates, Ralph. *Scientific Societies in the United States.* Cambridge: M.I.T. Press, 1945.

Bell, Whitfield, Jr. "The Relation of Herndon and Gibbon's Exploration of the Amazon to North American Slavery, 1850–1855." *Hispanic American Historical Review* 19 (1939), 494–503.

Bemis, Samuel Flagg. *John Quincy Adams and the Foundations of American Foreign Policy.* New York: Alfred A. Knopf, 1949.

———. *The Latin American Policy of the United States.* New York: Harcourt, Brace, 1943.

Bourne, Kenneth. *Britain and the Balance of Power in North America 1815–1908.* London: Longmans, Greene, 1967.

Brooke, George M., Jr. *John M. Brooke, Naval Scientist and Educator.* Charlottesville: Univ. Press of Virginia, 1980.

Brooks, Van Wyck. *Fenollosa and His Circle.* New York: E. P. Dutton, 1962.

———. *The Times of Melville & Whitman.* New York: E. P. Dutton, 1953.

Calvocoresses, George M. *Four Years in a Government Exploring Expedition.* New York: Cornish & Lamport, 1852.

Cole, Allan B. "The Ringgold-Rogers-Brooke Expedition to Japan and the North Pacific, 1853–59." *Pacific Historical Review* 16 (1947), 152–62.

———, ed. *A Scientist with Perry in Japan.* Chapel Hill: Univ. of North Carolina Press, 1947.

———, ed. *Yankee Surveyors in the Shogun's Seas.* Princeton: Princeton Univ. Press, 1947.

Corbin, Diana. *Matthew Fontaine Maury: A Life of Matthew Fontaine Maury.* London: Sampson, Low, Marston, Searle & Revington, 1888.

Corner, George W. *Dr. Kane of the Arctic Seas.* Philadelphia: Temple Univ. Press, 1972.

Coulson, Thomas. *Joseph Henry.* Princeton: Princeton Univ. Press, 1950.

Dana, Edward S., et al. *A Century of Science in America.* New Haven: Yale Univ. Press, 1918.

Daniels, George. *American Science in the Age of Jackson.* New York: Columbia Univ. Press, 1968.

Dozer, Donald M. "Documents: Matthew Fontaine Maury's Letter of Instructions to William Lewis Herndon." *Hispanic American Historical Review* 28 (May 1948), 212–28.

Dupree, A. Hunter. *Asa Gray.* Cambridge, Mass.: Harvard Univ. Press, 1959.

———. "Science vs. the Military: Dr. James Morrow and the Perry Expedition." *Pacific Historical Review* 22 (1953), 29–37.

"Free Navigation of the Amazon River," 33rd Cong. 1st Sess., *Misc. Doc. 22*, 1854.

Friis, Herman. *The Pacific Basin.* New York: American Geographical Society, 1967.

Gates, W. B. "Notes and Queries: Cooper's *The Crater* and Two Explorers." *American Literature* 23 (1951), 243–46.

Gilliss, James Melville. *Origin and Operations of the U. S. Naval Astronomical Expedition.* Washington: A.O.P. Nicholson, 1858.

———. "The U. S. Naval Astronomical Expedition to the Southern Hemisphere During the Years 1849-'50-'51-'52." 33rd Cong. 1st Sess., *HR Doc. 121* (1855). 3 vols. (See especially Vol. I.)

Godfrey, William C. *Godfrey's Narrative of the Last Grinnell Arctic Exploring Expedition.* Philadelphia: J. T. Lloyd & Co., 1857.

Goetzmann, William H. *When the Eagle Screamed: The Romantic Horizon in American Diplomacy 1800-1860.* New York: John Wiley & Sons, 1966.

———, and Sloan, Kay. *Looking Far North: The Harriman Expedition to Alaska, 1899.* New York: Viking, 1982.

Graff, Henry F., ed. *Bluejackets with Perry in Japan.* New York: New York Public Library, 1952.

Gray, Jane Loring, ed. *The Letters of Asa Gray.* 2 vols. Boston: Houghton Mifflin, 1893.

Habersham, Alexander W. *The North Pacific Surveying and Exploring Expedition, or My Last Cruise.* Philadelphia, J. B. Lippincott, 1857.

Harrison, John P. "Science and Politics: Origins and Objectives of Mid-Nineteenth Century Government Expeditions to Latin America." *Hispanic American Historical Review* 35 (1955), 175-202.

Hawks, Francis L. *Narrative of the Expedition of an American Squadron to the China Seas and Japan.* New York: D. Appleton, 1856.

Hayes, Isaac I. *An Arctic Boat Journey.* Boston: Brown, Taggert & Chase, 1860.

———. *The Open Polar Sea.* New York: R. Worthington, 1869.

Headley, J. T. "Darien Exploring Expedition." *Harper's New Monthly Magazine* 10 (1853-54), 433-58; 600-15; 745-64.

Herndon, William Lewis, and Gibbon, Lardner M. "Exploration of the Valley of the Amazon." Parts I, II. 33rd Cong. 1st Sess., *Exec. Doc. No. 53*, 1854.

Hine, Robert V. *Edward Kern and American Expansion.* New Haven: Yale Univ. Press, 1962.

Idyll, C. P. *Exploring the Ocean World.* New York: Thomas Y. Crowell, 1969.

Kane, Elisha Kent. *Arctic Explorations: The Second Grinnell Expedition in Search of Sir John Franklin, 1853, '54, '55.* 2 vols. Philadelphia: Childs & Peterson, 1856.

Kazar, John Dryden. *The United States Navy and Scientific Explorations, 1837–1860.* Ph.D. dissertation. Univ. of Massachusetts, 1973. Ann Arbor, Mich.: University Microfilms, 1977.

Lewis, Charles Lee. *Matthew Fontaine Maury.* Annapolis: U. S. Naval Institute, 1927.

Lurie, Edward. *Louis Agassiz.* Chicago: Univ. of Chicago Press, 1960.

Lynch, William F. *Narrative of the United States Expedition to the River Jordan and the Dead Sea.* Philadelphia: Lea and Blanchard, 1849.

———. *Official Report of the United States Expedition to Explore the Dead Sea and the River Jordan.* Baltimore: John Murphey, 1852.

Maury, Matthew Fontaine. "Amazon Valley." *DeBow's Commercial Review* 14 (1852).

———. *The Amazon and the Atlantic Slopes of South America.* Washington, D.C.: F. Taylor, 1853.

———. "Atlantic Submarine Telegraph." *DeBow's Commercial Review* 16 (1853).

Merk, Frederick. *Manifest Destiny and Mission in American History.* New York: Alfred A. Knopf, 1963.

Mirsky, Jeanette. *Elisha Kent Kane and the Seafaring Frontier.* Boston: Little, Brown, 1954.

———. *To the Arctic.* New York: Alfred A. Knopf, 1948.

Montague, Edward P. *Narrative of the Late Expedition to the Dead Sea.* Philadelphia: Carey and Hart, 1849.

Morison, Samuel Eliot. *"Old Bruin": Commodore Matthew C. Perry.* Boston: Little, Brown, 1967.

Page, Thomas J. *La Plata, the Argentine Confederation and Paraguay.* New York: Harper & Bros., 1859.

Perry, Matthew C., ed. *Narrative of the Expedition of an American Squadron to the China Seas and Japan.* 3 vols. Washington, D.C.: A.O.P. Nicholson, 1856.

Philbrick, Thomas. *James Fenimore Cooper and the Development of American Sea Fiction.* Cambridge, Mass.: Harvard Univ. Press, 1961.

Pineau, Roger, ed. *The Japan Expedition, 1852–54: The Personal Journal of Commodore Matthew C. Perry.* Washington, D.C.: Smithsonian Institution Press, 1868.

Rasmussen, Wayne D. "The United States Astronomical Expedition to Chile, 1849–52." *Hispanic American Historical Review* 34 (1954), 101–13.

Reingold, Nathan, ed. *Science in Nineteenth Century America: A Documentary History.* New York: Hill & Wang, 1964.

Schlee, Susan. *A History of Oceanography: The Edge of an Unfamiliar World.* London: Robert Hale, 1973.

Strain, Isaac G. *Sketches of a Journey in Chile, and the Argentine Province in 1849.* New York: Horace H. Moore, 1853.

Wallace, Edward S. *Destiny and Glory.* New York: Coward-McCann, 1957.

Walworth, Arthur. *Black Ships off Japan.* New York: Alfred A. Knopf, 1946.

Williams, Francis Leigh. *Matthew Fontaine Maury, Scientist of the Sea.* New Brunswick, N. J.: Rutgers Univ. Press, 1963.

Chapter X.   THE HEROIC AGE OF GEOLOGICAL
EXPLORATION

Much of the material in this chapter, in an earlier version, now revised and with a considerably different orientation, has appeared as "The Heroic Age of the Western Geological Survey" in *The American West*, Fall 1979, for which permission to publish in this volume is gratefully acknowledged. Beyond this, the most important published sources and authorities for the present chapter, some of which have appeared since 1979, are listed below.

Aldrich, Michele A. L. "New York Natural History Survey, 1836–1845." Ph.D. dissertation, Univ. of Texas, 1974.

Bartlett, Richard. *Great Surveys of the American West.* Norman: Univ. of Oklahoma Press, 1962.

Culbertson, Thaddeus A. "Journal of an Expedition to the Mauvais Terres and the Upper Missouri in 1850." *Annual Report of the Smithsonian Institution,* 1850–52, pp. 84–145.

Darrah, William Culp. *Powell of the Colorado.* Princeton: Princeton Univ. Press, 1962.

Dellenbaugh, Frederick. *A Canyon Voyage.* New Haven: Yale Univ. Press, 1908.

Desmond, Adrian J. *The Hot-Blooded Dinosaurs.* New York: Warner, 1975.

Dupree, A. Hunter. *Science in the Federal Government: A History of Policies and Activities to 1940.* Cambridge, Mass.: Harvard Univ. Press, 1957.

Dutton, Clarence. *Report on the Geology of the High Plateaus of Utah.* Washington, D.C.: Government Printing Office, 1880.

―――. *Tertiary History of the Grand Canyon District with Atlas.* U.S. Geological Survey Monograph, Vol. II. Washington, D.C.: Government Printing Office, 1882.

Fowler, Dan D., ed. *"Photographed All the Best Scenery": Jack Hillers' Diary of the Powell Expeditions, 1871–1875.* Salt Lake City: Univ. of Utah Press, 1972.

Gilbert, G. K. *Report on the Geology of the Henry Mountains.* 2d ed. Washington: Government Printing Office, 1880.

Gillespie, Charles C. *Genesis and Geology.* New York: Harper Torchbook, 1959.

Goetzmann, William H. *Exploration and Empire: The Explorer and the Scientist in the Winning of the American West.* New York: Alfred A. Knopf, 1966.

―――. "Limner of Grandeur: William H. Holmes and the Grand Canyon." *American West,* May/June 1978.

―――. *William H. Holmes: Panoramic Art.* Fort Worth: Amon Carter Museum, 1977.

Holmes, W. H. "Random Records of a Lifetime in Science and Art." Ms. and scrapbook. Smithsonian Institution.

Hovencamp, Herbert. *Science and Religion in America, 1800–1860.* Philadelphia: Univ. of Pennsylvania Press, 1978.

Howard, Robert West. *The Dawnseekers: The First History of American Paleontology.* New York: Harcourt Brace Jovanovich, 1975.

Jones, William A. *Report upon the Reconnaissance of Northwestern Wyoming Including Yellowstone National Park Made in the Summer of 1873.* Washington, D.C.: Government Printing Office, 1875.

King, Clarence. *Mountaineering in the Sierra Nevada.* Boston: James R. Osgood Co., 1872.

Leidy, Joseph. "On the Fossil Horse of America." *Proceedings of the Philadelphia Academy of Natural Sciences* III (January–February 1846), 262–68.

———. "The Ancient Fauna of Nebraska." In *Smithsonian Contributions to Knowledge.* Washington, D.C.: Smithsonian Institution, 1854, pp. 1–119.

Ludlow, William. *Report of a Reconnaissance of the Black Hills of Dakota Made in the Summer of 1874.* Washington, D.C.: Government Printing Office, 1875.

Macomb, John N. *Exploring Expedition from Santa Fe, New Mexico, to the Junction of the Grand and Green Rivers of the Great Colorado of the West.* Washington, D.C.: Government Printing Office, 1876.

Manning, Thomas. *Government in Science, the U. S. Geological Survey 1867–1894.* Lexington: Univ. of Kentucky Press, 1967.

Merrill, George P. *The First One Hundred Years of American Geology.* New Haven: Yale Univ. Press, 1923.

Morgan, Lewis Henry. *Ancient Society.* Cleveland: World Publishing Co., 1877. Reprint. New York: Meridian, 1969.

Nash, Roderick. *Wilderness and the American Mind.* New Haven: Yale Univ. Press, 1967. 2nd ed., 1977.

Newton, Henry, and Jenney, Walter P. *Report on the Geology and Resources of the Black Hills of Dakota with Atlas.* Washington, D.C.: Government Printing Office, 1880.

Osborn, Henry Fairfield. "Biological Memoir of Joseph Leidy,

1823–1891." In *National Academy of Sciences Biographical Memoirs*, Vol. VII. Washington: National Academy of Sciences, 1913.

———. "Joseph Leidy, Founder of Vertebrate Paleontology in America." In *Impressions of Great Naturalists*. New York: Charles Scribner's Sons, 1924, pp. 133–48.

———. *Cope, Master Naturalist*. Princeton: Princeton Univ. Press, 1931.

Powell, John Wesley. *Exploration of the Colorado River of the West and Its Tributaries*. Washington, D.C.: Government Printing Office, 1875.

———. *Report on the Geology of the Eastern Portion of the Uinta Mountains . . . with Atlas*. Washington, D.C.: Government Printing Office, 1876.

———. *Report on the Lands of the Arid Region of the United States . . .* 2nd ed. Washington, D.C.: Government Printing Office, 1879.

———. *Second Annual Report of the United States Geological Survey*. Washington, D.C.: Government Printing Office, 1881. Contains:

  C. Dutton. "The Physical Geology of the Grand Canyon District."
  G. K. Gilbert. "Contributions to the History of Lake Bonneville."
  S. F. Emmons. "Abstract of Report on Geology and Mining Industry of Leadville, Lake County, Colorado."
  George F. Becker. "A Summary of the Geology of the Comstock Lode and the Washoe District."
  Clarence King. "Production of Precious Metals in the United States."
  G. K. Gilbert. "A New Method of Measuring Heights by Means of the Barometer."

Pyne, Stephen. *Dutton's Point: An Intellectual History of the Grand Canyon*. Grand Canyon, Ariz.: Grand Canyon Natural History Association, 1982.

———. "From the Grand Canyon to the Marianas Trench." In Nathan Reingold, ed., *The Sciences in the American Context*. Washington, D.C.: Smithsonian Institution Press, 1980.

———. *Grove Karl Gilbert*. Austin, Tex.: Univ. of Texas Press, 1980.

Pumpelly, Raphael. *My Reminiscences*. 2 vols. New York: Henry Holt, 1918.

Rabbitt, Mary. *Minerals, Lands and Geology for the Common De-*

fense and General Welfare, Vol. I, *Before 1879.* Washington, D.C.: U. S. Geological Survey, 1979.

———. *Minerals, Lands and Geology for the Common Defense and General Welfare,* Vol. II, *1879-1904.* Washington, D.C.: U. S. Geological Survey, 1980.

Runte, Alfred. *National Parks: The American Experience.* Lincoln: Univ. of Nebraska Press, 1979.

Schmeckebier, Laurence F. *Catalogue and Index of the Publications of the Hayden, King, Powell and Wheeler Surveys.* 58th Cong. 2d Sess., *H. R. Doc. 606.* Washington, D.C.: Government Printing Office, 1904.

Schuchert, Clyde, and LeVane, Clara Mae. *O. C. Marsh, Pioneer in Paleontology.* New Haven: Yale Univ. Press, 1940.

Scott, William Berryman. *Some Memories of a Paleontologist.* Princeton: Princeton Univ. Press, 1939.

Stegner, Wallace. *Beyond the Hundredth Meridian.* Boston: Houghton Mifflin, 1953.

Sweeney, J. Gray. *The Artist-Explorers of the American West: 1860-1880.* Ph.D. dissertation. Ann Arbor, Mich.: University Microfilms, 1975.

Turner, Frederick. *Beyond Geography: The Western Spirit Against the Wilderness.* New York: Viking, 1980.

U. S. Geological Survey. *Yearbooks.*

Wilkins, Thurman. *Clarence King.* New York: Macmillan, 1958.

———. *Thomas Moran, Artist of the Mountains.* Norman: Univ. of Oklahoma Press, 1966.

Chapter XI.   "On, Beyond Greenland's Icy Mountains" to a
"Fire on the Moon"

The literature on Arctic and Antarctic exploration is vast. The titles listed below represent the sources and authorities upon which I have chiefly relied without making any pretense at relating the definitive account of exploration in these polar regions. In addition, though my allusion to Henry Morton Stanley in this chapter is brief—briefer than

I would have liked—it rests, not only on published works by or about Stanley, but also on the vast literature by or about British explorers in Africa, as well as African exploration accounts by the Americans Martin Delaney and Paul Du Chaillu, in whom I have long been interested.

I also wish to thank Dr. Stephen Spurr for allowing me to read the unpublished autobiography of his father, the Alaskan explorer Josiah Edward Spurr of the U.S. Geological Survey. I found this and his extensive unpublished "The Log of the Kuskokwim" most enlightening. The latter narrative records in a vivid manner the difficult and daring work performed by the Geological Survey as they mapped the vast mountainous interior of Alaska in the days before the airplane and the satellite. The chief sources used in this chapter are as follows.

Allen, Henry T. *Report of an Expedition to the Copper, Tanana, and Koyukuk Rivers in the Territory of Alaska in the Year 1885.* Washington, D.C.: Government Printing Office, 1887.

Bemis, Samuel Flagg. *A Diplomatic History of the United States.* New York: Henry Hall, 1953.

Bickel, Leonard. *Mawson's Will: The Greatest Survival Story Ever Written.* New York: Stein & Day, 1977.

Breton, Pierre. *Klondike Fever.* New York: Alfred A. Knopf, 1958.

Cameron, Ian. *To the Farthest Ends of the Earth: 150 Years of World Exploration by the Royal Geographical Society.* New York: E. P. Dutton, 1980.

Carter, Paul A. *Little America, Town at the End of the World.* New York: Columbia Univ. Press, 1979.

Collins, Perry McDonough. *Siberian Journey: Down the Amur to the Pacific, 1856–1857.* Edited by Charles Vivier. Madison: Univ. of Wisconsin Press, 1962.

Dall, William Healy. *Alaska and Its Resources.* Boston: Lea & Shepherd, 1870.

Delaney, Martin Robinson. *Official Report of the Niger Valley Exploring Party.* New York: T. Hamilton, 1861.

Diebitsch-Peary, Josephine. *My Arctic Journal: A Year Among Ice Fields and Eskimos, with an Account of the Great White Journey Across Greenland by Robert E. Peary.* New York and Philadelphia: Contemporary Publishing Co., 1894.

Dodge, Ernest. *Northwest by Sea.* New York: Oxford Univ. Press, 1961.

Du Chaillu, Paul Belloni. *Explorations and Adventures in Equatorial Africa.* London: John Murray, 1861.

———. *Stories of the Gorilla Country.* New York: Harper's, 1867.

Ellsburg, Edward. *Hell on Ice: The Saga of the "Jeanette."* New York: Dodd, Mead, 1938.

Ellsworth, Lincoln. *Beyond Horizons.* London and Toronto: William Heinemann, 1938.

Farwell, Byron. *The Man Who Presumed: A Biography of Henry M. Stanley.* New York: Henry Holt, 1957.

Fox, Stephen. *John Muir and His Legacy.* Boston and Toronto: Little, Brown, 1981.

Friis, Herman R., and Bale, Shelby G., eds. *United States Polar Exploration.* National Archives Conference, Vol. I, Papers of the Conference on United States Polar Exploration, held on Sept. 8, 1967, National Archives Building, Washington, D. C. Athens, Ohio: Ohio Univ. Press, 1970.

Fristrup, Borge. *The Greenland Ice Cap.* Seattle: Univ. of Washington Press, 1966.

Galey, Thomas M., ed. *The Far North: Earliest Exploration by Aircraft: A Few Articles from the National Geographic Magazine.* N.P., N.D.

Goetzmann, William H., and Sloan, Kay. *Looking Far North, the Harriman Expedition to Alaska, 1899.* New York: Viking, 1982.

Gough, Barry M. *To the Pacific and Arctic with Beecher: The Journal of Lt. George Peard of H.M.S. "Blossom" 1825-1828.* Cambridge: Hakluyt Society, 1973.

Greely, Adolphus W. *Three Years of Arctic Service: An Account of the Lady Franklin Bay Expedition of 1881-84 and the Attainment of the Farthest North.* 2 vols. New York: Charles Scribner's Sons, 1886.

Griffith, Cyril E. *The African Dream: Martin R. Delaney and the Emergence of Pan-African Thought.* University Park: Pennsylvania State Univ. Press, 1975.

Grosvenor, Gilbert. *The National Geographic Society and Its Maga-*

zine: *A History*. Washington, D.C.: National Geographic Society, 1957.

Habersham, A. W. *North Pacific Surveying and Exploring Expedition, or My Last Cruise*. Philadelphia: Lippincott, 1858.

Healy, M. A. *Cruise of the Revenue Marine Steamer Corwin in the Arctic Ocean . . . 1884*. Washington, D.C.: Government Printing Office, 1889.

Hooper, C. L. *Report of the Cruise of the U.S. Revenue Steamer Thomas Corwin in the Arctic Ocean 1881*. Washington, D.C.: Government Printing Office, 1885.

Hunt, William R. *Arctic Passage: The Turbulent History of the Land and People of the Bering Sea, 1697–1975*. New York: Charles Scribner's Sons, 1975.

Livingstone, David. *The Last Journals of David Livingstone in Central Africa from 1865 to His Death*. Edited by Horace Waller. Hartford: R. W. Bliss, 1875.

Loomis, Chauncey C. *Weird and Tragic Shores: The Story of Charles Francis Hall, Explorer*. New York: Alfred A. Knopf, 1971.

MacMillan, Donald Baxter. *Etah and Beyond, or Life Within Twelve Degrees of the Pole*. Boston and New York: Houghton Mifflin, 1927.

Melville, George W. *In the Lena Delta: A Narrative of the Search for Lieut. Commander De Long and His Companions, Followed by an Account of the Greely Relief Expedition and a Proposed Method of Reaching the North Pole*. Boston: Houghton Mifflin, 1892.

Mirsky, Jeanette. *To the Arctic!: The Story of Northern Exploration from Earliest Times to the Present*. Chicago and London: Univ. of Chicago Press, 1970.

Mountfield, David. *A History of Polar Exploration*. New York: Dial, 1974.

Muir, John. *Travels in Alaska*. Reprint. Boston: Houghton Mifflin, 1979.

Nansen, Fridtjof. *Fartherest North, Being the Record of Exploration of the Ship "Fram" 1893–96 and of a Fifteen Months Sleigh Journey by Dr. Nansen and Lt. Johnson, with an Appendix by Otto Sverdrup, Capt. of the "Fram."* 2 vols. New York: Harper & Bros., 1898.

Neatby, Leslie H. *Conquest of the Last Frontier.* Athens, Ohio: Ohio Univ. Press, 1966.

———. *Discovery in Russian and Siberian Waters.* Athens, Ohio: Ohio Univ. Press, 1973.

———. *In Quest of the Northwest Passage.* New York: Thomas Y. Crowell, 1958.

Newcomb, Raymond Lee, ed. *Our Lost Explorers: The Narrative of the "Jeanette" Arctic Expedition as Related by the Survivors and Last Journals of Lieutenant De Long.* Hartford and San Francisco: American Publishing and A. L. Bancroft, 1884.

Nordenskiöld, A. E. *Voyage of the Vega Around Asia and Europe.* London: Macmillan, 1881.

Northrup, Henry Davenport, *Wonders of the Tropics or Exploration and Adventures of Henry M. Stanley and Other World-Renowned Travellers, Including Livingston, Baker, Cameron, Speke, Emin Pasha, Du Chaillu, Anderson, etc. etc., Containing Thrilling Accounts of Famous Expeditions, Miraculous Escapes, Wild Sports of the Jungle and Plain, Curious Customs of Savage Races, Journles in Unknown Lands and Marvelous Discoveries in the Worlds of Africa, Together with Graphic Descriptions of Beautiful Scenery, Fertile Valleys, Vast Forests, Mighty Rivers and Cataracts, Inland Seas, Mines of Untold Wealth, Ferocious Beasts, etc. etcs., the Whole Comprising a Vast Treasury of all that Is Marvelous and Wonderful in the Dark Continent.* J. R. Jones, N. P. 1889.

Nourse, J. E., ed. *Narrative of the Second Arctic Expedition Made by Charles F. Hall: His Voyage to Repulse Bay, Sledge Journeys to the Straits of Fury and Hecla and to King William's Land and Residence Among the Eskimos During the Years 1864–69.* Washington, D.C.: Government Printing Office, 1879. Also 45th Cong. 3rd Sess., *Sen. Exec. Doc. No. 27.*

Parry, Ann. *Parry of the Arctic: The Life Story of Admiral Sir Edward Parry, 1790–1855.* London: Chatto & Windus, 1963.

Peary, Robert E. *Northward over the Great Ice.* 2 vols. London: Methuen, 1898.

———. *The North Pole.* New York: Frederick Stokes, 1910.

Reingold, Nathan, ed. *The Sciences in the American Context: New Perspectives.* Washington, D.C.: Smithsonian Press, 1979.

Roberts, David. *Great Exploration Hoaxes.* San Francisco: Sierra Club Books, 1982.

Robinson, Ronald; Gallagher, John; and Denny, Alice. *Africa and the Victorians: The Climax of Imperialism.* 1961. Reprint. Garden City, N. Y.: Doubleday/Anchor, 1968.

Rouse, Irving C. *Cruise of the Revenue Steamer Corwin in Alaska . . . 1881.* Washington, D.C.: Anglin, 1883.

Savage, Thomas S., and Wyman, Jeffries. "Notice of the External Characters and Habits of Troglodytes Gorilla, a New Special of Orang from the Gaboon River [with] Osteology of the Same." *Boston Journal of Natural History* 5 (1847). In John C. Burnham, ed., *Science in America: Historical Selections.* New York: Holt, Rinehart & Winston, 1971, pp. 115–27.

Schwatka, Frederick. "Exploration of the Yukon River in 1883." *Journal of the American Geographical Society* 16 (1884), 346–81.

———. *Compilation of Narratives of Exploration in Alaska.* Washington, D.C.: Government Printing Office, 1900. Includes:
Ray, P. Henry. "International Polar Expedition Point Barrow, 1884," pp. 363–80.
Raymond, Charles P. "Reconnaissance of the Yukon River, 1869," pp. 19–44.
Schwatka, Frederick. "Exploration of the Yukon River," pp. 285–364.

Scoresby, William. *An Account of the Arctic Regions with a Description of the Northern Whale-Fishery.* 2 vols. London: Archibald Constable, 1820. Reprint. New York: Augustus Kelley, 1969.

Sherwood, Morgan B. *Exploration of Alaska, 1865–1900.* New Haven and London: Yale Univ. Press, 1965.

Spurr, Josiah Edward. *Through the Yukon Gold Diggings.* Boston: Eastern Publishing, 1900.

Stackpole, Edouard A., ed. *The Long Arctic Search: The Narrative of Lieutenant Frederick Schwatka, U.S.A., 1878–1880, Seeking the Records of the Lost Franklin Expedition.* Mystic, Conn.: Marine Historical Association, 1965.

Stanley, Henry M. *Through the Dark Continent.* 2 vols. New York: Harper & Brothers, 1878.

Stanley, Richard, and Neame, Alan. *The Newly Discovered Exploration Diaries of H. M. Stanley.* New York: Vanguard, 1956.

Sterling, Dorothy. *The Making of an Afro-American: Martin Robinson Delaney, 1812–1885.* Garden City, N. Y.: Doubleday, 1971.

Tarnovecky, Joseph. *Purchase of Alaska: Background and Reactions.* Montreal: McGill Univ. Press, 1968.

Tompkins, Stuart R. *Alaska, Promyshlennikii and Sourdough.* Norman: Univ. of Oklahoma Press, 1945.

Tuttle, Francis. *Report of the Cruise of the U. S. Revenue Cutter "Bear" and the Overland Expedition for the Relief of the Whalers in the Arctic Ocean from Nov. 27, 1897 to Sept. 13, 1898.* Washington, D.C.: Government Printing Office, 1899.

Vaucaire, Michel. *Paul Du Chaillu.* New York and London: Harper & Brothers, 1930.

Weems, John Edward. *Peary, the Explorer and the Man.* Boston: Houghton Mifflin, 1967.

———. *Race for the Pole.* New York: Henry Holt, 1960.

Whymper, Frederick. *Travel and Adventure in the Territory of Alaska.* London: John Murray, 1868.

Wolfe, Linnie Marsh. *Son of the Wilderness: The Life of John Muir.* New York: Alfred A. Knopf, 1945. Reprint. Madison: Univ. of Wisconsin Press, 1973.

Wrangel, Ferdinand von. *Narrative of an Expedition to the Polar Sea, 1820–23.* London: Madden, 1844.

INDEX